MARGARET FULLER AND HER CIRCLES

NEW ENGLAND IN THE WORLD

General Series Editor: Brigitte Bailey, University of New Hampshire

New England in the World promotes new directions in research on New England topics in a variety of disciplines, including literary studies, history, biography, geography, anthropology, environmental studies, visual and material culture, African American studies, Native studies, ethnic studies, gender studies, film studies, and cultural studies. In addition to its pursuit of New England topics in general, the series features a special emphasis on projects that situate New England in transnational, transatlantic, hemispheric, and global contexts. The series welcomes interdisciplinary perspectives, and it publishes books meant for academic readers as well as books that speak to a broader public.

For the complete list of books available in this series,
please see www.upne.com

Brigitte Bailey, Katheryn P. Viens, and Conrad Edick Wright, eds.,
　Margaret Fuller and Her Circles

Francis J. Bremer,
　First Founders: American Puritans and Puritanism in an Atlantic World

MARGARET FULLER AND HER CIRCLES

EDITED BY Brigitte Bailey, Katheryn P. Viens, and Conrad Edick Wright

Published in Association with
the Massachusetts Historical Society

University of New Hampshire Press
Durham, New Hampshire

University of New Hampshire Press
An imprint of University Press of New England
www.upne.com
© 2013 University of New Hampshire
All rights reserved
Manufactured in the United States of America
Designed by Vicki Kuskowski
Typeset in Caslon 540 by Copperline Book Services, Inc.

University Press of New England is a member of the Green Press Initiative. The paper used in this book meets their minimum requirement for recycled paper.

For permission to reproduce any of the material in this book, contact Permissions, University Press of New England, One Court Street, Suite 250, Lebanon NH 03766; or visit www.upne.com

Library of Congress Cataloging-in-Publication Data

Margaret Fuller and her circles / edited by Brigitte Bailey, Katheryn P. Viens, and Conrad Edick Wright.
   p. cm.—(New England in the world)
"Published in Association with the Massachusetts Historical Society."
Includes bibliographical references and index.
ISBN 978-1-61168-345-5 (cloth: alk. paper)—
ISBN 978-1-61168-346-2 (pbk.: alk. paper)—
ISBN 978-1-61168-347-9 (ebook)
1. Fuller, Margaret, 1810–1850—Criticism and interpretation.   2. Women and literature—United States—History—19th century.   3. Feminisim—United States—History—19th century.
I. Bailey, Brigitte.   II. Viens, Katheryn P., 1962–
III. Wright, Conrad Edick.
PS2507.M25 2013
818'.309—dc23   2012018382

5 4 3 2 1

CONTENTS

Acknowledgments ix

Introduction: Fuller at Two Hundred · *Brigitte Bailey* 1

1. Fuller's Lawsuit and Feminist History · *Phyllis Cole* 11

2. "Woes . . . of Which We Know Nothing": Fuller and the Problem of Feminine Virtue · *John Matteson* 32

3. Fuller, Feminism, Pantheism · *Dorri Beam* 52

4. Margaret Fuller, Self-Culture, and Associationism
   David M. Robinson 77

5. "More anon": American Socialism and Margaret Fuller's 1848
   Adam-Max Tuchinsky 100

6. Margaret Fuller and Antislavery: "A Cause Identical"
   Albert J. von Frank 128

7. Margaret Fuller on Music's "Everlasting Yes": A Romantic Critic in the Romantic Era · *Megan Marshall* 148

8. Sympathy and Prophecy: The Two Faces of Social Justice in Fuller's New York Writing · *Jeffrey Steele* 161

9. Margaret Fuller and Urban Life · *Robert N. Hudspeth* 179

10. Circles around George Sand: Margaret Fuller and the Dynamics of Transnational Reception · *Charlene Avallone* 206

Epilogue. "The Measure of My Foot-Print": Margaret Fuller's
Unfinished Revolution · *Mary Kelley*   229

Notes   245
Contributors   299
Index   303

ACKNOWLEDGMENTS

The Massachusetts Historical Society has become something of a center of programming on Transcendentalism over the past quarter century. Beginning in 1987, when the society investigated the liberal religious basis of Transcendentalism through a conference on American Unitarianism, 1805–65, it has held three-day meetings on Transcendentalism in its religious, intellectual, and cultural contexts (in 1997), on Ralph Waldo Emerson (in 2003), and on Margaret Fuller (in 2010). Most of the contributions in this collection first appeared at the last of these events, "Margaret Fuller and Her Circles," a commemoration of the two hundredth anniversary of Fuller's birth. The society's spring 2010 exhibition, "'A More Interior Revolution': Elizabeth Peabody, Margaret Fuller, and the Women of the American Renaissance," skillfully curated by Megan Marshall, rounded out these activities.

In acknowledging all those who made it possible to publish the collection now in your hands, the editors of the volume also want to thank everyone whose efforts contributed to the program that was its genesis. The conference grew out of a suggestion by Joel Myerson that Charles Capper then endorsed and promoted. Professors Myerson and Capper both served as commentators and active participants in the program, which took place in Boston at the society. We benefited also from the participation as commentators of Fritz Fleischmann and Larry Reynolds and of session chairs Susan Belasco, Bell Gale Chevigny, Helen Deese, and Joan von Mehren. Contributions from the Lowell Institute, the Department of English at the University of New Hampshire, Joan von Mehren, and an anonymous donor helped to underwrite the program.

Conferences are complicated to organize, but experience at the society since 1987 helped to ensure an event that functioned smoothly and rewarded those in attendance. For facilitating both the program and this collection, we owe special thanks to Dennis Fiori, Kathleen Barker, Bill Beck, Chris Carberry, Chris Coveney, Peter Drummey, Jayne Gordon, Tammy Hamond,

James Harrison, Emily Hogan, Peter Hood, Nicole Leonard, and Jennifer Smith, all from the society's staff. We are also grateful to Colleen Flannery, a volunteer who provided invaluable assistance during the event.

Brigitte Bailey
Katheryn P. Viens
Conrad Edick Wright

Introduction

FULLER AT TWO HUNDRED

Brigitte Bailey

Margaret Fuller (1810–50) has had three afterlives.[1] As a woman and a public intellectual whose contributions did not always fit within the dominant interpretations either of the Transcendentalist movement or of other nineteenth-century literary and cultural movements, Fuller became marginalized in academic studies of antebellum America in the century that followed her death. As scholars in this volume, from Phyllis Cole to Mary Kelley, have demonstrated, however, Fuller was an integral part of a tradition of women's education, writing, and rights advocacy that stretched from the late eighteenth century through the successful campaign for suffrage in the early twentieth. If, like other antebellum women writers, Fuller was purged from the literary canon by the end of the century, she remained a vivid presence to the club women attending Fuller birthday celebrations and to such women's rights activists as Elizabeth Cady Stanton.[2] The advent of Second Wave Feminism in the 1960s, which precipitated the emergence of women's studies and the recovery of women's texts, profoundly changed academic and popular views of the past and offered the opportunity gradually to integrate these alternative perspectives into the academy.[3] Beginning with the pathbreaking work of Bell Gale Chevigny and others in the late 1960s and the 1970s, Fuller has become central to a striking new account of antebellum literature, history, and culture.[4] This collection of contributions on Fuller, her works, and her contemporaries comes at a signal point of maturity in Fuller scholarship. Developments in the fields of literary and historical studies — as, for example, in gender theory, transatlantic studies, and archival excavations of the networks of reform — have converged with a renewed attention to Fuller's life and writings. Her very lack of "fit" in the traditional narrative has pushed scholars to rethink their understanding of the period and to redefine Fuller as a significant intellectual precursor, a critic who analyzed and challenged the dominant interpretive paradigms of her time. This volume marks the maturation of Fuller studies and indicates future directions of research and analysis.

Antebellum culture was characterized by an extraordinary burst of literary, social, and political reimaginings that had both national and transnational implications. In ways that often anticipated contemporary debates, American writers and activists questioned and revised definitions of citizenship, cosmopolitanism, the nation state, economic and social institutions, class, race, and gender—and they did so in the multiple genres of a rapidly proliferating print culture.[5] As a new understanding of this formative period in American culture grew among scholars, Fuller's significance as a writer and public intellectual in the 1830s and 1840s in New England, New York, and Europe resonated with critics and historians influenced by the social and political activism of the 1960s and 1970s and, in turn, helped to drive the emergence of this new understanding. Fuller was a Transcendentalist, teacher, translator, feminist theorist, book reviewer, literary journal editor, surveyor of reform institutions, journalist, traveler, political activist in the 1848 European revolutions, and foreign correspondent. As the editor of the *Dial*, the Transcendentalists' primary periodical, she drew out many of the literary implications of their movement. As one of the most visible of those New Englanders whose work carried them beyond the region, Fuller also shaped the language of such national projects as the women's rights movement and modeled cosmopolitan perspectives as she addressed America from Europe.[6] In sum, she was one of the central figures of this transformative period and one of those who most fully articulated its meanings.

The past three decades have seen the recovery, editing, and publication of all of Fuller's major texts and many of her smaller pieces, including her influential feminist work *Woman in the Nineteenth Century* (1845); her travel book on the Midwest, *Summer on the Lakes, in 1843* (1844); her letters; and her complete correspondence for the *New-York Tribune* (1844–50).[7] Several anthologies of her writings are now available for classroom use and include samples of these works as well as of her other pieces of criticism and her poetry.[8] This recovery process has stimulated an increase in teaching and graduate research on her life and works; while the 1960s, 1970s, and 1980s each produced a handful of dissertations in which Fuller played a major role, the next two decades averaged about twenty dissertations apiece.[9] The 1990s and 2000s have also been remarkable for their series of substantial biographies of Fuller that analyze her world and set her in the context of her period, especially those by Charles Capper, Joan von Mehren, and Meg McGavran Murray.[10] These decades have witnessed an expansion of literary criticism that unfolded the meaning of her texts, of the multiple genres she used, and of her dialogic engagements with writers and thinkers from Goethe to Emerson, to Douglass, to Sand. Christina Zwarg and Jeffrey Steele have authored critical monographs wholly or primarily on Fuller.[11] In 1992 the field witnessed the founding of the Margaret Fuller Society, and in 1995 the first Fuller conference.[12] The annual survey of research *American Literary Scholarship* retitled its regular essay on Transcendentalism to include Fuller in 1992.[13] Indeed, the academy has canonized Fuller, an event she might have viewed with some irony.

The bicentennial of her birth has prompted a further surge in scholarship. As of this writing, several of the contributors to this volume are completing book-length projects; John Matteson's biography has just appeared, Megan Marshall is finishing a shorter biography for general readers, David M. Robinson is at work on a study of Fuller and her relation with the Transcendentalist movement, and Phyllis Cole is writing a study of Fuller's legacy for subsequent women and, together with Jana Argersinger, editing a collection of essays on Fuller, Transcendentalism, and other nineteenth-century women writers.[14] In addition, Fuller has again become a historical figure who draws public attention. During 2010, events celebrating her bicentennial, especially those that took place in New England and New York, attracted a high level of public interest. Dorothy Emerson, the cochair of the Margaret Fuller Bicentennial Committee, centered in the Boston/Cambridge area, reported that the talks, historical reenactments, sermons, traveling exhibition, website, five plays, and other programs organized by her group and others across the country drew thousands of participants.[15] This book, also prompted by the bicentennial, is an opportunity to define the current state of Fuller studies and to examine her continuing relevance.

In the past two decades extensive research on other female antebellum New England writers has resulted in major biographies of Harriet Beecher Stowe, Lydia Maria Child, and the Peabody sisters, as well as important collections of scholarly essays on writers from Catharine Maria Sedgwick to Harriet Wilson. These provide a significant context for the scholarship in this volume.[16] In fact, these publications are mutually illuminating; the more we know about the writing, social contexts, and reform networks—that is, the "circles"—of one of these writers, the more we understand the expressions and life choices of the others. Together, these contributions deepen our understanding of women's far-reaching engagement with the social, political, intellectual, and literary cultures of antebellum New England and the nation.

THE CONTRIBUTIONS

Contributions to the volume address the central preoccupations of Fuller's career: the status of women, reform movements, urban culture, transatlantic exchanges, and—embedded in all these concerns—the liberatory potential of conscious acts of reading and writing. The contributions are arranged by subject, roughly in the order of the first four topics, although they frequently speak to more than one concern. Together they place Fuller more firmly than ever in the historical, cultural, geographical, and literary contexts in which she produced her work; this analysis enables illuminating interpretations of a wide range of her texts.

Phyllis Cole, John Matteson, and Dorri Beam explore Fuller's writings on women and gender ideology in three significant contexts: women's rights, sexuality, and feminist literary pantheism. Cole connects Fuller with transatlantic developments in feminism, from Mary Wollstonecraft to Stanton, and revises earlier interpretations of Fuller that set her apart from the women's rights movement. She shows how Fuller drew on the language of the law as well as on conventions of the political tract and the literary-religious essay to influence public opinion in *Woman in the Nineteenth Century* and in the *Dial* article on which it was based. In particular, Cole brings to light Fuller's surprisingly extensive "textual affinit[ies]" with both Wollstonecraft and the feminist abolitionist Sarah Grimké and, in doing so, reveals the fusion of the Enlightenment language of rights with the rhetoric of "religious perfectionism" that shaped First Wave Feminism. Matteson discusses Fuller's exploration of "the problem of feminine virtue" in the context of nineteenth-century concepts of women's sexuality. He pulls together three aspects of Fuller's life and writing in 1844–45: her portraits of three women in *Summer on the Lakes*, her visits to the prostitutes incarcerated in Sing Sing prison, and her discussion of sexuality and women's roles in *Woman in the Nineteenth Century*. While Cole's Fuller analyzes the ways in which legal and ideological structures inhibit women's aspirations, Matteson's Fuller describes the ways in which these aspirations are stymied by social pressures that "force women into an overly material, somatically centered existence," even as she wrestles with her own concepts of "chastity." Beam is interested in ecstatic modes of experience and expression that militated against these strictures. She observes that Fuller embraced a spiritual "ecology of 'self'" that extended beyond the individual, expanded when social obstacles were removed, and (borrowing from the practice of Mesmerism) "untethered" gender from the "overly material" body that Matteson discusses. This "Transcendentalist model of feminism," then, was not an escape from politics but rather prompted new understandings of gender and new modes of expression. Like Cole, Beam reconnects Fuller with a range of other women writers; in juxtaposing Fuller's mystical, erotically charged passages in *Woman in the Nineteenth Century* with writings by Elizabeth Oakes Smith, Harriet Martineau, and Mary Clemmer, she discovers a "widespread feminist allegiance to an accessible realm of spiritual energy that offered the opportunity to rethink subjective and social forms."

Contributions by David M. Robinson, Adam-Max Tuchinsky, and Albert J. von Frank capture Fuller's complex engagements with other antebellum movements, including Associationism and antislavery. Robinson explores Fuller's ideal of "self-culture"—her fusion of the Unitarian concept of spiritual growth through self-examination with Goethe's more secular imperative to develop all the capacities of the self—and, in a reading of her "Autobiographical Romance" and other texts, argues that for Fuller such development occurred most powerfully in relationships with others: "The self that Fuller sought to nurture . . . was a self-in-relation, unfolding its nature in association with others." Therefore, the individual self was intimately bound up with community (perhaps in ways related to what Beam calls Fuller's expansive "ecology of 'self'"). This insight led Fuller, along with fellow Transcendentalist William Henry Channing, toward the reform movement influenced by the French thinker Charles Fourier: cooperative Associationism, the organizing principle of the Utopian experiment at Brook Farm. In a related study, Tuchinsky places Fuller's thinking in the context of the socialist critiques of the market economy in the 1840s and analyzes her engagements with a range of thinkers and movements: Ralph Waldo Emerson, American Associationism, French Fourierists and Christian socialists, and Italian nationalists. Like Robinson, he breaks down traditional scholarly oppositions between Emersonian individualism and Transcendentalism's communitarian tendencies. Tuchinsky argues that, despite her radicalization in Italy, Fuller's brand of socialism remained a form of liberalism, as it aimed to eradicate class difference not through class struggle but with "incremental reforms" that would develop "self-reliant member[s] of an associated community."

Von Frank takes up a question that has dogged Fuller scholars: her belated interest in the antislavery movement. Although she knew a number of abolitionists in Boston and New York, she evinced her first public support for abolitionism later than some of her colleagues, and she grew most sympathetic with the movement as she covered the Roman Revolution for the *New-York Tribune* in the late 1840s. Von Frank engages in a nuanced reading of Fuller's relationship with her father, the congressman Timothy Fuller; of the emergence of Boston antislavery societies and the ensuing question of women's rights; and of Fuller's critique of the combative rhetoric of the movement. As a result, he identifies a shift from "her youthful notions of heroism" as "a masculine, even a fatherly attainment [that] . . . involved some triumphantly willful projection of force" toward a definition of heroism connected at once with a redemptive "femality" and with an antipatriarchal "revolt against the leader class"—"against the nation's wise fathers." As a result of this development in Fuller's definition of the heroic, "rhetorical parallels between antislavery and women's rights" shape *Woman in the Nineteenth Century*. These three contributions—by Robinson, Tuchinsky, and von Frank—illuminate Fuller's political and social thought by retrieving its highly specific autobiographical and historical contexts; they reveal Fuller and her contemporaries to be evolving thinkers and actors in a changing world.

Boston, New York, London, Paris, and Rome are the settings for contributions on Fuller's engagement with urban and transatlantic culture by Megan Marshall, Jeffrey Steele, Robert N. Hudspeth, and Charlene Avallone. Highlighting a relatively neglected area of Fuller's work, Marshall describes how Fuller moved beyond traditional gender roles in the arts and recovers the range and sophistication of her music criticism. Raised to play the piano as a part of her female (that is, amateur) education, Fuller reviewed professional musical performances for the *Dial* and the *New-York Tribune*. Her reviews of Beethoven symphonies in Boston, numerous concerts in New York, and Chopin's performance in Paris reinforced her conviction that music, even beyond poetry, was a universal language that embodied human aspirations and yearning for the infinite: "music exemplified human perfectability." But Marshall also traces the implications of Fuller's meditations on music back into her literary works; she notes that Fuller wrote her mystical fiction at the time she was developing her appreciation of music in the *Dial*, and she finds that musical metaphors pervade both Fuller's private and her public writings. Steele analyzes Fuller's strategies for representing urban social ills in her columns for the *Tribune*. Taking a different direction from Robinson and Tuchinsky, he argues that Fuller found the language of Transcendentalism, developed to discuss the individual, inadequate to shape "public attention" on the social issues of the emerging metropolis of New York. In response, Fuller fused Transcendentalism's capacity for imaginative vision with the language of Christian sentiment—that is, merged "vision" and "affect"—in a rhetoric of "sentimental Transcendentalism" to rouse middle-class urban readers from their complacency over slavery, materialism, poverty, and the mistreatment of immigrants. As a journalist seeking to overcome conventions of detached "urban spectatorship," Fuller imagined city dwellers as a "collective 'body'" that could create change through an "urban ethic of 'contact'" with social others.

Hudspeth points out that Fuller's life was essentially an "urban life" and that the cities in which she lived, especially Boston, New York, and Rome, are vital contexts for understanding her writings. As "the most cosmopolitan of the American Transcendentalists," Fuller experienced cities as arenas for collaborative growth. As does Marshall, Hudspeth emphasizes the importance of Fuller's experience of urban classical musical performances; like Fuller's Conversations for women, these concerts were collaborative in nature, with artists and audience members creating meaning together. At the same time, New York shifted Fuller's attention to questions of social justice, as Steele also notes, and provided a larger audience for her writing; the *Tribune* "helped Fuller become thoroughly urban" since it allowed her to speak as one urban "citizen" to others. In the end, though, Rome became the "home" she most fully "inhabited" even as it also represented revolution and loss: as Hudspeth observes, "Fuller's final urban experience in Rome was of war."

Taking a different approach to Fuller's immersion in a cosmopolitan culture, Avallone brings together gender concerns, political issues, and transatlantic exchanges in her closely researched account of the reception of the French novelist George Sand by Fuller and her intellectual circle in Boston. Avallone offers a "model of reading thoroughly embedded in local and transatlantic dialogue," that is, an approach that situates her reading of Sand in terms of Fuller's coterie's discussion of Sand's works, Sand's British reviewers, and other intellectuals of la jeune France (Young France). She argues that Fuller was not a lone voice championing Sand as a feminist and socialist thinker but rather was part of a transatlantic "progressive reception circle" around the author that included such other American Transcendentalists as George Ripley (the founder of Brook Farm) and Caroline Sturgis. As her reviews of Sand's books demonstrate, Fuller's thinking developed in dialogue with these figures and with such Sand partisans in Europe as Giuseppe Mazzini, but she remained reserved in her support of this politically avant-garde thinker and sexually transgressive woman. This contribution situates Fuller in the transnational intellectual milieu that prompted much of her thinking, even as it connects her more firmly with Boston intellectual circles.

In the epilogue of this volume, Mary Kelley returns to the feminist aspects of Fuller's life and writings and considers the work that Fuller left unfinished upon her premature death in 1850. She describes Fuller's legacy for the cause of women's progress and asks, "to what degree is her revolution unfinished?" Kelley gauges the twenty-first century status of American women by using Fuller's *Woman in the Nineteenth Century* as well as Fuller's own experience as benchmarks and by bringing recent books on the current status of American women into the argument. Citing statistics on women's tremendous gains in access to education, political office, reproductive self-determination, and the professions—but also recent analyses of abiding economic and professional inequities and a resurgence of sexism in popular culture—Kelley notes both the ways in which Fuller's vision of equal opportunities for women to learn, to use their full capacities, and to gain control over their bodies and lives has been realized in the United States and the ways in which it has not. She considers how the contributions collected here inevitably point to issues of social justice still very much alive today. By doing so, Kelley brings this volume back to the connection between intellectual inquiry and public life that Fuller so valued.

FUTURE WORK

All but one of the collection's contributions are revisions of essays originally presented at a conference honoring Fuller's bicentennial held at the Massachusetts Historical Society in Boston in 2010.[17] Like the essays, the conference was marked by the complexity of critical engagement and historical contexts—a fit celebration of Fuller.[18] The title of this collection, *Margaret Fuller and Her Circles*, points both to its contents and to future directions of work. This volume joins and hopes to provoke further growth in the current research that characterizes antebellum writers as circulating through multiple groups, intellectual affinities, and places; this approach is particularly appropriate for exploring the significance of Fuller's life and work.

Larry J. Reynolds has published a thorough assessment of the status of Fuller studies and prospects for future work; in his article he reviews publications up to 2004.[19] While noting the striking emergence of Fuller scholarship, he calls for extensive contributions in two areas. The first is the continued editing of her published and unpublished writings; in addition to the publication of a number of remaining manuscripts (including journals), he calls for a university press to commit to producing an authoritative edition of "The Collected Works of Margaret Fuller" and for her inclusion in the Library of America series. Both these projects still need to be undertaken; the contributions in this book, some of which draw on archival material, point to their importance. The second area is the further study of Fuller's personal and professional relationships in the context of her thought and writings: her friendships, intellectual circles, contacts, transatlantic travels, and influences on others. These connections illuminate the often collaborative evolution of her thinking on institutions, such as marriage and slavery, and on political developments, such as socialism and European republicanism, and they shed light on her significance in the nineteenth century.

Margaret Fuller and Her Circles speaks to the second area of Reynolds's analysis of gaps in Fuller studies and indicates lines of further research in this direction. Most contributions address the transatlantic turn in critical and historical studies in some way, whether they focus on Fuller's urban experience (Hudspeth), the kinds of socialism she encountered (Tuchinsky), or her place in the history of feminist expression (Cole). Transatlantic circulations of ideas—theories of political economy, of gender, of literature—defined much of Fuller's intellectual world and call for more investigation. In recent years Fuller's own circulations in Rome, Paris, and New York have been studied but not exhaustively so. Like the transatlantic world of the period, antebellum urban geography has also emerged for scholars as a place of transformation, exchange, and mobility that demanded literary innovation, as Steele points out, and held heightened opportunities for aesthetic response, as Marshall observes.

These contributions also highlight a revived understanding of Fuller's connections with other women: friends, students, other writers, activists, even figures glimpsed while traveling, as Matteson notes. Cole, Beam, and Avallone trace the sometimes elusive trail of women's influences and exchanges through correspondence, published writings, and allusions. This approach remains a productive line of research. Similarly, contributors outline networks of reform or movement culture, such as Associationism (Robinson) or antislavery groups (von Frank), with which Fuller either had contact or which she knowingly avoided. Fuller's world held many such circles—prison reform societies, New York literary salons, publishing networks, transatlantic Unitarian reform networks, radical republican and socialist groups in Europe—circles whose connections with Fuller would shed light on the rapidly evolving antebellum milieu.

In a related approach taken in a number of these contributions, a renewed attention to language as a medium of exchange uncovers the significance of acts of reading, translation, discussion, and writing in the nineteenth century. As Kelley states, "Fuller [and others] approached reading and writing not as separate and autonomous acts but instead as continually intersecting and mutually constitutive habits"; one might add that Fuller and her circle also understood reading and writing as collaborative acts. More reception studies are needed (as in Avallone's model) that trace the passage of texts, including Fuller's, across linguistic and cultural borders. Contributors in this volume also pay close attention to the uses of various types of rhetoric by Fuller and others and to the period-specific associations of language; the latter analysis appears in contributions as diverse as those by von Frank, Steele, and Beam. These conjunctions of finely grasped historical contexts with a close study of Fuller's words are fruitful models for future work.

Through its methodologies and the range of texts and contexts it addresses, this collection reveals a Fuller who is, interestingly, less exceptional yet more substantial and wide-ranging in her theoretical and representational writings than previously imagined. One aspect of Fuller scholarship holds constant; her work, as Kelley reminds us, continues to have implications for contemporary feminism. Fuller's decision in *Woman in the Nineteenth Century* to focus her analytical energies on a cultural critique of gender, to "offer," as Kelley says, a more "fluid . . . system of gender relations," makes her work available for the ongoing task of rethinking gender. As Reynolds points out, "this is an exciting time in Fuller studies."[20] Given the wealth of work in this volume and the ongoing projects, Fuller studies promise to be exciting for some time to come.

I

FULLER'S LAWSUIT AND FEMINIST HISTORY

Phyllis Cole

In their *History of Woman Suffrage*, Elizabeth Cady Stanton and her coauthors claimed Margaret Fuller as a "precursor" to the American women's rights movement, which began just three years after the 1845 publication of Fuller's *Woman in the Nineteenth Century*. Moreover, they specified, she had wielded this power by offering "a vindication of woman's right to think." By implication the phrase made her a disciple and partner of that other precursor, Mary Wollstonecraft, whose *Vindication of the Rights of Woman* had issued a galvanic call from England in 1792. Indeed, these feminist historians described Wollstonecraft by quoting lines about her from Fuller's manifesto. They suggested no comparable linkage between Fuller and American founders Sarah and Angelina Grimké, whose antislavery eloquence and resistance to clerical opposition provided the dominant foreground to their own massive record of conventions and public oratory. But all these individuals appear in a chapter titled "Preceding Causes," with Fuller positioned just after the antislavery women, and all are listed among the nineteen to whom the authors dedicate their work.[1] In this influential account of American feminist origins, Fuller both initiates and transmits a shared revolutionary discourse.

As Charles Capper comments, however, such a role has been "strangely missing from both Fuller biographies and feminist histories, which often assert or imply that her book floated somewhere above the movement's turbulent waters." One can easily see why. Not only did Fuller make her argument as a writer rather than a platform orator; in addition, her writing is difficult, an allusive literary and religious meditation as well as a feminist tract. Fuller understood what she had written even as she sent *Woman in the Nineteenth Century* to press, conceding that it would require "too much culture in the reader to be quickly or extensively diffused." She still hoped for influence, however, precisely through the literary means of addressing "a

11

mind here and there and through that others." Her successors soon testified to an impact of just this kind; by 1867, in an especially telling commentary on the proliferation of feminist ideas, Caroline Healey Dall paired Wollstonecraft and Fuller as structurally definitive "Lives That Have Modified Public Opinion" on two sides of the Atlantic.[2] Capper's point about Fuller's absence from movement histories applies less to the nineteenth century than to academic women's studies scholarship as it has become more specialized since the 1970s: students of Fuller have celebrated her feminist voice primarily within the history of literary and philosophical Romanticism, while students of feminist politics have focused on the Grimkés and Stanton without pausing for long over Fuller's elusive text.[3]

There have been exceptions to this academic division of labor, however. Political scientist Elizabeth Ann Bartlett helpfully distinguishes four foundational traditions of feminism: an Enlightenment strand, exemplified by Wollstonecraft; a Romantic strand, by Fuller; a utopian socialist strand, by Frances Wright; and a radical sectarian strand, by Quakers such as the Grimkés. Like Bartlett I find no evidence that Fuller knew Wright, though she acknowledged learning from the significantly different utopian socialism of Charles Fourier.[4] In this contribution, I consider Fuller especially through dialogue with her two other most important female precursors, Wollstonecraft in *Vindication of the Rights of Woman* and Sarah Grimké in *Letters on the Equality of the Sexes*. Even Bartlett leaves each of the four strands of feminist argument essentially separate from the others. But I argue for a Romanticism in *Woman in the Nineteenth Century* of sufficient depth and breadth to incorporate the Enlightenment reason of Wollstonecraft, the prophetic piety of Grimké, and the political urgency of both.

To make such an argument in no way denies the expressive power of Fuller's post-Christian religious myth making, elucidated in recent studies by John Paul Gatta and Jeffrey Steele. Fuller's persona was that of a questing Eurydice, a compassionate Mary, a goddesslike Minerva or Isis, as she gathered women's history toward the millennial future. Yet Gatta marvels at discovering the Virgin Mary in a "feminist polemic aimed at enlarging the scope of liberty and action," while Steele specifies that Fuller aimed "to summon the power of female myth into the public domain of social reform."[5] Here the obverse of that duality is emphasized, with liberty and reform in the foreground and spiritual power as motivation and means.

In particular, like her predecessors Fuller considered women's status within a wider civil rights discourse, and all three feminists self-consciously defined their arguments as public interventions on behalf of women. Wollstonecraft presented a "Vindication," as if clearing women's name from previous charges of innate deficiency. Though Sarah Grimké ostensibly wrote "Letters" to a sister abolitionist while in fact aiming them for newspaper publication, her sister Angelina specified that she was making an "Appeal" directly to the public.[6] Fuller encompassed and stepped beyond such rhetorical modes by calling her argument a "lawsuit."

In the structure and message of *Woman in the Nineteenth Century*, allusions to the law and courtroom were as important as Fuller's evocation of goddess-inspired spirituality, even intertwined with it. The first version of her essay, published in the *Dial* in 1843, featured the trope of legal complaint in its title, "The Great Lawsuit. Man versus Men. Woman versus Women." Immediately she extended the metaphor by telling of a human "inheritance" lost and now, despite delays for lack of counsel to plead the cause, pursued to higher courts for recovery. Fuller presented herself as the needed counsel in women's cause of regaining what was originally their own; by the essay's end, she had become prophet and legal advocate at once, seeing woman as the Virgin Mother of a renewed humanity "would she but assume her inheritance." The suit to regain this inheritance combined redemptive urgency with a call for change in and for the world. Although two years later Fuller entitled her expanded essay *Woman in the Nineteenth Century*, she began it by explaining and defending the old title for its affirmation of a shared human destiny to "ascertain and fulfil the law."[7] So the original judicial reference continued, both here and through her ongoing language of pleading, courts, and inheritance. She wished women and men to present this suit jointly rather than through mutual antagonism; their goal, however, would still be the restoration of an inheritance uniquely lost to the female half of humanity.[8]

The irony of the "Great Lawsuit" in either of its versions was that Fuller named a means of public remediation to which, in 1845, women had no access. Her freelance authorship introduced a metaphoric suit in the absence of any such literal prerogative. In the words of James Kent, America's foremost legal commentator of the nineteenth century, the essence of married women's civil nonexistence under the common law of coverture was the incapacity to "sue or be sued." A single woman like Margaret Fuller could in theory have exercised legal authority, but practice, especially in the absence of extraordinary wealth or status, constantly absorbed single women back into dependent status so that they were still dead to the law.[9] Grimké's "appeal," like the abolitionists' petition to Congress, was the resort of an outsider, and Wollstonecraft's "vindication" a stance of argument that did not specify its cultural location. Among the three manifestos, Fuller's "Great Lawsuit" implied the most audacious confrontation with power.

It did so, furthermore, without overt anger or defiance, but by calling forth the law that would overturn such dispossession. Fuller's lawsuit brilliantly combined a process of grievance and an invocation of restorative principles, because it referred less to the common law that would prevent her suit than to the higher law of divine nature whose aim was to restore humanity's inheritance. Universal law served as an agent of change, above civil inequity and yet open to perception by individual human consciousness.[10] Fuller positioned her quest for such principles amid political enunciations of liberty evoking the French and, even more, the American Revolution: America was "destined to elucidate a great moral law," and its Declaration of Independence had indeed "become a law," a "golden certainty" whose promise of freedom and equality lay open to fulfillment despite the nation's injustice to slaves and women.[11] Yet even more essentially, she identified with the artist whose vision would provide this impetus to fulfillment. Commentators have often recognized Fuller's presentation of Orpheus as a crucial figure in *Woman in the Nineteenth Century*, but no one has queried her description of him as a "law-giver by theocratic commission." Fuller did not refer to any civic role Orpheus played in ancient Greece, but specifically to his gift for expressing in music the secrets of nature "as seen in the mind of God." The artist gave the higher law, and Fuller's purpose in evoking Orpheus's powers was to set forth an equal commission for his female partner, Eurydice, who must no longer be left passive in the underworld but now would "call for an Orpheus, rather than Orpheus for Eurydice."[12] An Orphic woman would enunciate the law, and if Fuller was herself one incarnation of Eurydice, she called for others.[13]

In its metaphoric and mythic reach, its intellectual sophistication and audacity, Fuller's "Great Lawsuit" was her own uniquely Romantic pronouncement; however, it shared fundamental ground with Wollstonecraft and Grimké in religious perfectionism as well as in civil rights argument. Like Wollstonecraft, Fuller posited a divinely originated human nature that allowed for utopian imagination of the future: "It is time," her predecessor had written in 1791, "to effect a revolution in female manners—time to restore to [women] their lost dignity—and make them, as a part of the human species, labour by reforming themselves to reform the world." Like Sarah Grimké, Fuller entered the thickets of legal and ecclesiastical injustice in the American republic, building on Grimké's religious conviction that legal coverture and clerical edicts of silence "destroy the responsibility of woman as a moral being" as well as her most basic agency in the world.[14] Rather than surrendering to oppressive regulation, both women reclaimed their moral being through the very act of speech.

Such a triangulation of originating feminist texts is based on clear if not often examined biographical and cultural connections. Fuller grew up knowing of Wollstonecraft in two different guises. Before her tenth birthday in 1820, Margaret could read her father Timothy's contradictory judgments of the Englishwoman in his letters home, which within the same week described *Vindication* both as a "sensible and just" guide to female education and as a book that, on account of its author's scandalous life, "no woman dares to read."[15] Wollstonecraft the apologist for education seems to have won out, for Timothy significantly based his strenuous development of Margaret's mind on her ideas. Years later, in 1837, Fuller engaged with the Transcendentalists amid an uproar in Massachusetts over the Grimkés' abolitionist addresses to "promiscuous" audiences of women and men. Staying at the Emerson house in Concord, she met with Ralph Waldo Emerson's Transcendental Club the same week his wife, Lidian, hosted the Grimkés for tea and joined her townswomen in planning an antislavery society.[16] Eventually Fuller would represent these feminist predecessors by name within the text of *Woman in the Nineteenth Century*. But her partial portraits do not acknowledge the extent of either her lived affinity with them or her textual debts. The earlier writers provide valuable entry points into Fuller's work, and they also ground the argument for her place in an American and transatlantic feminist tradition.

FULLER AND WOLLSTONECRAFT

Building on Wollstonecraft was a risk, and in the search for a new enunciation of women's being, Fuller did not claim her as a full partner. Significantly, both versions of her "Great Lawsuit" name this predecessor among "outlaws" whose lives ran tragically against the walls of circumstance.[17] Timothy Fuller's letter of 1820 encapsulated cultural judgments that still hung over Wollstonecraft's reputation as woman and writer more than two decades later: her "conduct with [Gilbert] Imlay, of America, whom she loved so ardently & would not marry, but had a child by him . . . must completely discountenance her 'Rights of Woman.' . . . She should be charged with libertinism."[18] Margaret Fuller showed considerably more sympathy than her father for Wollstonecraft's "genius" and capability of "virtue," key terms in her description of an ideal woman of the future. But daughter, like father, seems to have been reading Wollstonecraft's life more than her book when she declared, "Mary Wollstonecraft . . . was a woman whose existence better proved the need of some new interpretation of woman's rights, than any thing she wrote." Fuller even drew a moral of deep resonance for her vision of change, claiming that anyone wishing to reform others must be "unstained by passionate error; they must be severe lawgivers to themselves. . . . Their liberty must be the liberty of law and knowledge."[19] She held both her authorial voice and the cause she pleaded apart from "libertinism."

In fact, Fuller's portrait of Wollstonecraft did not arise amid her primary case for feminist change in the opening or closing pages of *Woman in the Nineteenth Century*, but exemplified "intellectual companionship" in her classification of marital types. Fuller's ambivalence about Wollstonecraft herself turned to celebration of the posthumous defense written by her husband, William Godwin: "He loved her, and defended her for the meaning and tendency of her inner life. . . . The champion of the Rights of Woman found, in Godwin, one who would plead that cause like a brother." Such a testimony—written after the publication of Wollstonecraft's feminist book and her unconventional motherhood—was the true "sign of a new era."[20] Fuller could only hope for such a "brother" in her own life.

Ironically, this rehabilitation of Wollstonecraft's life by way of spousal loyalty alluded to the very book, Godwin's *Memoirs of the Author of the Vindication of the Rights of Woman*, that fueled antifeminist reaction over two generations by issuing frank details about her union with Imlay, motherhood, and attempted suicide when Imlay abandoned her.[21] Godwin was not defending his wife's virtue against previous defamation, as Fuller asserted, but unwittingly opening the door to it with such disclosure. Fuller declined to address this tangle of motives and results, but instead conflated the *Memoirs* with Godwin's fictional image of Wollstonecraft in his novel *St. Leon*, claiming that anyone who could portray "the form of woman" so purely was also true to the romance in his own life.[22] Though the heroine of *St. Leon*, Marguerite, truly was based on Wollstonecraft, here she became a wife and mother of intellectual strength rather than an iconoclast; indeed, perhaps in a Gothic refraction of Imlay, the hero-narrator St. Leon deserts her and their children to pursue male dreams of alchemical power.[23] Fuller drew an ideal feminist form out of Wollstonecraft only through a highly selective representation of Godwin's memorials.

Such balancing of praise and judgment of a controversial predecessor does not, however, reveal the depth of textual affinity between Fuller and Wollstonecraft. Mary Kelley remarks that, even though discredited, the British radical's influence in nineteenth-century America remained "there in the shadows," her ideas still productive; the comment might apply as well to Wollstonecraft's influence on *Woman in the Nineteenth Century*. Even where there is no question of scandal, of course, literary art need not specify its sources: Fuller's book, for example, leaves her mentor and foil Ralph Waldo

Emerson unnamed as well. But verbal echoes of Wollstonecraft (as of Emerson) can be discerned at crucial points in her text.[24] Fuller drew on the very language of Wollstonecraft's title when she called for a messianic woman "who shall vindicate their birthright for all women." Such vindication lay at the heart of her own lawsuit to recover the lost inheritance. Wollstonecraft declared that women were "placed on this earth to unfold their faculties," not to fulfill the "prevailing opinion, that woman was created for man." Fuller echoed as she expatiated, "Not one man, in the million, shall I say? No, not in the hundred million, can rise above the belief that woman was made *for man*.... What woman needs is not as a woman to act or rule, but as a nature to grow, as an intellect to discern, as soul to live freely and unimpeded, to unfold such powers as were given her when we left our common home."[25]

As this shared language reveals, both feminist writers urged women's intellectual development not just through formal education but through a remaking of the mind itself. Fuller's idealized alter ego, Miranda, represented the Wollstonecraft regimen that her father Timothy designed for her, the training that allowed clarity of thought, knowledge of the universe, freedom in the world, and above all "self-dependence," the alternative to living "*for man*." Such a "living mind" as Miranda's descended directly from Wollstonecraft, who urged women "to *think*, and only rely on God." As Fuller pronounced in the concluding pages of her argument, "I wish woman to live, *first* for God's sake."[26]

Wollstonecraft's explicit urging of "Reason" and "Virtue" as means to female self-dependence might appear to divide her irreconcilably from Fuller's celebration of the "electrical ... intuitive" element of woman's genius, which she called "Muse."[27] Gatta, for instance, would sharply distinguish Fuller's religious vision from Wollstonecraft's "secular rationalism" as means to emancipation: one belongs to the Enlightenment and the other to Romanticism.[28] But recent scholars identify the British feminist's thought as Enlightened theism on the brink of Romantic conviction, a mode of God-reliance also crucial to the Boston religious liberals who came to be known as Transcendentalists. As historian Barbara Taylor shows, Wollstonecraft found her intellectual voice within the London-area radical Unitarian community of Richard Price. Soon she shared his conviction that the free exercise of conscience and imagination led to virtue, in harmony with a God-given physical and moral universe. *Vindication* articulated a direct lesson for developing the lives of women: "Let us ... trace what we should endeavour to make them in order to co-operate, if the expression be not too bold, with the supreme Being."[29] It was just such Unitarian thought—whether expressed by Price or Wollstonecraft—that prepared the young men and women of Boston to extend their reach beyond Unitarianism.[30] Fuller's insistence on universal *law* had no parallel in Wollstonecraft, but the idea of self-dependence in cooperation with divine intent was strongly analogous.

Wollstonecraft herself found both a mentor beyond Price and her chief adversary in the early Romantic philosopher Jean-Jacques Rousseau. She raged against him in *Vindication*, because he explicitly excluded women from his vibrant conception of natural, independent virtue. "This was Rousseau's opinion respecting men," she declared; "I extend it to women." Far from simply ignoring woman, Rousseau would make her into "a coquettish slave in order to render her a more alluring object of desire, a sweeter companion to man. . . . What nonsense!" A distorted and immoral sexual politics determined his choice of "sensibility" for her instead of reason and virtue. If all the human virtues were "manly," Wollstonecraft expostulated, let us have more masculine women. Fuller followed her in such conviction, even while redefining the "great radical dualism" of sexes as a continuum open to negotiation, and she gave the divine-feminine name "Minerva" to women's male-identified powers of thought and action. Though she also celebrated capacities of feeling and intuition in the complementary "Muse," a term far beyond "sensibility" in its rise to independent ecstasy and vision, Fuller also internalized Wollstonecraft's warning that feeling might imprison. She called women "rather to the Minerva side" out of "love for many incarcerated souls."[31]

The two feminists' urgency to release the incarcerated reflected their common grounding in revolutionary liberty. Each asked not only for freedom of self-determination, but also for the wider social transformation necessary to foster it. Wollstonecraft experienced the French Revolution as her immediate scene of commitment, springing to Richard Price's defense when his favorable view of affairs in France was attacked by Edmund Burke. *Vindication of the Rights of Men* (1790) led to its more famous feminist sequel two years later; she dedicated the second book to Charles Maurice Talleyrand, who had set forth a revolutionary agenda for education that left women, in Wollstonecraft's words, "immured in their families groping in the dark." Half a century later, Fuller found in the French Revolution her first evidence that "as the principle of liberty is better understood, . . . a broader protest is made in behalf of Woman." Indeed, her conception of this revolution paralleled her understanding of Wollstonecraft, since she conceded the impurity and lawlessness of both even while insisting that "truth was prophesied" thereby.[32] To Fuller, Wollstonecraft *was* the French Revolution as applied to women. Her predecessor's case against Rousseau and male prerogative unmasked tyranny and enslavement, and she proclaimed the political alternative to be "emancipation of the whole sex."[33] Fuller held up liberty without equally decrying tyranny, and she found her ultimate expression of liberty in the American Revolution rather than the French. But when she referred to America's "monstrous display of slavery," from knowledge of the social institution more literal and immediate than Wollstonecraft's, she still recalled that earlier moment of revolutionary radicalism: abolitionists, she declared, were "coldly regarded as the Jacobins of their day."[34]

Prophesying an internal revolution in the relationship of women and men, Fuller found her most important model in Wollstonecraft's utopian feminism. In different generations, both writers were futurists. Wollstonecraft affirmed that "all will *be* right" rather than "was" or "is" right. Such hopefulness did not arise just from enlightened reason, but also, as Barbara Taylor points out, from passion and imagination, once these were freed from women's fixation on men. "A wild wish has just flown from my heart to my head," Wollstonecraft wrote, "and I will not stifle it though it may excite a horse-laugh.—I do earnestly wish to see the distinction of sex confounded in society, unless where love animate the behaviour."[35] Not only the content of that "wild wish" but its very flight from heart to head constituted Fuller's debt to her. Neither writer set out a platform of specific demands or expectations for the future, but both looked ahead to public influence or "civil existence" for women. Before Fuller wrote, "Let them be sea-captains," Wollstonecraft suggested that women pursue medicine, politics, or business, both to free themselves from marriages of economic need and to exercise their "benevolence" more widely. And while Fuller transformed Wollstonecraft's "wild wish" into a transhistorical religious search, Wollstonecraft also affirmed the divine intent behind her own vision: "These may be termed Utopian dreams.—Thanks to that Being who impressed them on my soul."[36]

Such a reading of Wollstonecraft sets in relief both Fuller's grounding in the age of revolutions and her leap beyond that earlier utopian wish into fully Romantic constructions of the soul and universe. To a large extent, male mentors led Fuller to apprehend the soul's organic relationship to nature and divinity. She had Miranda describe herself in Ralph Waldo Emerson's preeminent term "self-reliance" and detailed the heroines of Johann Wolfgang von Goethe in a female typology, adding the lyrical Mignon to the "perfected intelligence" of Macaria. Her first epigraph for *Woman in the Nineteenth Century* evoked a universe of dynamic order through words of Friedrich Schiller: the breast concealed a soul that was "free through reason, strong through laws."[37] Wollstonecraft, however, was her feminist model in appropriating male terms for woman's soul while also resisting the Romantic masters' messages of female subordination. Emerson remained unnamed but was probably the most immediate target of Fuller's charge that "works intended to give a permanent statement of the best experiences" included the "contemptuous phrase 'women and children.'"[38] Goethe scholar Carol Strauss Sotiropoulos points out that Fuller's celebrations of his heroines were made possible only after she edited out the patronizing lines in his text.[39] And even though she quoted Schiller, Fuller was direct in her critique of his "Dignity of Woman": it exhibited only "a great boy to be softened and restrained by the influence of girls." How could ordinary men see beyond such conventions, she asked, if this visionary poet "was not more prophetic as to what women must be?"[40] Wollstonecraft's vehement attack on Rousseau in *Vindication* foregrounded and permitted Fuller's own subtler acts of opposition. Women's "prophetic" priority was to be themselves rather than to soften men.

Of course, Wollstonecraft did not offer the only model of woman as writer and prophet; more contemporary female Romantics contributed in particular to Fuller's ecstatic sense of women's potential. Germaine de Staël first imagined a heroine of "genius" and rhapsodic speech, and Fuller hailed her as a "benefactress" to New England girls. But the tragic life of de Staël's Corinne, ending fatalistically with the loss of both voice and love, made her less than exemplary for purposes of feminist argument. The more vital partner to Wollstonecraft was George Sand, so much so that Sand intruded with no reference to marriage on Fuller's account of the union between Wollstonecraft and Godwin. Together these women writers of past and present showed that "some new interpretation of woman's rights" was needed beyond the actual work of either. Fuller suppressed the influence of Sand's writing on her own feminist development as much as she did the influence of Wollstonecraft. Gary Williams has recently made an impressive case that Fuller's engagement with Sand's *Spiridion* and *Les sept cordes de la lyre* informed her conceptions of the spiritual quest and cosmically attuned female musicianship. But the most striking aspect of Fuller's portrayal of Sand was her pairing of the French novelist's male affectations with Wollstonecraft's assault on sexual convention. Both were signs of "outlaw" status. Along with Elizabeth Barrett Browning, whose sonnets on Sand she appended to this account, she would have had new wings drawn from the defiant woman's strong shoulders to "amaze the place/with holier light." Her own Orphic, lawgiving voice would also bring that light.[41]

Fuller's rejection of outlaw women would come back to haunt the memory of her own life after the publication of *Woman in the Nineteenth Century*. Wollstonecraft had written *Vindication* as a single woman and nowhere urged the flouting of marital convention, but composing the book drew her straight to the French Revolution, which she experienced intimately through her liaison with Imlay and bearing of a child. Through an equally urgent self-propulsion, Fuller relocated her single life by way of New York and journalism to revolution in Rome, where she met Giovanni Ossoli and also bore a child. She must have thought of Wollstonecraft, even followed her predecessor's life plot on a conscious or unconscious level, but she left no written recognition of what Meg McGavran Murray has called a "peculiar symmetry" between them.[42] Certainly *Woman in the Nineteenth Century*, with its insistence on moral law, did not prefigure such outcomes except in its implicit desire for a fulfilled personal life, sexual as well as spiritual. The two women's tragically premature endings—Wollstonecraft's death of puerperal fever at thirty-eight, Fuller's drowning with her family at forty—lent further poignancy to these feminist biographies. But for better or for worse, Fuller had no Godwin to defend her unconventional life course. Surely her earliest biographers, the authors of the 1852 *Memoirs*, wanted instead to protect her from any charge of likeness to Wollstonecraft, normalizing her "private marriage" to Ossoli and emphasizing her dedication to the Roman cause without themselves endorsing revolution.[43]

Mid-Victorian feminists publicly recognized the pioneering roles of both Wollstonecraft and Fuller by setting aside possibly scandalous biography and paying critical attention to their writing. In 1855 George Eliot, serving a journalistic apprenticeship before her career in feminist fiction writing, wrote the first comparative study of these two founders. She acknowledged that readers might harbor a "vague prejudice against the *Rights of Woman* as in some way or other a reprehensible book," but still she recommended it as "eminently serious, severely moral," if also "rather heavy." No comparable prejudice detained her even temporarily as she considered *Woman in the Nineteenth Century*. What she found was "strong understanding" in both books, a reappearance of Wollstonecraft's ideas in Fuller's more literary form, and an especially fine response by Fuller to "the folly of absolute definitions of woman's nature." At least, this was Eliot's opinion for public consumption. An earlier letter, written after she had read the *Memoirs*, sympathized with Fuller's plea that life as well as intellect might be sweet. "I am thankful, as if for myself, that it was sweet at last," Eliot confided.[44] The private woman not only reserved judgment but positively seized upon Fuller's romantic and domestic happiness.

Within a few years Boston feminist Caroline Healey Dall began lecturing on both Wollstonecraft and Fuller as part of an ambitious project in feminist history, one that eventually informed her own feminist argument in *The College, the Market, and the Court* (1867).[45] Rather than ignoring the shadow under which Wollstonecraft's reputation remained, Dall sought explicitly to "clear the memory of a much-abused woman" by carefully studying the primary evidence of her adventures in France, exonerating her of blame in avoiding marriage with Imlay, and (like Fuller) finding beauty in Godwin's memorial. Strikingly, she made no parallel study of Fuller, though the recent publication of the *Memoirs* would have allowed her to do so; a veritable minefield of conflicted personal feelings about both her mentor and her own marriage probably kept Dall away from such scrutiny. Her positive point, however, was idea driven, seconding Eliot's public embrace of the two feminists within a wider historical context. Dall sized up Wollstonecraft's "startling energy" and advocacy of women's education in the explicit context of her Price-directed Unitarianism and her immersion in the French Revolution; she described Fuller in terms of both the uniquely "*complete* statement" of *Woman in the Nineteenth Century* and her personal role as "Truth-teller and Truth-compeller" to Boston women.[46] Through the voices of both women, she claimed, an influence on their respective generations allowed women's literature to rise to feminist consciousness.

Neither Dall nor Eliot, however, embraced Fuller's Romanticism without qualification, as they criticized the allusive complexity of her prose even while valuing its moral plea for liberty. Dall found *Woman in the Nineteenth Century* too learned for the average reader, even as she cherished such axioms as "Let them be sea-captains" that put her "in everybody's hands." Eliot spoke loftily as a British critic of the "vague spiritualism and grandiloquence which belong to all but the very best American writers," so that Fuller's mind seemed like the American wilderness itself, requiring a reader to step "from the sunny 'clearings' into the mysterious twilight of the tangled forest."[47] Both critics were undervaluing Fuller's "Orphic" pronouncement, either its transhistorical sweep or its messianic offering of divine law. But they were still offering a real and usable Fuller to the burgeoning feminist movement of their day on both sides of the Atlantic.

FULLER AND THE GRIMKÉ SISTERS

Sarah and Angelina Grimké were neither conscious revolutionaries nor sexual rebels. From the grounding of Quaker faith, however, they dared to undertake the equally radical act of speaking publicly the dictates of conscience on the abolition of slavery. Their 1837 Massachusetts lecture series, which eventually reached more than forty thousand listeners of both sexes in sixty-seven towns, had further seismic repercussion, because the state's Congregational clergy issued a "Pastoral Letter" condemning public speech by women as a violation of their biblically defined sphere.[48] Sarah memorably responded in *Letters on the Equality of the Sexes*, drawing battle lines for an immediate and long-term struggle over women's right to a public voice. Fuller did not directly participate in these early controversies. Several years later, however, her deep attention in *Woman in the Nineteenth Century* to both the injustice of American slavery and the need for women's speech drew vitally on the Grimkés: they located the emergence of Eurydice's voice and the collective lawsuit of women in a foundational scene of American politics.

Like Mary Wollstonecraft, Angelina Grimké appeared in Fuller's text as an allusive figure of argument, occurring at moments in midstream that suggested rather than encompassed Fuller's larger debt to the two sisters. Cataloging current motions that "overflow upon our land," Fuller proceeded from England's new queen, Victoria, to the "deep questions" of faith put by young girls, as well as to "women who speak in public . . . for conscience' sake." Then appeared the contemporary phenomenon of Angelina Grimké—along with her friend and ally Abby Kelley, who sustained the impact of the 1837 lecture tour after the Grimkés withdrew, through ensuing years of division within antislavery ranks over the "woman question." Fuller's foreshortened historical narrative introduced the speech of both as an example of "moral power" in "a cause which they hold sacred," invariably overcoming audience prejudice and awakening the nation to its needs. Alongside Fuller's potent cultural memory of the French and American Revolutions, this image epitomized moral reform as present reality, with women as its agents. Later in the unfolding argument of *Woman in the Nineteenth Century*, moreover, the image of Angelina Grimké's first appearance in 1837 recurred, now in association with the nearly contemporary visits to America of Englishwomen Harriet Martineau and Anna Jameson: collectively these women had created a moment of challenge to the nation's subordination of its female half. Echoing William Ellery Channing's question of that time about "what the coming era would bring to woman," Fuller also restated the query for the 1840s.[49] She was at once recalling a moment in her own feminist formation, celebrating the emergence of women's public speech, and offering a sign of millennial promise.

This portrait bore all the more weight, furthermore, because it contributed to a structurally vital thread of argument throughout the essay that concerned abolitionist women and their public speech. Fuller built on her earlier allusion to Quaker preachers, implicitly antislavery orators, in characterizing those who demonstrated the beauty of women's appearing in public. Here she justified her own authorship as alternative and equivalent to the Quakers' oral address: claiming that the use of the pen had previously aroused opposition equal to that of the present-day use of the lecture hall, she found woman's "free agency" and prerogative to "plead her cause" to have been at stake in both. By the time her argument returned to Grimké and Kelley in particular, the transhistorical litany of pleading voices had risen to a crescendo and included representatives of women's spiritual power who ranged from religious founders Joanna Southcott and Mother Anne Lee to the Greek Cassandra and the Seer of Prevorst. Traditions of the "Ecstatica" led to the present historical moment when women were speaking in public with sacred authority. At the book's end, moreover, Fuller offered the force of this female company, especially its antislavery orators, directly to readers in a rousing call for all American women—"Exaltadas! if such there be"—to exercise moral authority by condemning the growth of slavery through the annexation of Texas. "You have heard the women engaged in the abolition movement accused of boldness, because they lifted the voice in public.... But were these acts ... so bold as to dare before God and man to partake the fruits of such offense as this?"[50] Fuller was amplifying the voice of Angelina Grimké toward Romantic registers of transformation for herself and readers alike.

But Fuller never named Sarah Grimké, the writer who decisively turned woman's moral agency to feminist pleading and provided her with an invaluable ideological source. Fuller's "lawsuit" significantly depended on Sarah's arguments in *Letters on the Equality of the Sexes*, composed for the *New England Spectator* amid the speaking tour of 1837; Sarah actually datelined her pivotal letter "Legal Disabilities of Women" from Concord the week that Fuller crossed paths with her there. Never as confident or persuasive as her younger sister in public speaking, Sarah was the legal analyst of the pair, laying bare the common law coverture of married women in a cogent form that would echo through subsequent American and British feminist arguments. British legal commentator Sir William Blackstone provided her text: *"The very being, or legal existence of the woman is suspended during the marriage,* or at least is incorporated and consolidated into that of the husband under whose wing, protection, and cover she performs everything." Not only did this render a wife's property her husband's without legal redress, Grimké insisted; it amounted to a form of abuse and degradation at one with slavery, so that a woman might be physically chastised by her husband and, as a child innocently suggested, classified after angels, men, and beasts in God's order of creation.[51]

Legal coverture was key to the destruction of woman's "responsibility ... as a moral being."[52] Grimké nowhere spoke of tyranny or revolution and never revealed any knowledge of Wollstonecraft's manifesto. This second major opening of feminist argument, however, hinged equally on abuse of power and expressed kindred if more controlled rage. Both its content and its tone were crucial to Fuller. As Jeffrey Steele comments, Fuller was nearly ventriloquizing parts of Grimké's letter in *Woman in the Nineteenth Century* as she made her primary case for woman's need. "It may well be an Anti-Slavery party that pleads for woman," Fuller asserted, "if we consider merely that she does not hold property on equal terms with men."[53] Grimké's exposure of women's legal deprivation of being met Fuller's concerns at the heart and led to a crucial alliance.

That alliance was based on a common familiarity with civil law and an association of it with patriarchal rule. In a pattern of startling frequency, early American feminist leaders were the rebellious daughters of American law. The Grimkés and Fuller—as well as Elizabeth Cady Stanton—had all been girls close to prestigious lawyer-fathers and thereby learned early of the social forces restricting them. In the home office of her father, Daniel Cady, Stanton overheard women's cases that awoke her heart to injustice; when he showed her the "inexorable statutes" in his books, she first planned to cut out the offensive lines, then received his memorable advice to instead "go down to Albany and talk to the legislators." For Sarah Grimké, the status of her father, John Faucheraud Grimké, as a South Carolina judge was intimately associated with the realities of his simultaneous plantation management and slave ownership. Educated by her older brother, Sarah vowed to study law and readily joined in the debates between father and son. Yet her personal introduction to the statute book followed a defiant effort at age twelve to teach her own maid to read; father John ended the enterprise with a stern lecture on its legal consequences. "Perhaps," Gerda Lerner comments, "the child was already then sensitive to the irony that the very books of law cited against her were the books denied her because she was a girl, denied her maid because she was a slave."[54]

Such anecdotes offer a clarifying framework for Fuller's experience as the daughter of Massachusetts congressman Timothy Fuller, whose eight years of letters from Washington directed her education, detailed national floor debates, and influenced her prose style.[55] In his controlling way the senior Fuller encouraged his daughter's education more than either of the other two fathers, both of whom expressed conventional regret that their aspiring girls were not boys. Whereas both Stanton and Sarah Grimké responded by vowing to comprehend the masculine domain of law, Fuller overtly rejected Timothy's "Roman," public sphere for the more "Greek" world of mythology, literature, and philosophy.[56] But she also returned to a certain identification with her father: after his sudden death, she struggled at the age of twenty-five to control the financial disasters resulting from his debts and the absence of a will. "I have often had reason to regret being of the softer sex," she wrote to a friend. "If I were an eldest son, I could be guardian to my brothers and sister, administer the estate, and really become the head of my family." Though ignorant of skills in managing property, Fuller added, "I am now full of desire to learn them."[57] In a real sense the "lawsuit" of Fuller's feminist essay addressed the disenfranchisement first recorded in her earlier letter. Pleading the cause of a new franchise, she expressed hard-won knowledge and assumed her father's mantle.

In this role she incorporated crucial aspects of Grimké's argument while always expanding on it as well. In the passage that most fully reflected Grimké's case against the law of coverture, Fuller joined her in a repetitive litany of first-person witness to cases of husbands' robbery of their wives' earnings, which "count up by scores within my memory." Even though she promised rhetorically not to speak, she could not resist speaking, "for the subject makes me feel too much."[58] In fact, the feeling rose in intensity beyond Grimké's, especially as it focused newly on mothers' deprivation of their children. Though Fuller had experienced no such loss personally, she raised the emotional register with that most poignant of womanly losses.

Her shifting emphasis, however, may also have reflected the rapid development of the woman's rights debate after 1837. Just as Fuller updated her image of Angelina Grimké the orator by pairing her with Abby Kelley, so she explicitly acknowledged recent developments in the legal contestation of property rights. These developments ranged from legislative debate in Rhode Island to a *Democratic Review* article that offered the same topic "more largely considered." The latter piece dwelled at length on the grievances of mothers, for instance the increasingly notorious British case of Caroline Norton, whose estranged husband had barred her from her children. But it also expressed "large" ideals of personhood within marriage similar to those that Fuller went on to express.[59] "If principles could be established," she concluded, "particulars would adjust themselves. Ascertain the true destiny of woman, give her legitimate hopes, and a standard within herself; marriage and all other relations would by degrees be harmonized with these."[60]

Fuller was a Romantic in both "feeling too much" and in moving beyond mere feeling to principles. This statement, arising directly out of the "particulars" of women's plight, epitomized her idealism as a means of at once releasing the inner self from emotional turmoil and addressing problems at the root: trust in self and universal justice amounted to a nonconflictual strategy for change. Her argument and Grimké's might be considered complementary, sequential steps in such a strategy. Grimké cleared space with a negative critique, responding with lawyerlike patience to the edicts of male authority: first the Massachusetts "Pastoral Letter" and its attempted prohibition of women's speech, then Blackstone's legal definition of women's moral nonbeing. While alluding knowledgeably to both controversies, Fuller rehearsed neither one, but instead stepped beyond them by evoking women's voices, as they arose from podium and printed page, and their consonance with the harmony of natural law. She called on this law but did not write like a lawyer. Rather than rebutting her opponent in the manner of Wollstonecraft or Grimké, she worked, as Steele points out, through indirection, allusion, and shifting subject positions. Her early "woman's rights speech" was preceded by a satiric portrait of the "irritable trader" as a possessive husband and followed by her conversation with Miranda, the self-reliant woman who would have all women share her riches of knowledge.[61]

In the religious substratum that made such self-reliance possible, *Woman in the Nineteenth Century* also advanced a conversation begun by *Letters on the Equality of the Sexes*. Grimké's tract was intensely scriptural, a feminist commentary on America's Second Great Awakening orthodoxy. "I am in search of truth," she avowed on her first page, and "shall depend solely on the Bible to designate the sphere of woman." No aspect of her mentality was further from Wollstonecraft's Enlightened faith in the communication of mind and divine order. Interestingly, Quaker "inner light" was not a direct resource of argument. But Grimké's reading of Genesis and Paul was highly revisionary, critiquing the "perverted interpretation" that underwrote women's subjection with apparently sacred authority. She affirmed the equality of female and male in God's creation and found Adam and Eve equally guilty in the fall; furthermore, she read as mere prediction rather than command God's word to Eve, "Thou wilt be subject unto thy husband, and he will rule over thee." Later, addressing Paul's command for women to "keep silence in the church," Grimké curtailed the universal authority of this line by recalling women's "gift of prophecy" throughout the Bible and Paul's own positive guidelines for its practice. Such a reading of scripture framed her withering response to the "Pastoral Letter," where she bypassed clerical authority in favor of Jesus's injunction to "Come unto me and learn of me," then recalled the direct word of God, "Cry aloud, spare not, lift up thy voice like a trumpet, and show my people their transgression."[62] Given such scriptural words, no woman of faith would dare be anything but a public reformer.

Immersed in New Critical and Romantic approaches to the Bible as poetry rather than revelation, Fuller did not join Grimké in patient exegetical argument. But she was more like Grimké than Wollstonecraft in engaging with the Bible's patterns of prophecy and millennial possibility. Acknowledging the fall only as a projection of the "severe race" that created the Bible, she found that "even they greeted, with solemn rapture, all great and holy women as heroines, prophetesses, judges in Israel." Instead of a fall, there had been a *loss* of the divine "inheritance"; still, however, a "future Eden" awaited its recovery. In that recovery Fuller combined elements of the Judeo-Christian tradition with that of "other nations" by affirming Aspasia and Sappho, Isis and the Greek pantheon, alongside Eve and Mary. Fuller laid out the content as well as the capacity of woman's holy voice across world cultures and eras. But, as with Grimké, the language of Jesus provided a touchstone for her hope: "This is the law and the prophets. Knock and it shall be opened, seek and ye shall find."[63]

In Fuller's hands prophecy turned from Grimké's indictment of iniquity primarily to exemplify such seeking and finding. She wrote with a utopian confidence outside of her predecessor's range; neither Quaker conviction nor antislavery politics gave Grimké such possibility. The *Letters* end without a vision of God's kingdom, but only with a call for woman to labor against sin in a fallen world; Grimké could pray for opportunity to advance "the glory and honor of Emanuel's name" but could not say what that opportunity would bring.[64] Each letter closed identically, "Thine in the bonds of womanhood"; her arguments did not loosen those bonds. In this sense Fuller's greater affinity lay with Wollstonecraft, who saw the world opening to revolutionary change. But Fuller's confidence in transformative possibility surpassed both. Souls could discover their own power and their creator's law, allowing the prescriptions of church and state simply to be overwhelmed by the higher truth of equality. "There is but one law for souls," enfranchising both women and African slaves, and "this law cannot fail of universal recognition."[65]

Possibly Fuller's greatest gift to nascent feminism was this rhetoric of expectancy as a means to its own fulfillment. Such expectancy both arose from self-reliance and directed the self outward to social change. Both of her predecessors asked for the support of powerful men in changing the status quo. "As these abuses do exist, and women suffer intensely from them," Grimké wrote, "our brethren are called upon . . . by every sentiment of honor, religion, and justice, to repeal these unjust and unequal laws." Wollstonecraft concluded similarly, "Let woman share the rights and she will emulate the virtues of man. . . . Be just then, O ye men of understanding!"[66] Fuller asked men for attention but did not depend on their power. When she used the verb "let" it was to proclaim rather than ask permission: "But if you ask me what offices [women] might fill; I reply—any. I do not care what case you put; let them be sea-captains, if you will." The potential resistance of a lawyerlike "case" was simply bypassed. Likewise, she used subjunctive forms in a queenly mandate of hopefulness: "We would have every arbitrary barrier thrown down. We would have every path laid open to woman as freely as to man."[67] Giving voice to possibilities was her unique way of pleading the cause.

Sarah Grimké's subsequent response to such messages offered a compelling sign of Fuller's effectiveness in lifting the aspiration of the feminist community. Though both sisters retired from the public stage after Angelina's marriage to Theodore Weld in 1838, Sarah did not give up her plan for a systematic study of the law and the development of her own intellectual capacity. Fourteen years later, looking ahead to a "winter in Boston to stir up my latent powers if there are any," she wrote to her friend Harriot Hunt of one possible enticement in that quarter: "I should dearly love to attend the Conversations."[68] Fuller had died two years before, but the sixty-year-old Grimké was entertaining the wishful thought of engagement with her. Clearly such an impression of Fuller's Conversations with Boston women had arisen from reading the newly published *Memoirs*, because earlier that year Grimké had concluded a letter to the West Chester Woman's Rights Convention with a message taken from those same volumes: "If we adopt as our watchword the language of Margaret Fuller, we can not but overcome all obstacles, outlive all opposition: 'Give me Truth. Cheat me by no illusion. Oh, the granting of this prayer is sometimes terrible; I walk over burning plowshares and they sear my feet—yet nothing but Truth will do.' "[69]

In her 1838 *Letters*, "truth" meant a right perception of scripture; now Grimké recommended Fuller's devotion to "Truth" as a transcendent principle and resource, precisely the resource for overcoming oppression that earlier she could not articulate. But the convention address revealed her immersion in Romantic ideas far beyond this single quotation, as Grimké spoke of women's emerging from their chrysalis and awaiting a "glorious destiny."[70] Recently published manuscript essays from the same period show the extent of such development in work she intended to publish: her late "Essay on Laws" positioned law as preexistent in God's mind, though needing fulfillment through the awakening of human reason, while "The Education of Women" spoke of an unloosening of the soul far beyond her former moral and religious beliefs.[71] Grimké's new creed of self-fulfillment surely had many literary sources; allusions within these essays reveal her interest in Elizabeth Barrett Browning, Charlotte Brontë, and Anna Jameson. But key affirmations in her "Sisters of Charity" derived quite clearly from Fullerite Transcendentalism: "By asserting and claiming her natural Rights [woman] assumes the prerogative which every free intelligence ought to assume, that she is the arbiter of her own destiny, and if her soul is filled with this godlike sentiment she will strive to reflect in her life the representation of all that is pure and noble. *Self-reliance only can create true and exalted women.*"[72] Grimké had taken on the attributes of Miranda and the Exaltadas from *Woman in the Nineteenth Century*, just as surely as Fuller previously had incorporated the abolitionist persona and arguments of the Grimkés into her text.

FEMINIST HISTORY

In the years of conventions that produced a politically active transatlantic feminist movement, between Stanton's 1848 gathering at Seneca Falls and the Civil War's opening, none of our three "precursors" was personally in attendance. Wollstonecraft had of course long since died, and Grimké stayed in retirement except for occasional letters to conventions and a secret production of new essays, none of which would reach publication in her lifetime. Fuller had gone to Europe and in 1850 met her catastrophic death, just weeks before Paulina Wright Davis gathered the first national convention in Worcester, Massachusetts. Davis had written to Fuller in Italy soliciting her leadership, but instead was "left to mourn her guiding hand—her royal presence." Regardless, as Davis testified twenty years later, "she was, and still is, a leader of thought." Davis's collapsing of past and present suggests the persistence of Fuller's afterlife in the nineteenth-century woman's rights movement, as do the testimonies of Eliot, Dall, and Grimké already quoted in this contribution. The 1852 *Memoirs* of Fuller surprised the editors by becoming a best seller, and in 1855 the new edition of *Woman in the Nineteenth Century* immediately sold three times as many copies as the first.[73] A change of climate was producing more of those specially attuned readers than Fuller had dared hope for when her book was new.

Elizabeth Cady Stanton, who both led change and wrote its history, built on the ideological force of Wollstonecraft, Grimké, and Fuller alike. Her 1848 "Declaration of Sentiments" followed Wollstonecraft's lead most directly in attributing to men the "tyranny" that justified revolution, and she joined Grimké in detailing ways in which the law rendered women "civilly dead." Dall made the case for Fuller's influence with the zeal of a disciple, claiming that she had "stated with transcendent force the argument which formed the basis of the first 'Woman's Rights Convention' in 1848." At the very least, an affinity with such force might be discerned in the declaration's insistence on self-respect, God-given conscience, and education. But Stanton's immersion in Fuller's text was absolutely manifest in the first speech she delivered after the 1848 convention, where she echoed Fuller's words without attribution. Speaking of self-dependence, Stanton amended just slightly: "let [woman] live first for God and she will not make imperfect man an object of reverence." Exhorting her listeners to heroic action, she quoted from the concluding poem of *Woman in the Nineteenth Century*:

> Persist to ask and it will come,
> Seek not for rest in humbler home
> So shalt thou see what few have seen
> The palace home of King and Queen.

Indeed, Stanton's quotation from Fuller's poem rings like prophecy, for while Fuller would have her life cut short two years later, Stanton would "persist to ask" through an embattled half-century career, with Fuller as an explicit and implicit resource. Both the term "self-reliance" and the broader value of individualism remained in her arsenal from 1848 through major works of the 1890s, the post-Romantic address "Solitude of Self" and the commentaries in her *Woman's Bible*.[74]

Fuller provided a utopian resource in her feminist reading of law and self-reliance, as well as her spirituality of goddesses and women prophets who endorsed change. She modeled an integral feminism, however, by also incorporating and building on the contributions of her predecessors. At a conference celebrating the bicentennial of *Vindication of the Rights of Woman*, Joan W. Scott argued that "great figures like Wollstonecraft become great through their incorporation into a feminist tradition, and . . . we can learn a great deal about them by studying the creation of that tradition."[75] Fuller's struggle with Wollstonecraft's life story and embrace of her ideas contributed to the tradition that Scott celebrates, and her conversation with Grimké likewise carried the agenda of abolitionist feminism forward. In turn, the use of Fuller by others is part of her greatness, a use that we are still in the process of discovering.

2

"WOES... OF WHICH WE KNOW NOTHING"

Fuller and the Problem of Feminine Virtue

John Matteson

On a cold winter night in Groton, Massachusetts, just a few months after the death of her father, Timothy, Margaret Fuller walked past bare trees to sit at the bedside of a dying girl. The girl suffered from tuberculosis, but it was not that disease that was soon to end her life. Rather, the girl, pregnant and unmarried, had sustained fatal injuries in a botched abortion. In a letter to Caroline Sturgis five years later, Fuller used ornately delicate language to address the matter. She wrote, "It was said she had profaned her maiden state, and that the means she took to evade the consequences of her stain had destroyed her health and placed her on this bed of death." But Fuller's stately tone did little to conceal the horror she had felt upon witnessing the scene. Recalling her patient as "wretched," Fuller described the sick chamber as "full of poverty, base thoughts, and fragments of destiny." The rest of her recollection merits quotation in full:

> As I raised her dying head it rested against my bosom like a clod that should never have been taken from the valley. On my soul brooded a sadness of deepest calm. I looked, ay, I *gazed* into that abyss lowest in humanity of crime for the sake of sensual pleasure, my eye was steadfast, yet above me shone a star, pale, tearful, still it shone, it was mirrored from the very blackness of the yawning gulf. Through the shadows of that night ghost-like with step unlistened for, unheard assurance came to me. O, it has ever been thus, from the darkest comes my brightness, from Chaos depths my love. I returned with the morning star.[1]

Fuller's letter to Sturgis is, it seems, a useful corrective to anyone who falls into the lazy but seductive habit of supposing that the heroes of American Transcendentalism were simply a crowd of twenty-first century liberals who fell into a time warp. It is hard to imagine a figure much more pitiable than the wretched girl in Fuller's recollection, racked by pain, smitten by shame, and breathing out her final breaths in a desolate room and an almost friendless condition. Yet Margaret's judgment was striking in its firmness. In choosing to abort her fetus, the girl had, in Fuller's view, committed a crime in the name of sexual license that had plunged her into what Fuller frankly termed "that abyss lowest in humanity." After such a pronouncement, any claim to modern political correctness on behalf of Margaret Fuller must surely lie in tatters.

But this fact is very much beside the point. Recall that the wretched girl in Groton died in an *almost* friendless condition. Almost, but not quite, and not quite for the simple reason that Fuller was there. Margaret Fuller had not a feather's weight of sympathy for the girl's conduct; it even occurred to her that the girl ought never to have been born. Yet what deserves to be remembered and repeated about this story is the fact that she was there. Her principles did not override the dictates of simple kindness. Fuller's ability to hold both condemnation and compassion in her mind at the same moment was indeed remarkable. What is still more striking is her statement to Sturgis about how essential to her being was a sense of moral chiaroscuro—the intimation that if she could not walk in darkness, she would never be able to rise into the light. It was only the experience of the depths that could unleash her full capacity for love.

This quality of Margaret Fuller's spirit related powerfully to her thinking about the state of women in society. Fuller's ideal notion of herself and of women in general could not be separated from her credo of aspiration and advancement. Her understanding of a life well lived was one of upward striving, in which the person sought ceaselessly to evolve and to know herself better. Such a life, she believed, was in keeping with the progressive nature of the universe. But, perhaps more than any of the other important writers whom we consider Transcendental, Fuller could not ignore the contradictions between her ideal theory of humankind and the evidence she saw around her. True, she was adept at surrounding herself with aspiring souls. Nevertheless, she realized that, as a metaphysician, she needed somehow to account for those souls who showed little or no inclination to ascend, and, as an advocate for the rights of women, she knew that she must address the causes and appetites that drove girls like the wretched one in Groton not to the apex, but into the abyss.

In this search for understanding, it was incumbent on Fuller to try to understand the nature of authentic virtue. She required little convincing, of course, that much of what her society deemed virtuous for women had limited and demoralized them instead of encouraging them either toward a higher concept of themselves or toward the largest possible usefulness to society. The more difficult question was one that Fuller came to regard quite seriously: Was there any objective basis for an idea of expressly feminine virtue, or were such notions merely a matter of perception conditioned by social position and prejudice? Furthermore, even if those ideas of virtue lacked an authentic basis, did they retain value as a species of Platonic "noble lie," objectively untrue but nonetheless philosophically essential to maintaining a necessary order in society? The search for the dividing line between truth and illusion led Fuller where no New England congressman's daughter had likely gone before, and if her visits to the deathbeds of sexual outlaws and the prison cells of prostitutes finally gave her no definitive answers, they gave rise to some of the most fascinating reflections in which she ever engaged.

As Margaret Fuller addressed the problem of feminine virtue, she was forced to confront a potentially devastating irony. Although the very idea of feminine virtue ascribed certain positive qualities to female identity, such as gentleness, modesty, and maternal love, it seemed evident to Fuller that the moral downfall of a woman was too often linked to a concomitant of gender identity, namely sexual desire. Yet even if desire were written out of the equation, the very fact and perception of sexual difference were potential barriers to the attainment of a pure soul. According to Emerson, the culture of the soul and the proper understanding of religion could take place only when reality was regarded as spiritual instead of physical. If one wrongly supposed that divine truth were dependent on externalities, only a short time would pass before one's religiosity descended into medieval brutality. The base impulse "to whip that naughty heretic," Emerson told his journal in 1838, "is the natural feeling in the mind whose religion [is] external." Yet Emerson wrote from within a culture that firmly associated womanhood with externality, both because perceptions of women were too often inseparable from female sexual characteristics and because women themselves were generally supposed to maintain a worldview fixated on outward appearances.

Indeed, Emerson revealed much about his own suppositions when he called the impulse to scourge the heretic a "feminine vehemence." "The life of women," he noted in his journal, was "unfortunately so much for exhibition." Emerson was right to hold "the accomplishments of vulgar[,] pretty women" in low esteem, and his more intellectual experiences with women such as Fuller, Elizabeth Peabody, and his own aunt Mary eventually led him to expect somewhat more from femininity. Nevertheless, he could not wholly dispense with the idea that the excellence of a woman's character depended heavily on her worldly condition. He observed, "I have thought that the perfection of female character seldom existed in poverty, at least where poverty was reckoned low."[2] The reason, he surmised, was that women typically lacked will, and wealth could bolster the will as meaner circumstances could not. In Jacksonian America, a man such as Emerson or Alcott could find ways of regarding and presenting himself as a sexless mind and spirit. For a woman, identified first and foremost with the corporeal and the materialistic, the positing of self as spirit was an invitation to skepticism and ridicule.

The trouble with sex was, of course, not merely one of gender identity. The matter of how the soul was to ascend in spite of sexual passion was thornier still. Sexuality—as well as the pains and follies to which sexual urges could lead—was a personal and perplexing problem for Fuller. A prodigiously quick study in most aspects of life, she seems continually to have made the same mistakes in a love life too often more imaginative than actual. Until she was thirty-seven, when her romance with Giovanni Ossoli finally brought her a measure of satisfaction, Fuller's attempts at romance followed a pattern of frustration: a precipitous fall into infatuation; the premature and overly enthusiastic declaration of the same; and an eventual, wrenching divide, laden with accusations of bad faith and regal statements of self-justification. Yet if Fuller's ineptitude in communicating her most tender feelings to young men caused her repeated discomforts, these were nothing compared to the sufferings caused her by objects of affection to whom she dared not breathe a word. Chief among these was Anna Barker, a girl whose innate loveliness and unaffected grace Fuller found it impossible to observe without a tremor. The feelings prompted by Anna and, to a lesser extent, other young women appear to have found expression only in Fuller's journal, where she strove earnestly to reason out the powerful and sometimes confusing emotions of same-sex attraction. "I loved Anna for a time I think with as much passion as I was then strong enough to feel—Her face was always gleaming before me,—her voice was echoing in my ear, all poetic thoughts clustered around the dear image. This love was a key that unlocked for me many a treasure which I still possess, it was the carbuncle (emblematic gem) which cast light into many of the darkest caverns of human nature.... That night when she leaned on me ... we both felt such a mystic thrill and knew what we had never known before."[3]

That Fuller's attraction to Anna Barker was largely erotic seems difficult to deny. And yet, when Fuller scrutinized her feelings, she tried to purge them of any association that she might have considered base or unworthy: "It is so true that a woman may be in love with a woman, and a man with a man. It is so pleasant to be sure of it because undoubtedly it is the same love that we shall feel when we are angels when we ascend to the only fit place for the Mignons where 'Sie fragen nicht nach Mann und Weib'—It is regulated by the same law as that of love between persons of different sexes, only it is purely intellectual and spiritual, unprofaned by any mixture of lower instincts, undisturbed by any need of consulting temporal interests."[4] Significantly, Fuller did not anathematize same-sex attractions or consign those who felt them to an afterlife of punishment or regret. Very much to the contrary, same-sex attraction was for her an exalted love, precisely as she expected to find in heaven. Yet—and this is an indispensable point—it was a love capable of being fully expressed and truly enjoyed only where, in the words of Mignon's song from *Wilhelm Meisters Lehrjahre*, "Sie fragen nicht nach Mann und Weib." That is to say that, paradoxically, homosexual love in Fuller's view could exist only where physical bodies no longer existed and the outward signs of gender identity had been swept away by death and transfiguration. Curiously, in Fuller's ideal afterlife, the *feelings* of same-sex attraction lived on in glory, but the gendered bodies that originally inspired them were nowhere to be seen.[5]

Fuller's musings on the nature of love in the afterlife were in every way consistent with her theories about the destiny of humankind and the nature of the universe as a whole. Fuller's philosophy of nature was deeply informed by the work of Friedrich Wilhelm Joseph Schelling, an associate of Goethe's who posited that physical nature was in a process of spiritual evolution in which creation was constantly struggling toward a greater consciousness of itself and toward an ever more ideal form. Fuller's own experience of life coincided brilliantly with Schelling's natural philosophy; just as Fuller the child had become convinced that academic self-improvement was the goal of her existence, so did the mature Margaret espouse the belief that the task of her soul, as well as that of the Weltgeist, was to follow an ever-upward trajectory. Yet this ascension involved not just her mind, but also her passions. The attainment of heaven did not mean, as some philosophies would have it, the extinction of desire; rather, desire, too, was to be perfected.

Fuller assayed her own formulation of Schelling at the outset of her "Credo," a statement of beliefs that she hastily composed one evening in 1842 and never published. Fuller's "Credo" begins with the assertion, "There is a spirit uncontainable and uncontained.—Within it all manifestation is contained, whether of good (accomplishment) or evil (obstruction). To itself its depths are unknown. By living it seeks to know itself, thus evolving plants, animals, men, suns, stars, angels, and, it is to be presumed[,] an infinity of forms not yet visible."[6] Because nature is aspirational, Fuller averred, humankind remained consonant with nature only when it, too, sought eternally to improve and spiritualize itself.

True adherence to one's nature thus did not mean surrendering to one's animal impulses. Rather, in a fascinating paradox, it was in the authentic nature of men and women to overcome the baseness that one might ignorantly mistake as natural. Fuller put it this way: "Wherever man remains imbedded in nature, whether from sensuality or because he is not yet awakened to consciousness, the purpose of the whole remains unfulfilled, hence our displeasure when man is not in a sense *above* nature. . . . [Man] must be at once the highest form of nature and conscious of the meaning she [Nature] has been striving successively to unfold through those below him."[7] Seen in the light of this passage, one of the more obscure phrases from Fuller's letter about her night beside "the yawning gulf" in Groton becomes clear. Fuller described the girl's sick chamber as being filled with "fragments of destiny." *This* was the culminating sin of the girl from Groton: embedded in base nature, sunk in sensuality, she had failed to heed the summonings of a higher consciousness, and she had trampled on the law of life that leads away from selfish sensuality and toward the glittering, ineffable Good. In Fuller's mind, one who failed in this way offended more grandly than merely against herself or even her unborn child. "While any one is base," she was to write in *Woman in the Nineteenth Century*, "none can be entirely free and noble."[8]

Yet, as Fuller well knew, it was hard to argue that the universe was following a law of spiritual progression when it seemed that more people were breaking it than obeying it. The argument became still less tenable when the woman who proclaimed it had cause to wonder whether it was true even within her own breast. In reference to Anna, Fuller wrote, "The secret of my life is sealed to her forever."[9] But that secret was well known to Margaret herself, and the mystery of why it should exist remained unresolved. On the one hand, Fuller regarded women as the potential redeemers of society. On the other, she knew that they—and she herself—were unredeemed. Much of her most significant writing was to wrestle with this contradiction.

Fuller embedded her first protracted effort to discover the moral essence of womankind in the text of *Summer on the Lakes*, the idiosyncratic memoir of her waterborne journey to Chicago in the summer of 1843. One of the features that has given *Summer on the Lakes* its reputation as a baffling text is its inclusion of three episodes that bear no evident relation to Fuller's travel narrative. Each longer than the last, the three passages describe three highly unusual women, each of whom, for a different reason, stands outside the moral mainstream of her society. Taken together, the three panels of the triptych represent an Inferno, Purgatorio, and Paradiso of female spiritual life. Implicit in their portraits is a spectrum of the soul that ranges from carnal sensation to transcendent vision. In each case, the proximity of the woman to an ideal condition of character relates directly to the extent to which she lives her life as an expression of the spirit. The more dominated she is by bodily appetites and urges, the more limited her moral usefulness. Fuller's triptych effectively dramatizes the core contention of her *Dial* essay "The Great Lawsuit," the precursor of *Woman in the Nineteenth Century*: that the most important struggle that women face is not between women and men, but between women and Woman.

In his critique of the "women of genius" whose stories are embedded in *Summer on the Lakes*, Jeffrey Steele has argued that they, as well as Fuller herself, derive their chief motivations from a desire for "equilibrium in the face of oppressive ideologies" and a need "to harmonize [their] inner and outer worlds." This contention, while appealing on its face, may benefit from some refinement. It would seem the better argument that Fuller went to the frontier to *escape* from settled conditions, not to find them. Her journey to the geographical limits of white America was, indeed, a metaphor for her continual pressing against the limits of the soul. She had written to William Henry Channing of her belief "that every man must struggle with ... enormous ills." On the prairies of Illinois, she sought not a refuge from that struggle, but rather the largest possible theater in which it might be carried forward. She was looking for, but did not find, the kind of *destabilizing* conditions that stimulate the formation of culture. As Cheryl J. Fish aptly observes, Fuller's narratives of misfit women in *Summer on the Lakes* reflect her own desire "to travel out of bounds, into that wild zone where women make direct contact with nature and truth."[10] It would seem evident that the besetting threats to the inner lives of Mariana and the Seeress of Prevorst appear not in the form of disharmony, but in the shape of *too much* harmony: the false comfort and corpse-cold stasis that comes from marriage to a conventional man like Mariana's Sylvain or from life in the lonely, culturally desiccated hamlet of Prevorst. Fuller argued forcefully in *Summer on the Lakes* that the great and ultimate task for any woman was not to seek stability, but, when the need arose, to flee it—to cast aside her material distractions and petty cravings and to rise toward a spiritual, transcendent ideal of womanhood. She had to trade the limitations of existence for the glories of essence. Men were the foes of women precisely insofar as they treated them as material aggregations of physical desires and impulses. To the extent that they regarded women as spiritual beings and potential expressions of perfect womanhood, they befriended them.

For Fuller in the early 1840s, the ultimate goal of freedom was never mere physical gratification. The destiny of woman, she believed, must be something other and better than either the indulgence or the taming of unruly energies. If, as Fish has hinted, Fuller was searching for a community that would embrace her transgressive desires, this seeking was secondary to her quest for a milieu that would support her striving for spiritual transcendence. Fuller rejected the definition of freedom as the mere absence of social constraint, as evidenced by her disapproving treatment of the first of her three transgressive women, the depraved alcoholic wife of Captain P. Of the three, Captain P.'s wife is the least recognizably human. Grossly material, incapable of self-restraint, she is endowed by Fuller's text with a prodigious capacity for crudeness, but very little else. The reader is likely to forget that, apart from being known as Mrs. P., she has her own name: Fanny. Her character, only briefly developed, seems to function solely on the level of base, animal impulse. Her only ecstasy derives from alcohol. Devoid of higher yearnings, she is a personified id before the letter. Her moral significance is twofold: first, rather obviously, as an example to be avoided, and, less evidently, as the dark backdrop against which her husband's long-suffering virtue is able to shine. She affords, like the disgraced girl in Groton, a glimpse into the moral abyss. Like her, too, Mrs. P. supplies the "Chaos depths," as Fuller put it in her letter to Sturgis, from which a truly disinterested love may emerge. Indeed, her story truly belongs to Captain P. and his uncomplaining self-sacrifice, significantly characterized by Fuller as a "holy" atonement.[11] For his debased and vulgar wife, however, there is no hint of a possible redemption. Thoroughly carnal, she is the countertype of Fuller's theory of moral progression, and the only path open to her leads further downward.

Fuller gave the middle figure in her threesome, Mariana, the dignity of both a much longer treatment and a more appealing ecstatic dimension. Hers was, by Fuller's admission, the most autobiographical of the three sketches. Supremely "rich in energy and coloring," Mariana engages in "wild dances and sudden song" and, dervishlike, spins her way to a state of exhilaration. Physical motion is her means toward mental and spiritual elevation. Her excitements thus emanate from a place midway between the spirit and the body, and her being also occupies an unresolved state between extremes. The contentment that fills her heart just before her cruel humiliation at the hands of her boarding-school classmates, we are told, is the same "pure blue" as the heavens. Yet she is also a distinctly earthbound creature, capable when provoked of "doing what the demon prompted, without scruple and without fear." From an ethical viewpoint, the key difference between her story and that of Mrs. P. is that, whereas Mrs. P.'s descent into sin provides the necessary though negative foundation for Captain P.'s redemption, Mariana's disgrace precedes *her own* moral resurrection. In the wreck of her pride, in the stained, sad "bottom of her soul," she discovers "the moral nature which never before had attained the ascendant."[12] Within her character lie both the abyss and the means of surmounting it. Mrs. P.'s baseness requires an external agent to give it meaning; unlike her, Mariana, partaking of both the degraded and the divine, evinces a self-consciousness of sin. Her moral dualism entails a hope for salvation that Mrs. P. entirely lacks.

Although Mariana's experiences of chastisement and suffering bestow on her a benign dignity and she appears, for a time, ripe for earthly sainthood, she at last can rise no higher than what Fuller terms "a fine sample of womanhood." Denied the necessary food for her spirit and intellect, afforded no means of developing the "secret riches within herself," Mariana remains a stunted being, subdued at last by a weakness that she might have conquered, Fuller tells us, "had she known more of God and the universe." When Fuller speculates that, through death, Mariana "perhaps, has entered into a larger freedom," that freedom is not heaven, as one might guess, but knowledge.[13] Even to the last, Mariana is a creature of the middle kingdom.

She is not held there by her own inclinations. She is kept in place, instead, by a husband, Sylvain, capable of seeing her only in the social identity typically reserved for women. Uninterested in "explor[ing] the little secret paths" from which the true fragrance of her spirit emanates, Sylvain lives in ignorance of "a whole province of her being to which nothing in his [being] answered."[14] Though not a cruel husband in the typical sense, he can conceive a place for her only in the social world, in which Mariana finds it impossible to heed the inner law of her growth and expression. Sylvain's spiritual blindness efficiently undermines and kills his wife, who dies, no less than the real-life girl in Groton, amid the fragments of destiny.

"Secret" is a word that arises twice in Fuller's discussion of Mariana's and Sylvain's failure to divine their essential nature. The word also appears earlier in the book during Fuller's conversation with James Freeman Clarke, in which she identified herself with a race of underground gnomes, who "work in the secret . . . because only there such marvels could be bred." Cheryl Fish has identified the three women of Fuller's triptych as "grotesque," invoking the modern sense of the word, meaning misshapen or distorted.[15] Perhaps more important, they are also grotesque in the more literal sense that pertains to grottoes and caves; the spiritual strivings of a woman such as Mariana take place in a hidden region, one metaphorically underground. Fuller implied that, because unfeeling men such as Sylvain had driven them there, the true, wonder-producing virtues of women were subterranean and unknown. Perhaps only an earthquake in the existing expectations regarding women might suffice to bring these values to the surface.

Mariana prepares us for the last and most fully explored of Fuller's uncanny, outlaw women: Frederica Hauffe, the "almost disembodied" Seeress of Prevorst. Although Fuller's stronger autobiographical ties were with Mariana, there is little question that she somewhat identified with the Seeress as well. Shortly before commencing her account of the Seeress's life, Fuller observes of herself, in the persona of "Free Hope," "I never lived, that I remember, what you call a common natural day. All my days are touched by the supernatural, for I feel the pressure of hidden causes, and the presence, sometimes the communion, of unseen powers."[16] In the Seeress, Fuller presented a figure who, though strangely otherworldly, was by no means entirely alien to Fuller's own Transcendental nature. Like the Seeress before her, albeit to a decidedly lesser extent, Fuller passed through her own protracted period of psychic illumination in 1840 and 1841, during which, as she later recalled, she had known "glorious hours."[17] During this time, Fuller assumed that an early death might well be the logical outcome of her spiritual ascent. Unlike the Seeress, however, Fuller had pulled herself back from the point of dissolution. Fuller's affinity with the Seeress was therefore quite strong, and she saw in Frederica Hauffe an ontological problem that connected the latter with both Mariana and Fuller herself: how could a woman continue to live a spiritual and intellectual life that was true to her inner nature while the material world insisted on regarding her body as her true self and was forever imposing limits that were geared to her identity as a physical being?

It is hardly a coincidence that, as with Mariana, the Seeress's ontological crisis becomes acute after her marriage, in which she is "obliged hourly to forsake her inner home, to provide for an outer, which did not correspond with it." Also, as in the case of Mariana, it soon becomes impossible for the Seeress "to conceal the inward verity by an outward action"—the disparity between authentic and performed self is so tremendous that harmony between the two cannot even be feigned. Whereas Mariana's escape from her domestic imprisonment comes through death, the Seeress undergoes a peculiar divorce of mind and body in which "the body sank . . . and the spirit took refuge in the inner circle." As with Mariana, Frederica's condition is made worse by those who persist in regarding her nature as primarily physical; Frederica edges nearer to death as long as Dr. Kerner insists on ignoring her imaginative dimension and on treating her as a material, medicalized body. As Fish has observed, it is only when Kerner decides to respect her etherealized nature and abandons his effort to control her that Hauffe achieved her apotheosis.[18]

Residing as near as one could to the world of the spirit without actually dying, the Seeress conformed to Fuller's theory of a hierarchical, self-improving nature; she represented, in one sense, an upward bound of human existence. She was among the highest creations of what Fuller called "the fashioning spirit, working upwards from the clod to man." Evidently because of her estrangement from her body, the Seeress was gifted with a clear spiritual vision; she would seem to encourage us to equate the renunciation of the physical with moral excellence. Yet the story of the Seeress was also cautionary. She had deviated too far in the direction of pure spirit. As Fuller warned, "The fashioning spirit, which loves to develop and transcend, loves no less to moderate, to modulate, and harmonize; it did not mean by thus drawing man onward to the next state of existence, to destroy his fitness for this.... When we see excess either on the natural ... or the spiritual side, we feel that the law is transgressed."[19] Fuller must have observed in Frederica Hauffe a tragic variation on her own experience of the infinite a few years earlier, during which "angels certainly visited" her, but whose raptures had brought her perilously close to madness or death.[20] Distrustful as she was of the corrupting and corruptible flesh, she also knew that overly exuberant impulses of the spirit could drown and destroy "the common human existence of the person."[21] So long as this life continued, one's spiritual ascent would forever be encumbered by the nagging but necessary body.

Beyond question, though, the example of the Seeress was far more the exception than the rule. If the world erred occasionally in driving a woman too far away from the flesh and toward the spirit, its more besetting tendency was to force women into an overly material, somatically centered existence. For Fuller, the core problem of feminine virtue remained the same: the social definition of a virtuous woman was both alien and hostile to the imperative of spiritual growth and intellectual striving that, in Fuller's view, was the authentic summum bonum of life. It was becoming evident to Fuller that the efforts of individual women to transform themselves into higher beings would be largely doomed to failure until society relented in envisioning women as principally carnal beings.

Fuller's quarrel with gender was, in part, analogous to Emerson's complaint about language in general; once plainly defined, all things lose their fluidity and life, and the verbal formulation that has captured them becomes a prison. In the Seeress, Fuller was fascinated to find a woman whose essence so perfectly evaded definition. Her discussion of the Seeress is full of allusions to floating, to double identities, and to unstable, evanescent electric fluids; it tries to describe a mode of existence that, by evading definition, preserves both freedom and unlimited possibility. In "The Great Lawsuit,"

Fuller similarly sought to escape definition as it applied to male and female. Declining to accept the idea that maleness and femaleness are physical classifications, Fuller instead regarded the genders as collocations of emotional and intellectual qualities, but even these, she averred, were neither stable nor predictable. Masculinity and femininity, she assured the readers of the *Dial*, were "perpetually passing into one another. Fluid hardens to solid, solid rushes to fluid. There is no wholly masculine man, no purely feminine woman." This being so, she exhorted, "Let us be wise and not impede the soul. Let her work as she will. Let us have one creative energy, one incessant revelation. Let it take what form it will, and let us not bind it by the past to man or woman."[22] Fuller's characterization of the soul as feminine in this passage did subtle but important work. Well aware that men were presumed to be more capable than women of cultivating spirits not tainted by carnality and materialism, Fuller was more than happy to turn the tables. Even while attesting that the spirit was fluid and neuter, she was quick to claim it as essentially feminine.[23]

Fuller obviously knew, however, that the body could not be theorized away. Her pleading for a vision of a unitary human spirit, of which "Sie fragen nicht nach Mann und Weib," would count for nothing so long as women remained in the eyes of the many a creature of flesh instead of philosophy, of indulgence rather than ideality. This problem was very much on her mind as she prepared for a transformative experience a few months after the publication of *Summer on the Lakes*: her interactions with the inmates of Mount Pleasant, the women's division of Sing Sing Prison in Ossining, New York. In late 1844, as she revised and expanded the text of "The Great Lawsuit" into *Woman in the Nineteenth Century*, Fuller could not at all be certain about the actual destiny of the female spirit. She herself was, she knew, no Seeress of Prevorst; her earthly passions were every bit as developed as her vatic propensities, perhaps more so. Before she could finish transforming "The Great Lawsuit" into a more comprehensive statement on the nature of woman, she needed to know more about the forces of passion that drew women away from the fulfillment of their divine destinies.

In large part this need explains Fuller's surprising fascination with the female inmates of Mount Pleasant. As her correspondence reflects, Fuller was particularly captivated by the thoughts of female sexual criminals, those who had been jailed for acts of prostitution. Prior to her visits to the facility, Fuller's principal source of information about the inmates was Georgiana Bruce, a late resident of Brook Farm who, at Fuller's prompting, had signed on as an assistant to Eliza Farnham, the prison's recently appointed matron. Farnham, a liberal reformer, had taken immediate steps to better the moral condition of the prisoners, but prior to her arrival, the more indecent of the inmates had routinely "made [the] night hideous by singing blasphemous and obscene songs" and had eventually attacked the previous matron, ripping the clothes from her body.[24]

In her letters to Bruce, Fuller was frank and highly specific: she wanted to know what the prisoners thought about the tenets of morality that, to some, were the indispensable adhesive that held society together but which, to Fuller's open mind, were quite possibly no more than serviceable fictions. Having asked Bruce to share some of the inmates' journals with her, Fuller was particularly impressed with the account given by an African American woman named Satira, whose "idealizing of herself in the face of cruelest facts" belonged, according to Fuller's estimate, "to the fairest, most abused part of feminine Nature."[25] That Satira could retain a favorable view of herself despite her erstwhile profession and the penal price she had paid for it astonished Fuller. Here was a woman who stood little different in the sight of the world from the girl in Groton, yet who seemed confident enough to shrug off any suggestion of reproach.

Whereas most people surely would have credited a depravity in Satira's ethical opinions, Fuller wanted to know whether the ex-prostitute's self-idealization arose from a moral possibility that Fuller herself had previously failed to consider. She inquired of Bruce, "You say few of these women have any feeling about chastity. Do you know how they regard that part of the sex, who are reputed chaste? Do they see any reality in it; or look on it merely as a circumstance of condition, like the possession of fine clothes? You know novelists are fond of representing them as if they looked up to their more protected sisters as saints and angels!"[26] Fuller never asked any questions with greater seriousness; having acquired much of her knowledge of life by bookish means, she hoped through Bruce to identify and correct her romantic misconceptions. Still, however, her precise reasons for asking these particular questions are open to interpretation. On the one hand, she surely understood that part of the failure of the women of Mount Pleasant to live within the law had been their inability to attach reality to a concept that, although abstract, was essential to social respectability and, in that sense, quite real. Another possible angle to her thought is more intriguing. She was evidently willing to entertain the possibility that chastity *was* merely an appurtenance of social standing, imbued with only that degree of value that one's fellows were inclined to acknowledge.

Bruce obligingly passed Fuller's queries on to some of the inmates, though she was skeptical of receiving any honest answers. Bruce was quite astonished when one of the more intelligent women spoke her mind. Of course, the prisoner explained, "everybody in the world knew that promiscuity was wicked." But "if no one knew" that a woman was promiscuous, it was as if the sin did not exist; rather, "you did not seem a bit different from anybody else. In fact, you did not stop to think of yourself at all." It was very curious, the woman reflected, "that your being ashamed was caused by people knowing your life, not by the life itself." When pressed, the woman added that she and her fellow inmates recognized Farnham and Bruce as "good," but not at all because of their sexual conduct. In the eyes of the inmates, the goodness of their overseers consisted of their refinement, sincerity, and selflessness, not their reputation for being "chaste." These observations were far from comfortable for Bruce to contemplate, and she concluded her account of the episode in her memoirs with the peremptory statement, "It is not best to dwell on this subject."[27]

Fuller, however, wished to dwell on the subject as long as she had more to learn, and her education continued when she visited Mount Pleasant in October 1844. Fuller told a group of inmates that she was writing about Woman and, since her path had been a favored one, she hoped "to ask some information of those who had been tempted to pollution and sorrow." Fuller's record of the women's specific responses, if there were any, has been lost, but her description of the tone of the meeting is itself revelatory. She observed that her listeners "were among the so called worst, but nothing could be more decorous than their conduct, and frank too." To her evident pleasure, the time passed "much as in one of my Boston Classes."[28]

If she were adhering strictly to her theories regarding human nature, Fuller would not have been overly surprised by the gracious reception she received from the inmates. In a midsummer letter to Bruce, Fuller had emphasized her belief that there was much more that united different classes of women than there was to divide them. The prisoners, she had already decided, were representative, not anomalous. She had written, "These women in their degradation express most powerfully the present wants of the sex at large. What blasphemes in them must fret and murmur in the perfumed boudoir, for a society beats with one great heart."[29]

The fact that Fuller was unwilling to see the women of Mount Pleasant as fundamentally different from herself speaks volumes for her liberality of spirit. It is important to realize, however, that Fuller saw womankind as indivisible not only in a social sense, but also in a spiritual one. This fact added another level of complication to her ideas. Fuller, as has been observed, believed that humankind was destined to rise to an ever more rarified condition of moral purity. But the women of Mount Pleasant, particularly those who, like Satira, were wholly capable of justifying and idealizing their lives of debauchery, suggested the possibility of a fearful alternate destiny. If, as the presence of women like Satira seemed to suggest, chastity were no more than a subjective, artificial construct, then it could be done away with by a mere shift in mass opinion. Moreover, if there really were, as Fuller feared, a quietly, murmuring version of Satira in every boudoir, then all of womankind shared in a terrible corruption, and it was only a tacit agreement not to confess that corruption publicly that kept chastity intact as a moral ideal. It also seemed more than likely that the Satiras of the world would always be with us. If, as Fuller was soon to affirm in *Woman in the Nineteenth Century*, "While any one is base, none can be free and noble," then how would it be possible for womankind to fulfill its progressive destiny? As Fuller wrote soon after her first visit to the prison, she felt great interest in the inmates' welfare and hope for their improvement. That concern was not distinct from her hopes for society at large.

Fuller's experiences with the women at Mount Pleasant also affected her personally, for it is clear that if Fuller worried about the frettings and murmurings of the perfumed boudoir, she was all the more troubled by the ones in her own heart. Her own belief in the reality of chastity, while challenged by the inmates' assertions and examples, was not displaced. When she wrote to the women after her first visit with them, she urged them toward an "acquaintance with purer thoughts and better purposes" than they had previously known.[30] She wished to bring the inmates over to her view of the matter, not to go over to theirs. The principal change that her visit had effected was that Fuller now saw more deeply into the causes of lapses in female morality than she had before.

In her memoir, immediately after she recounted the results of having put Fuller's questions to her charges, Bruce wrote of an inmate named Martha Hallam, who at fifteen had been abducted by thugs and carried away to a brothel, where she was drugged and subjected to treatment that Bruce delicately refrained from elaborating. Thereafter, Hallam stayed in the bordello, having been persuaded that her family would drive her out and none of her old acquaintances would speak to her. After her mind began to give way in prison, Martha was transferred to an insane asylum. Thereafter, however, she reversed her direction and, by means that Bruce did not detail, gradually restored herself to a respectable place in society. Years later, she was proud to reintroduce herself to Farnham as the wife of a mechanic and as a woman loved and respected by a small but devoted circle of friends. Bruce remarked that if Fuller had now asked her if Martha considered herself inherently defiled and impure, she would have decidedly answered, "No." It was clear that Martha had believed and proven that "while the soul could aspire and the body perform its functions, ruin was out of the question."[31]

Though Fuller was dead long before the happy denouement of Martha's story, it seems overwhelmingly likely that she heard from Bruce or the inmates themselves similar tales of degradations not of one's own choosing and of spirits who refused to let prevailing notions of chastity compel them to regard themselves as "ruined." In July 1845, now well settled in Horace Greeley's home, Fuller wrote to Bruce of seeing, in a little wood somewhere in Manhattan, "finely dressed, painted courtesans playing at being insulted by swearing men, whose lightest repartee was 'God damn your soul!'" She added, "Oh, these are woes cancerous, horrible, of which *we* know nothing."[32] Fuller was exaggerating; by then, Bruce indeed knew much of these woes, and Fuller was coming to comprehend them too.

The understanding that Fuller had acquired in the fall of 1844 came to her just in time, as she revised "The Great Lawsuit" into *Woman in the Nineteenth Century*. Examining the two works side by side, one can only be impressed by the change in Fuller's consciousness that took place between the publication of the essay in the *Dial* in July 1843 and the appearance of the book in February 1845. After meeting the inmates in Ossining, Fuller believed in the reality of chastity as much as ever, and she was even convinced that it was linked to the survival of liberty; among the new passages in *Woman in the Nineteenth Century* is the assertion, "The power of continence must establish the legitimacy of freedom."[33] Chastity, indeed, is a far more salient theme in *Woman in the Nineteenth Century* than it had been in "The Great Lawsuit," in large part because Fuller's experiences with the inmates had helped to broaden her thinking about the problems of women in society.

When "The Great Lawsuit" addresses the social disadvantages of modern women, it most often imagines the typical woman as a middle-class housewife, confined and frustrated by her lot in life but at least not immediately financially threatened. In that essay, the stereotypic man who resists the movement toward equality is a "sorrowful trader" who fears that women's rights will break up his family.[34] In *Woman in the Nineteenth Century*, the trader remains, but he has been joined by a more dissolute cousin, a systematic flatterer and breaker of promises, to the likes of whom Fuller attributed the fall of "nine thousand out of the ten [thousand]" misguided, maltreated women. When Fuller turned her attention in the later work to the class of men who were directly or indirectly responsible for "the degradation of a large portion of women into . . . sold and polluted slaves," there was an anger in her voice that was largely absent in "The Great Lawsuit"—a vengeful, righteous fury that was possible for her only after she had beheld the Satiras and Marthas of her country with her own eyes. When Fuller called down wrath on the despoilers of women, "your forms degraded and your eyes clouded by secret sin; natural harmony broken and fineness of perception destroyed in your mental and bodily organization; God and love shut out from your hearts by the foul visitants you have permitted there," she wrote with the outrage of an inflamed prophet.[35]

Yet when Fuller turned to the subject of sexual degradation in *Woman in the Nineteenth Century*, a subject she had generally skirted in "The Great Lawsuit," it was not merely to vent her rage; rather, she meant to elaborate with care and precision the reflections on morality that her recent experiences had prompted. As to the idea of chastity as a mere socially constructed perception, she cited not Satira, but the norms of other cultures. The polygamous man of the East or the tribal chief of the American plains, Fuller observed, "did not wrong according to his own light.... [His] women were not lost, not polluted in their own eyes, nor those of others." These examples, however, did not lead Fuller to adopt the idea that chastity was *mere* perception, and no more. To the contrary, Fuller was happy to remind her readers that, in nations that "own the Christian rule . . . there is a standard to appeal to."[36]

The significant problem for Fuller was how that standard, which seemed inescapable, was to be honored. A bit surprisingly, her most pointed advice on this subject was not addressed to the men whose lusts had spawned a culture of sexual exploitation; she left the men to teach and warn one another. Instead, Fuller appealed to women—not to the prostitutes themselves, but to the creatures of society in easier circumstances, who had corrupted the lower orders by their subtly meretricious examples. In a devastating juxtaposition, Fuller set a description of a fashionable resort for ladies alongside a recollection of her recent visit to Ossining. At the former place, she had seen women dressed "without regard to the season or the demands of the place," in mindless imitation of what was taken to be European fashion. In this parade of folly, jealousy, and vanity, Fuller thought she had witnessed a kind of crime that was not down in any statute book, a crime made all the worse because it was perpetrated by "American *ladies* . . . of that class who have wealth and leisure to make full use of the day, and confer benefits on others."[37] It was women like these whom Emerson had accused of living too "much for exhibition," deriving their will only from the false confidence created by easy circumstances. It mattered not to Fuller whether such women might have no lovers other than their husbands. Call them whatever else you might, they were not chaste.

In this passage there finally emerges a less than obvious meaning in Fuller's questioning of the inmates regarding chastity. When Fuller asked whether the unhappy women of Mount Pleasant regarded the reputation for chastity "merely as a circumstance of condition, like the possession of fine clothes," she had more in mind than the idea that chastity was a virtue that only the economically comfortable could afford.[38] She was evidently thinking as well about the ladies of the voguish resort, who, in their tasteless sensuousness and love of lowly pleasures, had not a grain more of chastity than Georgiana Bruce's charges. For these women, as much as for those immured at Ossining, chastity was no more than a name and a reputation; nothing about their lives or demeanors had given it an ounce of substance. In the failure of the comfortable classes to find better uses for their privileges, Fuller saw the origins of the greater evil. The motives that had started the Ossining inmates on the road to prison were simply imitative. Like the women of the resort whose manners were a vulgar burlesque of European fashion, the women of Mount Pleasant had begun by wanting what an unreliable model had held up to them as valuable. They, too, had been betrayed by "love of dress, love of flattery, love of excitement."[39] Lacking the dresses of the other ladies, they had stolen them; avid for cheap and transitory pleasures, they had bartered their bodies to get them. It was entirely evident to Fuller that the women of the fashionable house were answerable for the women in the prison.

Fuller was above all concerned, as always, with the maladies of the spirit, but if the malaise that she observed had a social cause, then she did not hesitate to seek a social solution. The antidote for both the jaded society woman and the abused, discarded prostitute was, she believed, to bring them together. To the pampered women of the boudoir, she urged, "Seek out these degraded women, give them tender sympathy, counsel, employment. Take the place of mothers, such as might have saved them originally." Such a seeking to benefit the unfortunate, Fuller knew, was an act of salvation not only for the recipient but for the giver, and she enjoined her readers to give without reserve: "Offer beauty, talents, riches, on the altar; thus shall ye keep spotless your own hearts, and be visibly or invisibly the angels to others."[40] Again, the aspirations of which Fuller wrote were to the angelic, but these were to be fulfilled not through scholarship or the attainment of a transcendental union with the All, but by charity.

From the outset, Fuller's efforts toward equal rights were more a struggle on behalf of the minds and souls of women than a quest to win them economic and political power. Although perhaps the most frequently repeated line from *Woman in the Nineteenth Century* is the wonderful "Let them be sea-captains, if you will," the book as a whole is no more fundamentally about employment opportunities than Swift's *A Modest Proposal* was about dietary reform. What is to be liberated is not a gender, but a thing naturally without gender: a spirit that was potentially divine but that was at every turn brought back to earth by the narrow bigotry that sees a person not as a spirit, but as a piece of mortal flesh with sex organs. Even at its end, *Woman in the Nineteenth Century* seeks to make clear that its ultimate aim has been to encourage the development and perfection of the ideal spirit. In one of her final paragraphs, Fuller insisted, "It is not woman, but the law of right, the law of growth, that speaks in us, and demands the perfection of each being in its kind, apple as apple, woman as woman."[41]

And yet, as her book also makes clear, however, Fuller's meditations on the imprisonment of the human soul had led her to realize that the spirit could not be separated from the life of the body or from life in society. To regard human beings as exclusively spiritual was to turn them all into Seeresses of Prevorst. To isolate them from their social contexts was to deny something obvious: that poverty and physical abuse and neglect can destroy a soul as efficiently as any more metaphysical devil. The Margaret Fuller of earlier years had been much concerned with the state and elevation of the spirit qua spirit; it had been the inner, individual life that had mattered above all. In *Woman in the Nineteenth Century*, however, she evinced the understanding that the social *is* the spiritual and the personal *is* the political.

In *Summer on the Lakes*, Fuller expressed her doubts that limited, human experience permitted anyone "to settle the origin and nature of sin, the final destiny of souls, and the whole plan of the causal spirit with regard to them."[42] Nevertheless, Fuller's thinking and writing on behalf of women were very much concerned with what she took to be the destiny of souls. Confident as she was that the spirit of humankind would gradually transform its fleshly appetites into a less carnal, more angelic form of love, she told her readers in both "The Great Lawsuit" and *Woman in the Nineteenth Century* that those who would reform the world must lead lives "unstained by passionate error; they must be severe lawgivers to themselves."[43] But Fuller herself was to learn the difficulty of heeding her own prescriptions. Despite her formidable capacity for discipline and self-governance, she was, at last, unable fully to restrain her own implacably passionate nature, nor could she foresee the outcome toward which her passions were leading her. In Rome in 1848, expecting a child who had been sired by a man she had not yet married, Fuller concealed her pregnancy from her friends and family in America. More than she likely ever would have imagined, she had cause to reflect on the observations of the female prisoner at Mount Pleasant who had told Georgiana Bruce that it was the reputation for chastity, not its actual possession, that was significant in the world of manners. In miles and in years, Fuller traveled a long distance from the bedside of the dying girl in Groton. The distance she traveled in her thinking about feminine virtue was no less substantial.

3

FULLER, FEMINISM, PANTHEISM

Dorri Beam

In a classic essay on American Transcendentalism, "Jonathan Edwards to Emerson," Perry Miller traces a strain of interest in pantheistic and mystical energies from Edwards to the Transcendentalists, and especially to Emerson and Margaret Fuller. Asking why Emerson and Fuller would recommit themselves to beliefs in a pantheistic force and influxes of power, Miller notes that the rational attack on Calvinism by the Unitarians seems only to have released "energies" entirely "opposite to rationalism." In a broad cultural phenomenon that reached beyond Transcendentalism, even to the "emotionalism" of Harriet Beecher Stowe and Elizabeth Stuart Phelps, these energies sought new forms of expression in the mid-nineteenth century: "mystics were no longer inhibited by dogma" and "there was nothing to prevent them . . . from identifying their intuitions with the voice of God, or from fusing God and nature into the one substance of the transcendental imagination." Miller asks, "Why should Emerson and Margaret Fuller, almost from their first reflective moments, have cried out for a philosophy which would reassure them that matter is the shadow and spirit the substance, that man acts by an influx of power—why should they deliberately return to the bondage from which [William Ellery] Channing had delivered them?"[1]

Miller's characterization of Emerson and Fuller as subjecting themselves to mystical and spiritual energies, "reeling and staggering" with the most colorful New England fanatics and heretics, is as provocative today as it was seventy years ago. It calls into question a model of self-possessive individualism that has been alternately cherished, in Miller's midcentury moment, and in more recent political turns, reviled as a core element of the "American" character that the Transcendentalists purportedly helped build. Miller's association of Emerson and Fuller with irrational and undisciplined mystical modes furthermore provokes discomfort for the modern secular sensibility, both in his time and ours. But Miller's remarks are salient precisely for his wry but frank acknowledgement of a "tradition of emotion and ecstasy" and its particularly energetic manifestations in the middle years of the nineteenth century.[2] Rather than amputate the mid-century avidity for the mystical experience of immediate access to spiritual truth and a merger of the self with a world infused with pantheistic, immanent spirit—enthusiasms that formed the very "body" of Transcendentalist philosophy—Miller seeks to knit this sensibility to intellectual history. In doing so, he historicizes Transcendental idealisms that otherwise rejected any relation to historical specificity in their commitment to universalism, transpersonality, and "spirit." He also unearths some reasons that mystical experiences and beliefs in a world of energies might have attracted Emerson and Fuller: these metaphysical constructs allowed the subjective forms and experiences for which they and others longed, due to their intense dissatisfaction with conventional, dogmatic religion and the authoritarian social structures it institutionalized.

My contribution offers a close-grained historical treatment of such mystical enthusiasms and asks not "whence they came" in the long arc of American history, but rather probes how they served their authors' social vision and purpose, a question that for too long has been foreclosed by suppositions that such modes are not only personal but evasive of social engagement and immune from history.[3] In particular, my contribution focuses on the feminist interests that such enthusiasms served, beginning with Fuller's desire to harness a world of energies and spirit for her theory of gender, then panning out to encompass a constellation of women who, directly or indirectly, contributed to, reflected on, and extended Fuller's philosophical project. The double lens is essential: the breadth of participants beyond the Transcendentalist coterie reveals the resonance and meaning of a widespread feminist allegiance to an accessible realm of spiritual energy that offered the opportunity to rethink subjective and social forms. Rather than delineating direct lines of influence, it brings into focus a common and complex response to the spirit of the times, one that Fuller helped to shape, but of which she was far from the sole architect.

Yoking Fuller's feminism with her mysticism has never been an easy task. Although Miller tolerated Emerson's concepts of the Oversoul, Compensation, and Self-Reliance with sympathetic irony, it is well known that he participated in the kind of convenient amputation he castigated when he endorsed the continued excision of mystical passages in Fuller's *Summer on the Lakes* in his edition of the work. Likewise, he lamented that Fuller could not be separated from the "hyperbolically female intellectualism of the period," phrasing by which Miller, like many critics before and after him, registered his disdain for Fuller's oracular posturing and highly wrought visionary fantasies, thought to be inappropriately intense in a "feminine"—and also sexual—way.[4]

Since the twentieth century, Fuller's mystical modes have been problematic because they seem an evasion of the "real-world" feminist work that critics have sought in her writing. Yet to attempt to focus on her plan for clear social action at the expense of her Transcendental idealism is to risk missing the philosophy on which her social vision was built. Similarly, discrediting the sexual charge of Fuller's participation in a "tradition of emotion and ecstasy" surely evades a fundamental arena of feminist intervention—sexual cultures. Nor can Fuller's mysticism continue to be understood in terms of her biography, as a psycholinguistic symptom of her personal alienation from a patriarchal culture or as an effect of her personality. Too many others similarly indulged in visions of a world throbbing with spirit and passional energy for the historicity and cultural resonance of such a sensibility to be ignored.

Rather than amputate and ignore, or isolate and personalize, it is wise to acknowledge the tradition of emotion and ecstasy in Fuller's writings—and beyond—and attempt to understand the work it is doing. Readers are thereby, as Miller maintains, "not required to persuade ourselves" to indulge in mystical flights.[5] It is, however, useful to return to and remind ourselves of the central role of spirit and ecstasy in Transcendentalist thought, take it on its own terms, and ask how the concept and experience of transcendence served Fuller's feminism. If the purely rationalistic and progressive approach of Western secular feminism has repeatedly come under fire for its narrowness and failure to address the complexities of sex and gender systems, first from theoretical and continental feminisms and more recently from non-Western feminisms that demand the recognition of diverse spiritual systems, nineteenth-century feminist thought provides a surprising vantage point from which to exercise more capacious forms of feminist inquiry.[6]

First, Miller's characterization of Emerson and Fuller in which they posited themselves as subject to mystical and spiritual energies requires an adjustment in the understanding of how notions of the self and person worked in Transcendentalist writing, away from a self-possessive individualism. The pantheistic vision with which I am concerned was not devoted to a religious divinity, but was instead an endorsement of the immanence of spiritual phenomena and the relation to the world that such a notion of circulating energies indicated. Denying that spirit was "other" from the self or the world involved a reciprocal erosion of the bounded person. Fuller's writing represented a specific application of the Transcendentalist view of self as both part of and an instance of a larger field of energy, or spirit—an ecology of "self" that extended beyond the person; thus, a notion of integral, possessive personhood, such as one now associates with individualism, was not at stake in Fuller's feminism. Fuller pulled gender into this model of self, making gender part of the spiritual phenomena experienced within its ecology rather than a fixed identity rooted in the body.

Second, this contribution examines the pleasures and social possibilities, as found in a wider array of women's writing, that were available to the expanded but nonpossessive self. Writers from the feminists Elizabeth Oakes Smith and Harriet Martineau, to the trance medium Cora Hatch, to popular novelists Caroline Chesebro' and Mary Clemmer constructed an ecology of self that pleasurably extended and expanded when social obstacles were removed in dream or vision and the self poured out of its bounds, especially the body. At the same time, such a model opened the self to forces outside of it. This need not be a form of subjection, but a nuanced and empowering manifestation of gender and sexuality as forces that one did not fully contain, that were part of a shared existence with others, and that were idealities—shared constructions—that one experienced as realities. Thus the value of a popularized Transcendentalist model of feminism in which recourse to a realm of vision or ideas was not an escape or evasion of political realities becomes apparent: it provided a basic theoretical framework for lived experience.

In fact, Miller's indexing of the fervencies of the period touches on a wider understanding of access to a shared medium of spirit, one reinforced by the dynamic interchange between the philosophies of Transcendentalism and the practices of Mesmerism, which proposed a scientific basis for metaphysical phenomena. Mesmerism was an attempt to develop a science of spirit—one that could capture the spirit's irreducibility *and* its materiality, arguing indeed that "spirit was the substance and matter the shadow," as Miller phrased the mystical commitments of Emerson and Fuller. A closer study of Mesmerism, through both the manuals its practitioners wrote and its representation in nineteenth-century personal writing, reveals a cultural phenomenon less centered on the act of hypnotism, with which Mesmerism is now synonymous, than on the experience of the trance state—a state unfettered by social and physical limitations and affinitized to "spiritual" realities.

In the remove to the realm of the ideal, which the writers I examine negotiated in an explicitly visionary mode, one could experience the "truths" of subjectivity shorn of social conventions—an attempt to distinguish and rethink the very basis of how "realities" were understood. Their access and connection to "spirit" allowed the women examined here to imagine and unfold other ways of being, a process that replicated on a large scale the trance state as they experienced it. Read in the context of such experiences, the concept of self-culture to be found in Fuller's feminist circle, broadly conceived, was much more than Channing's Unitarian project of rational, individual uplift, for the mandate to allow the soul to "unfold" was far more radical when the soul was seen as an alternative form of embodiment, one that entailed new forms of relation to the world and to others.

These writers were particularly emphatic that ways of being were not based in anatomical understandings of sex and gender. This was not a displacement of sexuality and gender but a reframing of them with a political charge, posing such questions as: What if desires are not determined by gendered anatomy or social roles? What if gender has no basis in bodily morphology? What new ways of living would such a reframing allow? How can life—pleasures, body, feelings, power—be imagined differently and perhaps more justly? These were the stakes of the project in which Fuller, Oakes Smith, Clemmer, and the feminist philosophy they elaborated were involved as they worked to make idealism and spirit their most powerful tools for engaging and transforming material realities.

Fuller's interest in Mesmerism is by now well known. Like many women, she encountered Mesmerism as a healing practice. Fuller's 1845 *Tribune* review of Stanley Grimes's *Etherology; or, The Philosophy of Mesmerism and Phrenology* speaks of her encounter with a "blind somnambulist" who immediately sensed the headache from which she was suffering and offered a compelling remedy.[7] Fuller claimed that she "saw my true state more clearly than any other person did." She was also successfully relieved of chronic back pain in two months of sessions with a magnetic physician, Dr. Theodore Leger, in New York.[8] Considering the variety of poisons in the regular doctor's pharmacy (Sophia Hawthorne, for instance, was dosed with mercury, arsenic, opium, and morphine, to which she acquired an addiction), it is hardly surprising that many women turned to alternative notions of the body and noninterventionist techniques to understand and treat their symptoms.[9] Many, including Fuller, discovered a more capacious and nonempirical understanding of the body as well as a language for articulating their own less culturally admissible energies and uncodifiable feelings.

In her review of Grimes's *Etherology*, Fuller expressed concern for what she saw as Grimes's excessively materialist approach to spirit but recognized that "man is always trying to get charts and directions for the super-sensual element in which he finds himself involuntarily moving"; thus, she saw Grimes and his ilk as part of a valuable "corp" of "workmen" investigating "the power of this more subtle and searching energy" that all "prescient souls . . . more or less . . . share the belief in." Fuller's *Woman in the Nineteenth Century*, also published in 1845, forged connections between Mesmerist descriptions of vital fluid and Transcendentalist faith in an Oversoul, an energy that connected each individual soul to the larger life of the universe. Mesmerist findings in fact gave Fuller's conception of universal energy a gendered specificity, and even a sensational effect, that departed from Emerson's exalted force transcending the material world of social or bodily experience.

If Fuller's Oversoul had more tangibility than Emerson's, so her version of the social barriers to its free flow had more bulk. In Fuller's feminist view, such energies were impeded by social identities, relations, and institutions that women could not peel off as easily as Emerson could "shun father and mother and wife and brother."[10] But rather than dwelling in the present of difficult impediment, the tendency of Fuller's feminist writing was to seek routes to an unhampered future, and Mesmerism was one conduit to such an alternative. Her own experience with a clairvoyant, she remarked in the review of Grimes, was a clue to "the mysteries of future states of being" in which all could be brought into palpable contact with a realm of spiritual truth.

Fuller was not alone in her thinking. In her *Letters on Mesmerism* (1845) Harriet Martineau, like Fuller, denounced the clank and twaddle of much that passed for Mesmerism, particularly the "performances," but in lofty tones she propounded the great possibilities of Mesmerism for uncovering new "faculties" for accessing spirit and developing the potential greatness of the human race.[11] Martineau's utopian anticipation echoed one of the most influential and widely read accounts of Mesmerism (one she recommended to her readers): Chauncy Townshend's 1841 *Facts in Mesmerism*. Townshend claimed to approach Mesmerism not as a medical problem, but as a "phenomenon of our nature." He asserted that the trance state is "capable of eliciting the highest state of moral and intellectual advancement, to which man, in this existence, can probably attain."[12]

Unlike Grimes or Mesmer before him, Townshend was less interested in whether "such a *power* as mesmerism exists," but rather "whether there is a *state* so denominated." His approach was a persuasive one: like Fuller, many believed in Mesmeric phenomena, but few were entirely satisfied with the accompanying explanations. Townshend was able to provide rafts of empirical evidence concerning the states produced by Mesmerism, and he thus lured the reader toward an admission of the fact of Mesmeric trance itself, if not all of its controversial explanations, which he downplayed. But in his emphasis on and descriptions of the trance state itself, he also tapped into a vein of intense midcentury interest that has been overlooked in modern preoccupations with the Hawthornian magnetic relations that induced trance.

For Townshend and his contemporaries, the trance was more than involuntary motions and physiological changes; it was "a *state* which appears to possess its own laws of perception and action; and, in this point of view a Mesmerized person may be considered as learning a new language in which he cannot express himself with eloquence or with ease until he has mastered its idioms and possessed himself of its copiousness." This state was "a rise in man's nature," a "link in the eternal chain of things," not a result of a diseased condition (as others maintained, especially of the trances of female mediums): "Separated from the usual action of the senses, the mind appears to gain juster notions, to have quite a new sense of spiritual things, and to be lifted nearer to the fountain of all good and of all truth." Those in trance "seem to be taken out of common life, with all its heartless forms and plausible conventions" and reoriented toward a spiritual realm. It had the "elements of a future existence."[13] It was not, then, any particular clairvoyant account of the future that attracted Fuller and her contemporaries to Mesmerist discourse but the new mode of being, requiring in turn new "forms" of expression, that the trance state seemed to herald.

Joseph Haddock's 1850 *Psychology; or, The Science of the Soul, Considered Physiologically and Philosophically* identified the many levels of trance, further revealing what was at stake in its representation at midcentury. The highest level was "clairvoyance or magnetic vision, or to speak more truly and plainly, the internal sight of the soul." This higher state was to be distinguished from the now more frequently cited states of "Phantasy" or "Transfer of State and Feeling," in which the thoughts and responses of the magnetizer became those of the patient. In the lower magnetic state, the cerebrum (front brain) of the subject was dormant, so the subject's cerebellum (back brain) was guided by the magnetizer's cerebrum, which had become the "common cerebrum of both parties." In clairvoyance, by contrast, the patient's "soul" was not relying on the relay of images from the magnetizer's cerebrum; it was using its own unique senses. Nor did this mean that it was relying on the subject's physical senses. Rather, the soul "acts independently of the external visual organs, so it is not trammeled by those natural laws to which they are necessarily subject. . . . Things may be seen which are out of the range of natural sight, and altogether above its nature." The "rotundity and opacity" of the earth were barriers to the visual range of the eyes, but the soul ultimately was not limited to the body, so it was not bound by its senses. "To the higher stages of clairvoyance there seems, comparatively speaking, no bounds," and so the clairvoyant could see across oceans or within bodies "as if the external and internal parts were alike as transparent as glass."[14] Townshend, also speculating on the mechanisms of clairvoyance, suggested that the physical senses were actually "masks" for "blunting, not for heightening, sensibility," but in trance one could dispense with the sense organs and experience an expanded sensibility.[15]

As he moved from magnetic relations to clairvoyance, Haddock's language shifted from that of the physiology of the mind to what he called "the science of the soul," because "physiology as such, that is, as the science of our outward organism" could not explain the activities of the inward organism, which were better discussed in the terms of "psychology and philosophy." Nonetheless, the soul could be studied scientifically; it was not "that simple entity, that abstract nothingness so generally represented by metaphysical writers." It was "a subject of the laws, and possesses the properties of that world which have nothing in common with *time, space,* or *common matter,* it displays those powers which can be explained by no merely natural or psychological knowledge."[16] The trance in its highest state provided the opportunity to experience such other worlds, or to encounter this one on very different terms.

The trance state, then, posited access to an ideal realm and to other ways of being that were not just conceptual but could be experienced in trance. Mesmerism provided a way to imagine self and body otherwise, allowing Fuller, her peers, and her literary protégés to conceive of reframing gender in ways untethered from the body and to explore what such reframing might have to offer to the lived experience of women. Feminist and literary writer Elizabeth Oakes Smith framed her feminist theory in much the same way as Fuller; the similarity points to the wider interest in the applicability of Mesmerist philosophy to questions of gender, body, and self and its foundational importance to midcentury feminist theory, as well as to Oakes Smith's clear philosophical debt to her predecessor.

Both writers explored notions of what Fuller called the "the electrical, magnetic element," the "especial genius of woman," and conceptualized their dreams and desires according to Mesmerist notions of self and body using Mesmerist vocabulary.[17] "It has been a part of my experience several times to become clairvoyant of a sudden—when I have prophesied and such predictions have always been true," Oakes Smith wrote in her unpublished autobiography.[18] Her 1852 publication, *Shadow Land; or The Seer,* is an astonishing account of her dream life, in which she tours several continents with clairvoyant accuracy, forecasts events, anatomizes her spouse's aura, and gets a look at her own spiritual body. As Barbara Welter has noted, Fuller's "mystical feminism" extended to her self-presentation, for Fuller "gloried in her role of Sibyl, and relished all reference to her as delphic and/or Oracular."[19] That Fuller and Oakes Smith experienced their visions as particularly feminine dispensations is clear from their deployment of semiautobiographical portraits of exceptional, electric women throughout their writing. Yet this gendered essence was not one that inhered in the biological body, nor even in one's personal psychology, and that distinction gave their concept of gender a degree of innovation and possibility.

In their feminist conception, the soul was infinitely more diverse than a dimorphic model of the sexed body. A woman's or a man's soul could take an infinite number of shapes; thus, the unimpeded soul was the basis from which to argue a feminist agenda of expanded action and intellect rather than of separate spheres. The treatment of women as soulless bodies, according to Oakes Smith's 1851 feminist monograph *Woman and Her Needs*, was the central problem with their condition: "It is the making of woman a creature of luxury—an object of sensuality—a vehicle for reproduction—or a thing of toil, each one, or all of these—that has caused half the miseries of the world. She, as a soul, has never been recognized."[20]

Oakes Smith incisively captured the self-annihilation that seemed to her the central tenet of "woman's sphere": "it is a sphere by which every woman creature, of whatever age, appending to [a man], shall circle very much within his own—see and hear through his senses, and believe according to his dogmas, with a sort of general proviso, that if need be for his growth, glorification, or well-being, in any way, they will instantly and uncompromisingly become extinct." "Let woman learn to take a woman's view of life," and she would learn to see differently, Oakes Smith argued. We see the importance of Mesmerism to Oakes Smith's feminism: women must release themselves from their assigned sphere, itself a kind of Mesmerized slavery in which they "see and hear through [man's] senses."[21] Once women achieved the higher visionary encounter with their own souls, however, they would slough off the "effigies" of the socially defined women's sphere. They would be endowed with Townshend's "new sense," where the soul's different vision would allow women to see beyond what Townshend called "heartless forms." Women must look to the soul to produce a new embodiment of self.

But Oakes Smith's argument moved beyond Townshend's more general claim for visionary access to a just future. She wished women to access "a difference in the soul as in the bodies of the sexes," which she variously dubbed "woman-thought," "woman-perception," and "woman-intuition." In language that sounds strikingly current, Oakes Smith postulated, "I see no way in which harmony can result in the world without entire recognition of differences." In contrast to the "woman's sphere" of popular phraseology, in which, according to Oakes Smith's text, a woman rotates around a man like a dark star around a sun, that is, she "must merge her being, be absorbed and annihilated in marriage—be an extinct world, a gone-out soul, in the chaos of a household," Oakes Smith proposed different, noncomplementary, bodily alignments. "There is a Woman's sphere—harmonious, holy, soul-imparting," but since its orbits were independent of the "private circle" it could not be defined in relation to that system. "Let [women] not feel disparaged at the difference which I have recognized; it is a difference that crowns women with a new glory," she asserted.[22]

The different vision and new senses to which Oakes Smith alluded were more than metaphor for her and for Fuller. In *Woman* Fuller contended that women had "far more" of "the electrical, magnetic element" than men. She claimed, "the especial genius of woman I believe to be electrical in movement, intuitive in function, spiritual in tendency" and borrowed the term "femality" to label such feminine energies.[23] Fuller regretted the fact that this element had never been fully developed in women and looked to it as a future source of power for them. While Emerson directed his listeners to heed a universal "Genuine Man" or "Universal Man," accessible to every individual in his growth, Oakes Smith and Fuller posited access to energies they asserted were feminine.

A long history of Fuller scholarship has debated the status and location of the feminine in Fuller's feminist theory. For many years, Fuller was cherished for promoting androgyny, an amorphous merger of masculine and feminine traits that makes gender ambiguous. Since then, Fuller's feminist stance has alternately been linked to the masculine or feminine sphere, but in either position she has often still been made to disavow herself from the feminine.[24] Taking issue with such views, Cynthia J. Davis argues that "in the final analysis Fuller disavowed *both* femininity and masculinity for an identity that transcended or at least incorporated both." For Davis, Fuller's disavowal was evident in her escape from gendered form, specifically the body. In Fuller's *Woman*, Davis argues, "an abstract generic 'soul' displaces concrete gendered essences as that which is contained within bodies, whether male or female." Examination of Fuller's theory of gender, however, reveals that although Fuller moved out of body to formulate her concept of woman, that move did not entail a loss of gender nor a "resistance to materiality."[25] While Fuller detached gender from the body, she nonetheless preserved it as an essence available to, though not inherent in, the soul. Fuller proposed a thoroughly Transcendentalist model of gender in which gender, and particularly femininity—while a powerful force in the world that interests Fuller in its pure, essential form and in its alloyed forms as it reveals its presence in nature—is not something that belongs to anyone personally by virtue of their body or their psychology.

In the following passage, significantly located in the center of her discussion of the "electrical element in woman," Fuller articulated this concept of gender:

> Male and female represent the two sides of the great radical dualism. But, in fact, they are perpetually passing into one another. Fluid hardens to solid, solid rushes to fluid. There is no wholly masculine man, no purely feminine woman.
>
> History jeers at the attempts of physiologists to bind great original laws by the forms which flow from them. . . . Nature provides exceptions to every rule. She sends women to battle, and sets Hercules spinning. . . . Of late she plays still gayer pranks. Not only she deprives organizations, but organs of a necessary end. She enables people to read with the top of the head, and see with the pit of the stomach.[26]

In this view, pure gender is never resurrected in the flesh; instead, the spheres of Fuller's great radical dualism are permeable bodies that pass into and out of each other, mingling in various amounts and at varying locations. Fuller thereby defeats the compartmentalization of gender into separate spheres by releasing gender into "the spheres," where bodies are permeable, shifting, and transmuting versions of their former state. In this heaven that gets gender right, essences of souls are made plain and are freed from the limiting binary of biology to occupy a zodiac of possibilities. The passage mocks physiologists for whom only bodies, "forms," are legible, whose theories could never account even for scenes such as Hercules spinning or women battling. Men and women should not be confined to exclusively masculine or feminine roles, since "in *fact*" their constitution, in which gender traits are "perpetually passing into one another," reflects more diversity.[27]

At the same time, there are, the passage maintains, in *principle* essential feminine and masculine "energies." Though *Woman* asserts that both men and women can tap into either energy, it also maintains that women's souls are more likely to be modified to partake of femality. Fuller's final task in this passage was to embody her vision of this truer world. She accomplished this by moving from "organizations" to "organs," from social body to individual body. If first she scrambled the signifying power of the body politic by disbanding its organization into gender spheres or parts, she next worked at the level of the individual body, depriving organs of their usual functions. Here she was rearranging the body to replace its orientation toward the physical world with an orientation toward the spiritual or interior realm, just as the trance state did. In a manifestation of Oakes Smith's "new senses" for women, Fuller imagined the scalp reading and the stomach seeing. Fuller went on to show that these other senses "enabled Cassandra to foresee the results of actions passing around her; the Seeress to behold the true character of the person through the mask of his customary life"; and "the daughter of Linnaeus to see the soul of the flower exhaling from the flower," a vision ranged against Linnaeus's anatomizing gaze.[28] Fuller's concept of gender, then, is characterized by an emphasis on the soul and its different senses, and a will to tinker with the body, to reorganize its organs.

For Fuller, each person is pervaded by and a part of a "great radical dualism," the immanent divine spirit that holds masculine and feminine in balance but is obstructed by contemporary social barriers. This cosmic "dualism," in other words, was akin to Emerson's Oversoul, but it was gendered. Fuller also claimed in *Woman* that the feminine soul "breathes, it sings, rather than deposits soil, or finishes work, and that which is especially feminine flushes, in blossom, the face of earth, and pervades, like air and water, all this seeming solid globe."[29] Again in this passage, the feminine self is not the "seeming solid" earth, despite formulations of the female body as just such utter matter; rather, it is that which troubles solidity, which points to another dimension. This feminine principle can be felt within the body, but it does not originate there; it is a transpersonal force existing beyond the confines of the person. Fuller's notion of a gendered "essence" was neither biological nor psychological; in practice, each person partook of different portions of each gender through spirit, despite their biological sex. Spirit was the location of a feminine "essence," but, as Judith Butler has noted, an essence in the traditional metaphysical sense is opposed to appearance; it is "something that strictly speaking does not appear" and is not available to description.[30] That essence cannot finally be captured to describe a fixed feature of femininity or its "place." Fuller's and Oakes Smith's feminism sought to acknowledge a sense of the feminine as a force—in the material world, in language and literature, and within each person, while simultaneously freeing women from socially prescribed versions of femininity that failed to acknowledge internal gender diversity and linked women to a single reductively defined and lesser social identity.

Feminists today abjure any notion of a gendered essence as playing into "essentialist" notions of gender that tie biology irrevocably to identity. It can be difficult to see how Fuller's belief in essence could serve feminism. But the notion of essence has its own historicity. In this case, a notion of an essence of the feminine, here a model of spirit akin to Emerson's Oversoul, allowed Fuller and her contemporaries to formulate a version of gendered resistance that was facilitated through the notion of spirit, that allowed for the imagining of alternative models of gender that could not be tied to the body and thence to the anatomic dualism that made the masculine the primary value. In a rich and productive paradox, they constructed a positive presence based on spirit—one that formulated a different way of being in the world, as did the experience of trance. They posited a way of being embodied as spirit, with a different set of senses that peeled away the barriers to one's interaction with the world and its essential truths. Vision became an arena for reframing femininity as an uncategorizable presence, an energy that could unravel the logic of the separate spheres by undoing social categories based on the body. Fuller separated gender from the body to make it available for examination as an idea while nonetheless admitting its power as such. If, Fuller seemed to suggest repeatedly, one reframed the feminine as equal to the masculine at the level of ideality or thought, what might that have to offer one's conception and experience of gender?

Women's descriptions of the trance state in both fictional and nonfictional accounts provided important answers by giving a wider sense of the alternative forms of experience and embodiment available through the framework of trance. In her model of organs without necessary ends, Fuller suggested that the body and senses were conceptually available for rethinking and that those reconceptualizations opened onto transformative social arrangements. Women's fictional and autobiographical accounts of trance suggest to us the insights made available by an experience of the self not limited to or contained by the body, including an altered perspective on gender and the new social configurations, as well as the kinds of pleasure, such an experience unfolded.

In fact, much Mesmeric discourse was explicit about the existence of a material, embodied soul, what Spiritualists called "the electrical body" and author Lydia Maria Child, in her 1855 *The Progress of Religious Ideas, through Successive Ages*, described as "the sensuous soul" — "a subtile [*sic*] invisible body, the seat of the spiritual faculties, the mediator between the soul and the senses." Child found evidence of such a spiritual body in the example of "the soul of Hermotimus, the Greek philosopher, [who] frequently left his body apparently lifeless, and wandered all over the earth, bringing tidings from remote regions, and foretelling futurity."[31]

In her *Shadow Land*, Elizabeth Oakes Smith related a similar tableau: "We may imagine the spiritual being laying down its material companion tenderly to slumber, withdrawing itself gently from the exhausted receptacle, and rejoicing in its freedom from the frettings of daily life; while itself, needless of repose, goes out into new untried spheres, filling its urn at divine fountains, lighting the torch of its existence in the glories of the Infinite Source; holding its companionship with undying affinities, and enlarging itself by ranging through illimitable space."[32] The passage describes the experience of leaving the body behind and the consequent ability to "enlarge" the self and extend into "new untried spheres" to enjoy freedom of movement and a negation of gendered boundaries. Likewise, popular author Caroline Chesebro's 1851 story "The Clairvoyant" describes an out-of-body flight as simultaneously an escape from the body and from male control: "He had looked upon me, and I know not how it was, but his strange gaze overpowered my nervous system, inducing a sleep of the animal life, and then this panting, struggling soul escaped his influence, as it had that of the body."[33]

But the soul's mobility, clairvoyance, and prophecy in these conceptions were made possible only by its embodiment: Child noted that the ancients sometimes called it an "aerial body" and sometimes a "sensuous soul," describing such an entity as "exercising *all* the functions of sense, in *every* part of it; that it was 'all eye, all ear, and all taste.'"[34] The protagonist of Oakes Smith's 1854 women's rights novel *Bertha and Lily* is able to self-induce a trancelike state, a state that "is so delicious, that one of less integrity of life might be tempted to repeat it. I seem to float in air—my senses are cottoned upon me—faint music and exquisite odors float about me."[35] In all of these examples, the sensuous soul offered a range of possibilities. The soul's escape from the body allowed an exploration of interiority free from gender prescription, but, being embodied, it provided an arena in which to explore sexuality free from the entrapments of a specular, culturally scripted and "sexed" body. This version of the soul, described by Chesebro' as "panting" and Oakes Smith's Bertha as "delicious," impedes the critical impulse to chalk these instances up to conventional Christian feminine spirituality.

It would be misguided to think that any sexual or erotic register of the soul that one might detect here was lost on nineteenth-century readers. The *Christian Enquirer*, for instance, in an anxious review of Oakes Smith's *Bertha and Lily*, suggested that some new configuration of sense and spirit was the implicit project of the novel: "As might be expected, coming from the pen of Mrs. Oakes Smith, there is in it at times, a tinge of *transcendentalism*; yes, and of *spiritualism* too; to say nothing of a strong flavor of *Swedenborgianism*, all through. It makes us ask the question, whether sensualism may not be spiritualized, and so made fascinating? The accomplished authoress seems to us to prove the possibility."[36] We have seen that Mesmerism sought a new relation of matter and spirit—to see and feel the soul in trance and, conversely, to reencounter the material world through the vision of the soul. Hence, figures of the soul were just that: conceptions of the soul as a tangibility and even a body.

An embodiment of Fuller's organs "without necessary end," freed from utilitarian, limited applications in the physical world, the sensuous soul as incarnated in women's midcentury accounts involved a rearrangement of the body and its faculties. Mesmerist manuals described the clairvoyant state in just such terms, as "a *closing* of the common external of our being, a *transfer* of the *sensational* perceptions from the *ultimate of the body* to the *ultimate of the spirit*—and thence, and simply from this transfer of ultimates, arises an awakening of the conscious sensational perception of the inner man, or spirit."[37] While the bodily senses were shut down, encountering the soul through the trance state depended on the notion that it could be sensed, that is, physically encountered precisely because the soul was sensate, capable of sensing and of being sensed.

Harriet Martineau's description of the trance state in her *Letters on Mesmerism* provides a model of erotic experience that quite literally avoids the snares of the physical body:

> As the muscular power oozes away under the mesmeric influence, a strange inexplicable feeling ensues of the frame becoming transparent and ductile. My head has often appeared to be drawn out, to change its form, according to the traction of my Mesmerist; and an indescribable and exceedingly agreeable sensation of transparency and lightness, through a part or the whole of the frame, has followed. Then begins the moaning, of which so much has been made, as an indication of pain. I have often moaned, and much oftener have been disposed to do so, when the sensations have been the most tranquil and agreeable. At such times, my Mesmerist has struggled not to disturb me by a laugh, when I have murmured, with a serious tone, "Here are my hands, but they have no arms to them:" "O dear! what shall I do? here is none of me left!"[38]

Here, the body is exaggerated and attenuated, weirded and rearranged, at the same time. Finally Martineau's body melted away in inverse proportion to the ascendancy of her pleasure, until there was nothing, leaving her to experience the most intense pleasure at the moment of utter self-abandonment.

Cora Hatch, the famous trance medium whose lectures even Henry James and Nathaniel Parker Willis attended, described (while channeling Epes Sargent's spirit) the experience of encountering the spirit's body after the death of the material one: "Suddenly and with full power, I sprang upright, and was aware immediately of being a form, a being whose intensity pervaded and thrilled me, until I seemed a part of all the universe around; a form that was so unlike the form that lay at my feet that I was startled."[39] Hatch's grammar conveys a dispersion of self and even a confusion of selves: Is the speaking "I" that springs up as a new form the same as the "being" whose "intensity" pervades and thrills her? The dispersion of self, nonetheless, leads to an experience of concentrated sensations—of power and thrilling intensity. Hatch and Martineau described disembodied states of transparency and dispersion, even as they narrated distinctly sensual responses—the "moaning" and "the sensation of transparency," and the "thrill" and "intensity" to be accessed outside of the physical body.

Oakes Smith, in *Shadow Land*, also described the experience of seeing "her spiritual anatomy" in a dream, including

> the nerves, a perfect forest of them, but beautiful in themselves, like threads of pearl; next I saw the bones, and these were of the purest ivory. Palpable as these parts were, they were exquisitely beautiful to the eye, and made up a floating, transparent, white shape, affecting me with a sense of pleasure; but within all these—breathing, and diffused through all, and making up the solidness of what here, in this world, is flesh and blood, for I saw none in my dream—was a rosy light that seemed to live of itself, imparting completeness to the whole body.[40]

Here again is the semantically and grammatically impossible feat of seeing and describing the experience of one's (spirit) body from a place outside of bodies. One gets tangled in the language of the passage because the metaphor and logic break down: how do these parts work together? In the attempt to map the spiritual body back onto the bones, flesh, and blood of the physical one, the imagery baffles, as if the process of being mapped back onto a physical body denied the spirit its integrity. Without the semantic knitting of the images, one loses track of the way this spiritual body is put together. Perhaps, however, that is the point. As one wanders through these clauses, which provide such an inadequate anatomy, one nomadicizes the body described and gives it extra, unmapped dimensions. As it was for Hatch, the "thrill" of diffusion is palpable. This passage describes—but also acts as a conveyance for—a feeling of the self's pouring out of its bounds. The move out of the body is a move into a space newly alive to pleasure. The self has become uncontained but yet is substantive and accessible in ways it had not been before.

The model of self reconstructed here was important not only for reconfiguring individual women's pleasures and desires in their experiences and descriptions of trance, but also, as Fuller and Oakes Smith after her had insisted, for reframing social and sexual relations. A forgotten but fascinating novel by author Mary Clemmer fleshed out these possibilities in ways that resonated with and extended their vision. A protégé of Alice and Phoebe Cary, Clemmer is now best known for writing a memorial biography of the sisters after their death. During her life, however, Clemmer was notable as the Washington, D.C., correspondent for the New York *Independent*. In the 1850s and 1860s, she attended the Carys' salon in New York, where she arrived too late to meet Fuller but encountered her legend; it inspired her to write a commemorative essay on Fuller published in an 1872 collection titled *Outlines of Men, Women, and Things*. Clemmer's 1864 novel, *Victoire*, explored a variety of feminist issues: it was an exposé of difficult working conditions for women in New York City, a critique of marriage as women's vocation, and a fraught exploration of free love.

The eponymous protagonist of Clemmer's *Victoire* harbors ambitious longings to be a painter, but when her parents die before her maturity, a family friend, Henri Rochelle, insists that she needs his protection and asks for her hand in marriage. Yet in the midst of Henri's proposal, which she is expected to accept, Victoire reflects on the "rights" of the soul, much as Fuller and Oakes Smith had, and muses on the open spaces it requires: "Every soul holds an inner life and this should be allowed to expand, to grow, safe from the pressure of any outward hand." Nonetheless, she goes on, "that bent of the mind, which can neither be given nor taken away, which distinguishes its possessor from every other human being, is generally regarded as a fault." The outward life, especially of women, does not unfold according to the soul's unique shape. During this reverie, Victoire receives what she calls the "prophecy of an individual mission," a vision instructing her to be an artist rather than a wife, and she subsequently refuses Henri. Here Victoire demonstrates the feminist-Mesmerist tenet that locating a self in the soul, rather than in a social body that needed protection and a mate, or in a heart that needed a head as the Victorian sentimental formulation posited, paradoxically allows her to maintain control over her body.[41]

The radical implications of Victoire's statement, which free lovers were also exploring, were that although social contracts attempted to bind her body, her soul remained free to range arenas outside of them. Her desire does not necessarily follow into the spaces assigned to her gendered, embodied self. This is made explicit in the proposal scene when, as Henri presents his suit, she closes her eyes and "sees," in the "trance of [her] new vision," not only alternative career paths but the face of someone whom she clearly prefers to the present applicant, a man she has glimpsed only once but for whom she conceived an immediate passion. Her visions transport her to the lush bounty of Les Delices, her childhood garden in France and now the mise-en-scène for her rapturous visions of the face of a stranger. As Victoire mentally wanders from the proposal scene to her garden, she clears a space in which she experiences the "tremble" of "the pulses of life," even as her suitor drones on about her "needs" for protection, for money, and so on.[42] She thus counters her seemingly docile (according to her status as female and ward) and passionless body by abandoning it and manifesting her pleasure at another location altogether.

In fact, the status of Victoire's visions as imaginary is complicated by their frequent grounding in reality: the reader later discovers that the man Victoire sees in the garden was really there at the time of at least one of her visions. His presence in what she calls the "soft spring realm" of this inner garden and the electricity of their out-of-body connection charges this vision with sexual overtones. Since the two had exchanged only a fleeting glance prior to Victoire's visions of him, her out-of-body encounters with him in fact provide the material for their subsequent attraction when they do meet. That is, her visions precede and explain the intensity of the reunion when they meet again, as if the visionary encounter had the status of an actual event. In the mystical space opened up by Victoire's sixth sense, a space that need not correspond to the spatial or temporal limitations of her physical body any more than her clairvoyance does, what constitutes a sexual encounter becomes ambiguous.

Victoire's visions offer an experience much like the highest trance state the Mesmerist manuals describe, in which she can "see" more; she can in fact apparently see from New York, where she goes to practice her art, back to France and her garden. She can also see or sense that "future state of being" Mesmerists had promised: a world geared to spirit, rather than to the body or the forms of convention. Strikingly, the spiritual reality to which Victoire has access encompasses a full-scale sexual alternative that reaches beyond the personal limits of autoerotic reverie. In the novel, the stranger, appropriately named Ambrose, appears in America after Victoire has finally consented and married Henri. In the chapter titled "Free Love," Victoire refuses to act on Ambrose's proposal to flee with him to Europe. Yet the eponymous principle of the chapter is everywhere validated. Victoire portrays another reality in which

> we wake to find ourselves possessed with a mysterious feeling of kinship for one standing without the sphere of our individual life, with whom we are never to enter into any intimate personal relations, yet the vines of alliance, reaching out from that soul, cling closely to our own. . . . So illusive is the tissue, we cannot sunder it, so tense is the subtle fibre, we cannot lengthen it. . . . There are hours when longings for the absent presence pierce the soul as the wondrous vision of unattainable joy . . . the mocking glory of the "Might Have Been."[43]

Victoire describes spheres of desire and affection—haunting, spectral, flowing outside and through social and physical structures. In the novel, human desire moves in mysterious, unpredictable ways; it cannot be manipulated or projected by the individual. It is "spontaneous and independent of our volitions." Persons with no evident role or significance in one's life can yet impinge on and impress that life more than those who are physically proximate and involved: "Souls separated by a thousand barriers yet act and react upon each other; that beings who seem far distant from us sometimes exert a deeper influence over our lives than the companions who walked by our side."[44] The novel offers a radical and strict configuration of a love so free that it roams about of its own volition, taking little heed of persons, spatial relations, social circumstances, or the self's instructions to it. Attraction that surpasses all bounds, circulates outside of the marriage contract, exceeds the companionate love of the domestic circle, and is fundamentally antithetical to social institutions pervades the novel and challenges its marriage plot.

Like Fuller's feminine principle, the free love the novel portrays operates as a spirit that can have social impact and can be felt in the body but does not originate there. Free love amounts to a kind of pantheistic force; the force of spirit depicted in the novel is so radical that it cannot be conjured or contracted. In Clemmer's construction of it, this dynamic has risks: the bonds created by free love are not of one's own making. One's sexuality is not something that can be projected in private or shared at will; sexuality comes from outside of the self and threatens to—perhaps pleasurably—undo one's self. One who is responsive to such spirit, however, can partake of its radical freedoms.

Victoire was remarkable not only for probing and developing an alternative space of free love and the agony of living outside it but also for not finally renouncing or eradicating it. The spiritual lovers, Ambrose and Victoire, resign themselves to separation, but although Victoire has conducted rigorous experiments in the asceticism of seventeenth-century French mystic Madame Guyon, among others, the conclusion suggests that Victoire will not purge her feeling, but harbor it, and the text suggests that it may find the light of day again. Renunciation would have denied the spirit of free love; the conclusion instead allowed Clemmer to offer the socially correct maintenance of the marriage vow as a kind of "meantime" in which the spirit of free love exists as an immanent future.[45] Withdrawal into and indulgence in one's vision has had the power to destabilize the social structures, especially marriage, that were momentarily abandoned. The visionary realm is not shown to be private, isolated, and contained; indeed, in featuring extramarital desire it reveals another reality that conventions have masked. Victoire's visions produce another plane of experience for her and likewise compete in the novel's diegetic space and time with the marriage plot, causing the narrative to break open around marriage, which takes place at the halfway point of Victoire's narrative, rather than resolve with it.

Just as Mesmerism granted access, not to separate worlds or afterlives, but to previously inaccessible regions of this one, so Clemmer's novel posits through Victoire's visions other itineraries for women that are temporally and spatially coincident with the realities of Victoire's plotted, normative existence; these alternative possibilities are presented as "here" not elsewhere, ready for those who know how to access them. Clemmer operated under the recognition that, as Judith Butler writes, the critical promise of fantasy "is to challenge the contingent limits of what will and will not be called reality," because such visionary possibility "is what allows us to imagine ourselves and others otherwise; it establishes the possible in excess of the real; it points elsewhere, and when it is embodied, it brings the elsewhere home."[46]

One can in fact locate in the visionary landscape that Victoire accesses a final example of the sensual soul—a configuration of body, spirit, and energy that is linked to and allows for the exploration of alternative sexual arrangements in the text. Clemmer's highly stylized language was the site for her experiment with making such energies palpable and requiring the reader's apprehension of the alternatives suggested—an embodiment that "brings the elsewhere home." In the vision in which Victoire sees the stranger in Les Delices and the reader learns that he was actually there, Victoire's visionary description of the garden carries the weight of a charged sexual experience. At the very moment that she is transported from her body, in fact, she employs an utterly sensual vocabulary:

Before my second inmost sight [the garden] stood in the trance of a summer noon. The mountain summits burned in smouldering clouds of electric crimson. The cascade fell in sheets of crystallized sunshine—trailed its glory over blistering rocks, dropping at last on the cool hearts of purple mosses which waited its coming in the humid gorges below. Again the fruits in the hands of Ceres flushed with mocking mellowness. More than ever the redolent flowers blushed above the mirrors of the fountains. Waters trickled in the throats of marble lilies—tinkled, gurgled in myriads of murmurous jets.[47]

On the one hand, abandoning the body in visionary ecstasy has resulted not in an attenuation of sense but in a multiplication of female erogenous zones encountered at every turn. Yet the dizzying proliferation of pleasure, the manic movement from one sensual event to another, confuses any reading that stops with the notion that the passage operates as a metaphor for the physical body. The language of the passage is highly deliberate, but reference did not determine the language chosen here; it seems instead to have been chosen according to an aesthetic grammar in which words are *arranged* not according to their meaning, but to the aesthetic qualities they offer or the syntactical events they might orchestrate.

The intensive consonance of the passage insists on the phonic qualities of language and the arrangement of words according to an aesthetic grammar of sounds and imagery. The sibilance that marks the entry into trance and second sight and connects it to the hiss of heat (in "summer," "smouldering," "crimson," "sunshine," and "blistering") yields to the repeated joining of the sibilance with a hard *c* in four consecutively stressed words ("clouds," "crimson," "cascade," "crystallized") that imitates both the crackle of fire and the hard "cascade" of water, which in turn gives way to the softer sounds of the second half, where the flowing of water is a sound the words make even before the onomatopoeic "murmurous" appears in the last phrase. The brash crescendo of consonance in the final sentence, which seems to flaunt the loud but unspecified sexuality ringing through the syllables of the passage, brings together the three predominant sounds, *s*, hard *c*, and *m*, in a baroque waterworks of hard and soft sounds. Rather than using metaphor to figure alternative embodiment, this language seeks to wring from language's material qualities—here, its sounds—a palpable form for the sensuous soul.

If the final crescendo of consonance brings hard and soft together, that phonic event points to the primary semantic event in the passage—the oxymoronic meeting of opposites. The movement of the passage is from high mountains and clouds to humid gorges and the throats of lilies, where hot also meets cool, and the directed action of sunshine and cascade finds receptivity and response in open hands, blushing flowers, and waiting mosses. In the spasmic spray of the final sentence, however, such distinctions between active/passive, hot/cool, up/down, or top/bottom and the sexual distinctions we believe we read therein are confused and made nonsensical.

The conjoining of oppositions occurs at a syntactical level as well, especially in the strange "crystallized sunshine," but also in the decadent "marble lilies," where things ethereal are substantialized by their modifiers. Likewise, solids melt, as in the "burning mountain summits" and "blistering rocks." If bodies might be said to lurk behind this imagery with its clear sexual charge—to wait, open, seek, and release—such activity is not easily sexually divided, as such oppositions are transformed by their conjoining. Here it might be said that Clemmer's Les Delices may well take as its intertext Hieronymous Bosch's infamous fifteenth-century painting, *The Garden of Delights*, as part of the mystic canon that interweaves the text, but also as a figure of free love. Bosch's central ornate fountain is surrounded by bodies in every configuration of union and hybridity, just as Clemmer's central cascade is surrounded by these strange syntactical figures of union.

As in Fuller's conception, spirit facilitates a more capacious and pleasurable sense of embodiment: organs are found to have no "necessary end," anatomy is susceptible to rearrangements that enlarge one's capacity for sensory receptivity and activity, and a diversity of gender and sexuality configurations are made available. Clemmer's wedding of opposites envisions a new kind of sexual union, one that can acknowledge difference rather than subsuming it, and one in which coupling does not rely on anatomies but on the unassigned pleasures of receptivity and activity.

The passage in fact closely tracks Fuller's conception of gender at the heart of *Woman*, where "fluid hardens to solid, solid rushes to fluid," a passage in which Fuller registers her own interest in a pleasurable loosening of fixed social categories. Fuller wished to claim these metamorphic energies for the feminine and to articulate a new order of experience in which the spiritual and the sensual were brought into dynamic relation through its agency, as when she claimed "that which is especially feminine flushes, in blossom, the face of earth, and pervades, like air and water, all this seeming solid globe."[48] If Mesmerism offered "a conceptual model for affirming a lawful relationship between matter and spirit," then in Fuller's passage, femininity is the vital fluid that connects and transforms matter and spirit—an elemental essence leaving its mark as a particular sensation—a flush, blossom, breath.[49] Less material and just beyond incorporation, it infuses bodies but is not incarcerated there.

Just as Fuller casts femininity as an immanent transformative energy pervading and transforming "seeming solid" entities and persons without being contained by them, in Clemmer's novel Victoire's sexual desire is best embodied in the vigor of the cascading language of the passage that crashes on the ear, that pervades semantically opposing features to bring them into syntactical relation and diffuses distinctions in a spray of words. Like Fuller's, Clemmer's passage is buttressed by feminist-Mesmeric vision, which took as its premise the ability to unlock a nonbiological but gendered essence in an out-of-body state, an essence that can go on to confound gendered oppositions.

As Judith Butler has argued, the "human body is not experienced without some recourse to ideality, to a frame for experience." In the texts shaped by feminist-Mesmerist idealism, vision did not clear a space apart and away from social life but instead granted a new vantage point from which to reengage the social world. Clemmer's vision, premised on feminist understandings of the trance state, provided a crucial alternative framework through which to experience embodiment, and it was not an escapist or private one. In Clemmer's novel, the pantheistic energy accessed through vision entails the essence of human relations itself. To experience sexuality in the way that Clemmer's principle of free love suggests is to understand sexuality as involving a dimension of the self that cannot be fully possessed or determined, one that comes from outside of the individual person. Sexuality, in this framework, is a "mode of being disposed toward others," one that involves risk and exposure.[50] This dynamic, while transpersonal, need not be imagined as blandly universal or politically disinterested; rather, Clemmer's principle of free love proposes an exhilarating dynamic that constitutes the self in and by the social.

If ideality, a mental frame or imagining, is essential to an experience of one's own body, or another's, as gendered, the writers examined here accessed that space with an intent to grasp and shape that experience on behalf of feminist politics. Visionary space as it was understood by Fuller, Clemmer, Oakes Smith, Martineau, and others was a framework not only for rethinking embodiment but also for understanding and experiencing other, less observable ways in which selves were constructed. To be undone in trance was to relinquish conventional anatomies of both social forms and the individual body; it also entailed surrendering a bounded or even possessive notion of the self. If Fuller imagined the feminine principle as a pantheistic energy that did not originate in and was not contained by the female body, then sexuality and gender were not features one possessed or directed at will; they came from outside of the individual and were larger than the self.

These were no self-contained, privileged fantasies of an integrated and enriched personhood. Reflecting on the ways one "does" one's gender or sexuality, that is, chooses to perform or improvise each, and on the ways gender or sexuality simultaneously "undo" the person, because each is part of a larger field of socially constructed ideas beyond ourselves, Judith Butler poses questions that seem also to have been suggested by Martineau, Hatch, or Oakes Smith about their experiences of the sensuous soul in trance. Butler asks, "But what if sexuality is the means by which I am dispossessed? What if it is invested and animated from elsewhere even as it is precisely mine? Does it not follow, then, that the 'I' who would 'have' its sexuality is undone by the sexuality it claims to have, and that its very 'claim' can no longer be made exclusively in its own name?" Strikingly, Butler herself draws on figures of spirit and ecstasy to describe the way that sexuality and gender work to "do" and "undo" the person. Butler continues, "If gender is for and from another before it becomes my own, if sexuality entails a certain dispossession of the 'I,' this does not spell the end to my political claims. It only means that when one makes those claims, one makes them for much more than oneself."[51] For Clemmer or Fuller, of course, spirit did not operate only as metaphor—but then, our experience of the ideality of sexuality and gender is not simply a metaphor for Butler either.

Perry Miller's questions return at this point: why, then, did Fuller and her contemporaries "return to the bondage" of a subjective disposition that held them to "act by an influx of power"? The authors treated in this contribution appear to have found it more tenable to understand both gender and sexuality as modes of dispossession, as dimensions of the self that are not entirely chosen, that are constituted by what is before or outside of the person in a shared, immanent imaginary. Agency was not to be found by wishing these conditions away. Instead, Fuller and her contemporaries harnessed their insight to push at the limits of rationalist accounts of reality and to rework sex and gender norms. Their detailed, phenomenological accounts of being out of body sought to rework the norms by which bodies could be understood and experienced, and their descriptions of selves open to influxes of power sought to revise the terms by which the self opened to others in all relational forms, from social gender relations to sexual union. When these writers render their experience of the trance state, and readers participate through the aesthetic experience of their writing, they make a claim about the body that is inherently political and inherently social: feelings of sensateness, receptivity, activity, and pleasure can involve us in a realm not compassed by our bodies. These writers understood that realm as one through which to access new ways of experiencing gender and sexuality that exceed the body and can thus open onto alternative social configurations.

4

MARGARET FULLER, SELF-CULTURE, AND ASSOCIATIONISM

David M. Robinson

Let me begin with two anecdotes. The first describes Elizabeth Palmer Peabody, lost in thought one afternoon as she walked directly into a tree. Concerned witnesses asked her if she had not seen the tree in front of her. "Yes, I saw it," she replied, "but I did not realize it."[1] The second concerns Amos Bronson Alcott, who was said to have told of an experience he had "in his early days, [when he] devoted some time to peddling books, making his way on foot from village to village, from house to house. One hot summer day, walking along the country road, which ran by the side of a swift-flowing stream, he overtook another peddler, going the same way. They fell into conversation, and as the sun rose higher, and the heat became oppressive, [Alcott] said 'Here is a cool stream, let us go in and bathe.' The other peddler answered, 'But I cannot swim.' 'No matter for that,' said [Alcott], 'I can swim, I will take care of you.' Then . . . [Alcott] looked round on the circle of listeners and said blandly, 'But I lost him!'"[2]

These stories, particularly the latter, suggest one of the problems inherent in any consideration of the political dimensions of Transcendentalism, the image of the Transcendentalists as feckless dreamers disconnected from reality, whose detachment rendered them either irrelevant or downright dangerous as political agents on the American scene. While by no means a unanimous view, this perspective is the current against which one must swim in arguing for a consideration of Transcendentalism as a movement with important political dimensions and consequences. One prominent Melville scholar is said to have declared the term "minor Transcendentalist" redundant. Similarly, some would, no doubt, regard the term "political Transcendentalism" an oxymoron.

NEW ENGLAND SELF-CULTURE

As it emerged as a theological movement in the early nineteenth century, Transcendentalism was fundamentally a doctrine of religious empowerment that gave the individual confidence that a spiritual life could be lived in resistance to prevailing norms and expectations. Emerson's "Self-Reliance" (1841), an essay that calls for a skeptical, hard-edged determination to set a nonconformist direction, is perhaps the definitive statement of this emphatic individualism. This affirmation of the potential of the self accounts in large measure for the continuing cultural appeal of Emerson and Thoreau in particular, but such radical individualism has also been troubling to some of its critics. Such individualism can seem both resistant to the claims of community and profoundly anti-institutional. To those who believe that progressive social change is best achieved through the formation of institutions that can foster and sustain such change, Transcendentalism has often seemed a problematic movement. "Wherever a man goes," Thoreau wrote in *Walden*, "men will pursue and paw him with their dirty institutions, and, if they can, constrain him to belong to their desperate odd-fellow society."[3] Obviously, this is a distinctly unpromising attitude to anyone committed to institution building, and though one always has to allow for a measure of rhetorical exaggeration in Thoreau, the remark captures the defiant attitude that made him both an articulate political dissenter and a problematic recruit for progressive politics.

"Self-Reliance" was, however, only the most radical articulation of a larger cultural ethos, the Unitarian redefinition of religion as a process of "self-culture," a principle most closely connected with the influential preaching of William Ellery Channing. Self-culture was the ideology with which New England liberals overturned Puritan Calvinism, reversing the core doctrine of innate depravity on which both the creedal edifice and the resilient psychological authority of Puritanism had been founded. Self-culture affirmed spiritual expansion through the realization of the soul's innate capacities, but it was a philosophy of potential rather than privilege, grounded in a process of spiritual practice enabled by self-examination, self-discipline, and perseverance. "Self-culture is something possible. It is not a dream. It has foundations in our nature," Channing wrote, noting that both a "self-searching" power and a "self-forming" power within the individual made continuing development possible.[4]

No one believed in the principle of self-culture more deeply, or embodied it more completely, than Margaret Fuller, for whom it stood as the guiding principle. "*Very early I knew that the only object in life was to grow,*" she wrote. James Freeman Clarke invoked this declaration in the Fuller *Memoir* as the essence of Fuller's character, making clear that her "aim, from first to last, was SELF-CULTURE," a purpose that explained her "profound desire for a full development of her whole nature, by means of a full experience of life." In addition to the Unitarian culture that molded them both, Clarke cited another aspect of Fuller's life that gave crucial support to her commitment to growth. It was a pursuit that he also shared: the "study of Goethe, the great master of this school." In Goethe Fuller found a "recognition of a high standard of duty" and an accompanying belief in humanity's "high destiny," articles of faith that enabled her "to do and bear, with patient fortitude, what would have crushed a soul not thus supported."[5] Empowered by the Unitarian rehabilitation of the potential of human character, and bolstered by Goethean principles of duty and high destiny, Fuller thus embodied the new self of Transcendentalism, the individual who set out, as Emerson's "Orphic Poet" would have it, to build her "own world."[6] One can read Fuller's accomplished yet heartrending life as a narrative of the revitalized soul's confronting a still-sleeping world and its resistant institutions, a tragedy perhaps, but one, like all great tragedies, that is both cathartic and empowering.

There is, however, a counterpoint to this interpretation, a strand of ideology that complicates any attempt to construct a linear narrative of Fuller's thinking or her life. In December 1849, after Fuller had aided the rise of the Roman Republic and then seen it fall, she wrote to Marcus and Rebecca Spring, telling them, "I have become a[n] enthusiastic socialist," and adding, "elsewhere there is no comfort, no solution for the problems of the times."[7] That declaration was long in coming for Fuller, and while it owed much to her experience in the first phase of the Italian Risorgimento, it was rooted in studies and conversations that were by no means divorced from her advocacy of self-culture. This interplay between the demands of self-development and the duties of cooperative association that defined Fuller's thought stands as the most significant dialogue within the Transcendentalist movement. Indeed, Fuller's chief contribution to the development of Transcendentalist thinking might well be described as her persistent interrogation of the concept of "self." Fuller redefined that concept in gendered, relational, associative, and ultimately political terms, thus shaping an intellectual path toward political critique and engaged social reform.

While Fuller built on a cultural foundation laid by Channing and reinforced by her reading of Goethe and other modern German authors, she also had, as scholars are beginning to recognize, important female mentors. Charles Capper elucidated Fuller's friendship with Ellen Kilshaw, an important figure in the "Autobiographical Romance," as the first of a series of quasi-maternal attachments that Fuller developed with women who provided her the sympathy, example, and guidance that she did not seem to receive in sufficiency from either of her parents.[8] The most important of these was with Eliza Farrar, an author and influential figure in Cambridge society while Fuller was growing up. Fuller's biographers, early to late, have characterized Farrar as a crucial formative influence on Fuller during a pivotal period in her life.[9] Farrar was, as Thomas Wentworth Higginson wrote, "a woman of uncommon character and cultivation, who had lived much in Europe, and who, with no children of her own, did many good services for the children of her friends."[10]

Farrar recognized in Fuller a young woman whose intellectual brilliance was marred by gracelessness and an impulsive lack of self-restraint; she vowed to remake her. "Something in Margaret's earnest awkwardness and sincerity," Joan von Mehren explained, moved Farrar to take her "permanently in charge."[11] Fuller found in Farrar not only a genuinely kind and supportive friend, but access to a cultured and artistic world. Farrar's intellectual attainments, cosmopolitan sophistication, and firm self-confidence were important models for Fuller. Farrar was also a woman with a genius for sociability, and among her greatest gifts to Fuller were her introductions. Three of these would have a powerful impact on Fuller's development: Farrar's niece Anna Barker, her young friend Samuel Gray Ward, and a minister and lecturer of rising prominence, Ralph Waldo Emerson.

Given Fuller's emerging ambitions as a writer, it was also significant that Farrar was a successful author. She took Fuller under her wing during the early 1830s, a very productive literary period in which she published several children's books and an influential book of manners, *The Young Lady's Friend* (1836). This guidebook to household management, social etiquette, and personal development was written by a "friendly stranger" to "a young woman just entering upon life." Farrar entered "into the most minute details of every-day life," providing advice on bed making, nursing the sick, diet and exercise, dress (including strictures on tight shoes), sibling and parental relations, correspondence, friendship, and courtship. She did not, however, present herself as a stern and controlling supervisor, but as an experienced voice on time management and the conduct of relationships. "Far from wishing to abridge the pleasures and privileges of the young," she "is only desirous of showing them how they may use without abusing them, and so prolong the happiness of their early days."[12]

While the modern reader is likely to become engrossed, for better or worse, in the aspects of nineteenth-century upper-class housekeeping detailed by Farrar, her real goal, announced prominently in the book's opening pages, was of particular importance to Fuller: "The great business of early education is to form habits of industry, to train the mind to find pleasure in intellectual effort, and to inspire a love of knowledge for its own sake." She was disdainful of the attitude that attending school was merely "something expected of you" and warned that "if you have regarded your studies as daily tasks to be performed till a certain period, when you will be released from them, you are still *uneducated*." Farrar regarded manners and social forms, modes of experience that her culture regarded as part of the feminine sphere, as in fact dangerous obstacles to women's self-development. That development must, she insisted, be primarily intellectual, and *The Young Lady's Friend* championed both wide-ranging education and ongoing intellectual cultivation for women. She cautioned her readers that leaving school early was "the great mistake" and regarded continuing self-education as an imperative for women, one that could be threatened by the many responsibilities that they would face in maturity. "Self-education begins where school-education ends; and with this additional responsibility, she is placed in new circumstances of temptation and trial." She advocated efficiency and the capable management of time, including a resistance to frivolities, as means to free young women to continue their reading, writing, and intellectual development. As a cautionary example, she cited a young acquaintance who said "she never could find time to read" but nevertheless spent "two hours every morning in arranging the glasses of flowers that adorned her mother's parlour." Farrar's biblical condemnation was pointed: "Better would it have been for her never to have had a flower in the house, than thus to neglect the more important duties of mental culture."[13]

The lengthy discussions of practical daily advice and instruction in *The Young Lady's Friend* are subsumed by the larger goal of promoting disciplined reading as the core of the process of self-culture. Farrar closed the book with a chapter on "Mental Culture," describing the work of serious and engaged reading bolstered by consultation with reference books, note taking, "written abstracts," and "the frequent exercise of the mind in composition," which she considered "one of the most important means of mental culture."[14] Given these assumptions, Farrar's attraction to the intellectually gifted and earnestly striving young Fuller is easy to understand. Farrar's emphasis on self-education and mental culture reinforced the Unitarian ethos of "self-culture." By applying this religiously grounded principle to her analysis of the domestic vocation of women, she adapted self-culture into a strategy of domestic self-possession and liberation for women.

THE CREATIVE SPIRIT

Though guided by the principle of self-culture, Fuller was never an uncritical ideologue, and this code of living presented her with challenges both theoretical and practical. Her considerations of the problematics of the concept may be traced in two important early texts, the 1839 introduction to her translation of *Eckermann's Conversations with Goethe* and her "Autobiographical Romance," written in 1840 but not published in her lifetime. The first of these, appearing in George Ripley's series of translations, *Specimens of Foreign Standard Literature*, signaled Fuller's arrival as an important voice within Transcendentalism and secured her reputation as a linguist and authority on modern European literature.[15] It is one of the movement's most fluent and astute critical essays, although it has been surprisingly little noted in Transcendentalist criticism and historiography. The second, a compelling feminist document, is better known, though it has been consulted more frequently as a biographical source document than as the self-consciously constructed work of literary art and feminist theory that it surely is.

In her preface to the Eckermann translation Fuller explained lucidly why Goethe had become for her "an object of peculiar interest and constant study" and, more broadly, why modern German literature, despite the concerted opposition to it in America, provided the best access into "the workings of the spirit in the European world these last fifty years or more."[16] Fuller countered the determined resistance of religious critics by conceding that Goethe was unwilling to subordinate "the intellectual to the spiritual" and grounded himself in classical authority rather than the conventional formulations of Christianity. He held a "love of form" that was "Greek" in nature, and his theory of ethics was "'the great Idea of Duty,'" which "'alone can hold us upright.'"

Yet he was more than an aesthetician and more than a moralist. "His God was rather the creative and upholding than the paternal spirit," she explained, and his religion was "that all his powers must be unfolded."[17] By defining God as a spirit of "creativity" and religion as the "unfolding" of the powers of an individual, Fuller had, through her exposition of Goethe, forged an important link between creative expression and self-culture. The spiritual law of creativity, expression, and perpetual metamorphosis was the cosmic version of the effort of self-development that Channing had advocated for the individual. Such growth was not wholly internal and passive; it required communication, relationship, and resourceful effort. Fuller was coming to recognize the relevance of this law to her identity as a woman and would soon declare, in *Woman in the Nineteenth Century*, a theory of unobstructed self-development and self-expression as the ethical grounding for women's rights.[18]

While Fuller's "Autobiographical Romance" is much different in form and tone from the Eckermann preface, it expounded through a literary narrative the laws of creativity and unfolding sacred to Goethe and the arduous effort that these laws demanded. Fuller took her own life as her subject and portrayed not only her immense hunger for wider experience and self-development but also the barriers that she confronted in the values and attitudes of her father, Timothy Fuller. The "Autobiographical Romance" was conditioned by his sudden death in 1835, a traumatic blow that set in motion a complex process of mourning and rebellion, the beginning of Fuller's work toward what one can now understand as a theory of gendered identity.[19] A wealth of feminist literary theory in the last decades of the twentieth century brought new recognition to women's self-writing—in fiction, autobiography, and the essay—as crucial acts in the reformulation of the concept of gender. The act of self-writing that Fuller undertook was bold and required analysis of the unitary "self" that was the foundation of the notion of identity itself. As Sidonie Smith has argued, the "self" that women had to take up in the process of self-writing had been conceived principally as "male" throughout history. To articulate her particular experience, a female author had to interrogate, explicitly or implicitly, this culturally inscribed maleness of the narrated self. The self-revelatory writing of nineteenth-century women was thus an implicit "poetics of resistance," Smith maintained, in which writers acted as both "creative sign makers" and "agents of contestation."[20] Fuller's autobiography seems a remarkably self-aware example of this dynamic, particularly in its analysis of self-development as a struggle against paternal authority.

The words "My Father" open the "Autobiographical Romance," a recognition of Timothy Fuller's central role in the early shaping of his daughter's identity and an acknowledgment that she had to measure herself against her father and his expectations to come to a complete self-understanding. Fuller's portrait of him is a stinging rebuke, but also carries a certain respect and sympathy. Most important, Fuller understood and portrayed her father as a man whose character and experience revealed cultural barriers and limitations that he was unable, or unwilling, to overcome. Her struggle with him, therefore, was also a struggle against deeply rooted cultural values and expectations and an embedded hierarchy of social power. Timothy Fuller was, she wrote, "a lawyer and a politician" who was "largely endowed with that sagacious energy" typical of New England culture. His own father, who had been denied a college education, had viewed this privilege as his "great object and ambition" for his sons and that passion for formal and institutionalized education was clearly imbued in Timothy, who hoped to make his first child "the heir of all he knew." This ambition was grounded, Fuller contended, not only in her father's character, but also in the society that formed it. "As a Lawyer, again, the ends constantly presented were to work for distinction in the community, and for the means of supporting a family. To be an honored citizen, and to have a home on earth, were made the great aims of existence." Fuller's carefully crafted language should be noted. Her father's "ends" were "presented" to him; some external force "made" or constructed his "aims of existence."[21]

Fuller's larger purpose was to make her father a representative figure, a man who embodied culturally accepted values and practices that were much more powerful than those of any individual. Her capacity to see him in this light was an important intellectual breakthrough; it meant that she understood that her battle for self-possession was not with a particular man, but with a social structure and its ingrained assumptions about the nature and differing roles of women and men. Those assumptions had, she believed, rendered her father a man of duty and social place without access to "the deeper fountains of the soul," a man of surface but not depth, of "outward relations" but without an interpersonal or spiritual dimension. "In the more delicate and individual relations, he never approached but two mortals, my mother and myself."[22] This inner poverty, which Fuller came to see as a signpost for American culture as a whole, was alarming.

Thus, through the figure of her father, Fuller was able to sketch the gendered partition of modern society, a world in which the attainment of social place and political authority was a male prerogative that came at a high cost to the development of emotion, empathy, and an inner life. Fuller grappled with the ironic fact that her educational experience, largely the work of her father, had given her a limited form of access to male authority, but in so doing complicated and in some senses threatened the development of her female identity. Fuller dramatized this loss in her account of the death of her fourteen-month-old sister Julia in 1814, which traumatized her mother and left a lasting wound in Fuller herself. "My earliest recollection is of a death," she wrote. While she remembered being shown her dead sister and experiencing certain parts of the funeral preparation and procession, "I have no remembrance of what I have since been told I did, — insisting, with loud cries, that they should not put the body in the ground." In this narrative Fuller seems at times to be both herself and her sister, both bereaved and buried. It is as if in the funeral of her sister she witnessed the burial of the female part of herself. This event also seemed to mark the early end of her childhood, as if in her sister's death she witnessed her own childhood terminated. Her grief-stricken father, "all of whose feelings were now concentrated on me," responded to his loss by initiating an intense tutelage of her. She thus confronted an enormous task. She must fill the void that her sister left, while also performing, in her studies, the role of a son. She survived, one might say, by becoming her missing sister and also her father's as yet unborn son. Fuller's early grief, with the pain and disorientation that it brought, was the first of a series of wrenching separations from those closest to her and the beginning of a life-long struggle with isolation: "Thus my first experience of life was one of death. She who would have been the companion of my life was severed from me, and I was left alone."[23]

Fuller recalled her childhood as isolated, a condition amplified by the pressure of her father's overwhelming expectations. The attention that he gave her came at a painful cost. In a section entitled "Overwork," which again begins with "MY FATHER," she detailed the severe "discipline" of Timothy Fuller's tutelage and identified his "one great mistake" of attempting to bring "forward the intellect as early as possible." Pushed to the limit of her capacity and denied necessary rest because of her father's lengthy workdays, Fuller suffered, she believed, "a premature development of the brain, that made me a 'youthful prodigy' by day, and by night a victim of spectral illusions, nightmare, and somnambulism." Shifting from the first person perspective with which she had constructed the foregoing narrative, Fuller began to describe the fate of "this child," misunderstood by parents and other relatives and driven into a state of extreme stress and agitation. Fuller's shift of narrative perspective is notable and somewhat puzzling. It may reflect her personal reluctance to deal directly with her terrifying nightmares, and it may also signal her intention to make herself a representative figure, the "child" who corresponds to the "father" of the narrative. Her description of her psychic trauma borrows from the Gothic, making the mind and its dreams a chamber of horrors. "The child" was forced to bed, to confront "colossal faces advancing slowly towards her, the eyes dilating, and each feature swelling loathsomely as they came." She described "horses trampling over her" and "trees that dripped with blood" (an image she ascribed to her reading of Virgil). "No wonder," she commented, "the child arose and walked in her sleep, moaning all over the house."[24] Ghostlike, the injured "child" haunted the broken household, signifying the loss of her own well-being and of the family's domestic harmony.

While Transcendentalism is associated with a sunny optimism, a body of writing in which images of dawn, awakening, light, and transparency set the tone, Fuller's nightmarish images are the kind of dark Romanticism that one might expect of contemporaries such as Poe and Hawthorne. In her darker version of Transcendentalism, the aspiration toward self-culture and perpetual spiritual expansion sours into hallucinatory horror and intense suffering and suggests extreme stress rather than fulfillment. Fuller was familiar with the key visual image of Transcendentalism, Emerson's "transparent eye-ball" in *Nature*, which embodied seeing, transparency, and an empowered transcendence of material barriers.[25] The "child" that Fuller described had been rendered insecure and vulnerable. Her natural path of development was distorted. The "colossal faces" with "eyes dilating" that she described seem to be a deliberate reversal of Emerson's depiction of transcendent elation and vision, and her account of her dreams is notably material and corporeal—faces, eyes, and pools of blood that "plashed over her feet" and expanded until "she dreamed it would reach her lips."[26] Rather than dissolving rapturously into a benign countryside, as Emerson imagined, Fuller slowly drowned in a rising pool of blood.

The weirdest of these nightmares were the "often" repeated images of a funeral in which "the child's" mother took the place of her sister in burial: "Often she dreamed of following to the grave the body of her mother, as she had done with that of her sister, and woke to find the pillow drenched in tears."[27] Where does one begin with this entanglement of identities and deaths? At once a means of revisiting her grief for her sister, the dream is also an expression of fear for her mother and, perhaps, a hidden resentment of her as well. In its motif of a return to the graveside, the dream also suggests Fuller's concern with her own mortality, the continuing sense of insecurity that her sister's death had brought. It is of course significant that all three of the figures connected with death—the child, her mother, and her sister—are female. The dream seems to suggest Fuller's fear of the extinction of the female principle in a world made utterly masculine by her father's powerful will. This aspect of the dream echoes Fuller's disquiet with her transformation into her father's surrogate son and emphasizes the problem of gender as a crucial, but unarticulated concept in her account of herself.

The sudden death of her father had been traumatic for Fuller and had unleashed a torrent of grief and remorse, as well as a prolonged self-examination. She had come to believe that her father's intervention in her early development had deprived her of a "natural childhood" and set her on an unbalanced course of future development. His rigorous methods "had prevented the harmonious development of my bodily powers, and checked my growth," thus causing her "continual headache, weakness and nervous affections, of all kinds."[28] Fuller's sense of "harmonious development" grew out of her pursuit of self-culture and her understanding of the organic and horticultural connotations of the term "culture." "To cultivate any thing, be it a plant, an animal, a mind, is to make grow," Channing had written. "Growth, expansion is the end. Nothing admits culture but that which has a principle of life, capable of being expanded."[29] This process entailed a balanced development of the various aspects of the mind, body, spirit, and personality of the individual. Arising from the potentiality for divinity, innate within the soul, this process defined the practice of religion for nineteenth-century Unitarians and was embraced in an even more radical way by the Transcendentalists. By 1840 Fuller had come to realize that her father had thwarted this process with his demanding mentoring and unrelenting expectations. His intention had been to discipline and train his daughter's mind, but he had in fact injured her body in doing so. Fuller identified her wounds not only as "nervous affections," but as physical or corporeal ailments as well. Her "masculine" accomplishments as a scholar and master of languages and texts thus came, she reasoned, at the price of her physical health and fortitude.

Fuller eventually recognized that this kind of learning was alien to her in important ways. In the "Autobiographical Romance" she provided a vivid account of her submission to her father's demands for "accuracy and clearness in everything" and to a way of speaking and thinking that absolutely forbade complexity, nuance, or uncertainty. "He had no conception of the subtle and indirect motions of imagination and feeling" and thus pushed her against "the natural unfolding of my character, which was fervent, of strong grasp, and disposed to infatuation and self-forgetfulness." Fuller had thus "put on the fetters" (a dramatic image in the slavery-haunted 1840s) of a "discipline of heroic common sense" focused on Latin and Roman history, while "my own world sank deep within, away from the surface of my life." She had been chained to a utilitarian world, "a world of deeds."[30]

The medium of this world of "deeds" was, however, books, and through them Fuller found ways to nourish an inner life. In Ovid's mythology, she found glimpses of a world in which "the law of life . . . was beauty," and in Shakespeare she found even more sustenance for her imagination.[31] Her reading of *Romeo and Juliet* at age eight epitomized her hunger for the imaginative and the aesthetic and her determination to take her own path despite her father's strictures. Finding her rapt in a book on a Sunday afternoon and discovering that she was reading Shakespeare, her father rebuked her, "that's no book for a Sunday; you put it away and take another." Fuller complied, briefly, but as the Shakespearean characters and dialogue "burnt in my brain," she returned to the banned volume. Her defiance resulted in an early dismissal to bed, but there she continued to remember "the free flow of life, sudden and graceful dialogue, and forms, whether grotesque or fair, seen in the broad luster of [Shakespeare's] imagination." The play ignited her, and she saw in it, as she would later see in the work of many other authors, "the life I seemed born to live." While he thwarted her with his narrow discipline, her father also, despite himself, empowered her as an impassioned reader and thus an imaginative and independent spirit. "I had too much strength to be crushed," she asserted.[32] Fuller's strength was of will and determination, a fortitude that her extensive reading would nurture. Her command of books and language, particularly after her father's death, remained her ultimate resource.

Although writing the "Autobiographical Romance" marked a major breakthrough in Fuller's recovery from the trauma of her father's sudden death, and in the self-recognition required in this process of healing, the work also led to another important personal and philosophical discovery. After honest and courageous analysis of her father and the unintentional but grave injuries that he had inflicted, Fuller described her discovery of a crucial refuge from his Roman world of law, civic duty, and discipline. This was the garden, "the happiest haunt of my childhood years." This small enclosure was for her a maternal and nurturing place, "my mother's delight," as she remembered it.

Fuller's "Romance," however closely it hews to "Autobiographical" reality, is clearly a polemical text, and the interposition of this female alternative to her father's masculine world signals her awareness of gender as a shaping force in her experience and in that of other women. "Here I felt at home," she wrote, expressing a sense of belonging and peace utterly absent from her accounts of her dealings with her father. She contrasted the "socially utilitarian" house of her father, and even the "proud world" she found in her reading, with "the teachings of the little garden," which provided a measure of the security and expressive release that she had been denied. In the garden, "my thoughts could lie callow in the nest, and only be fed and kept warm, not called to fly or sing before their time."[33] In the garden, and especially in its flowers, whose beauty was the basis for one of the most richly meaningful aspects of nineteenth-century women's culture, she found emotional expression denied her in the masculine realm of her father, where she struggled to keep her welling emotions pent up.[34] "I loved to gaze on the roses, the violets, the lilies, the pinks; my mother's hand had planted them, and they bloomed for me." She embraced the flowers as a sister, kissed them, and "pressed them to my bosom with passionate emotions, such as I never dared express to any human being."[35]

TRAVEL AND CULTURE

The associations among aesthetic perception, personal affection, and emotional release remained fundamental to Fuller's sensibility and her quest for a harmonious self-culture. Her "Autobiographical Romance" concludes with a discourse on friendship, the first of three important Transcendentalist explorations of the topic, which include Emerson's 1841 "Friendship" and the "Tuesday" chapter of Thoreau's 1849 *A Week on the Concord and Merrimack Rivers*.[36] Fuller's depiction of Ellen Kilshaw, a young English friend of the Fuller family who dazzled the seven-year-old Margaret with her talent, charm, and special personal kindness, suggests the centrality of affectionate and open friendships to the development of the possibilities of life.[37] "I remember very little," Fuller wrote, "except the state of feeling in which I lived. For I *lived*, and when this is the case, there is little to tell in the form of thought." Her relationship to Kilshaw, even at this early age, brought her to a peak of intensified experience and intimacy, a condition that she would continually seek in later relationships.

For Fuller, this kind of deep and rapturous bond was the defining state of the soul, the best self, the ultimate end of the process of culturing the self. The self that Fuller sought to nurture, therefore, was a self-in-relation, unfolding its nature in association with others. There were, she wrote, "beings born under the same star, and bound with us in a common destiny. These are not mere acquaintances, mere friends, but, when we meet, sharers of our very existence. There is no separation; the same thought is given at the same moment to both,—indeed, it is born of the meeting, and would not otherwise have been called into existence at all."[38] The premise that "there is no separation" would guide Fuller's thinking to the end of her life. She shared this belief with other like-minded seekers, seers, and reformers who came to champion "Association" as the defining idea of their era.[39]

Fuller's growing interest in association, cooperative relationship, and community is evident in her writings for the *Dial*, a crucially important medium of self-expression and literary experimentation for her in the highly charged and productive years of the early 1840s. In its pages she was able to extend in new forms the discussions that she had initiated in the Eckermann translation and the "Autobiographical Romance." Jeffrey Steele has established the importance of fictional pieces such as "Leila," "The Magnolia of Lake Pontchartrain," and "Yuca Filamentosa," highly symbolic and myth-drenched experiments in the short story.[40] Fuller also expanded her discussion of Goethe in the *Dial* and in an essay titled "The Great Lawsuit," which provided the initial form of what would become her signature work, *Woman in the Nineteenth Century*.[41] While best known for its ringing call for full legal rights and vocational opportunities for women, the work also presented the empowerment of women as a process that would rejuvenate society as a whole.

Fuller's effort to reimagine self-culture in terms of the relational and communal is also an important recurring theme in the book with which she claimed her identity as author, *Summer on the Lakes*. A travel narrative based on her 1843 journey to the frontier areas near the Great Lakes, Fuller's wide-ranging book returns again and again to the possibilities of a new existence in the West. In assessing life as she encountered it on the borders of the frontier, she was measuring an important component of the "American Dream," the capacity to begin anew to build the ideal society. She pondered, is the West a potential setting in which to satisfy this hunger? It is therefore instructive to read *Summer* as sharing the historical moment in which the Transcendentalist utopian experiments Brook Farm and Fruitlands emerged, and in which the theories of the Associationist movement, heavily influenced by Charles Fourier, were the essential parts of the intellectual discourse in New England. In *Summer* Fuller was testing the limits of solitude and self-reliance and coming to a firmer conviction that meaningful social progress must be generated and sustained by organization, cooperation, and the formation of benevolent social institutions.

Like her friends James Freeman Clarke and William Henry Channing, who had had deeply disillusioning experiences in their attempts to establish Western ministries, in the end Fuller found no encouragement for her hopes for a purified democracy in the West. Her observations of the frontier were neither pure advocacy nor pure description, but a narrative in which she measured her utopian hopes for the promise of the frontier against the actual life that she had seen there. *Summer* dramatized the clash between her utopian enthusiasm for the potential of the West and her mercilessly honest observations of the way that the frontier enchained rather than liberated the men and women who settled it. The trip itself as well as the writing of the book played an important role in her determination to engage questions of social reform more deeply in her work. In this sense they are signs of the increasingly political orientation of the Transcendentalist movement in the 1840s. In late 1844, shortly after the publication of *Summer*, Fuller moved to New York to begin a new career as a correspondent for the *New-York Tribune*, a pivotal decision in her intellectual career.[42] In the surge of determined energy that this move generated, she expanded her *Dial* essay "The Great Lawsuit" into *Woman in the Nineteenth Century* and began to use her *Tribune* post to campaign for attention to several critical social issues in this heart of emerging American economic power, including swelling immigration and extreme urban poverty.

Fuller's use of the travel narrative as a form of cultural analysis and social critique is evident in her impressions of the rapidly growing city of Milwaukee and her description of a journey into the Wisconsin countryside, where she observed the isolated cottage and farm of a European immigrant couple. Fuller noted that Wisconsin was at this point "a territory, not yet a state" and was, in its early stages of development, "nearer the acorn than we were."[43] The metaphor signaled her assumption that the journey into the West was not, as one would conventionally think of it, a journey into the future, but instead a return to origins, an opportunity in effect to reconstruct the beginnings of America's social organization and perhaps initiate the process of creating a new and purer form of democracy. Fuller's journey reflected her growing disillusionment with the American democracy as a whole, an attitude that was fueling the hot discussions of communal experiments such as Brook Farm and Fruitlands.

Fuller observed the "torrent of emigration" in Milwaukee, which brought "poor refugees" who were "travel-soiled and worn" and must spend the night in "rude shantees" before they "walk off into the country—the mothers carrying their infants, the fathers leading the little children by the hand, seeking a home where their hands may maintain them." With its tone apprehensive rather than triumphant or even hopeful, this was an inversion of the mythical portrait of the bold and self-sufficient pioneer. Fuller recognized these immigrants as courageous and determined, but also as men and women forced to the margins. They had been denied a home and now had to try to construct one themselves. Fuller's description mixed respect for the fortitude of the immigrants with a troubled recognition of the social forces that would put that endurance to the test. Deeper shadows were thrown over the utopian West in Fuller's description of the encampment of a wandering band of Pottawattamie Indians, whose extreme destitution had forced them back toward the edge of the white settlements so that they might attempt to barter for their survival. As Fuller reported, they had "neither food, utensils, clothes, nor bedding; nothing but the ground, the sky, and their own strength."[44] Like the uprooted European immigrants, the wandering Pottawattamie reflected a western frontier that was less the sign of hope and new beginnings than a symbol of oppression, loss, and displacement, a clear indictment of the stability of a damaged social order.

These and other moments of dystopian recognition overshadowed Fuller's attempts to glimpse an image of hopeful new origins in the West. She offered them with a minimum of commentary and analysis, as if she intended the experiences themselves to do their own explanatory work. She was more explicit, however, in the culminating episode of this part of her narrative, her description of an immigrant couple working out the terms of their new lives on an isolated Wisconsin farm. Part of the impact of this narrative moment is that Fuller provided a glowingly appreciative description of the idyllic beauty of the couple's woodland cottage. "As we approached," she wrote, "it seemed the very Eden which earth might still afford to a pair willing to give up the hackneyed pleasures of the world, for a better and more intimate communion with one another and with beauty." Their cottage was embowered in woods where "flowers waved, birds fluttered around" and the entire scene "had the sweetness of a happy seclusion." This was the kind of felicitous scene that Fuller had hoped to find, and her expectations were high as she approached the cottage and prepared to meet its inhabitants, feeling that all who might see the scene would say, "All hail ye happy ones!"[45]

Finally, however, one must open the door. When Fuller did so, she found two persons "evidently rich in personal beauty, talents, love, and courage" who nevertheless found themselves ensnared in a seemingly inescapable impasse. The husband had seriously injured his foot on the voyage to America and had become an invalid. "His beautiful young wife," Fuller explained, "was his only attendant and nurse, as well as a farm housekeeper." Clearly Fuller had great sympathy for this promising young woman imprisoned by circumstance. She recognized that such a confinement, intensified by the couple's geographical isolation, would be an entombment for both of them. While both husband and wife seemed to be bearing up resolutely under the circumstances, Fuller could not but observe that the young wife, who looked "as if she could bear anything for affection's sake," would also "feel the weight of each moment as it passed."[46]

Fuller made this concern more tangibly persuasive when she described looking through an "album full of drawings and verses which bespoke the circle of elegant and affectionate intercourse they had left behind." That cultured, convivial, and community-grounded past was now only a memory in the isolated woods. As a sign of the powerful necessity of the support and affection of a wider circle of friends, the album is a memorable image. "The young wife must sometimes need a sister," Fuller imagined, "the husband a companion, and both must miss that electricity which sparkles from the chain of congenial minds."[47] "Electricity," an important symbol in *Woman in the Nineteenth Century*, evoked the power of women's perceptions in a transformed, egalitarian society. Here it reminds us of the energy generated by relationship and association, without which human experience loses its vitality. The extreme isolation of this couple is magnified by the husband's incapacitation, but even if both husband and wife were in the best of health, they would be challenged to endure this separation from their past society. Fuller's implicit question is whether an individual can thrive without the supportive connections and the enriching responsibility provided by a larger community. What Fuller had expectantly called "the sweetness of a happy seclusion" is placed under critical scrutiny, and the dream of utopian solitude gives way to a larger hope for a more harmonious and mutually supportive society.

ASSOCIATION AND SOCIAL PROGRESS

Fuller's growing support of egalitarian reforms in the highly politicized 1840s reinforced a crucial intellectual affinity with William Henry Channing (nephew of William Ellery Channing), the most important theorist of Associationism among the Transcendentalists. Channing was a friend of James Freeman Clarke and had known Fuller only distantly in Cambridge in the late 1820s. Their friendship became much closer a decade later, as they identified themselves with the Transcendentalist movement. Channing was an important influence on Fuller's awareness and support of egalitarian politics. They shared a sense of cultural disorientation and felt themselves weighed down with "unemployed force," as Channing wrote in an 1840 letter.[48] Channing felt something hollow in his ministerial work and Fuller shared this unease, even though she had established herself as a critic, translator, and leader of public "Conversations" for women. That missing element seemed to be political in nature. Neither was able to intervene effectively against the pressure, competitiveness, disharmony, and distrust that they confronted in 1840s America. Emerson described the restless ennui of "The Transcendentalist" in his 1841 essay by that title, and Fuller and Channing could well have modeled for his portrait. "We are miserable with inaction," the young Transcendentalists declared to the world. "We perish of rest and rust. But we do not like your work."[49] The problem, Emerson went on to explain, was that they had not yet found fulfilling work of their own to substitute for the paucity of alternatives that American society offered them.

Emerson's recognition that Transcendentalism was rooted in an acute sense of vocational crisis, one that he also shared, provides an important biographical perspective on the key members of the movement. Fuller and Channing, the cultivated fruit of a long New England tradition of learning and leadership, both seemed to question the purpose of their work in modern American culture and groped for a way to translate their intellectual attainments into pragmatic, socially relevant action. The relationship between society and the intellectual was entering a period of crisis in the American 1840s, just as Fuller and Channing were coming into their intellectual maturity. "We know that somewhere in Nature this vitality stifled here is manifesting itself," Fuller wrote to Channing. "But individuality is so dear we would fain sit beneath our own vines and fig trees."[50] Their cultivation threatened to become an entrapment.

The friendship of Fuller and Channing was based in this mutual effort to find a way out of their individuality, to forge a path beyond their "own vines and fig trees." While Fuller was making herself an authority on German literature and establishing herself as an author in the 1830s, Channing held Unitarian ministries in Boston and Meadville, Pennsylvania; toured Europe; served as a minister to the poor in New York; took another pastorate in Cincinnati; and finally returned to the Unitarian ministry in New York. In 1847 he formed the Religious Union of Associationists, signifying his deepening engagement with Associationist and Fourierist political theories. Both his ministry-at-large and his work in Cincinnati had an experimental and missionarylike quality as they took the liberal religious and reform message outside the ordinary bounds of the New England Unitarian parish, which Channing found deadly despite his auspicious lineage. Fuller's term "vitality stifled" captures nicely Channing's experience with parish ministry. He was pursuing something bigger, and a religiously tinged version of Fourierism that entailed a repudiation of the developing market economy in America was his best approach to it. Those who went to Brook Farm hoped not only to change the world but to find fulfilling work, to be able to engage in a worthy enterprise with their whole heart, to be able to redeem their commitments and their labor into ennobling projects rather than dreary and demeaning tasks of necessity. Fourier promised them a way to accomplish this.

"Life is a long torment to one who pursues occupations without attraction," Fourier wrote, but he believed that men and women could find fulfillment in work if society were organized to optimize each individual's engagement with attractive or desirable tasks and if that work were also constantly rotating. "In work, as in pleasure, variety is evidently the desire of nature," he wrote.[51] He believed that attractions to all the necessary forms of human labor were present within every group of some 1,600 persons and that, if such groups were divided into cooperating subgroups focusing on tasks that revolved frequently, work would become a pleasure. Such occupation would fulfill the attractions or desires for activities suited to human nature and temperament and remove the frustration and hostility that arose from uncongenial work.

One need not swallow the whole theory to believe that it revealed the felt problems of a society transformed by the industrial revolution and the modern market economy. Channing, George Ripley, and other Brook Farmers took Fourierism as a directive to devise a new social organization in which men and women could fully express their natures and be freed from the restrictions and oppressions arising from labor that was unchosen, repetitive, trivial, boring, exploitative, or demeaning. They heard Fourier say that while men and women were made to work, they were also made to enjoy that work, and that unreflectively traditional or calculatedly greedy social structures stood in the way of this natural gratification.[52]

Fourier also believed that ever-changing attractions led to fulfillment in love as well as fulfillment in work. He was a decided opponent of marriage as an oppressively stifling arrangement and applied his doctrine that "variety is evidently the desire of nature" to the realm of sexuality. This was not a doctrine that the Transcendentalists emphasized, and chastely genteel flirtation seems to have been the limit of any such experimentation at Brook Farm. Channing himself never actually joined Brook Farm, apparently because his wife objected.[53] She seems not to have been alone in this resistance, as an 1843 entry in Emerson's journal suggests. "Married women uniformly decided against the communities," he observed. "It was to them like the brassy & lackered life in hotels."[54] Even so, it was clear to many women that the institution of marriage needed reform. Fuller set out a thoughtful and extensive discussion of the forms of marriage in *Woman in the Nineteenth Century* that was an important element of the book's overall argument for women's rights. As she posited, "a religious recognition of equality" between husband and wife was the foundational requirement of the success of marriage, a standard that had not been achieved in the nineteenth century. She called for a conception of marriage as "pilgrimage toward a common shrine," in which husband and wife were equal partners in a shared aspiration.[55]

Fuller and Channing entered a period of highly productive utopian speculation at roughly the same time, 1843 to 1845, and the convergence of their thinking suggests the political awareness that was beginning to characterize the Transcendentalist movement as a whole. In 1843 Fuller published "The Great Lawsuit," an important contribution to the discourse of women's rights, and in the next year wrote her critical observations of the American westward migration in *Summer on the Lakes*. In 1843 Channing launched a journal called the *Present*, in which he asserted "the triumphant power of good, of forbearance, forgiveness, fidelity, mercy" and the principles of an enlightened "Asceticism" and "sympathetic labor" that would transform American culture.[56]

Channing articulated an aura of dissent and heightened political awareness that marked this second phase of Transcendentalism, a mood that one also finds in the works of Emerson, Theodore Parker, and, eventually, Thoreau. Channing was an impassioned utopian; he made the case for "Heaven on Earth," the title of one key essay, more boldly than perhaps any of the Transcendentalists. In an important sense, his was a representative voice whose assumptions one also finds, in different form, in Fuller. Channing offered a vision of human progress achieved through the work of "CO-OPERATION." Such harmonious association would lead to "a Divine Order of human society; a justice so perfect, that every individual man shall be a member with all his brethren of a larger Man, which is the Nation; and Nations members together of the Universal Man, which is the reunited race."[57]

These "men" and "brethren" also included women, and in fact were led by women, in Channing's view. "History proves one fact in letters of light, that according to the measure of Woman's Freedom has been the elevation of manners. How imagination lingers over a Zenobia, a Boadicea. The earth waits for her Queen." Channing's growing radicalism in these years is evident in his explanation of the basic cause of war, the greatest manifestation of human disunity and self-division: "*War broke the unity of the Human Race*," Channing argued, "and ever since sorrow has been heaped upon sorrow, and ruin on ruin. *And War originated in the unjust division of labor, and of the profits of labor.*"[58] Though few of the Transcendentalists had working-class backgrounds or were much at ease within working-class social settings, Channing was among the first to recognize that issues of labor and economic class divisions were central to the advancement of social justice in the American 1840s.[59]

Fuller listened sympathetically, but responded skeptically at first, to the utopian prophesies of Channing, Ripley, and others. "I do not believe in Society," she remarked to Channing in an 1841 letter concerning Brook Farm. "I do not know what their scheme will ripen to; at present it does not deeply engage my hopes."[60] Yet *Woman in the Nineteenth Century* suggests how deeply utopian thinking was transforming her outlook. Man is "still a stranger to his inheritance, still a pleader, still a pilgrim," Fuller wrote. "Yet his happiness is secure in the end. . . . Whatever the soul knows how to seek, it cannot fail to attain." But this aspiration, Fuller contended, "is better understood, and more nobly interpreted, [when] a broader protest is made in behalf of Woman."

The core of Fuller's argument is that human progress becomes more certain when women are free to pursue their own perfection. Women in the United States, Fuller observed, "have time to think, and no traditions to chain them, and few conventionalities compared with what must be met in other nations. There is no reason why they should not discover that the secrets of nature are open, the revelations of the spirit waiting for whoever will seek them. When the mind is once awakened to this consciousness, it will not be restrained by the habits of the past, but fly to seek the seeds of a heavenly future." Her call for women's full participation in all aspects of society was uncompromising, and her confidence in the result of such equality was complete: "We would have every arbitrary barrier thrown down. We would have every path laid open to Woman as freely as to Man. Were this done, and a slight temporary fermentation allowed to subside, we should see crystallizations more pure and of more various beauty. We believe the divine energy would pervade nature to a degree unknown in the history of former ages, and that no discordant collision, but a ravishing harmony of the spheres, would ensue."[61]

When Fuller arrived in New York to take her position at the *Tribune*, Channing was immersed in the work that would eventually lead to his formation of the Religious Union of Associationists in 1847. Channing's support of Fuller was of great importance at this transitional moment. She had corresponded with him before her arrival about "our round of visits to the public institutions," and it is evident that both of them saw such work—visiting prisons, asylums for the insane, reform schools—as a fundamental step in their own development and in the betterment of society in the United States.[62] This was the "real" America that neither of them had fully apprehended in their Boston upbringing. Their thirst for the truth about American institutions and public life, and of the lives of the poor, was notable. As Bell Gale Chevigny has written, Fuller's work for the *Tribune* "gave her access to worlds hitherto closed to a woman of her class," and thus "a deepening concern for other oppressed groups—immigrants, blacks, the poor, the blind, the insane—followed."[63] Fuller's New York period, and the range of her *Tribune* essays, have recently become an important focal point for Fuller studies.[64] As scholars are beginning to understand, once Fuller had come to know New York she could no longer hold mildly sunny and uncomplicated views of the American democracy.[65] This wrestling with the American idea became even more intense when she went to Europe.

THE NEW ERA

Fuller's experiences in France and Italy loom ever larger in our sense of her achievement and her continuing influence. The growth of her academic reputation has been somewhat thwarted because she has been largely the property of Americanists in literary studies and in history, a situation that has resulted in an underappreciation of her connections with the international democratic movement that transformed Europe in the 1840s. Larry Reynolds's groundbreaking 1988 book *European Revolutions and the American Literary Renaissance*, a transatlantic study before Transatlanticism, introduced an important perspective on Fuller, and the collection of her European dispatches that he edited with Susan Belasco has been an enormous benefit to all Fuller scholars. We now also have, in the second volume of Charles Capper's biography and in Joan von Mehren's illuminating research on Fuller's marriage, a much more detailed picture of Fuller's life in Italy.[66] This research is leading us to a more complete understanding of Fuller as an international figure deeply engaged in a movement of world-historical significance. Despite the suffering that she at times endured in Italy, Fuller found in France and Italy the measure of deep thinking and engaged social participation of which she had caught only glimpses in New England. She recognized that she was part of a movement of social reformation with world-altering potential. As she wrote to Channing in reference to the 1848 revolution in Rome, "It is a time such as I always dreamed of, and for long secretly hoped to see. I rejoice to be in Europe at this time, and shall return possessed of a great history."[67]

There remains much to say about Fuller as part of this international movement of egalitarian reform and socialist revolution, but two lines of inquiry deserve emphasis as particularly auspicious for further investigation. First, one should recognize that a reconsideration seems to be under way in the historical interpretation of early French socialism, as indicated in Pamela Pilbeam's 2000 rereading of *French Socialists before Marx* and Jonathan Beecher's 2001 study of Victor Considerant, whose work Fuller knew and read while in Paris.[68] Considerant, who would attempt to establish a utopian community in Texas, seems to have been one of the most articulate advocates of the tone of Associationism that Fuller and Channing were exploring before Fuller left for Europe.

One should also recognize the importance of another strand of radical political theory that Fuller encountered in Paris, the apocalyptic utopianism of Polish poet and revolutionary Adam Mickiewicz, whose political theories were bound up with an odd form of mystical cultism, Towianism, which centered on the nationalistic visionary Andrzej Towianski. Mickiewicz is the subject of a recent biography by Roman Koropeckyj, and Ursula Phillips has recently published a detailed and quite insightful article on the profound impact of Mickiewicz's "Apocalyptic Feminism" on Fuller.[69] Though Fuller was a rational advocate of a planned and disciplined self-culture, she was drawn to the mystical and the transrational, as her attraction to the German mystic Novalis suggests. Phillips offers an astute analysis of the way that Mickiewicz received Fuller as a fellow spirit and even an example of the kind of heroic female figure who foretold the coming changes in the world social order.

To view Fuller through this European lens will certainly enhance our sense of the importance of the last years of her career, when, like Thoreau, she was cut down while in the midst of an intellectual project of potentially enormous consequences. These sources suggest that Fuller's gradual process of political education converged with the political forces reshaping Europe and that Associationist theory was for her a key to the intellectual friendships and sense of belonging that she found in France and Italy. While Fuller became the most radical of the Transcendentalists, her political development also illustrates that the Transcendentalist movement as a whole, rooted as it was in the history of New England's religious disputes, moved steadily toward political theory and reform in the turbulent 1840s and 1850s, pursuing a more partisan sense of Emerson's vision of a "new world." "The next revolution, here and elsewhere, will be radical," Fuller declared in her January 1850 *Tribune* dispatch. "The New Era is no longer an embryo; it is born."[70]

5

"MORE ANON"

American Socialism and Margaret Fuller's 1848

Adam-Max Tuchinsky

When Margaret Fuller arrived in Italy in the spring of 1847, she wrote that although it was cold and gray, she had at last "touched those shores to which I had looked forward all my life." Fuller spent the remaining years of a life cut short by shipwreck in an Italy that was the scene of multiple revolutions, and there seems to have been a great Romantic correspondence between her own maturing sense of self and the political events that surrounded and engaged her. In Italy, Fuller likely married (though the circumstances were murky) and had a child, but even so, this was not the sort of self-realization anticipated by the antifeminist Sophia Hawthorne, who once remarked that if Margaret were "married truly, she would no longer be puzzled about the rights of woman."[1] Rather, it was her rejection of Victorian gender conventions in Italy that led, ironically, to romantic fulfillment and a child. More generally, she seems to have found in Italy a national and political home, and a new sense of public engagement. Italy and foreign travel helped her to "see the pattern of the stuff, and understand the whole tapestry."[2] Italy brought to the surface submerged psychological and political currents. As Bell Gale Chevigny suggests, Italy united Fuller to her "material reality," her "sexuality," her body, and her social "condition."[3] If Italy was, for Fuller, a site of radicalization, what form and substance did this radicalization take?

By now it has become almost historically orthodox to assume that American Transcendentalism, which began as a religiocultural movement in the 1830s, took a social turn in the 1840s, when many of its leading figures and some second-generation disciples became increasingly absorbed in the dilemmas of market culture. To some observers, a social and intellectual chasm that opened up between Emersonian individualism and a more community-conscious socialism precipitated this shift. Margaret Fuller's life trajectory, in many cases, has been layered on top of this supposed division. Her movement from New England, to New York, and then to Europe, which literally and perhaps figuratively distanced her from Emerson, has been read ideologically, as a change in political and social consciousness, from individualism to socialism, from culture to politics, from American exceptionalism to cosmopolitanism, from conservatism to radicalism, from Transcendentalism to revolution. As Larry Reynolds puts it, "her experiences in Europe during 1846–49 . . . led her farthest away from Emersonian individualism and gave her new values, new concerns, and new forms of expression."[4] For Margaret Allen, who helped initiate feminist scholarship on Fuller, the Transcendentalism of her formative years was "otherworldly" and genteel, and it was only by repudiating Emerson personally and intellectually that could she grow politically and ideologically. In most of these accounts, the core component of these "new" counter-Emersonian values was socialism.[5]

This contribution argues something different. Though it concurs with earlier scholarship that contends that Europe and especially the Italian revolution radicalized Fuller politically and personally, it rejects the notion that socialism was a substantive component of this turn. Moreover, it takes issue with scholarship on Fuller that embeds her intellectual development within a larger historical construction of Transcendentalism that imagines a decisive break between Emersonian individualism and an emergent socialism. Such an interpretation depends on a misreading of the historical context. In Italy, Fuller became a *radical* republican and a *liberal* socialist. Fuller wrote of socialism in the same voice that she had used to write of prison reform. She thought that some concentrated effort could be made to relieve poverty and squalor and that this would happen in concert with, or because of, a dramatic transformation of the political and cultural order. Politics would be the way to realize social transformation, through the elevation of the lower orders. Though she wrote that throughout Europe, "the political" was "being merged in with the social," she never became a social revolutionary of a Marxist kind. Her radicalism was defined by her embrace of political violence, her anticlericalism, her late (and perhaps timid) rejection of moral and sexual respectability, and her contempt for compromise, an immediatism that she finally shared with an abolitionist movement that she had long kept at a distance.

Fuller's socialism, then, was an outgrowth of a larger Transcendental commitment to self-culture, but it was also incidental and peripheral. Fuller came to identify herself privately and publicly as a socialist, but in many respects her transformation was only skin deep. It did not shape the manner in which she understood or interpreted the revolutionary events unfolding around her in any fundamental way. Fuller never developed a detailed political economy, and this framework never structured her journalism or her understanding of events. Moreover, most of the socialist discourses that were available to her, and to which she was by temperament drawn, were of a distinctly unradical sort. They were essentially liberal. Fuller was as familiar with Marxism as any American, but that was mostly because it was a marginal force on both sides of the Atlantic. Only Fuller's close attention to German culture resulted in what was likely the first account of Marxist thought to have appeared in an American publication, but even so, nearly all of her references to "communism" were vague and undeveloped. Although Marx and Marxism remained largely anomalous, the socialism circulating in Fuller's circles was counterrevolutionary in most respects. Liberal socialists did raise the specter of revolution, but only to promote peaceable and voluntary reform. They rejected the very notion of class struggle and most of all aimed to establish friendly, fraternal feelings between the classes. They hoped that incremental reforms would cause classes to disappear, ironically, by making everyone a capitalist after a fashion, a self-reliant member of an associated community.

Making socialism a polestar of Fuller's radicalization, however, simply ignores her context. Fuller and her contemporaries lived in a moment when in most places—Italy especially, but even New York and New England—the contours of industrial society had not yet taken shape completely. Therefore, any imposition of a left-right spectrum on the era's political economy has to be considered problematic. So-called Emersonian individualism can be easily marshaled to defend a later social order, but such a construction is anachronistic and fails to acknowledge the diverse ways in which antebellum critics responded to the spread of market culture. To build a biographical trajectory for Fuller based on her ostensible movement from Emersonian individualism to Italian revolutionary ideals simply exaggerates the conservatism of the former and the radicalism of the latter. The relationship between Fuller's radicalization and her incipient socialism can be understood, in short, only against the background of her intellectual and economic environment.

TRANSCENDENTALISM AND SOCIALISM

Fuller's socialism and, more broadly, her political economy, cannot be considered apart from her milieu. Two main influences shaped, and in some cases circumscribed, her inchoate understanding of this intersection of the economy and politics. Her worldview was rooted in Emersonian Transcendentalism, which by the 1840s had been challenged and reshaped by transatlantic socialism and other related social movements. The scope of Fuller's political economy was also conditioned by the very fact that, except for a few pockets mostly in England and the United States, the advanced economies of the West were largely pre- or protoindustrial. The combination of these two factors explains in many respects the contours of Fuller's response to the political and social upheaval that she witnessed in Europe.

As a religious, social, and intellectual movement, Transcendentalism was clearly responsive to the cultural and economic changes that historians have labeled a market revolution.[6] Throughout the 1840s, after the religious controversies that were Transcendentalism's initial thrust had ebbed, first- and second-generation Transcendentalists turned their attention to social, cultural, and communal reform. Some of their endeavors, such as Brook Farm, are well known, while others, such as Bronson Alcott and Charles Lane's vegetarian commune, Fruitlands, are less so. Yet there were other initiatives born of Transcendental engagement with the social question that are often ignored, perhaps because they did not cross a communitarian threshold or because they mixed cultural uplift with reform.

Alcott, Fuller, and Elizabeth Palmer Peabody, for example, all pushed for progressive schooling. Peabody became a publisher and the owner of a countercultural bookstore, and most of the Transcendentalists supported the *Dial*, Transcendentalism's countercultural magazine. Emerson's career as a public lecturer and Fuller's as a working journalist reimagined the relationship between elite intellectuals and the democratic public. Even Henry David Thoreau, hardly a socialist to be sure, challenged market culture in both a literary and a participatory way with as much rigor as the West Roxbury socialists. All of these experiments sprung from a collective disenchantment with market culture—sentiments shared by Transcendentalism's leading light, Ralph Waldo Emerson.[7]

In some accounts of Fuller's life, as in histories of Transcendentalism, the figure of Emerson looms large, for obvious reasons. Emerson facilitated Fuller's emergence as a public intellectual, and he has been the pole against which Fuller's radicalization and commitment to socialism have been measured. Scholarship on Transcendentalism has focused on its ideological fissures, between, as Perry Miller put it, the "two opposing poles in Transcendentalism—the associationists and the Emersonian individualists."[8] But what James Freeman Clarke once said of Fuller, "What a Sphynx is that girl," was equally true of Emerson.[9] To imagine that Fuller's political realization demanded a repudiation of Emerson begs the question: which version of the man? A convincing case can be made that Emerson, aphoristic rather than coherently argumentative, was a sort of reactionary prophet of American enterprise, a proponent of U.S. exceptionalism and an apologist for the emerging bourgeois and capitalist order. As David Leverenz has observed, Emerson's maxims have inspired figures as diverse as the author and Yale professor Harold Bloom and Ohio State football coach Woody Hayes: "Hayes affirmed the country's dominant gospel of competitive success, while Bloom delights in the mind's revelatory Gnostic leaps beyond social convention."[10] Emerson's politics and political economy are obviously a vast subject, and to imagine him primarily as a champion of bourgeois conservatism may make for an appealing contrast with Fuller. This ignores, however, the generally radical intellectual thrust of his work, the majority of the historical record, and, most important, the diverse modes in which antebellum intellectuals and social critics opposed aspects of market culture.

Though often remembered for making an American Romantic case against history, deference, habit, and conformity and a plea for intuition, instinct, and, most important, self-reliance and growth, Emerson, like contemporary socialists, was also a critic of individualism in a broadly French sense. This particular critique of market culture took a variety of forms. Fuller's journalism, especially during the New York years, focused on the impact of market inequalities on public institutions and spaces, but Emerson wrote more deeply about the psychic costs of the new economy. Like the socialists, Emerson argued that market culture stunted holistic growth in a basic sense. We "strut about so many walking monsters," he wrote, "a good finger, a neck, a stomach, an elbow, but never a man." Moreover, with contemporary communitarians, Emerson maintained that his culture's psychic crisis—and, more narrowly, its masculine crisis of specialization and debilitating overcivilization—could be healed by manual labor. In the *American Scholar*, he observed that "there is virtue in the hoe and the spade, for learned as well as for unlearned hands." In "Man the Reformer," he claimed that in an age tending toward market specialization and exchange, sources of renewal could come from craft, manual labor, and autonomy: "We must have an antagonism in the tough world for all the variety of our spiritual faculties, or they will not be born."[11] The ideological extension of Emerson's calls for physical labor was political sympathy for the manual classes: "For see this wide society in which we walk of laboring men. We allow ourselves to be served by them. We pay them money & then turn our backs on them. We live apart from them & meet them without salute in the streets. We do not greet their talents, nor rejoice in their good fortune, nor foster their hopes, nor in the assembly of the people vote for what is dear to them."[12]

Emerson believed that democracy would be the basis of a national culture and that for the scholar-intellectual the vocational counterpart of physical self-renewal was scholarly engagement with "the lowest class in the state"—not solely through cultivation and uplift but by making them subjects and giving them voice. "The literature of the poor, the feelings of the child, the philosophy of the street, the meaning of household life are the topics of the time," wrote Emerson. "I ask not for the great, the remote, the romantic. . . . I embrace the common, I explore and sit at the feet of the familiar, the low."[13] In these cultural addresses, the *American Scholar* and the "Divinity School Address," Emerson laid out the intellectual basis for public engagement by literary men and women. While Emerson became a lyceum lecturer, Fuller carved out this impulse toward public engagement more fully by becoming a progressive journalist. Writing for mixed audiences in one of the era's great cheap and national daily newspapers, the *New-York Tribune*, she participated "in the great work of popular education." Journalism became a "means of mutual interpretation" between cultures and classes.[14]

More so than Fuller's writings, Emerson's appeal for a comprehensive culture that included both manual labor *and* the manual classes resonated with the message and spirit of American socialism during the 1840s. Emerson called for a new religious culture, one that spoke vigorously and prophetically to mixed congregations, in which "the best and the worst men in the parish, the poor and the rich, the learned and the ignorant, young and old, should meet one day as fellows in one house."[15] In this, Emerson reflected the hopes of the Brook Farmers, who were determined "to insure a more natural union between intellectual and manual labor" and to "prepare a society of liberal, intelligent, and cultivated persons, whose relations with each other would permit a more simple and wholesome life, than can be led amidst the pressures of our competitive institutions."[16] The founding of Brook Farm is rightly regarded as a high point of Transcendental social engagement, but it is also often framed as opening up an ideological chasm between Emersonian individualists and the communitarians. Most of this discussion naturally has centered on Emerson's dithering but ultimate rejection of George Ripley's pointed invitations to join the Brook Farm community.[17]

Emerson's reasons were many and varied. He claimed that "the ground of my decision is almost purely personal," but he mourned privately that the experiment sounded to him like little more than "a room in the Astor House hired for the Transcendentalists." With more serious conviction, he wrote that he did "not wish to remove from my present prison to a prison a little larger. I wish to break all prisons." This anti-institutionalism would at times manifest a political economy even more radical than Brook Farm's. Emerson would even attack the institution of property as a convention that revealed a "want of self-reliance." Real property "is living property," he suggested, and "does not wait the beck of rulers, or mobs, or revolutions, or fire, or storm, or bankruptcies, but perpetually renews itself wherever the man breathes."[18]

Fuller's relationship to Brook Farm, however, deserves more attention. When Brook Farm was launched, Emerson was ensconced in an established household. Fuller, by contrast, was without a place to live. More than most associated communities, Brook Farm was a magnet for single women. Fuller's mother encouraged her to consider the community and even proposed to join her there. They thought enough of the settlement to send her emotionally troubled brother Lloyd there to attend its school. Fuller did visit the community often, though frequently on these occasions she stayed at the nearby home of the wealthy Shaw family. Yet, like Emerson, she declined to join. From a personal perspective, Brook Farm was simply a bad fit. For Fuller, labor and the direct experience of nature were never paramount concerns. Many women did find solace in the more egalitarian gender dynamics of the settlement, but their emancipation was also rooted in artisanal projects that, although unconventional, likely had little appeal to Fuller. One of the triumphs of Brook Farm was the women's "Fancy Group," a craftwork enterprise that was a financial success and grounded in the notion that women's emancipation rested on material autonomy, but Fuller was an intellectual and a writer first and foremost. Making caps and lampshades, even in a self-consciously political effort, held little appeal.[19]

If anything, ideologically, Fuller was yet more ambivalent toward the communitarian impulse than Emerson was, even as she became ever more attuned to the problems of the impoverished in the mid-1840s. She characterized Bronson Alcott and Charles Lane's Fruitlands experiment in associated community, for example, as "miserable," vain, and, in many of its methods, "puerile." She took Brook Farm more seriously but even it, she thought, was "premature." As Charles Capper writes, her "interest in the community was not especially ideological," and she doubted whether it was the right time to "reconstruct society." Moreover, she wrote William Henry Channing, she did "not believe in Society. I feel that every man must struggle with these enormous ills in some way."[20]

Though more sympathetic than Emerson and certainly Thoreau to philanthropic reform (and that chasm would widen over time), she shared their instinct that self-reform should precede communal reform. Fuller sympathized with the "heroism that prompted" the community, and she considered it "an *experiment* worth trying," but she was committed to an association of "destiny," not of "effort": "It is a constellation, not a phalanx, to which I would belong." Though she believed in the "dignity of labor," she thought it fruitless to try to "eradicate evil"—misguided, too, because evil was also a "growth of nature, and one condition of the development of the good." William Henry Channing described Fuller's misgivings about Brook Farm as thoroughly "Transcendental," hostile to institutions that threaten the heroic and the individual.[21] As Channing summarized,

> Her objections, to be sure, were of the usual kind, and turned mainly upon two points,—the difficulty of so allying labor and capital as to secure the hoped-for cooperation, and the danger of merging the individual in the mass to such degree as to paralyze energy, heroism, and genius; but these objections were urged in a way that brought out her originality and generous hopes. There was nothing abject, timid, or conventional in her doubts. The end sought she prized; but the means she questioned. Though pleased in listening to sanguine visions of the future, she was slow to credit that an organization by "Groups and Series" would yield due incentive for personal development, while ensuring equilibrium through exact and universal justice. She felt, too, that Society was not a machine to be put together and set in motion, but a living body, whose breath must be Divine inspiration, and whose healthful growth is only hindered by forcing. Finally, while longing as earnestly as any Socialist for "Liberty and Law made one in living union," and assured in faith that an era was coming of "Attractive Industry" and "Harmony," she was still for herself inclined to seek sovereign independence in comparative isolation. Indeed, at this period, Margaret was in spirit and in thought preeminently a Transcendentalist.[22]

In the end, Fuller mirrored Emerson's and Thoreau's misgivings about the impact of association on individual self-culture but shared a developing social consciousness with the Transcendental movement as a whole. For communitarian and noncommunitarian Transcendentalists, Brook Farm and the social realities that inspired it were a challenge that demanded a response.

The provocation of Brook Farm received, if anything, an even more pronounced reply from Emerson than from Fuller. During the 1840s he commenced a series of parallel experiments as a rejoinder to Brook Farm's indictment of market culture. In 1840 he proposed a free-form university, "built out of straw" in Concord. He also launched a series of domestic reforms. "Impatient of seeing the inequalities all around me," Emerson hoped to join his own family to Alcott's, asked his servants to join the family at a common dining table, and eventually brought Henry David Thoreau into his home under nearly explicit Fourierist conditions.[23] Thoreau had "his board &c for what labor he chooses to do."[24] In all, Emerson hoped to make Concord and his own home a kind of social experiment. Emersonian and Transcendental individualism, to put it simply, have been misread. The dichotomy between Emersonian individualism and Brook Farm Associationism, while real, is exaggerated and, most important, ignores the connection between the sort of midcentury socialism common in America and Transcendental self-culture. Emerson's Romantic individualism, as Dorothy Ross so cogently puts it, was "very different from the kind of libertarian and hedonistic models that gained force through the twentieth century."[25] Emerson's political economy was complex—and often frankly contradictory, but mid-nineteenth-century political economy itself was inherently multifarious.

The 1840s and 1850s was an era in which the left-right, radical-conservative divide in political economy lacked meaning. During the late 1860s and early 1870s, with the Paris Commune and the birth of Marx's International, industrialization, the creation of industrial unions and the growth of an immigrant proletariat, corporate consolidation, and the emergence of modern, free-market individualism in the hands of Liberal Republican ideologues such as Edwin Lawrence Godkin, the outlines of a left-right divide in political economy became more plausible. But during the 1840s and 1850s, in the United States and especially in central and southern Europe, multiple forms of traditional and modern political economy coexisted. Even throughout the advanced economies of the West, most people still lived within the context of a slave or domestic economy, where the culture of contract and incentive was largely unknown. Against the framework of traditional political economy, where nearly all labor was "unfree" after a fashion, "liberals" such as Fuller and "radicals" such as Marx attacked long-established structures of social organization. In England Fuller joined the country's liberals in denouncing the Corn Laws and the landed aristocracy that fought to maintain them.

Marx likewise observed, with almost undiluted awe, the speed with which "the British principle of free competition, of *laissez-faire*" destroyed traditional Indian agriculture and civilization—social forms he characterized as "undignified, stagnatory, and vegetative."[26] In this transition moment, the laissez-faire principle was not yet fully marshaled on behalf of the emerging industrial order, and even the socialists—or most of them—were still trying to protect a system that included private property, profit, and incentive, even if they were using communitarian means to do so. The mainstream of the American socialist movement was in part a realistic alternative to the emerging market society, but it was also rooted in it. The socialists, as Emerson could plausibly argue, were only the "describers of that which is really being done. The large cities are phalansteries; and the theorists draw all their arguments from facts already taking place in our experience."[27]

The radical nature of the Emersonian inheritance, along with the transitional context of American political economy at midcentury, are revealed even more clearly by one of Fuller's fellow second-generation disciples of Emerson: Henry David Thoreau. In some respects, Thoreau's years at Walden Pond can be grouped with the other contemporary Transcendental social experiments, but they were also an archindividualist rejoinder to them. *Walden* documents symbols of market modernity such as the global ice trade, the arrival of the railroad, and the ubiquity of debt, yet Thoreau was still enough of a witness to unself-conscious self-reliance and economic autonomy that in "Resistance to Civil Government" he could imagine that a total abdication of property was a realistic response to political malfeasance. Nonetheless, in the mid-1840s Thoreau was resolutely earnest that genuine self-reliance and autonomy remained a possibility, illustrating how incomplete the penetration of the market actually was. At the same time, the Walden experiment was also a literary device, a figurative exercise through which Thoreau could critique the larger community, his neighbors, and the complexity of market society.

Walden and *Walden* both were practical guides to individualist resistance to the market, but also requiems of lost independence. Thoreau's determination that a "government that governs best governs least" was a last gasp of Jacksonian radical individualism within the context of a political economy in which property ownership was still plausibly universal, even if it was diminishing and there were clearly visible pressures in opposition. In this moment when the ideal of propertied independence was giving way to market interdependence, *Walden* rendered them both essentially strange. In tone and temperament, Thoreau was even more radical than the socialists who surrounded him. Thoreau shared the socialist worry of a future dominated by alienating specialization, but his solution was to say, "no!" rather than to carve out novel ways to combine freedom, social justice, and economic specialization and complexity. Historically, though, Thoreau—and Emerson and Fuller—still lived in a moment when propertied self-reliance remained a credible and genuine alternative. That day, however, was disappearing; their message would later be adapted to a postbellum fantasy of Algeresque upward mobility, and this was why a Thoreau or an Emerson could be cited approvingly by Woody Hayes and other proponents of an industrial capitalist social order.

Transcendentalism's social and political consciousness and engagement, which included among other things Brook Farm, Emerson's domestic experiments, Walden, and Fuller's New York journalism—much of which focused on the plight of that city's poor and moral outcasts—took a radical turn in the late 1840s. For most Transcendentalists, the signal event was the Mexican-American War, which seemed to many northerners to be orchestrated by a slave-power conspiracy. Questions surrounding the status of slavery in an expanding West eventually resulted in a political compromise that included the Fugitive Slave Act, which implicated Massachusetts in the institution of slavery and inspired a decade of passionate civil disobedience. The debate over the future of slavery was connected to, but also a diversion from, the question of class and the rise of market culture.[28] For socialists and those whom they influenced, including Fuller, the late 1840s witnessed another decisive event that had a radicalizing effect: the revolutions of 1848. In years prior, the future of labor and social organization had been a matter of reform, distinctly separate from politics. But, as Fuller put it, during the convulsions of 1848 "the political" was "being merged in the social struggle."[29]

Within the long transition from a largely domestic, patriarchal economy to one organized on the basis of contract, incentive, and consent, the revolutions of 1848 proved to be a breaking point. Prior to the 1840s the United States had witnessed the first stirrings of modern union activity and class consciousness, but socialism was virtually unknown. Starting in 1840 the work of Charles Fourier reached American audiences through the writings of Albert Brisbane, the son of an affluent land speculator who was tutored by Fourier and other French socialists while completing his education in Europe during the 1830s. Brisbane's distillations of the work of Fourier and his contemporaries in books, pamphlets, newspapers, and magazines soon resulted in a large-scale social movement.[30]

The American Fourierists, quickly reborn as Associationists to distance themselves from the French theorist's speculations in the realms of cosmology, marriage, the family, and sexuality, began agitating on behalf of communitarian reorganization. They proposed "phalanxes" of roughly 1,600 people, among whom private property would be retained, but labor and profits would be distributed according to more egalitarian, scientific formulas. They proposed that manual and mental labor be alternated and that work could be assigned according to the laws of passional attraction. By the mid-1840s, American Fourierists numbered in the tens of thousands, had launched a major national organization and journal, and, most important, started more than twenty planned communities. Yet Associationism's fall was as rapid as its rise. By the late 1840s most of the Associated communities had failed, even though their influence on American political economy was profound. In particular, their contention that to cope with the complexities of national and global markets, workers required cooperative organization remained the core demand of the American labor movement into the late 1860s. Moreover, the socialist indictment of market inequality helped shape the way some Americans understood the crisis of 1848. When Fuller started to hint that she was increasingly persuaded by socialist arguments, it was likely some variant of Fourierist Association that she had in mind.

1848, SOCIALISM, AND FULLER'S ITALY

Fuller was an accidental witness to the turmoil of 1848. Some American socialists such as Brisbane and Charles Dana went to Europe with the explicit intention to witness the great upheaval, but Fuller arrived in Europe much earlier, in August 1846. Between 1844 and 1846 she had been a journalist with the *New-York Tribune*, where she wrote on literary topics but also made frequent excursions to the city's philanthropic institutions. In New York she became increasingly sensitized to the problem of poverty and to sexual and racial inequality. While Fuller never became a full-blown participant-observer in the world of benevolence, and although she admitted that her columns may not "do much, practically, for the suffering," she hoped that by raising awareness in "an organ of expression" such as the *Tribune*, she "may be of use." Nonetheless, Fuller left New York for Europe, but it was not her growing interest in social politics that drove her departure. Rather, according to Fuller, it was "the culture I sought in going, for with me it [was] no scheme of pleasure but the means of needed development."[31] Thus, when she arrived in England, she continued the pattern that she had established in New York. She wrote, in essence, about culture and society. She wrote of "Zoological Gardens," literary celebrities, museums, and music. Interspersed between these more conventional travel accounts were letters on reformers, poverty, and revolutionaries in exile. This pattern continued into the autumn of 1846 when Fuller left England, first for Paris, and then for Rome in the early spring of 1847. Things changed in 1848.

In that year revolution rocked nearly all of Europe. The conservative political order that had been carefully constructed in 1815 in the aftermath of French revolutionary turmoil seemed to come crashing down with lightning speed. In just the first four months of 1848 nearly fifty instances of political violence inflamed various small duchies and principalities, and these events were all dwarfed by what happened in France, where after an escalating succession of street demonstrations and political banquets, the people of Paris went to the barricades to overthrow a state that proved to be spectral. Just days into the uprising, the army and police refused to defend the regime, King Louis-Philippe fled the country, and a coalition of liberals and socialists, radicals and moderates, proclaimed a provisional government. Within weeks of the outbreak, it became clear, though, that the revolution in France was something different than nearly anything that had preceded it. A republican uprising had become a social one. Within days of Louis-Philippe's abdication, the provisional government followed up on one of the revolution's rallying cries—the "right to work"—and formed "National Workshops," modeled after Louis Blanc's manifesto, *The Organization of Labor*, and a "Workers' Commission," whose mission was to establish social rights under the new constitution.

The National Workshops were intended to be the basis of future producer and consumer cooperatives, but their goals were never fully realized. They enrolled close to a hundred thousand workers by May, but they were almost impossible to sustain, as the national government was almost totally bankrupt and had little prospect of improvement in an economy that was completely paralyzed. It was not long before the infant socially democratic republic began to fall apart. On May 15 a demonstration in support of Polish independence turned violent following provocative speeches by Armand Barbes and Louis Auguste Blanqui. Though the National Guard contained the unrest and took some leaders into custody, the uproar anticipated the more violent events to come. In late May national elections replaced the progressive provisional government with a new National Assembly, which resulted in a government more conservative than the one Parisian demonstrators had established in the original revolution. The assembly would soon issue a series of reports that on June 22 culminated in the closing of the National Workshops. The order ignited class violence in the capital that would come to be known as the June Days. In three days of street fighting, more than a thousand soldiers and demonstrators perished, and there were upward of ten thousand arrests and four thousand deportations. Afterward, the revolution would take a conservative turn. The French 1848, which began with such optimistic promise but unraveled in violence, shaped in many respects what would follow in Italy.[32]

Much of what unfolded in Fuller's revolutionary Italy took place, from an American perspective, in the shadow of the June Days violence in France. During the heady spring and summer months of 1848 Italy was a backwater. News was seldom reported from the region, and Fuller, in fact, went silent for more than seven months during the heart of the European 1848. Nonetheless, the revolutionary ambitions of Italy's nationalists had been smoldering for years. At midcentury the region was politically, economically, and culturally fragmented. Many of the states on the peninsula, itself divided by the Apennine mountain range, were ruled by foreign-born kings and princes, each under a separate system of laws. Economically, Italy was hardly a unit, and the royals who governed the region kept it that way. Internal customs duties plagued commerce, and most states were too small to support much of a home market. Communication was virtually impossible because of the near total absence of press freedom, and conservative and absolutist rulers within Italy (and even without) resisted railroad construction because they feared its politically liberalizing effects.[33] Italy, furthermore, lacked a robust middle class, and for many of the country's peasant majority, their world did not extend beyond their village or even their estate.

In the century prior to 1848 there were sporadic efforts, practical and theoretical, to initiate some kind of Italian national unification, but the most promising and progressive was launched, somewhat unintentionally, by the election of Pope Pius IX. Pius, who replaced the authoritarian Gregory XVI, began a thawing in Italian politics. He invited nonclerical participation in the temporal government of the Papal States, released a sizable number of political prisoners, loosened restrictions on the press and the right of assembly, and, perhaps most important, seemed to resurrect the idea of a loose-knit Italian nation or confederation under the leadership of Rome. Very quickly, a spirit of liberalization and reform began to spread throughout the Italian states, along with a few minor revolts and boycotts.

Given the nearly endemic nature of warfare, dynastic strife, imperial conflict, and revolt in Italy, it is difficult to separate Italy's "1848" from what preceded it. Nonetheless, in January of that year, longstanding liberal and nationalist aspirations in Italy ignited into open revolt in Palermo, where protestors seized control of the city. When Austria declined the Kingdom of the Two Sicilies' request for aid in putting down the revolt, the kingdom was forced to grant a written constitution. The success of the rebellion and its intimations of Austrian weakness emboldened Italy's liberal nationalists. Soon after, the rulers of Sardinia and Tuscany pledged to issue constitutions, and in March so did the pope himself. Later that month, Vienna witnessed its own uprising, which brought forth an Austrian constitution, the exile of Prince Metternich, and further revolts in the northern Italian states of Piedmont, Lombardy, and Venetia, ultimately igniting a war against Austrian rule.

Unfortunately, the tide of revolution soon turned and thwarted the ambitions of Italy's nationalists and republicans. In April, facing pressure from Catholic monarchs around Europe, the pope refused to support Piedmont's war against Austria. In July the empire defeated Piedmontese troops at Custoza, and not long after King Charles Albert signed a peace treaty that acknowledged Austrian rule in northern Italy. Piedmont's retreat undermined the cause of home rule throughout the region, although some hope remained in Rome. In November the pope abandoned the city, and by February 1849 a republic was established that restored most of the major exiled revolutionaries to the peninsula. The Roman Republic survived for more than half a year, but it soon fell victim to foreign invasion. Naturally, Austria publicly advocated the pope's restoration, and the conservative English press indirectly circulated inflammatory reports about bloodthirsty mobs roaming the city. The real villain, however, was France, which equivocated and then pretended to act as a neutral force but finally invaded the city, destroying the republic at the very moment that its own republican revolution was taking a reactionary turn.

Margaret Fuller's socialist awakening, such as it was, came about in the context of a European-wide revolution, but in some respects it was limited by Italian particularities. Nonetheless, Fuller began to lean in a more socialistic direction after arriving in Europe. Horace Greeley, her editor at the *Tribune*, urged her to meet with Europe's leading socialists, and in England, still more progressive than radical, Fuller praised experiments in worker housing and education. She lauded, for example, the "excellent spirit" and the "desire for growth" that she witnessed at the Mechanics' Institute in Liverpool, which offered basic instruction in languages and math, along with "lectures and concerts" and a circulating library. She found all of this praiseworthy, which was not surprising given how consonant it was with the sort of Emersonian and liberal Whiggish cultural uplift that had surrounded her for most of her professional life. In England, however, Fuller also saw for the first time an even more advanced form of the squalor that had horrified her in New York. Upon observing "swarms of dirty women and dirtier children . . . one has to grow insensible or die daily," she wrote that no one could "dare to blame the Associationists for their attempt to find prevention against such misery." "Poverty in England," she noted, "has terrors of which I never dreamed at home."[34]

In Paris Fuller met an even greater array of socialists, but few were revolutionaries or associated with workers' parties or clubs. Rather, they were Fourierists such as Victor Considerant and Clarisse Vigoureaux, cultural radicals such as George Sand, Christian socialists such as Félicité Robert de Lamennais, and Romantic socialists such as Pierre Leroux.[35] Her commentary on these encounters was limited, but consistent with what she had said before arriving in Paris and what she would write afterward. She argued that experiments on the order of Fourier's—"the need of some radical measures"—were both inevitable and a necessary response to Europe's squalor. She also maintained that the social and economic crisis that she was witnessing in England and France was a glimpse into the American future and that only the "selfish" or "stupid" refused to see it. Finally, influenced by the religious and Romantic socialists whom she had met in France, she explained more clearly her long-standing objections to Fourier's "gross materialism," his "error of making soul the result of health of body, instead of body the clothing of soul."[36]

After 1848 Fuller became more committed to socialism but never really explained in a developed way what it meant to her personally. Privately, she shared with Mary Rotch that she was a "firm believer that the next form society will take in remedy of the dreadful ills that now consume it will be voluntary association in small communities" but that she had not had the "force and time to explain in print."[37] To William Henry Channing, she wrote of her interest in "*our* socialism . . . for it has become mine, too," but she also confessed that her "interest is shallow as the plans." She admitted that although she thought socialism "serve[d] this great future," she "like[d] no Fourierites; they are terribly wearisome here in Europe."[38] At the same time, the revolution in France prompted her to announce publicly not only "that the political is being merged in the social struggle" but that she welcomed the coming violence: "whatever blood is to be shed, whatever altars cast down. . . . whatever be the cost." Most important, she identified clearly and vigorously with working-class revolutionaries, "the true aristocracy of a nation, the only really noble—the LABORING CLASSES."[39] Yet she would not really return to this final statement in a pronounced way.

Fuller never took the opportunity to elaborate what socialism actually meant to her. When the nationalist leader Joseph Mazzini returned to Italy from his long exile, she cheered, but also noted that Mazzini's vision was limited to "political emancipation." Fuller hinted suggestively of some more comprehensive social revolution that would follow, some new elaboration indicated by "the cry of Communism, the systems of Fourier," but she would not write of it "to-day nor in the small print of the *Tribune*." "Of this more anon," she concluded as she had to Mary Rotch a year earlier, but "anon" would never be.[40] In both her public and her private writings, her commitment to Fourierism or socialism more generally was, as Larry Reynolds and Susan Belasco Smith write, rather "cryptic."[41] More than likely, her socialism would have taken the form shared by her patrons, Marcus and Rebecca Spring, or her friend Cristina Trivulzio di Belgioso, the Milanese aristocrat. The Springs were wealthy reformers who were committed to socialism and abolitionism but who spent much of their energy on elite philanthropic ventures. As Charles Capper notes, they had few "compunctions about having many servants and enjoying fine clothing and hotels."[42]

Likewise, in Italy, Fuller became an intimate of di Belgioso, a wealthy princess who devoted some of her fortune to socialist "experiments" in "education," "labor," and "household affairs," but nonetheless "confessed once that she could not cook an egg, hem a handkerchief, or even order a meal."[43] Fuller, too, moved somewhat awkwardly among "the rabble." When the social and cultural complexities of her pregnancy forced her into a rural exile, she was drawn to the "simplicity" of the people and loved the spectacle of "their patriarchal ways . . . remote from the corruptions of foreign travel."[44] Yet she also complained repeatedly of boredom. She initially maintained a Roman servant because "the country people are too dirty" and would later call them "the worst people whom I have ever seen."[45] The radical cultural politics of other Transcendentalists, such as Emerson or Thoreau, took an experiential form, mingled with ordinary speech and labor, and expressed a longing for unself-conscious authenticity and simplicity. In contrast, Fuller's radicalism was mixed with noblesse oblige; the "people" were objects of radical gestures rather than subjects to be emulated in their own right.

In some respects, Fuller's Fourierism was one of the least radical things about her Italian period. The version that she had encountered in America was in the spirit of the period's many benevolent societies, and not that distinct in tone from abolitionism, prison reform, and houses for fallen women. As Carl Guarneri put it, "Fourierism originated with the middle class," and few utopians were class-conscious industrial workers for a very simple reason: the United States simply was not yet close to being an industrialized country during the 1840s.[46] Even by the Civil War, few manufacturing firms employed more than fifty workers. Beyond certain pockets, the proletarian moment had not yet come. Association did, however, attract distressed artisans; they formed its rank and file and in some contexts had been radicalized by the economic changes taking place around them. Nonetheless, Fuller was closer in spirit to the reform community's elite leadership, people like the Springs. At bottom, Fourierists in the United States and abroad were on the revolutionary margins, and class violence conflicted with the movement's core values. The organ of the Associationist movement, the *Harbinger*, for example, barely acknowledged the June Days violence and remained persuaded that socialism, to use Fuller's language, was "preventative." "The Associative system points out the way, by which that peril can be averted, and unity of interests guaranteed with no sacrifice of individual rights."[47] More than the Fourierists, Fuller embraced revolutionary violence, but her perspective was largely political and national rather than social.

There simply is very little evidence that socialism shaped, in an integral way, the manner in which Fuller viewed the world, particularly in contrast to the other intellectuals influenced by the movement. For Fuller political conflict was primarily an epic romantic struggle between individuals, of representative men, of heroes and villains. She was engaged with European squalor but never really pulled back from it to see it as a humanitarian problem that socialism could address. Her socialism, never fully articulated, was ameliorative. It did not inform the way she understood the political condition of Italy, the sources of imperialism and nationalism, or the trajectory of the revolution. In only one dispatch did Fuller offer a structural analysis of the Italian political situation. She noted that the Italian nobility had resisted the "lures" of foreign and imperial "pleasures," observed the contrast between the intellectual fertility of the country's "middle class" and its incapacity "in the present system," and wrote that the "lower part of the population is in a dull state," stupefied by "the censure of the press," the lack of "public meetings," and restricted "access to . . . more instructed and aspiring minds."[48] Yet only here did she reflect on the social sources of political conflict and revolution. She would later write that political transformation must come "from the people themselves . . . and not from princes," but what she imagined was not, in effect, a social democracy but a natural aristocracy, "none but natural princes, great men."[49]

A comparison with other witnesses to the 1848 revolutions is instructive. Initially, 1848 did not represent a revolution for socialists only, and most Americans received the news of the various European outbreaks enthusiastically. Some Americans wore the French "liberty cap" and others Kossuth "hats" and "boots," named for the Hungarian revolutionary. Most Americans believed that 1848 symbolized the way in which the United States was leading a world governed by despots toward a republican future; this initial consensus was true for both the press and the government.[50] Rallies were held in cities across the country. The mayor of New York City convened a citywide demonstration that included delegations from the city's French, Irish, Polish, Italian, German, and even English populations. On their, and the city's, behalf he tendered "sympathy and warm congratulations to the citizens of the new Republic in Europe."[51] The federal government broke with its usual hands-off posture toward European political conflicts and took the radical step of recognizing the provisional French government, something it would not later do for the Roman Republic, much to Fuller's chagrin. Congress voted in March to "congratulate" the French people, and in April President Polk gave the new republican government formal sanction. Officially, the American foreign minister, unlike his British counterpart, almost immediately recognized the provisional French government, with James Buchanan even serving as an informal adviser.[52]

Americans' unity, though, proved to be temporary. In the second half of 1848 a number of dissenters began to emerge. Southerners opposed the decision of the provisional French government to abolish slavery in its colonial holdings.[53] More careful scrutiny by some observers, such as Francis Bowen, found that some national movements concealed more insidious motives. To Bowen the Hungarian independence movement, for example, was not driven to uphold liberal and republican ideals but to preserve the "masterdom . . . [of] the Magyars" and the "subjection and dependence" of various Slavic "races."[54] By the time the Italian Risorgimento became a focus of public attention, many American conservatives had come to believe that Catholics, peasants, peoples long subject to foreign rule, and "dark-skinned races . . . are only fit for military governments."[55] These doubts were exacerbated by the fact that much of the initial reporting on the various uprisings came from conservative newspapers such as the London *Times*. Margaret Fuller and the *New-York Tribune*, the paper for which she wrote for the last five years of her life, turned out to be a key democratic alternative for that "large class of readers who are not satisfied with seeing France and Europe presented through British Conservative spectacles."[56]

Although race and citizenship were important, the main fault line in American opinion proved to be political economy and socialism. France's social revolution, naturally, divided observers in the United States. Throughout the spring, American socialists remained supportive of the French Left's social democratic ambitions, despite the fact that many of its factions embraced doctrines more explosive than anything advocated in their own country. The *Harbinger*, for example, commented, "How can any intelligent person imagine for a moment, that the political relations of a country can be established on a sound and permanent basis, while its industrial relations are in confusion and disorder?" "No mere form of government, however excellent," it concluded, "[can] clothe the backs or fill the mouths of naked, hungry Frenchmen."[57] Albert Brisbane noted that German radicals admired American political democracy, but dreamed of a "Social" rather than a "Bourgeois Republic," such as the one "in the United States, where Labor is the prey of Capital, where free competition ruins the laboring classes, where you have the same distinctions of classes in Society, the same contrasts of wealth and poverty that we have here."[58] Even a conservative socialist such as Horace Greeley, though he labored to distinguish French and American Association from the unruly ferment on the ground, was consistent in his view that "from the hour that the fall of Louis-Philippe was known here to this moment,

[we] profoundly rejoiced in the Revolution itself, and more especially in its Socialistic aspects."[59] Greeley went to great lengths to emphasize that practical Fourierism would preserve private property, diminish class antagonism, reduce social and economic instability, and not threaten the traditional family or the moral framework underlying it.

But France's social revolution resonated with the *Tribune*'s well-established social democratic sentiments, embracing its "right to work" slogan and its protections for "Rights and Interests of Labor, the Reorganization of Industry, the Elevation of the Working-Men, the Reconstruction of the Social Fabric." Even Greeley asserted that revolutionary violence was not an indicator of a people's incapacity for self-government but rather of their desperation under an oppressive social and political regime; class violence only augmented the argument for socialism as a means of forestalling conditions where "revolution is the only resource left." To nearly all American socialists, including Fuller, European class conflict simply foreshadowed a situation that would one day emerge in the United States; the precipitating conditions, as one socialist would put it, were mitigated only by "the sparseness of the population [that] prevents the appearance of the evils which belong to the principle of Individualism, and otherwise we should have our Laborer's Riots and Revolutions."[60]

For conservative American critics of socialism, on the other hand, France's violent turn underscored the dangers of the movement. The Boston *Advertiser* depicted French and American socialists as the enemies of liberty, of "legislating the details of life." The *Courier*, which had long been the most stridently antisocialist voice in the American press, feared that French socialism portended something even more hazardous than the experiments that had already been launched in the United States: "*Socialism* in France is seen to be something more than a mere *abstraction*.... It has life, and power, and may do infinite mischief." Most ominous, socialism, the *Courier* cautioned, taught "the poor,—the ignorant,—the degraded . . . that they were the victims of a *false society*. Their sufferings and their vices were charged to the account of the social organizations.—They were taught that society owed them employment, with ample wages;—and that they would never enjoy their rights until the present order of things should be overthrown."[61]

The most obvious point of comparison to Fuller's 1848 journalism was the work of the *Tribune*'s Paris correspondent, Henry Börnstein. The German-born Börnstein remains not widely known. With a touch of perhaps false modesty he titled his autobiography the memoir of an "unimportant person." But, as a founder of *Vorwärts*, a cultural and political journal for Paris' radical expatriates, a community that included Karl Marx, Arnold

Ruge, Friedrich Engels, Heinrich Heine, and Michael Bakunin, he was present at the creation of Marxist politics and thought. Börnstein never produced an original work of political economy or social criticism—and Marx and Engels considered him little more than a business agent and possibly an informer—but during the mid-1840s, he became a correspondent for the *Deutsche Schnellpost*, a German-language newspaper published out of the same building as Fuller's *Tribune*. It was mostly likely his correspondence that Fuller translated as "The Social Movement in Europe," probably the first English-language survey of Marxism published in the United States. In it, Börnstein anticipated, and perhaps helped shape, the general approach that the *Tribune* would take to the 1848 revolutions. Börnstein wrote that he "would give not a farthing for political revolutions, even if as radical as those of 1793 . . . that leave the poor poor, the hungry hungry, the ignorant ignorant, and all kinds of miserables as they were before." Politics, he contended, could "correct neither the faults nor vices of individuals nor the errors of the masses, nor the false relations of our present society, nor the woes that spring from them, and that we must have a grander, wider, more comprehensive principles on which to base a new order."[62]

Börnstein's reporting on 1848, unlike Fuller's, was not merely sympathetic to what Fuller somewhat obliquely termed "the cry of Communism, the systems of Fourier"; it actively imposed a socialistic framework on the events of the day.[63] As was the case with Fuller's dispatches, the *Tribune* viewed Börnstein's direct reports as a corrective to the conservative English press whose correspondence dominated the field. Following erroneous reports in the London *Times* on the violent excesses of imagined Roman mobs, Fuller remarked that "there exists not in Europe a paper more violently opposed to the cause of freedom than the *Times*, and neither its leaders nor its foreign correspondence are to be depended upon."[64] Likewise, the *Tribune* self-consciously positioned Börnstein's correspondence as an eye-witness and progressive alternative to "English Tory papers" that were unremittingly hostile to workers' movements.[65] When conservative papers such as the Whig *Express* complained of Börnstein's "ultra-Revolutionary and War-invoking sentiments," the *Tribune* answered that it had "engaged 'H.B.' to let our readers know what the ultra-Radical party of Europe are meditating and doing, which is neither fully nor fairly set forth through the other channels of information accessible to us."[66]

What made Börnstein's correspondence distinct from Fuller's was not its radicalism but rather the more careful attention Börnstein paid to the foundational elements of the revolution. Unlike Fuller, he carefully documented the French 1848's political, ideological, and social factions. He described, for example, the way in which the "late Revolution in France was the work almost exclusively of the Labouring class especially the so called—the Workmen for Hire in Paris." He noted that under Louis-Philippe's rule, the government had acted only on behalf of the "Bourgeoisie or Middle class" and "against the Laborers in every struggle they made to improve their condition." Börnstein further cataloged the variety of workers parties: "at one extreme is the absolute Communism of Cabet, Blanqui, etc., at the other is the Associationism . . . of Considerant." "Between these," Börnstein finished, is a "distinct" third, Louis Blanc and Albert's plans for "the Organization of Labor," the idea "that the nation shall provide vast workshops, purchase materials, prosecute various branches of manufacture, and furnish employment to all who require it."[67] And as the republican coalition between workers and the French bourgeoisie began to unravel in May and June, Börnstein began to argue openly that "revulsion," "bankruptcy," and "bloodshed" were but a prologue to "a vastly improved social order." Social progress depended on "the Revolution of the Laboring Class," a sentiment well removed from the Associationist commitment to class harmony and reconciliation.[68] Both Börnstein and Fuller called for revolution in Europe, a fact that placed them both on the radical end of the American ideological spectrum, but when the former called for a social revolution, he was explicit, a clarity rooted in a comprehensive worldview.

A decade of French social criticism shaped Börnstein's correspondence and analysis of the French 1848. Perhaps the most influential of these thinkers was Louis Blanc, whose historical works, like Börnstein's correspondence but in contrast to Fuller's, set out a collection of premises that would become pervasive among socialist commentators throughout 1848. These general assumptions included the notion that history was shaped by economic forces, that law and custom expressed the interests of ruling elites, and, more pointedly, that capitalist individualism was a "system of extermination," moving relentlessly toward concentration, stratification, and moral bankruptcy.[69] Blanc's macrohistorical approach to politics and political economy was not even exclusive to socialists but was endemic among writers with a certain cast of mind. Alexis de Tocqueville, for example, who like Blanc was both a theorist and a participant in the French 1848, wrote social commentary in the 1830s and history in the 1850s even more abstract than Blanc's, a landscape almost completely denuded of individuals or identifying detail. But it was Blanc who offered the plausible model, and during the last months of her life, Fuller took to reading Blanc's histories, along with Alphonse Marie-Louis de Lamartine's, as she continued to write her own history of the Risorgimento.[70]

France's 1848 transformed both the vocabulary of the Left and the way it processed the trajectory of history and politics, and this new language was mostly absent in Fuller's correspondence. As the Associationist *Harbinger* pointed out, "'Organization of Labor,' 'Unity of Interests,' [and] 'social Science,' are henceforth destined to be common words in all prints . . . with all editors and all who minister to public opinion."[71] Typical were newspaper series such as "Philadelphia in Slices," which sketched the urban landscape's social types; this number, undoubtedly modeled after George Foster's *New York by Gaslight*, noted specifically the novelty of this new social scientific sensibility. Its portrait of the city's "Bourgeoisie" began with the apology, "the last few months have rendered all readers of newspapers familiar with this word, although we do not undertake to say that even the Editors themselves who are most in the habit of using it know what it means."[72] Even the dilettante Donald Mitchell, a correspondent for the antisocialist *Courier*, would write of the conflict between the "bourgeois" and the "strange and incongruous men" who made up the socialist parties.[73] When Albert Brisbane wrote about the June Days, which he witnessed, he instinctually wrote of a desperate "working-class" without "middle or upper class" leadership and of its sources in the "stagnation of commerce" and the absence of concerted government action.[74] The revolution brought to the surface wide-ranging treatments of what French radical intellectuals self-consciously called "social science" and the "social question," which made its core subject the relationship of individuals to the institutions, laws, and practices that governed their lives. In particular, radical thinkers investigated "the problem of labor and its organization."[75] Socialism became not solely a political commitment but a new lens through which social conflicts could be interpreted and understood.

In contrast, the Romantic style of Fuller's correspondence can to some extent be explained by her subject—Italy. As Bell Gale Chevigny points out, conditions in Italy were different from those in France and especially Paris. Italy lacked France's republican revolutionary tradition, its "social theorists," and especially "an industrial proletariat and consequently . . . class consciousness."[76] The fault lines of Italy's several revolutions were primarily political and religious. Most Italians were united against foreign rule, but beyond that they were divided. What would be the role of the church in the new Italy? Would the peninsula be united under a single government? Would Italy become a republic or a constitutional monarchy? The social question was simply not paramount.

Still, there were socially revolutionary elements in the Roman Republic that mirrored those that had arisen the prior year in Paris, but these are largely invisible in Fuller's correspondence. There were mass demonstrations orchestrated by radical democrats, so successful that they managed to drive more moderate elements from the government. Some of these demonstrations were organized by class, in some cases dominated by artisans and in others by peasants from the countryside. The so-called *capipopolo* rallied for public works, in particular railroad and building restoration projects, and successfully convinced the provisional government to outlaw imprisonment for debt. In Tuscany there were strikes by peasants and dockworkers, and the liberal revolutionary government had to resist more radical calls to seize church property and to displace the clergy. There were also appeals for land reform.

In addition to these events, Fuller could have analyzed the sources of counterrevolutionary resistance by the rural peasant population to the south of Rome, which remained loyal to the papal regime. In some villages, inhabitants tore down all of the symbols of the republic and replaced them with the insignias of the church. This symbolic violence became more than metaphoric—a social war—when pro-Republican and papist groups organized themselves into militias and fought several small skirmishes with one another. One could speculate that Fuller largely ignored Italy's social conflicts because of her commitment to the political program of Mazzini. To Fuller Mazzini's name was synonymous with "the cause of human freedom," but he was only vaguely committed to various programs of worker association.[77] He had an abstract commitment to "the people," but his first priority was national unification and liberation, even if it meant a temporary alliance with counterrepublican forces such as Piedmont's King Charles Albert.[78]

In the end, Fuller's radicalism had less to do with her socialism, which was largely benevolent and philanthropic, and more to do with her politics, her anticlericalism, and her Romantic nationalism, all of which by the autumn of 1848 were, to be frank, sanguinary. Fuller's relationship to both Catholicism and nationalism is complex, and it is an ambivalence derived largely from her Transcendental-socialist anti-individualism. Like many of her Romantic contemporaries, Fuller's posture toward tradition and organic community was mixed. As Charles Capper writes, among American intellectuals sympathetic to Italian culture, Fuller was alone in recognizing that "if Italy was to have a future, much of the country's feudal order underlying its admired culture required destruction or drastic reordering—and that was a good thing."[79] She was committed to a modern Italy, an Italy that was not a living—or dead—museum of the past. Appreciative of the country's classical and more recent heritage and true to her Emersonian roots, she rejected the notion of an Italy that was merely about the "dry bones of the past" and instead embraced the country's political present and future.

Perhaps even more thoroughly, Fuller's gender politics were tied to the idea of revolutionary self-making of a fashion that could transcend habits, social forms, and even nature. She wrote famously that "masculine" and "feminine" "are perpetually passing into one another."[80] In short, she refused merely to "accept the universe" as it was. Fuller was particularly critical of lower forms of nationalism, especially when her own country "betrayed" its "high commission" and dithered in its official response to the Roman Republic. She compared the "spoliation of Poland" to the "conquest of Mexico" and excoriated the "cancer of Slavery."[81] Most of all, she despised American materialism, the pervasive "lust of gain" that she feared was written into the national character. Writing of Harro Harring's political exile in liberal America, Fuller identified him—and by extension herself—as an international cosmopolitan, emancipated from "any local standard of orthodoxy" and a part of an "advanced guard in all liberal opinions."[82]

Nonetheless, Fuller's radical cosmopolitanism was mixed with her Romantic sympathy for the ties of tradition, community, nation, and even ethnicity and race. When Fuller landed in Italy, she felt that she had "touched those shores" that were her natural home, and even before revolutionary violence broke out, she commonly spoke of an "Austrian race" and an "Italian character."[83] She discovered in Italy a kind of rootedness and solidarity, a commitment to national self-emancipation, even though, ironically, she found it principally among a community of revolutionary exiles. Fuller's sense of the centrality of nation, culture, and race was not new, however. While in New York, Fuller described Frederick Douglass as both "a specimen of the powers of the Black Race" and as a symbol of the promise of a cosmopolitan, transnational America, one that could "assimilate" the low and "peculiar element" of the "African Race" and the higher elements of "those imported among us from Europe."[84]

Her thoughts on religious traditionalism were similarly contorted. Fuller also condemned New York's social segmentation, particularly as it was reflected in its churches. She contrasted the "fashionable" splendor of Grace Church to the dignity of traditional Catholic cathedrals, where decorative grandeur glorified "brotherly love" and "rich and poor knelt together upon their marble pavements, and the imperial altar welcomed the obscurest artisan."[85] Fuller wielded pro-Catholic sentiments not only against the city's high bourgeoisie but against its nativists and nationalists and more broadly against the culture of individualism and materialism. This was a sentiment shared by a number of Romantic intellectuals, most famously by Orestes Brownson; his class-conscious radicalism eventually carried him to Catholicism, which "assumes that the evil originates in man's abuse of his freedom" and, unlike the Fourierists, teaches that "our appetites, passions, and affections are disordered, depraved, and therefore not to be trusted."[86]

Fuller's Romantic nationalism, like the radical political economy of other intellectuals, was a counterweight to the culture of individualism and, as with political economy, resists description along a left-right continuum. Fuller was among a wide range of midcentury intellectuals who recoiled from the individualism and materialism rampant in the advanced economies of the West. Tocqueville mourned the manner in which market cultures "make every man forget his ancestors, but it hides his descendants, and separates his contemporaries from him; it throws him back forever upon himself alone, and threatens in the end to confine him entirely within the solitude of his own heart." Marx simultaneously welcomed and critiqued the market's capacity to erase "all fixed, fast-frozen relations, with their train of ancient and venerable prejudices and opinions." Others, such as Emerson or Thomas Carlyle, preached heroic individualism to counter the splintering effects of modernity.[87]

It was this background of anti-individualism that encouraged Fuller to trust the early, church-enabled flowering of the Italian 1848. Italy's national and democratic ambitions were wrapped up in the fate of the church, and this was particularly true of Fuller's Rome. In a general way, Fuller arrived in Italy with a certain amount of receptivity to Catholicism. Like many liberals throughout Italy and the rest of the continent, Fuller initially embraced Pope Pius, praising his political reforms and trusting "his tenderness of heart." She celebrated the optimism that his elevation unleashed and hoped that the symbolic power of his position would unify the country, but she also anticipated "how hampered and inadequate are the means at his command" and that he would never live up to "all this noise of expectation." "Doubts were always present," she later wrote, "whether all this joy was not premature."[88]

By 1848 Fuller's forebodings were becoming manifest. By January a "shadow" had "fallen" on the pope's "popularity" and the untenable nature of his position was becoming increasingly clear. Catholicism would be an enemy not only of democracy but of nationality in any form. By early summer the pope had repudiated the political thaw that he had initiated, but in Fuller's mind this was a blessing because it discredited Italy's conservative nationalists, led by Vicenzo Gioberti, who hoped to nationalize the country under the leadership of constitutional monarchs and the papacy. The failure of elite nationalism made room for Mazzini and an Italy confederated and ruled from below: "It seems as if Fate was at work to bewilder and cast down the dignities of the world and democratize Society at a blow." Later Fuller would write that the revolutionary dynamic itself would transform the political consciousness of the peninsula. When she arrived, the revolutionary impulse was latent, but the "vast majority" had no desires beyond "limited monarchies" and written constitutions. They "despise the priests" but were "attached to the dogmas and rituals of the Roman Catholic Church." The treacheries of the church and secular rulers, however, persuaded the "people that no transition is possible between the old and the new. *The work is done; the revolution in Italy is now radical*" and would not end until Italy became both an independent nation and a "republic."[89]

As Italy's many revolutions reached a crisis point, any ambivalence that Fuller once had about Catholicism disappeared. Like almost any other American Protestant, she recoiled from the church's debased splendor. She related one anecdote of a priest who refused to say masses on behalf of a poor orphan's dead uncle without monetary compensation but exhorted worshippers to "imitate Christ" during the Liturgy. Like most European liberals, she was an avowed opponent of the Jesuits, the enemy of the "free progress of humanity," "emissaries of the power of darkness," and a "cancer." Fuller called for their "extirpation," though she was resigned to the fact that even without the Jesuits, "there would remain Jesuitical men." When the church turned against Italy's and Rome's political emancipation, she questioned publicly, "how any one can remain a Catholic . . . I cannot conceive." She termed republican Rome and Romans "Protestant" and noted that the "New Testament has been translated into Italian." She watched approvingly as the people set fire to "the Cardinals' Carriages" and made "mock confessions in the Piazzas" using the "confessionals" that they had ripped from the churches. If the classical republican narrative was of swords beaten into ploughshares, for Fuller, it was of confessionals transformed into "barricades."[90]

From the summer of 1848 forward, Fuller's political and anticlerical rhetoric became increasingly violent and extreme. She wrote of a pope "shut up . . . in his palace," surrounded by a "crowd of selfish and insidious advisers" and carrying out "infamous treacheries." These were "scarlet men of sin." She called Charles Albert a "traitor" and a coward: "Had the people slain him in their rage, he well deserved it at their hands." As the French army prepared to destroy the Roman Republic, she wrote, "The struggle is now fairly, thoroughly commenced between the principle of Democracy and the old powers, no longer legitimate. That struggle may last fifty years, and the earth be watered with the blood and tears of more than one generation, but the result is sure. All Europe, including Great Britain, where the most bitter resistance of all will be made, is to be under Republican Government in the next century." As she watched the revolution to which she had devoted every scrap of her being crumble, she publicly declared her socialism. But in her view the root of Italy's problems was not political economy but Europe's imperial system and especially religion: "The next revolution, here and elsewhere, will be radical. Not only Jesuitism must go, but the Roman Catholic religion must go. The Pope cannot retain even his spiritual power."[91]

Margaret Fuller's occasional and elusive public and private commitments to socialism were indicative of, but hardly constituted, her radical turn. The Italian revolutionary experience had radicalized her, but socialism as she understood it was "preventative" and served only to mitigate rather than advance fundamental social conflicts. It was, arguably, distinctly counterrevolutionary. One can only speculate whether her socialism might have taken a new form in her history of the Roman Republic, whether it would have embodied a thorough intellectual transformation and produced something very different from her newspaper dispatches. Her friend Elizabeth Barrett Browning wrote that the book she "was preparing upon Italy would probably have been more equal to her faculty than anything previously produced by her pen (her other writings being curiously inferior to the impressions her conversation gave you); indeed, she told me it was the only production to which she had given time and labour." Moreover, Browning speculated, it would have been "deeply coloured by those blood colours of Socialistic views, which would have drawn the wolves on her, with a still more howling enmity, both in England and America."[92]

As Fuller moved physically farther from New England and the Transcendental orbit, she certainly became more radical, but always in ways that were connected to her past. In Italy she became nothing less than a Jacobin, embracing violence, revolution, and a measure of anticlericalism far beyond what one could have expected. In other respects, however, she followed a trajectory that anticipated and matched that of other second-generation Transcendentalists who remained at home.[93] Her Italian revolutionary commitments foreshadowed Bronson Alcott and Thomas Wentworth Higginson's storming of Boston's federal courthouse to free the fugitive slave Anthony Burns. They anticipated Theodore Parker's efforts to arm free soil settlers in Kansas. They looked forward to Emerson's canonization of John Brown. They portended Henry David Thoreau's counsel to his compatriots to "let your life be a counter-friction to stop the machine."[94] Margaret Fuller's radicalization did not leave behind her Transcendental past but instead carved out and anticipated its more radical political future.

6

MARGARET FULLER AND ANTISLAVERY

"A Cause Identical"

Albert J. von Frank

I wish to be a true & free man, & therefore would not be a woman, or a king, or a clergyman, each of which classes in the present order of things is a slave.
—*Ralph Waldo Emerson*, Journals and Miscellaneous Notebooks, *July 15, 1834*

Who ain't a slave? Tell me that.
—*Herman Melville*, Moby-Dick, *1851*

Only late in her short life did Margaret Fuller come to a creditable, appreciative understanding of the American antislavery movement. There was never a time, of course, from childhood on, when slavery did not draw from her at least a measured disapproval, as befitting the alert daughter of cautiously antislavery parents. For a long while, however, the bondage of Africans in America elicited no outrage, and among the complex reasons why it did not was that, until she discovered revolution in Europe, she simply had not grasped with any firmness the meaning of chattel slavery, either in political or in human terms. Ironically, the idea came fully home to her only when she went abroad in 1846. In this regard the progress of her thought might be seen as coincident with or even slightly in advance of changes in popular feeling among educated New Englanders. Especially is this so if one were to grant that it was only with the annexation of Texas in 1845, or the commencement of the Mexican War in 1846, or still more decisively with the passage of the Compromise of 1850 and the Fugitive Slave Act (virtually at the moment of

Fuller's death) that abolitionism ceased being a predominantly moral and religious crusade and finally emerged as a revolutionary movement.[1]

Fuller's earliest attitudes about race and slavery are not well documented, but to the extent that they can be known or reasonably inferred they appear to have been shaped by the views of her parents, especially those of her father, Congressman Timothy Fuller. In two widely reported speeches delivered in the House of Representatives in February 1819, Fuller had supported a provision (the Tallmadge amendment) for the gradual emancipation of slaves in Missouri should that territory be admitted to the Union, and he excoriated General Andrew Jackson for his aggression against the Seminole Indians in Florida. Representative Fuller believed that the framers of the Constitution had granted slavery a "temporary indulgence" in exchange for measures protecting northern commerce, but he, like many others, expected that the institution would soon disappear, given that it was the prerogative of the federal government to bar it from the territories. His position on the Seminoles may have had as much to do with political antipathy to Jackson as with solicitude for Native Americans, but his defense of Indian rights is a matter of record and worth noting in view of his daughter's recurrent attention to the subject. Indeed, Margaret Fuller would often feel profounder pangs over America's dealings with its indigenous population than over its treatment of enslaved blacks, catching at the significance of the fact that the former seemed threatened by racial extinction even as the latter were fruitful and multiplied.[2]

In the American republic as Margaret Fuller knew it through most of her life women had no opportunities, much less responsibilities, of a political sort. If they exercised power they did so indirectly, in the private sphere, through influence on whatever voters or shapers of public opinion their households might contain. Even this proxy power, unfacilitated by particular educational, religious, or political institutions and uncoerced by anyone's expectations, had in each local instance to be extemporized. There was no formula—certainly no generally recognized formula—whereby women might manufacture political force. As Catharine Beecher would write in 1837, "it was designed that the mode of gaining influence and of exercising power [by women] should be altogether different and peculiar."[3] Female influence might on rare occasions have been offered to or been enlisted in some cause of reform, but it was "peculiar" in never being a representation of the coalesced opinions of any party or association. That is to say, the value of any woman's political views did not depend on the number of other women who shared it. Where it existed, it was the projected effect of individual moral character and of the respect, large or small, in which that character was held. These conditions obtained most universally during Margaret Fuller's youth or, in other words, until 1836–37, when Sarah and Angelina Grimké began their northern lecture tour and female antislavery societies sprang up in their wake. By a different reckoning, they existed until 1833, when Fuller's friend Lydia Maria Child published her *Appeal in Favor of That Class of Americans Called Africans*, which had a widespread converting effect on male and female readers alike.

Both of these pioneer instances of female influence were in explicit affiliation with the public crusade of Boston-based abolitionist William Lloyd Garrison. His campaign, effectively begun with the establishment of the *Liberator* in 1831 before Fuller's twenty-first birthday, benefited from the way in which Child and the Grimké sisters practically subverted the idiosyncrasy (or isolation, or guardedness) of female moral authority. Because antislavery had so much to do with what it meant to be a New England woman in the nineteenth century—and indeed with what it meant to be a woman's rights advocate—the whole complex question of Fuller's relation to abolitionism has to be canvassed if her total accomplishment is to be understood.[4]

The obvious way to approach this task would be simply to assemble the statements that Fuller from time to time made on the subject, and yet to do so would likely disguise both their infrequency and the context that gave them, in almost every instance, a crucial supplemental meaning. Given that she was by no means a historically important source of antislavery ideology, the operative question becomes not what did she say, but rather why, in light of her known sympathies, did she not say more? What, indeed, were the effective, mostly constraining, conditions of her discourse? Tracing out this line of inquiry sheds light on a variety of issues, including the much debated question of whether "Transcendentalism" was so inner-directed as to be incompatible with the personal maintenance of a social conscience.

One begins with the premise that the ambient culture at any moment has within it factors that call out and factors that inhibit the activity of the social conscience so that reform is often an effect of personally readjusting their relative proportions. Margaret Fuller's modest first publication, composed at the age of twenty-four, is a fascinating, complexly nuanced case in point. In October 1834 the historian and Democratic activist George Bancroft published an article in the *North American Review* titled "Slavery in Rome." In their home in Groton, Massachusetts, Timothy and Margaret Fuller read this essay. Father encouraged daughter to write a brief reply, which, perhaps with a boost from Timothy's sponsorship, duly appeared on an inside page of the *Boston Daily Advertiser and Patriot* on November 27, signed "J."

Bancroft's provocative essay is notable as the most unqualified denunciation of slavery that its author ever wrote. Reading it today one has the impression that he anticipated virtually every secular argument that later writers would raise against the utility or morality of the slave system. His thesis that slavery was the immediate cause of the decline and dissolution of the Roman Empire is transparently couched as a cautionary tale for modern times. Yet just three years earlier, in a review of Philipp August Boeckh's *Economy of Athens*, Bancroft had passed up an opportunity to make similar claims about another equally egregious slave society. The motive to allegory may have been less pressing in the early months of 1831, a year that, owing to Garrison's efforts, changed how slavery would henceforth be discussed. Bancroft's 1834 essay clearly rode on the energy of that change.

In her response, written at her father's request, Fuller proved almost entirely oblivious to the subject of the essay on which she commented.[5] In the first paragraph Fuller perfunctorily acknowledged the unnamed writer's "liberal" views and conceded that they were "such as must meet with warm approbation from most enlightened minds in this part of the world." But she otherwise passed them by. What captured her attention (and her father's, too, as may be inferred) was the virtually parenthetical and argumentatively irrelevant denigration of the figure of Marcus Brutus, the patriot who famously conspired against the life of Caesar. To Bancroft Brutus was a man of "headstrong, unbridled disposition," "time-serving, treacherous," "avaricious and cruel," who in the end showed himself to be "the dupe of more sagacious men."[6] To the young Fuller, who knew her Plutarch and her Shakespeare, Brutus was the moral hero par excellence, so Bancroft's unhandsome and gratuitous stroke of revisionist history necessarily "occasioned [her] a painful surprise." Her dismay over the impugned character of this hero ("the noblest Roman of them all") effectively removed the subject of slavery from her sight. Thus, in correcting the judgment of the historian, Margaret Fuller began her literary career in the very act of overlooking slavery.

She was entitled, of course, to object to any detail in Bancroft's essay as she saw fit. Yet there is a real significance in the reasons why, given her circumstances in the fall of 1834, she was compelled to argue the trivial antiquarian point at the cost of ignoring what was fast becoming the great moral question of contemporary American life. The species of sentimentalism involved in her outsized regard for Brutus was rooted not just in the classical education that Timothy Fuller saw to it she possessed, but in the quasi-private mythology that Rome, as a foundational moral construct, offered to her. She would make a great deal of this myth in her "Autobiographical Sketch," in which Rome, associated with civic virtue, "stern composure," and the force of masculine willfulness, functions as the sign of the father, just as counterpointing Greece, with the "enchanted gardens" and "sunny waters" of its more beautiful, more moderate mythology, functions as the sign of the mother.[7] Charles Capper notes that her youthful reading of Plutarch promoted a lasting respect for the Roman ideals of "'an earnest purpose, an indomitable will,' 'hardihood' and 'self-command.'"[8] Fuller necessarily received the attack on Brutus, then, as entailing an attack on her own father, both in his capacity as a public man (like Brutus a framer of laws, a self-denying conservator of the state) and in the heroic light in which Fuller privately regarded him. To the daughter, Timothy Fuller's masculine, character-driven, born-to-command moral authority verged in these mythic terms on the imperial, intrinsically proslavery Roman ethos that Bancroft deplored.

Margaret Fuller's defense of this particular vision of the moral-heroic, which she found objectified in the patriarchal virtues of the classic Roman politician, was already, in 1834, an old-fashioned position, an inheritance from her father, whom she pointedly called "a Queen Anne's man."[9] It was not, in any event, a position well calculated to bring her personally into conflict with the laws that in her own time made an institution of human bondage. What was most remarkable about the early antislavery movement and its many female adherents was a tendency to look to private and subjective sanctions for behavior and at the same time to be aggressively skeptical about claims advanced with the historically established political authority of male "heroes." To be an abolitionist in the mid-1830s meant taking the part of the despised and lowly against the nation's wise fathers, both the founders in a foregoing generation and the apologist sons currently in government—and, for that matter, in the pulpit as well. First and foremost abolitionism was a revolt against the leader class, one reason why it resonated so strongly with women; in this milieu being abashed at an iconoclasm that demoted Brutus would have to be seen as retrograde, as motion against the tide. Fuller's own antislavery views had very little chance of emerging until her antislavery father (who, in commissioning a defense of Brutus, effectively decommissioned an attack on slavery) dissolved his immediate and personal leader-class influence by dying in 1835.

Nevertheless, Fuller's obtuseness in her response to Bancroft is all the more puzzling when one considers that Lydia Maria Child's abolitionist *Appeal* had been issued, to immediate and widespread notoriety, only a year before. Oddly, there is no direct indication that Fuller so much as knew of Child's book, though it is highly probable that she did. The two women had been friends since 1825 when Child (or Miss Francis as she then was), author already of the novel *Hobomok*, befriended the fifteen-year-old Fuller and inspired her with a love of scholarship. By 1827 they had begun a course of reading together, which terminated sometime before Lydia Maria's marriage to David Lee Child in 1828.[10] Fuller did not again refer to her friend until 1837, when she made a brief disparaging comment on Child's historical novel, *Philothea*. Child attended some of Fuller's Boston Conversations in 1839, and the two women put their friendship on a still stronger footing five years later in New York.[11]

But Fuller never looked to Child as a model of what she might herself do either in literature or reform. Heroism, for Fuller, was not yet so broad and available a category as to cover that near case, lacking, as it may have seemed, the deep focal length of historical abstraction. The *Appeal*, if Fuller read it, drew no comment. Child's biographer, Carolyn Karcher, credibly asserts the heroism of her subject's willingness to antagonize public opinion by assuming the role of the abolitionist and more particularly by coinciding with Garrison in the repudiation of racial prejudice. The decision to write the *Appeal* cost Child the considerable literary reputation that she had already earned and, as it turned out, the financial security that her writings had promised. Because Fuller could make no similar commitment to the cause of the slave in the crucial 1830s, the careers of the two women diverged sharply: during the years when Child edited the *National Anti-Slavery Standard* in New York, Fuller edited the *Dial* in Boston. Even on the unlikely assumption that "martyrdom" could have been acceptable to Fuller as a young adult, the unfolding example of Child's plausibly heroic career must have suggested that abolitionism, once taken up, would foreclose other options, leaving, in particular, no room for literature or philosophy.[12]

An identical lesson was the upshot of Fuller's relationship with Harriet Martineau. Bringing a solid literary reputation with her on her visit to America (1834–36), the English writer proved helpful to the emerging Transcendentalist movement by promoting "Carlylism" and by embracing the movement's topics in general—encouraged in doing so by Emerson's Philadelphia friend William Henry Furness. As an established female author and as one actively fascinated by Goethe and German philosophy, as Fuller also was, Martineau seemed an ideal mentor. During several weeks in August and November 1835 (before and after Timothy Fuller's death on the first of October), Martineau stayed with John and Eliza Farrar, friends of Margaret's in Cambridge, and the two got to know each other.[13]

In mourning and justifiably concerned about her family's finances, Fuller had very little to say about the mounting violence directed at this time against the abolitionists, though it took profound hold of Martineau's attention. On October 21 an afternoon meeting of the Boston Female Anti-Slavery Society was brazenly attacked by a mob that had meant to assault the visiting English abolitionist George Thompson, but, missing that object, turned its tar-and-feathery purposes on a last-minute substitute speaker, William Lloyd Garrison. This mob might have seriously harmed or even killed the editor had city authorities not, with much dithering and difficulty, got him into protective custody in the Leverett Street jail. In the aftermath and partly at the suggestion of Fuller's friend Ellis Gray Loring, Harriet Martineau addressed the BFASS to announce her support for their abolitionist principles.[14] Given that the women had been blamed for provoking the violence (by the extraordinary, unladylike action of holding a mixed-race meeting in furtherance of political ends), Martineau's public endorsement was both courageous and widely railed against. As an obscure private individual Fuller could not, of course, have made any similar demonstration even had she wished to. Just then assuming the burdens of her bereft family, she had in effect to become her own father, the new "paterfamilias," as Capper notes.[15] Even so, she seemed oddly uncertain what to make of the public ruckus or, indeed, of its opposite and antidote, the judicious, tempest-stilling book on the subject of slavery just issued by William Ellery Channing.[16]

Fuller was temperamentally inclined to align with Channing's views, if only because she admired and trusted the mildness of his judgment.[17] Yet she was not, by the same token, among the many who were offended by the abolitionist talk of the much despised George Thompson: she had heard him speak at Groton the previous January and thought him superior as an orator to the currently fashionable New England heroes in that line, Edward Everett and Daniel Webster. Again, however, as in the case of Bancroft, her response managed to miss the main point: Thompson impressed her as a "fine speaker" and not explicitly as a moral force.[18] At the same time, she took brief note of the brewing controversy at the Lane Seminary in Cincinnati, where the student "rebels," led by Theodore Dwight Weld, had become obstreperously vocal about the injustice of slavery. In pressing the point, they opposed censorious school officials, including Lyman Beecher, and eventually seceded in favor of Oberlin, a school more tolerant of the doctrine of immediate abolitionism. Fuller seems to have admired the students' position. "That sounds from afar so like the conflict of keen life," she said from dull Groton and allowed that it made her want to go to the West.[19]

In point of fact, however, Fuller's appetite for conflict was, early in her career, never so great as her admiration for men such as Channing who found ways to avoid it. Like many antislavery moderates, she was disheartened by the abrupt and militant tone of common abolitionist rhetoric, its polarizing effect, its vulgarity, its invitation to respond in kind. Constitutionally more attentive to the rhetoric than to the appearance of morality in the cause, she was prepared to see that the hypermasculinity of the public debate was bound to issue (as in fact it almost immediately did) in brawls and assaults, fisticuffs, arson, and murder. What she found to praise most highly in Channing's 1835 treatise on slavery was "its calm, benignant atmosphere, after the pestilence-bringing gales of the day." It was only because the subject had "become so utterly bemazed and darkened of late" (notwithstanding Child's deep research and clear exposition in the *Appeal*) that Channing had been forced to make his question-settling opinion known over the span of so many pages.[20]

It seemed important to know what the judicious Channing thought of the matter, but the American public was by no means prepared to accept the scolding that Harriet Martineau gave it. When her *Society in America* appeared in 1837, Fuller was specifically aghast that her quondam mentor, whom she had so much admired, seemed to have sacrificed a brilliant opportunity in taking up the promising subject of the United States only to harp further on antislavery. "I do not like that your book should be an abolition book," Fuller told its author in a surprisingly frank, friendship-testing letter. Conceding that slavery "*is* a great subject," Fuller nevertheless pointed out that "your book had other purposes to fulfil." Once again, Fuller's unmet interest in the "other purposes" intensified her objection to the rhetoric of the ideologue, the deforming "intemperance of epithet," the "rashness and inaccuracy" of the author's judgment, and above all the fact that Martineau's fulminations against slavery "leaven[ed] the whole book." Fuller's disappointment was too profound to have been the consequence of a simple disagreement over slavery: in many respects the two women were agreed on that subject. Nor is it to be accounted for by the manifest clumsiness that resulted when Martineau's ideological bias collided with her characteristic haste in composition. Fuller's tone instead had to do with the painful discovery that she had been mistaken in her friend: that Martineau's advocacy of Carlyle, for example, did not portend the kind of idealism or acknowledgment of spirit to which Fuller's friendships with Emerson (whom she had met in 1836) and others of that circle increasingly drew her.[21]

If the letter faulted Martineau's fierce fundamentalism on the abolition question, its sharpest particular accusation concerned the book's "crude, intemperate tirade" against Fuller's friend and colleague Bronson Alcott and the educational principles deployed in his Temple School. The Platonic idealism that led Alcott to discount the body as body and focus on mind and meanings instead (stimulating curiosity but skimping on physical exercise) seemed especially ridiculous to an abolitionist reformer such as Martineau, whose objections demonstrated that her priorities were exactly the opposite. Her complaints, consistent with if not directly betokening the materialist construction of the antislavery argument, were ironically similar to those of Boston's proslavery conservatives, who in the end drove the Temple School into failure. Said Fuller, "They smile to hear their verdict confirmed from the other side of the Atlantic, by their censor, Harriet Martineau."[22]

Such performances confirmed Fuller in her prejudice against the typically counterproductive rhetoric of the antislavery movement, which led her as a rule either to oppose or, more frequently, simply to ignore its apostles. The degree of her disengagement was most striking and in some respects most puzzling in her failure to respond to the work of Angelina and Sarah Grimké, who, it has been argued, did more for women's rights than any others of that generation. Their antislavery lectures to mixed-gender audiences, beginning in New York in 1836 and moving on the next year to New England, challenged a verdict as old as Saint Paul that it was shameful for women to speak and teach in public assemblies. Converted to abolitionism by George Thompson and following William Lloyd Garrison's leadership, the Grimké sisters succeeded in drawing women by the tens of thousands out of their homes and beyond their "sphere," first to organize auxiliary societies and then to enter politics by petitioning for an end to slavery in the District of Columbia. The sisters began their career by addressing exclusively female audiences, but the men could not be kept out and soon what was not objected to in the arrangement began to feel comfortable. An important point had been made, and, gradually, in the years ahead, women speakers, addressing a variety of topics, were more and more to be found on the lyceum circuit.

As evidenced by the mobbing of the BFASS, however, and by the constant berating of activist women, rights of assembly and free speech had to be contended for as an immediate goal of gender politics: the campaign of such antislavery agitators as the Grimkés, Maria Stewart, Abby Kelley, Lucy Stone, Lucretia Mott, Maria Weston Chapman, and Lydia Maria Child was therefore simultaneously about enlarging women's public authority on the one hand and defending their right to speak and publish on the other. The petitions that arrived in the Capitol at Washington famously elicited a "Gag Rule," which tended to identify the obnoxiousness of women's speech with the obnoxiousness of attacks on slavery. Thenceforth, freedom for women and freedom for the slave would be close-linked objects. One sees that Fuller had no part in all this. In a popular casebook published by Kathryn Kish Sklar in 2000 titled *Women's Rights Emerges within the Antislavery Movement*,

1830–1870, the name of Margaret Fuller nowhere appears, marking the first time that a comprehensive interpretation of nineteenth-century American feminism could entirely — and not by any careless oversight — dispense with the author of *Woman in the Nineteenth Century*.[23]

"In toiling for the freedom of others, we shall find our own," said Lydia Maria Child, arguing in 1839 that a direct agitation of "the Woman Question" could only dilute the energies of the antislavery crusade.[24] When Angelina Grimké was cautioned on this point by fellow Quaker John Greenleaf Whittier, she replied, "And can you not see that women *could* do, and *would* do a hundred times more for the slave if she were not fettered?"[25] These two views as to the precedency of the woman question or the slave question fractured the abolition movement by 1840, leading on the one hand to the establishment of the "new organization," the American and Foreign Anti-Slavery Society, which did not admit women, and on the other to the Liberty Party, which in seeking a political remedy chose to proceed without the assistance of (nonvoting) women. These were alternatives to Garrison's movement, itself evolving toward a deep recognition of the organic relationship among various reform movements, including peace (or nonresistance), temperance, and women's rights, all increasingly subsumed under a banner of Christian perfectionism.[26]

So, while women's rights were a topic of heated discussion in the years just prior to the appearance of Fuller's "Great Lawsuit" (July 1843) and its book-length expansion in *Woman in the Nineteenth Century* (1845), her approach to the feminist subject involved essentially different principles. That is to say, Fuller's feminism was not logically obliged to fall into line behind antislavery feminism, which, had she stopped to analyze it, would almost certainly have struck her as more tactical and deferential ("How can we be the slave's slave?") than forthrightly radical in its womanist aims. Antislavery campaigning on behalf of women, very much centering at first on the right of white women to be agitators, effectively advanced a secondary or derivative entitlement to speak and move in public. Such a reform made its antislavery headway by upwardly revising public (i.e., male) estimates of female competence, thereby promoting a new understanding of women's moral and political agency. This last, which had little enough to do with antislavery, was separately alarming to conservatives. An important indicator of this discomfort was the "Pastoral Letter" of July 1837, a diktat issued by the Congregational clergy of Massachusetts to silence the Grimké sisters. In this document the ministers claimed that "the appropriate duties and influence of women are clearly stated in the New Testament," that such allowable duties and influence were naturally "unobtrusive and private, but the sources of mighty power," and that, in the end, "the power of woman is in her dependence"—that is to say, in a God-dealt incapacity that elicits protection. "We cannot, therefore, but regret the mistaken conduct of those who encourage females to bear an obtrusive and ostentatious part in measures of reform, and countenance any of that sex who so far forget themselves as to itinerate in the character of public lecturers and teachers."[27]

Thus, reactionary forces advised women not to comment on public matters at all but instead to refer them to their ministers, which is to say, to persons qualified to handle them. At the same time, progressive forces strongly committed to antislavery advised women not to speak in favor of women's rights lest they selfishly conceal the desperate cause of the slave behind trivial interests of their own. As sympathetic to the Grimké sisters as he was, Theodore Dwight Weld (who married Angelina in 1838) maintained that, although any woman of ordinary talent could write out the feminist argument, these specially gifted sisters, South Carolina refugees from the slaveholder culture, could not without guilt be excused from full-time, undiluted abolitionism.[28] In other words, in the reform communities of the late 1830s, the feeling was that antislavery speech and feminist speech were incompatible modes of unpopular expression, conceived of as primary and secondary modes of discourse, respectively.

Sarah Grimké nevertheless wrote her *Letters on the Equality of the Sexes* (1838)—including a chapter of rebuttal to the "Pastoral Letter"—on the well-founded belief that the opposition to woman's agency in antislavery work originated in a false (professional or masculinist) reading of scripture. The discovery was that women had been consigned to the margins by the very same religious history that justified slavery. Grimké's arguments, therefore, keeping within the conventional rhetorical bounds established by her clerical opponents, offered to clarify "the designs of Jehovah in the creation of woman." If she thus countered a religious prejudice with religious arguments of a reformed sort (as she, like Garrison, so regularly did in their respective antislavery work), she was ostentatiously proposing to teach the teachers. A little ironically, that was all that her opponents ever charged against her, though it did not go unnoticed that the allegation amounted nearly to a charge of witchcraft.[29]

It is surprising that Fuller hardly noticed the Grimké sisters or the controversy that swirled about them. Probably she found their way of asserting women's rights unappealing, given both its deployment as a prop to abolitionism and its Christian evangelical character and tone.[30] The fact remains, however, that the emergent synergy between antislavery and feminism was so strong and the contours of the movements so manifestly parallel that by 1840 Fuller's thinking about woman's place in the world could not simply extrapolate her private, apolitical, experiential history of self-orientation. Whatever might be said in 1843 or 1845 about the position of women unavoidably had to make use of analogies and metaphors drawn from the less "obtrusive and ostentatious" rhetoric of the antislavery movement. At the same time, one might concede that in *Letters on the Equality of the Sexes*, the religious discourse that most conspicuously connected the cause of woman and the cause of the slave had taken matters about as far in a certain direction as that special vocabulary could take them. Even had the case been well made for woman's right to agitate the cause of the slave, Fuller might have supposed that women's interests as such would not best be defined by searching the motives of Jehovah or by adducing the dubious clarities of the New Testament. What being a woman meant in the nineteenth century and what it might mean going forward remained, for all the buzz and clamor of the abolitionists, an orphan subject, its profundities still substantially unexplored—and those best equipped to explore it seemed all to be preoccupied.[31]

Fuller did mention Angelina Grimké, once, in *Woman in the Nineteenth Century*, in the course of suggesting that women who speak in public, "if they speak for conscience' sake, to serve a cause which they hold sacred, invariably subdue the prejudices of their hearers, and excite an interest proportionate to the aversion with which it had been the purpose to regard them." By placing the emphasis on the "cause which they hold sacred," Fuller testified to the value of genuine, conscientious self-expression rather than of abolition per se and called attention to what the holding sacred of any subject does (or ought to do) for the discourse that results. What elicited "interest" was not the compulsion of logic in an argument (on which the preacherly abolitionists so often relied), but the degree to which what was said connected one private conscience to another. At this point in her discussion Fuller approvingly quoted a letter describing a recent "heroic" performance by Abby Kelley on the antislavery platform: the letter writer had observed that "all heroism is mild, and quiet, and gentle, for it is life and possession; and combativeness and firmness show a want of actualness." This gentle sort of witnessing was preferable to male argument, Fuller's correspondent suggested, because "men speak through, and mostly from intellect, and this addresses itself to that in others which is combative."[32] Fuller believed that women "subdue" the prejudice against their speaking not, then, by combative rebuttal but simply by acting on the embraced principle of their own freedom.[33] In actions of that sort something essential was revealed about the nature of prejudice on the one hand and of heroism on the other.

Fuller would often speak of the tumultuous rhetoric of abolition as vulgar, as involving a lapse of taste; a great many others were of the same opinion. Modern readers are inclined to see this sort of objection as precious, given how high and substantial the stakes were. But the point is not the cringe in Fuller, but the implied faithlessness in the angry speaker. At the beginning of *Woman in the Nineteenth Century*—the text to which we now turn—Fuller laid out three reform modalities: first, acting out of the allegedly clear sight of the intellect (the "male" option); second, acting out of sympathy through imperfect life (the "female" option); and, third and best of all, the universal option, transcendental in regard to gender: "It needs not intellect, needs not experience, says a third. If you took the true way, your destiny would be accomplished in a purer and more natural order. You would not learn through facts of thought or action, but express through them the certainties of wisdom. In quietness yield thy soul to the causal soul. Do not disturb thy apprenticeship by premature effort; neither check the tide of instruction by methods of thy own. Be still, seek not, but wait in obedience. Thy commission will be given."[34]

Emerson was saying much the same thing at this time and for much the same reason, but one sees perhaps more clearly in Fuller's way of expressing it that "style" (or the mode of one's response in a controversy) has a significant, often overlooked moral content so that the speaker's distance from the "causal soul" will be signified by the fretfulness, desperation, and intemperance of his or her language. Fuller was language artist enough to know that not all rhetorics, even in a democracy, are born free and equal and that a harangue is not the local dialect of the kingdom of God. Often she praised William Ellery Channing for the endowment of serene confidence he enjoyed, based on his underlying "certainties of wisdom," and for the corresponding respect that he extended to his auditors.

The effects of the antislavery controversy on Fuller, as she carefully observed the responses of others, included an inevitable abandonment of her youthful notions of heroism—specifically the idea that heroism was a masculine, even a fatherly attainment; that it involved some triumphantly willful projection of force executed at great personal cost; and that it might best be exemplified in a paradigmatic figure such as Brutus. Over the course of the 1830s antislavery was advancing a rather different construction of the heroic, deriving it from Child's sacrifices, Garrison's mobbing, Elijah Lovejoy's murder, Prudence Crandall's persecution, and the general harassment of female abolitionists. If these events did not spontaneously imply a Christian narrative, Harriet Martineau would so interpret them by locating all this righteous suffering in what she called "The Martyr Age in the United States," the title of her brief 1839 survey of the American antislavery movement. Its reformers sought opportunities for martyrdom, a term evoking the highest reach of Christian heroism and irresistibly recalling the first centuries of saintly activity in the church. They sought it with ever-increasing deliberateness, climaxing with the apotheosis of John Brown in 1859. Garrison's response to the mob's attack on himself had been to call to mind Matthew 10:39: "he who loses his life for Christ's sake shall find it." On another occasion he saluted his *Liberator* colleague Isaac Knapp with the words, "My dear partner in the joys and honors of persecution."[35]

This was no more in Fuller's style than had been the related effort of the Grimkés to replicate "true" or orthodox Christianity and recover its prestige for the movement. Indeed, Charles Capper correctly insists that Fuller "detested" the "martyr-minded profile of Garrison and many of his associates."[36] It is a wonderfully suggestive point that, as Elaine Pagels has shown, the ancient church fathers were uniformly contemptuous of the gnostics (a heretical antinomian group having much in common with the Transcendentalists) on the specific ground that they rejected martyrdom, that great red badge and distinction among the orthodox. By centering the emergent church on the canonical narrative of the Passion and Resurrection, the fathers, as Pagels has noted, "affirm[ed] bodily experience as the central fact of human life.... But those gnostics who regarded the essential part of every person as the 'inner spirit' dismissed such physical experience, pleasurable or painful, as a distraction from spiritual reality—indeed, as an illusion."[37] Just as, in the Divinity School Address of 1838, Emerson had arraigned contemporary orthodoxy for its insistence on the "personality" of Christ, Fuller supposed that the abolitionists' immature fascination with embodiment, in respect equally to the suffering slave or the metaphorically or actually martyred antislave, was just another iteration of the materialist fallacy. The inner spiritual reality that the gnostics honored was close to what Fuller meant by the "certainties of wisdom" (*gnosis*) that she considered to be the admirably informing focus of Channing's life. To her he was potentially a new-style hero. It was as if Fuller knew that "martyr," etymologically considered, meant "witness." There is a wise passiveness at the core of the historical idea of martyrdom to which Martineau, a devotee of the dramatic gesture, was at bottom oblivious. "The genius of the day," declared Emerson in 1841, "does not incline to a deed, but to a beholding": that is to say, to the sort of "witnessing" that, amid the anger and agitation of others, constituted Channing's instructive example.[38]

Arguably, in regard to the language of controversy, certain ways of talking are better than others, and yet the same cannot be said of human beings, who, as the objects of legal discourse and of controversial talk, are famously "born free and equal." That proclamation, a "verbal statement" yet also a "golden certainty," was important to Fuller. To her it announced that America was itself a reform project, and at the same time constituted the entire ground for the bitter irony of American history, played out, she noted, in "what has been done towards the Red Man, the Black Man." In fact, "freedom and equality have been proclaimed only to leave room for a monstrous display of slave-dealing and slave-keeping." Fuller responded to this spectacle with the faith that "that which has once been clearly conceived in the intelligence cannot fail sooner or later to be acted out." She saw that the freedom and independence obtained with difficulty for the nation would in due course be obtained "also for every member of it."[39] If this should happen to be true in regard to racial justice, it could not fail to be so, too, in regard to justice for women.

American racial oppression was maintained and could only be maintained by the hypocrisy that honored freedom and equality while accommodating slavery. Yet Fuller's discussion of this point turned, characteristically, not so much on the "sorrowful brother" as on the effect that the "strife of words" had in creating a world of language morally distanced (by hypocrisy) from the world of earnest realities. Fuller's diagnosis paralleled that of Emerson in the "Language" chapter of *Nature* (1836), in which words became a "rotten diction" by losing their primary connection to nature amid the "roar of cities or the broil of politics."[40] For both Fuller and Emerson bad politics were a corollary to pathologies of language. Fuller deliberately extended this point to cover not only proslavery hypocrites, but sanctimonious abolitionists as well: "We sicken no less at the pomp than the strife of words. We feel that never were lungs so puffed with the wind of declamation, on moral and religious subjects, as now. We are tempted to implore these 'word-heroes,' these word-Catos, word-Christs, to beware of cant above all things; to remember that hypocrisy is the most hopeless as well as the meanest of crimes, and that those must surely be polluted by it, who do not reserve a part of their morality and religion for private use."[41] This is the case of the one to whom Emerson referred in "Self-Reliance" as the "angry bigot" who "assumes this bountiful cause of Abolition," whose "love afar is [nevertheless] spite at home."[42] One might doubt that "hypocrisy" could be "the meanest of crimes" where slavery was the issue, and yet there was a radical kind of penetration to original causes in this loyal regard for the moral stability of language. Certainly, with "heroism" so much in a cultural process of redefinition, the Transcendentalists aspired to be "word-heroes"—in fact and without the irony. "Those who would reform the world must show that they do not speak in the heat of wild impulse; their lives must be unstained by passionate error."[43]

Woman in the Nineteenth Century is peppered throughout with rhetorical parallels between antislavery and women's rights. One might almost say that these analogies "leaven the whole book." "In the advertisement of a book on America, I see in the table of contents this sequence, 'Republican Institutions. American Slavery. American Ladies.'" The "kidnapping" of a woman's children by the father in cases of divorce is not accounted a crime. Female infanticide seems a plausible euthanasia, not because the child is spared a life in slavery (as in the notorious case of Margaret Garner), but because she is spared "the life of a woman." Much of the argument is predicated on "Knowing that there exists in the minds of men a tone of feeling toward women as toward slaves." Fuller noted the hypocrisy of holding it unseemly for women to do public work, while making the most self-serving exceptions for "negresses" in "field work, even during pregnancy." The invisibility of the ongoing crime against women becomes visible specifically through the analogy with slavery: "In slavery, acknowledged slavery, women are on a par with men. Each is a work-tool, an article of property, no more! In perfect freedom, such as is painted in Olympus, in Swedenborg's angelic state, in the heaven where there is no marrying nor giving in marriage, each is a purified intelligence, an enfranchised soul,—no less!"[44] Marriage, considered in relation to slavery, is a patriarchal institution, not a divinely ordained one; the standard of heaven is in the direction of freedom and away from ideas of property, whether in the "acknowledged" or in the disguised ownership of one person by another.

For Fuller the marked interest by women in the cause of the slave was an outward and objectified sign of an inward desire that the world should conform to an unperverted standard of feminine character—or, to put it in Emerson's more familiar terms, that woman's "Not-Me" should come to match the feminine "Me." Here is how Fuller expressed it in *Woman in the Nineteenth Century*: "For woman, if, by a sympathy as to outward condition she is led to aid the enfranchisement of the slave, [she] must be no less so, by an inward tendency, to favor measures which promise to bring the world more thoroughly and deeply into harmony with her nature." By thus placing reform under the sign of gender, Fuller affirmed its broader ideal character, rationalized its dependence on individual as opposed to associated behavior, and showed the partial nature of any such particular reform as abolition. Her analysis of the public phenomena of opposition to slavery brought her not directly to a new stance on that question but rather to a new valuation of "Femality" as, potentially, the redemptive "harmonizer of the vehement [i.e., masculine] elements" evident in slavery and antislavery alike.[45]

Toward the end of her manifesto, Fuller's argument becomes more overtly millennial, not because she means to pursue a religious agenda in any conventional sense, but simply for the sake of the grand orchestral notes of Christian eschatology, already implicit in various kinds of Romantic reform, but useful here for rhetorical closure. The power to precipitate the end of time, Fuller suggests, belongs to a female messiah, the "immortal Eve." "Since the sliding and backsliding men of the world, no less than the mystics declare that, as through woman man was lost, so through woman must man be redeemed, the time must be at hand." This invocation of historical symmetry prepares the reader for allusions to recent reports of a movement of the Jews back to Palestine and to the millennial implications of that prophecy's fulfillment. She refers also to the recent deliverance from unjust imprisonment of Daniel O'Connell, the hero of Catholic emancipation and Irish independence, and then notes climactically that "last week brought news which threatens that a cause identical with the enfranchisement of Jews, Irish, women, ay, and of Americans in general, too, is in danger, for the choice of the people threatens to rivet the chains of slavery and the leprosy of sin permanently on this nation, through the annexation of Texas!"[46]

Fuller clearly recognized the world-historical significance of the Texas question, the outcome of which was to determine whether America's future would lie with its original commitment to freedom or with its latter-day embrace of slavery and its entailed hypocrisy. She notified the "Women of my country!—Exaltadas!" (representatives, each and all, of the "immortal Eve") that

> This cause is your own, for as I have before said, there is a reason why the foes of African slavery seek more freedom for women; but put it not upon that ground, but on the ground of right.
>
> If you have a power, it is a moral power. The films of interest are not so close around you as around the men. If you will but think, you cannot fail to wish to save the country from this disgrace. Let not slip the occasion, but do something to lift off the curse incurred by Eve.[47]

By the conclusion of *Woman in the Nineteenth Century*, antislavery has become the main context for the exercise of female redemptive power, even as the annexation of Texas becomes the immediate event that provokes and defines its significance. The mythologically "Roman" traits of "Energy,"

"Power," and "Intellect," developed first in man, are now to be modified by the progressive assertion of a principle of "femality," by which the mythologically "Greek" traits of "Harmony," Beauty," and "Love" will emerge to redeem the nation from an otherwise headlong descent into imperial mastery. The process by which female nature attains a historically belated equality with the masculine is figured, poetically, as the arrival of a messiah: "And will not she soon appear? The woman who shall vindicate their birthright for all women; who shall teach them what to claim, and how to use what they obtain?" Fuller's book, falling chronologically between Emerson's *Nature* and Thoreau's *Walden*, ends, as those books also do, with the world and the individual fully reformed, having attained the conditions of the kingdom of God. It finds Man and Woman where, in Fuller's perfectionist view, they ought to be: in "the palace home of King and Queen."[48]

Up to and including the period when *Woman in the Nineteenth Century* was written, Fuller sympathized with the burgeoning antislavery movement. Like Martineau before the Boston Female Anti-Slavery Society, she approved of its principles, but hesitated, as others did, before the spectacle of the associated measures and more especially before the combative language of the movement. She recognized, as apparently no one else then did, that this struggle on behalf of an oppressed group, the slaves of masters, had lessons to impart about what was properly analogous to it. She saw a movement on behalf of African American slaves, to be sure, but she also observed that the general critique of slavery held for any deliberate or conventional assertion of power over a class of persons. She chose, therefore, to understand and make use of antislavery as "a cause identical" to the enfranchisement of women.

Fuller's view of these matters changed significantly, however, in late 1847 and early 1848 under the provocation of the Italian revolution. The history of her altered opinion is succinctly laid out in Fuller's remarkable eighteenth dispatch in the *Tribune* series titled "Things and Thoughts in Europe." Conditions as she found them in Rome put her in touch not with the period of Brutus and Caesar, but with history as social struggle, as an effort by a disfranchised class to effect justice by improving the conditions of its own existence. This reminded Fuller of American revolutionary history, of the "early flight" of the American Eagle in the "clear sight of the Sun." "Thou wert to be the advance-guard of Humanity, the herald of all Progress; how often hast thou betrayed this high commission!" In Italy she saw that "high commission" undertaken not by "word-heroes" or "word-Christs," but in earnest action by revolutionists. She heard "the same arguments against the emancipation of Italy, that are used against the emancipation of our blacks.... I find the cause of tyranny and wrong," she said, "everywhere the same." Under this provocation, she could, for the first time, "say what I believe, that voluntary association for improvement ... will be the grand means for my nation to grow and give a nobler harmony to the coming age."[49]

For Fuller, this revaluation of associated or social action put the abolitionists in a completely new light:

> How it pleases me here to think of the Abolitionists! I could never endure to be with them at home, they were so tedious, often so narrow, always so rabid and exaggerated in their tone.
>
> But, after all, they had a high motive, something eternal in their desire and life; and, if it was not the only thing worth thinking of it was really something worth living and dying for to free a great nation from such a terrible blot, such a threatening plague. God strengthen them and make them wise to achieve their purpose![50]

In America antislavery had been offered to her as, in fact, "the only thing worth thinking of": this had been the discouraging impression that Harriet Martineau had created by the turn she gave to *Society in America*; this had been the impression left, as well, by Maria Weston Chapman, Martineau's lieutenant, who was impatient to divert Fuller's attention in the Boston Conversations to the better subject of antislavery, and by the Grimké sisters, who seemed to value justice for women solely for the advantage it bestowed on abolitionism.[51] It had been possible, under these conditions, to feel that the abolitionist campaign was an embargo on larger views and an immersion in sheer talk, often ugly and vulgar talk, and pretty much always unproductive— a charge that, indeed, Fuller leveled at Emerson after reading an early draft of his 1844 "West Indian Emancipation Address."[52] First-stage antislavery in the Garrisonian mold was abrupt and confrontational but it was not revolutionary, as it arguably became following the provocations of 1850. Fuller missed the practical demonstration and the qualities of high devotion in the hyperrhetorical American movement as she had known it; she found a better version of reform in Italy. One supposes that had she survived the voyage home, she would have been an increasingly powerful antislavery voice in the volatile decade of the 1850s.[53]

But of course she did not survive the voyage, and her reputation as an ambivalent, faint-hearted supporter of antislavery was all but sealed with the loss of the ship *Elizabeth*. In the 1852 *Memoirs* compiled by Emerson, William Henry Channing, and James Freeman Clarke, Fuller's old letter to Martineau was controversially made public, with its lament that the Englishwoman had fumbled her chance to be brilliant in her travelogue and had produced "an abolition book" instead. Martineau had also disappointed by exchanging the opportunity to be a mentor and a help to her young American acolyte for the self-appointed position of conscience in the matter of slavery. Though Martineau did not answer Fuller's letter when it first arrived, she did respond to the published text many years later in her *Autobiography*: "She who witnessed and aided the struggles of the oppressed in Italy must have become before her death better aware than when she wrote that letter that the struggle for the personal liberty of millions in her native republic ought to have had more of her sympathy, and none of the discouragement which she haughtily and complacently cast upon the cause."[54] Martineau was right in the main clause, but demonstrably wrong and unfair in the concluding supplement.

7

MARGARET FULLER ON MUSIC'S "EVERLASTING YES"

A Romantic Critic in the Romantic Era

Megan Marshall

An everlasting yes breathes from the life, from the work of
the artist.
—*Margaret Fuller*, Lives of the Great Composers, *1841*

We can safely add to the list of losses when Margaret Fuller went down with the *Elizabeth* her further contribution to the understanding and appreciation of classical music as its presence in American cultural life widened and deepened through the second half of the nineteenth century. Although as editor of the *Dial* she enlisted John Sullivan Dwight as the music reviewer for the first issue of the magazine, launching him on the career that would eclipse, if not erase, her own substantial early work in the field, Fuller performed that job ably for the *New-York Tribune* after she left Boston for New York City in 1844.[1] She continued to seek out opportunities to hear music in performance and to refine her critical perceptions of the art when she traveled to Europe two years later; this included her attendance at a piano recital by Frederic Chopin on February 14, 1847.[2] Before leaving the United States, Fuller had complained in the *Tribune* that it was impossible to know Chopin's works, "because we very seldom hear them adequately performed."[3] Now she could listen to them played by the composer and write with authority, "One must hear himself; only a person as exquisitely organized as he can adequately express these subtle secrets of the creative spirit."[4]

Fuller's achievement as a music critic is an aspect of her career that, with the exception of two important articles by Ora Frishberg Saloman, has received scant attention.[5] More typical is Michael Broyles's omission of Fuller's contributions to music criticism in his *"Music of the Highest Class": Elitism and Populism in Antebellum Boston*. Broyles recognizes that coverage of classical music in Transcendentalist literary journals "contributed to the growing prestige of music during the period" and explicitly mentions the *Dial* as one such publication, which printed "lengthy and carefully thought out statements on various aspects of American musical culture." Yet Broyles writes as if Dwight were the sole music critic producing essays for these publications, even though the lengthy *Dial* articles were mainly Fuller's. Dwight's more extended criticism appeared in the *Harbinger*, where, beginning in 1846, he honed his skills before founding *Dwight's Journal of Music* in 1852.[6]

Fuller's decision to write critically about music is one of the more dramatic examples of her resistance to, and lack of suitability for, normative gender roles. Like many daughters in prosperous families of her time and place, Margaret Fuller studied the piano from an early age. In her second extant letter, written to her father at age seven, she reported that she had "learned all the rules of Musick but one." Two months later, shortly before her eighth birthday, she wrote to Timothy that she had learned to sing two-part harmony with her aunt Abigail, "I geuss you will buy my pianno forte." He did, and before long, music joined the academic subjects that the young girl studied under her father's close scrutiny. While away from home in Washington, D.C., during one of his congressional terms, Timothy confided in a letter to his wife that he had dreamed of Margaret practicing the piano: that lesson "she could never play in true time."[7]

Fuller took drawing lessons at this time as well, but music was the art she studied and practiced consistently throughout her youth.[8] Perhaps she was inspired by her childhood mentor and early feminine ideal Ellen Kilshaw, who captivated drawing room audiences with her playing on the harp. The "tones" that Kilshaw drew from her instrument, Fuller later wrote, remained in her memory as "heralds of the promised land I saw before me then": the land of "accomplished" young women such as Kilshaw, who also painted in oils and spoke and moved as gracefully as her fingers plucked the harp strings.[9]

Fuller's efforts at the piano did not elicit quite the same response as had Ellen Kilshaw's at the harp. By age ten, she could proudly report that "Aunt Fuller has taught me to play 'Bounding billows' and sing it." But that same year her uncle Arthur complained that "he had as lieve see Mr Whittiers children take a cane and ride around the room as hear me play on the piano," and Uncle Elisha invited her to "play before him . . . [only] when he is asleep."[10] Nevertheless, she persisted.

At age thirteen Fuller performed three popular songs on the piano for a party of school friends at which there was "piano, singing, music, and chess." She had advanced to ensemble playing, for she accompanied—or, as she wrote to her father, "was accompanied by"—two other girls on "the flute and flageolet." At fifteen, after her return to Cambridge from Miss Prescott's school at Groton and the termination of her formal education, Fuller listed two daily hour-long stints at the piano—after her early morning walk and before the midday dinner—in her rigorous self-imposed schedule of studies, which also included "Greek . . . metaphysics, and French and Italian literature." The teenaged Fuller was still making music to be heard in her family circle. Before going to bed, she wrote to Miss Prescott, "I play or sing, for half an hour or so, to make all sleepy."[11] At least now family members started off awake, and she could play gently enough to ease them toward slumber.

This, however, was the last reference to regular piano practice that appears in Fuller's correspondence, and it cannot be known how long she adhered to the routine she outlined in her 1825 letter to Prescott. Evidently she did not become proficient enough at the piano or singing to teach music, even to her siblings; nine years later, when she cataloged the "daily lessons in three languages, in geography and history" that she was obliged to teach her younger brothers and sister in the family home at Groton, music was not among them. In 1839 when the Groton house was sold four years after Timothy Fuller's death, Fuller returned home to help pack and dispense possessions. During those final months in residence at Groton, she played the piano "five or six times," she wrote to her friend Caroline Sturgis, perhaps saying goodbye to the instrument that her father had bought for her in her childhood.[12]

Although Margaret Fuller was an American girl born in 1810, as a young female piano student she was participating in a widely familiar musical regimen with a distinctly extramusical purpose, aptly described in a Viennese music journal of 1800: "Every well-bred girl, whether she has talent or not, must learn to play the piano or sing; first of all it's fashionable; secondly, it's the most convenient way for her to put herself forward in society and thereby, if she is lucky, make an advantageous matrimonial alliance, particularly a monied one."[13] The rule still held in 1840 when Carl Czerny, the composer and pedagogue, published *Letters to a Young Lady, on the Art of Playing the Pianoforte*, claiming piano playing as "yet more particularly one of the most charming and honorable accomplishments for young ladies, and indeed, for the female sex in general."[14] The young Margaret Fuller understood this gambit. As a child, she had been keenly aware of the "accomplished" Ellen Kilshaw's search for a husband and that the "promised land" Kilshaw sought to gain through parlor displays of her accomplishments—the future that Fuller, too, "saw before me then"—was matrimony.

Increasingly through the nineteenth century, girls of Fuller's social class were urged on by their parents to "practice scales by the hour, by the year, in order to become acceptable players" until the young woman at the parlor piano—but not in the recital hall—became a stock figure of the time, sometimes idealized, sometimes scorned.[15] Thomas Carlyle grumbled about a neighbor who "spends all her young, bright days, not in learning to darn stockings, sew shirts, bake pastry . . . but simply and solely raging from dawn to dusk, to night and midnight, on a hapless piano which it is evident she will never in this world learn to render more musical than a pair of barn-fanners." Such girls were legion, he complained, and he wished "the Devil some good knight should take his hammer and smite in shivers all and every piano of our European world!"[16] (Carlyle would be unsettled, too, by the adult Margaret Fuller when they met in England.) Professional musicians worried about the effect these female amateurs would have on the art itself. In 1827 the Viennese composer Ignaz Moscheles, then living in London, was frustrated by his female pupils who "shrink from all serious study" and whose mothers demanded he write for them "something with a pretty tune in it, brilliant but not difficult."[17]

The scourge was not limited to London and the Continent, although by the time she wrote *Summer on the Lakes* Fuller recognized that the piano had become "the fashionable instrument in the eastern cities . . . merely from the habit of imitating Europe, for not one in a thousand is willing to give the labor requisite to ensure any valuable use of the instrument."[18] Fuller knew of those daunting requisite labors and their limited rewards firsthand. By 1875 a Boston edition of Sir Arthur Helps's *Social Pressure* was offering sympathy to the American father of piano-playing girls, who might "learn to bear with something like fortitude the practising of his own daughters on the piano" but could be excused for giving in to the impulse to "utter unbecoming language" when "for the sixth time, he hears C flat instead of C sharp played in an adjacent house."[19] Fuller might well have pointed out Helps's musical ignorance, however, had she lived to read his book; her years of piano study would have taught her that C flat is nearly always scored as a B natural and is unlikely to be mistaken for C sharp.

The female amateur pianist of the mid-nineteenth century might delight with her "accomplishment" or annoy with her incessant practice, but she never rose up from the piano bench, took pen in hand, and put the knowledge she had gained to use by writing about classical music for a general audience, as Margaret Fuller did. Yet Fuller appears to have experienced no conflict about her choice. She may not have been a child prodigy at the piano, but her critical impulse was as precocious when it came to music as to any other art form. In the same letter that announced her mastery of "Bounding billows" on the piano at age ten, she had written to her father, "Did you ever see Mozarts requiem[?] . . . There are remarkable circumstances about the writing of it which I will acquaint you with another time. The requiem is exceedingly beautiful and there is great variety in it."[20] These "tones," more than the strains of Ellen Kilshaw's harp, are the ones that truly stayed with her, to emerge decades later as dominant themes in her justly famous *Dial* essay "Lives of the Great Composers."

Fuller arrived at an early awareness that her talents lay in the direction of criticism rather than artistic creation as much through her experience of music as of literature. Her years of musical training enabled her to expand her mission to "aid in the great work of mutual education" as a critic who steeped herself in every available form of high culture by reading, looking, and listening to convey what she had learned to her audience. The "feeling that many are reached" made "the thoughts of every day seem worth writing down," Fuller explained to James Freeman Clarke shortly after taking up her post at the *Tribune*.[21] Quite often those thoughts came in response to music.

The years spent teaching at the Greene Street School in Providence were formative ones for Margaret Fuller's feminism; the same can be said of her music criticism. While living in Providence, Fuller wrote her first essay on music, "Some Remarks on Madame Caradori," in response to a vocal performance. She read the paper to the Coliseum Club in Providence on January 25, 1838. The essay is far more ambitious than the title suggests, opening with a general statement of Fuller's ideas on music's superiority among the fine arts and its singular usefulness to the improvement of life and character in a democratic society. The passage is worth quoting in full, as a prelude to her later writing on music:

> Music is the best language known to man,—the means of transmitting thought, best calculated to meet at once, the wants both of sense, and soul. For within this, lie types of all the other Arts. In this, we enjoy symmetry, color, and design, in as great perfection as in any of the Arts. All require that the observer should be educated to their full enjoyment. But Music, has more for all sorts of minds, than any other. For the simple heart, it has melody. For the mere man of taste, the thousand beauties of detail, both in composition, and execution. For the man whose taste is vitalized by genius, it has all these—all the enchantments of melody—all the miracles of harmony, and, beside, a poetry far surpassing, what can be expressed in words.—
>
> If in the olden day, Music lent her aid to charm the populace into

the reception of severe laws, or to fire the youthful bosom to heroic valour—if she built cities, when artificers were scarce, or won back beauteous darlings from the very footstool of glooming Dis;—do we need her influence less, in this so called enlightened age, to break the bonds of sensuality, or custom—to dissipate the fog of a narrow, dull ability, to call back souls, almost crusted over by the Actual, to a perception of the atmosphere, fresh in immortal fragrance of the Ideal? The man who has been blinking half his days at the dust beneath his feet, or the stone wall of his neighbor, hurled beyond the orbit of earth by the red thunderbolt of a Beethoven, or borne upward on the seraphic pinions of a Mozart, realizes for once, the relation borne by his little world, to the Universe. Man needs the insight of taste, and imagination, as much as that of mere understanding, to fathom the shallowest marvel of his existence.[22]

Fuller concluded that music "should be especially valued by us in this republic of mixed modes." At the same time Fuller was also grappling with music on a technical level, seeking to understand how a piece of music wrought its effects, as a passage from her private journal reveals. How did a musical work accomplish all that she experienced as a listener? "The Ton-Kunst, the Ton-Welt, give me now more stimulus than the written Word," she wrote, "for music seems to contain everything in nature, unfolded into perfect harmony. In it *all* and *each* are manifested in most rapid transition; the spiral and undulatory movement of beautiful creation is felt throughout, and as we listen, thought is most clearly, because most mystically, perceived."[23] Fuller's already well-formed musical aesthetic lay behind her early dismissal of critics whom she found unwilling to treat music's essential properties and powers in their writing. In an 1839 letter to Ralph Waldo Emerson, she complained about an article, "The Pianoforte," that appeared in the *London and Westminster Review*: "there does not seem to be any deep insight into the secrets of the art," despite the essay's "great descriptive power."[24]

When Fuller returned to Boston and became editor of the *Dial*, she wrote seven pieces on music for the publication; she would go on to write twenty-nine articles on music, mainly concert reviews, for the *Tribune*.[25] Fuller was fortunate to be in Boston for the best seasons of the short-lived orchestra of the Boston Academy of Music, organized in 1840, which performed Beethoven's Second, Fifth, Sixth, and Seventh Symphonies while Fuller was in residence.[26] Fuller's correspondence and published writings suggest that she heard all of these and was profoundly affected, although the movements of the symphonies were performed in different portions of each program, a practice Fuller instinctively deplored.[27]

On hearing the Fifth Symphony for the first time in April 1841, the first time it was heard in Boston, the second in the United States, Fuller wrote ecstatically to William Henry Channing, "what majesty what depth, what tearful sweetness of the human heart." It is difficult to imagine hearing Beethoven's now ubiquitous Fifth for the first time at age thirty, but Fuller's description brings the moment vividly to life: "Into his hands [Beethoven] drew all the forces of sound, then poured them forth in tides such as ocean knows not." Remarkably, Fuller knew Beethoven's dramatic life story from Anton Schindler's biography, which she would soon review for the *Dial*, before she heard his symphonies. "When I read his life I said I will never repine," she continued in her letter to Channing. "When I heard this symphony I said I will triumph more and more above the deepenin[g] abysses. The life is large which can receive a Beethoven. I lived that hour."[28]

This performance of the Fifth inspired Fuller's work on "Lives of the Great Composers," published in the *Dial*, October 1841, following the April concert. Beethoven carried the day among the five "high-priests of sound" Fuller discussed: Haydn, Bach, Mozart, Handel, and Beethoven. Fuller's Unitarian-Transcendentalist belief in the ever-improving human spirit, both individual and collective, seemed to her borne out in the biographies under review: "From the naive lispings of their uncalculating lives are heard anew the tones of that mystic song we call Perfectibility, Perfection." Of the five it was Beethoven whom she found to be "towering far above our heads," demonstrating that "there is the godlike in man."[29] This essay would remain Fuller's proudest achievement in criticism for the *Dial*. "I do not expect to write better than that," she confessed to James Freeman Clarke, as she began work for the *Tribune* in January 1845.[30] She heard the Fifth Symphony played again during the Boston Academy's next season and wrote about it, in comparison to the Sixth Symphony (the "Pastoral"), for the *Dial*: "we seem to have something offered us, not only more, but different, and not only different from another work of his, but different from anything we know in the clearness with which we are drawn to the creative soul, not of art or artist, but of universal life."[31]

Like many who practice an instrument for years but never quite attain mastery, Fuller glorified music above all other arts. "To-day," she wrote in the "Great Composers" essay, "Music is *the* living, growing art. Sculpture, Painting, Architecture are indeed not dead, but the life they exhibit is as the putting forth of young scions from an old root. The manifestation is hopeful rather than commanding."[32] Even literature was inferior. "Music is universal language," Fuller wrote, refining her Coliseum Club assertion that "music is the best language known to man."[33] It is capable of taking the listener "far beyond where words have strength to climb."³⁴ "Musical sympathy" underlay all great literature, she once wrote to James Freeman Clarke, and in her ideal school, "*My* pupil shall learn musick *before* poetry." She wished that books could be retained in the mind in the same way as "pieces of musick," she wrote in another letter to Clarke, so that they could be recapitulated as written—hummed, perhaps—while "taking a solitary walk."³⁵

Hearing the Boston Academy orchestra's performances set Fuller up for reviewing in New York City, where at last she heard an orchestra, the Philharmonic Society, founded in 1842, perform "with a degree of perfection worthy a great metropolis." Now she was able to admire a Haydn symphony in contrast to the works of Beethoven, with whom "we had so long been intoxicated and upborne by the passions and prolonged inspirations of that god of modern music." Here, Haydn's "minuet was really a minuet in its thought and form."³⁶

What was Fuller's musical aesthetic? In her article "Margaret Fuller on Beethoven," Saloman proposes that Fuller's music criticism "moved considerably beyond, and away from, other Transcendentalists of the 1840s" in two ways: by claiming an "intrinsic aesthetic autonomy" in music, "without the assumption of moralist values or religious intent," and in espousing "an atypical interest in fathoming the workings of genius . . . [which] led her to acknowledge the dual importance of intuition and intellection in Beethoven's creativity to counteract popular notions of the composer's sole reliance on inspiration."³⁷ Yet Saloman's conclusions betray a limited understanding of Transcendentalist spirituality and of the pliable notion of "genius" that drifted among the writers and thinkers influenced by and joining Emerson in formulating his rhetoric of "Representative Men."

Although Charles Capper does not treat Fuller's music criticism at length, his phrase "religio-aesthetic" seems an apt summation.³⁸ Fuller never struck the same pious notes as Dwight, for whom instrumental music was "the highest outward symbol of what is most deep and holy," with Beethoven "the most spiritual of composers."³⁹ Music affirmed Fuller's moral sense, however, as well as her particular spirituality. Her review of the Haydn symphony ended with observations on the "satisfaction" of "hearing something so truly good in its way." Listening to Haydn's music, ably performed by the Philharmonic Society, was not merely a matter of enjoying "sweet feelings and intellectual exhilaration"; rather, it was proof that "it is the office of the beautiful arts to remind man of what he ought to be, by giving back to him, in worthy forms, the aspirations of his better hours."⁴⁰ Music exemplified human perfectability, the bedrock of Fuller's theology.

Fuller's review "Entertainments of the Past Winter" contains lines so similar to Dwight's that one wonders whether the editor might have had a hand in his inaugural *Dial* review, "Concerts of the Past Winter." Dwight's oft-cited line, "Music is the aspiration, the yearnings of the heart to the Infinite," became Fuller's "We look out through this art into infinity."[41] Fuller's spirituality and musicality, however, were more personal: "Here [in music] will the inward spiritual movement of our time find its asylum, find its voice, and in this temple worship be paid to that religion whose form is beauty, whose soul is love." She achieved an almost Buddhist apprehension of life in the moment through music, which "not only raises but fills us, and hope and thought have ceased to be, for all is now."[42]

Fuller's great gift as a critic was in offering up her own passionate response to music's "everlasting yes" as a model for her readers. In "Lives of the Great Composers," she invited her readers to listen along with her, even if they had "a very slight knowledge of music." The "all-enfolding language" of music, she explained, was capable of expressing what other disciplines failed to convey: "Botany had never touched our true knowledge of our favourite flower, but a symphony displays the same attitude and hues; the philosophic historian had failed to explain the motive of our favourite hero, but every bugle call and every trumpet proclaims him. He that hath ears to hear, let him hear!"[43] Music, the universal language, could reveal primal truths and allow us to feel them; perception and reception merge in music as in no other medium.

If music was to her the superior art, writing about music moved Fuller to some of her more innovative critical responses to aesthetic experience. As Tess Hoffman observes of Fuller's Coliseum Club essay, "[Fuller] is impatient with the need to hold back the surge of emotion engendered by the encounter between artist and audience. Fuller is unwilling or unable temperamentally to accept critical boundaries." Fuller's essay had concluded with a sonnet, "Caradori's Songs," just as her *Dial* essay on the "Great Composers" was accompanied by her sonnets to Beethoven and Mozart. Writing about "Caradori's Songs," which summarized in verse Fuller's "reaction as a member of the audience to the artist's performance," Hoffman proposes, "The singing voice of the musician inspires a lyrical response from the writer. One voice answers the other—the musical voice turns into the poetic voice, a metamorphosis that suggests the inter-relationship between the fine arts as well as the intricate link and intense communication possible between the artist, the work of art, and the audience."[44] The romantic music of her day made Fuller's style of criticism possible: her reviews and critical essays were as personal, passionate, and charged with idealism as the music itself.

Anything less than full engagement in a performance by other reviewers continued to annoy her. In a short review for the *Dial* of *Music Explained to the World; or, How to Understand Music and Enjoy Its Performance* by the French musician and critic Francis James Fetis, Fuller snipped, "it is not music explained, for that were an impossibility." She accorded brief praise to the book's "account of the technical terms of the art, the scope and capabilities of the different instruments, and different kinds of composition" before leaving the work behind in favor of a summary of the season's musical offerings in Boston, paying no heed to Fetis's closing chapters on "How to Analyze the Sensations Produced by Music in Order to Judge of It"—questions Fuller repeatedly raised in her own writing on the subject. Presumably Fetis had failed there too.[45]

At the same time that Fuller was writing critically about music for the *Dial*, she was composing her mystical pieces "The Magnolia of Lake Pontchartrain," "Yuca Filamentosa," and "Leila." As her Providence journal passage indicated, Fuller already believed music communicated its ideas mystically. A later journal entry of 1840 expressed the converse, that the mystical could be experienced as music: "I grow more and more what they will call a mystic. Nothing interests me except listening to the secret harmonies of nature.... If I meet men for a brief time, they check and veil the music, like heavy draperies near an instrument, but if they stay near me long I fill them till they vibrate. But this music is sweet in my soul to very pain."[46] In late 1840 Fuller heard a performance of Bellini's *La sonnambula* in Boston. She had "loved every melody in it for years," she wrote to William Henry Channing of the opera, which featured a sleepwalking maiden; however, only after experiencing the entire work—"connectedly," as she described hearing a complete performance of Haydn's *Creation* that she attended the following year—could she appreciate how the music "expresses an extacy, a trance of feeling better than any thing I ever knew." Bellini had realized music's highest, extramusical, capabilities: "In him thought and feeling flow always in one tide, he never divides himself from your soul." Once such mystical heights had been reached, music was almost beside the point: music served as the "medium" that enabled one's apprehension of the mystical.[47]

Not surprisingly, all three of Fuller's *Dial* meditations employed musical metaphor to express heights of passion. The narrator who encountered the magnolia blooming on the shores of Lake Pontchartrain reported, "I stood astonished as might a lover of music, who after hearing in all his youth only the harp or the bugle, should be saluted on entering some vast cathedral by the full peal of its organ. After I had recovered from my first surprise, I became acquainted with the flower, and found all its life in harmony." When the two Yuca blossoms "burst into flower together. That was indeed a night of long-sought melody." Leila "bursts up again in the fire" to the accompaniment of "divinest music," releasing the narrator to become "fearless, and utterly free. There are to me no requiems more, death is a name, and the darkest seeming hours sing Te Deum."[48]

There were no similar mystical-musical effusions for the *Tribune*. Fuller's music criticism in New York took a more analytical, often sharply critical stance, but eloquent enthusiasm remained her strongest suit. In a January 1846 *Tribune* review of a piano recital at the Apollo Saloon, which offered "the fire and sweep of Liszt, the architectural majesty of Thalberg, and the tenderness and delicate fancy of Chopin," she wrote, "A juster mode of viewing music is beginning to prevail in this country. It is no longer viewed merely as an entertainment or means of stimulating one class of feelings, but truly as a Fine Art,—one of the highest mediums that the soul of man has ever found to express its entire scope and its noblest aspirations. . . . Now it has come to be the great and growing art, distancing all the others, and likely to supersede in a great measure the literature of books, by the better means it furnishes both for conception and expression."[49] Education remained her mission. Five years after "Lives of the Great Composers," she delivered much the same message, although with greater sophistication and authority, in a *Tribune* essay titled simply "Music": "There is no branch of culture more important, and in our own country and age there is no influence so desirable, as that of musical expression in its higher forms. It seems strange that it should be necessary to say this: and yet it is so, to reassure the many who obscurely feel, and confront the many who have no idea, of such truths."[50]

When she traveled to Europe, she kept saying it. Music became Fuller's measure of the engaged—or disengaged—tourist. She reviled "the conceited American": "with his great clumsy hands, only fitted to work on a steam-engine, he seizes the old Cremona violin, makes it shriek with anguish in his grasp, and then declares he thought it was all humbug before he came, and now he knows it; that there is not really any music in these old things; that the frogs in one of our swamps make much finer, for they are young and alive."[51] Being "young and alive" meant something very different to Fuller, as subsequent events revealed. During the months before she began her affair with Giovanni Ossoli, Fuller was plainly depressed. She expressed this feeling, too, in musical terms: "I have never yet loved any human being so well as the music of Beethoven yet at present I am indifferent to it."[52] Her first meeting with Ossoli followed a vespers service that they had both attended at Saint Peter's on Holy Thursday.

So fluent was Fuller in the musical idiom that virtually every important undertaking entered her imagination as musical metaphor. In her famous letter to Sophia Ripley that outlined her plans for the first Conversations series in 1839, Fuller wrote, "Should a class be brought together.... Let us see whether there will be any organ and if so note down the music to which it may give breath." When she began her work as editor of the *Dial*, Fuller described the project in musical terms. "I want to know what part you propose to take in the grand symphony," she wrote to William Henry Channing as she began to solicit the essays that would fill the first number, "and I pray you to answer me directly for we must proceed to tune the instruments." To Henry Hedge, she wrote, "I really hope you will make this the occasion for assailing the public ear with such a succession of melodies that all the stones will advance to form a city of refuge for the just."[53]

And if gender role resistance was an implicit aspect of Fuller's music criticism, music also informed her feminism. Records of the 1839 Conversations show that Fuller was troubled by the lack of women artists and composers and sought an explanation; her anguished draft of a letter to Beethoven written in November 1843 revealed the depth of her doubts about women's (and her own) capabilities for achievement. "I have not been true to my eventual destiny," she wrote, charging herself with a failure to "borrow" from her painful life experiences "the inspiration of ... genius," as Beethoven had. "Why is it not thus with me? Is it because, as a woman, I am bound by a physical-law, which prevents the soul from manifesting itself?"[54] Four months earlier, she had published "The Great Lawsuit." It may have taken the publication of the work as a book for Fuller to feel reassured by the answers that she had already provided; the book itself was an answer.

What would *Woman in the Nineteenth Century* be without the concept of harmony, first made personal in her mystical essays for the *Dial*, and then invoked knowingly for a wider audience by this writer with musical training? "Harmony exists in difference, no less than in likeness, if only the same keynote govern both parts," she wrote. When Fuller advised women to "leave off asking" men how to live and instead "retire within themselves, and explore the ground-work of life till they find their peculiar secret," it was so that when they emerged "then their sweet singing shall not be from passionate impulse, but the lyrical overflow of a divine rapture, and a new music shall be evolved from this many-chorded world." If men and women were to develop "in perfect harmony, they would correspond to and fulfil one another, like hemispheres, or the tenor and bass in music." But at present, "there is no perfect harmony in nature." Her concluding poem promised that eventually "the Power to whom we bow ... shall hear all music loud and clear."[55]

Summer on the Lakes, too, was everywhere alive to the musical impulse, from Fuller's early recommendation that frontier women learn to play the guitar rather than the piano (easier to tune, easier to play), to her enchantment with the "graceful sequence" and "light flourish" of the Winnebago courting flute.[56] She had traveled a great distance, in her own musical education, from her 1842 *Dial* "Entertainments" review, in which she had written, "music is not a plant native to this soil," noting that "Yankee Doodle" was probably derived from an English folk song and "Jump Jim Crowe" was the contribution of "those of 'ebon hue.'"[57] Finally, however, it was simply the "voice of sweet music" from the waters at Mackinaw that soothed her spirit. Even here in the wilderness, however, she wished for homemade "earthly music . . . some strains of the flute from beneath those trees, just to break the sound of the rapids."[58]

The verse this thought inspired in Fuller might have been inserted anywhere in her work—in her criticism, her travel writing, her idealistic feminism—or used as her epitaph:

> Music, be thy sails unfurled,
> Bear me to thy better world;
> O'er a cold and weltering sea,
> Blow thy breezes warm and free.[59]

8

SYMPATHY AND PROPHECY

The Two Faces of Social Justice in Fuller's New York Writing

Jeffrey Steele

When Margaret Fuller moved from Massachusetts to New York City at the end of 1844, this transition pushed her to a new stage of literary awareness. The deep fault lines of the city made her acutely aware of the ways in which earlier modes of Transcendentalist analysis, focused upon the reform of the self, were an inadequate vehicle to diagnose what seemed like a pervasive *social* injustice. Like her predecessor Lydia Maria Child, Fuller saw around her an acquiescence to slavery, a widespread materialism, and a general insensitivity to the poorer and weaker members of society. For many of Fuller's middle-class contemporaries, the inmates and patients housed on Blackwell's Island, the accelerating wave of European immigrants, and the poor were inconvenient intruders on the social scene — obstacles to be ignored or displaced into social invisibility, if need be. Addressing the blind spots of her contemporaries in her New York writing, she struggled to expand the field of public awareness to include those individuals who had fallen outside or below the threshold of respectability.

A growing cadre of writers who considered sentiment, the transmission of affect, to be the most effective means of connecting readers with urban problems preceded Fuller in her expanded commitment to social reform. Like Child, however, Fuller recognized that sentiment alone was not sufficient to change urban conditions. The awakening of what she termed "public attention" demanded that perception be reshaped, a process that involved both emotional and cognitive components. At the same time Fuller, along with Child, understood that the descriptive mode of writing pioneered by urban "flaneurs," who recorded the sights of the city, did little to lift readers beyond surface impressions. Following the footsteps of Child, Fuller realized

161

that urban complexity demanded multiple organs of perception: not just the eyes, but also the spirit, the heart, the imagination, and memory. Rather than addressing only the reform of the individual, Child and Fuller shifted attention to the *collective* existence of urban dwellers. It was necessary, they believed, to project luminous ideals of perfected being (a Transcendentalist ambition) but also to mobilize currents of public affect (a sentimentalist agenda) that might motivate social change. While one could often "see" through the heart, there were often moments when feeling became overloaded or blocked and the circuits of sympathy broke down. Visionary modes perfected in New England by Transcendentalist writers offered an effective way to move beyond such emotional blockages by projecting idealized zones of being that functioned as alternatives to the perceptible and emotionally felt world. This merger of vision with affect changed Fuller's writing in important ways. It eventually led her to prophetic moments in which sympathy transformed into anger, and the visionary manifested itself as a call for radical social change.

Fuller's transforming sense of the function of her writing led to a radical shift in her focus and authorial stance. Rather than positioning herself as an "exemplary persona" modeling the intellectual and spiritual expansion of the self, she shifted her attention to the condition of society as a whole. In the process, Fuller turned from classical mythology to the Bible as a source of insight, especially the prophetic books of the Old Testament and the social gospel of Jesus. Denouncing the ideological and physical "pollution" of society, she displaced the focus of her writing from the self-reliant individual to the image of a just society that might mesh social practice with public ideals. Given Fuller's commitment to the equitable development of women, this emphasis had been a part of her writing since the publication of "The Great Lawsuit" in 1843. But Fuller's revision and expansion of "The Great Lawsuit" into *Woman in the Nineteenth Century* revealed a dramatic shift of emphasis from the reformation of the self to the reform of society as a whole. A striking sign of Fuller's evolving awareness was the emergence of a new myth in her writing: a prophetic vision of the collective "body" that had been contaminated by the toxin of corrupt social values and materialized aims. Rather than challenging her readers to become independent individuals, she urged them to work toward a more functional and just society founded on a vision of collective social action striving toward the common good. A sign of this focused action, Fuller suggested, would be a marked shift in public decorum. Fuller urged her readers to develop a new sensibility modeled on sympathy, politeness, and concern instead of exhibiting apathy, hostility, or selfishness toward their fellow citizens. At some moments, she imagined a world based on principles of cohesion, not conflict, a society in which rich and poor, the respectable and the outcast, might meet on common ground.

Published in 1843, Lydia Maria Child's *Letters from New-York* started to define the pathway that Fuller would soon follow. Articulating a profound model of social justice, Child's book challenged her readers to move beyond the visible surfaces of the city into expansive vistas of spiritual, emotional, and historical awareness. As Bruce Mills points out, Child was deeply imbued with an Emersonian idealism that stressed "the divinity of the individual."[1] In the city, however, she discovered the difficulty of asserting the primacy of an Emersonian "transparent eyeball" able to celebrate a world that would present itself in all of its glorious transparency. Emerson had taught his generation to look through the surfaces of the world to a deeper truth shining within them. In New York Child quickly discovered that the urban environment, rather than aligning itself with vision, was filled with blind spots, fault lines, and unexplored alleys.

Unable to celebrate the spiritual "dominion" of a self glorying in a world laid out before her, Child found it necessary to attend to the material conditions that threatened to impede self-development and vision. Transposing the dual perspective of Transcendentalism to the urban situation, she documented disturbing conditions while she looked beyond the phenomena of metropolitan life to deeper layers of meaning. Unlike many of her urban contemporaries who could see only the surfaces of daily life in New York, Child realized that present social conditions could not be changed unless one could see beyond them to imaginable alternatives. Perceiving the city with the soul, the heart, and memory—as well as with the eyes—Child insisted that the "walls" of urban reality were only temporary obstacles. She showed her readers a realm of spiritual (and Transcendentalist) truth beyond the tangled impressions of daily life. In contrast to the hard-heartedness that founded the order of civic society on the high walls of the Tombs (the city's jail), she insisted on a mobility of sympathy that could cross the gap between middle-class citizens and those imprisoned behind the literal and figurative walls of institutions and prejudice. In response to an overwhelming awareness of "never-ceasing change" that threatened to annihilate her sense of identity, Child anchored her being in vivid countermemories of the city's past—a doubling of literary consciousness that opened up what she characterized as a "two-fold world."[2]

In reaction to the numerous visitors and journalists who recorded the sights of the city, Child showed Fuller that an effective literary response to New York involved much more than descriptions of the "great promenade" of fashionable Broadway or the "dirt and filth" of the nearby slum Five Points.[3] That had been Charles Dickens's response in 1842. But to Child (and later Fuller) such visual impressionism seemed hopelessly inadequate. For such a focus reinforced the status quo instead of promoting the imagination of a different city that was not structured according to the principles of profit, social display, and self-interest. A transplanted New Englander, Child encountered in New York a complex urban environment vastly different from the village culture of her previous home, Northampton, Massachusetts.

In New York, she recognized a city struggling with momentous changes. The population of Manhattan had rapidly increased from 197,000 in 1830 to nearly 312,000 in 1840, while the population density had skyrocketed from 9,600 to more than 15,000 persons per square mile in the same period.[4] The effects of the economic Panic of 1837 lingered in the early 1840s, manifesting themselves as urban poverty and homelessness. Increasing waves of immigration exacerbated the effects of a growing population. The widely publicized 1836 murder of Helen Jewett, a prostitute, as well as the supposed murder of the cigar girl Mary Rogers in 1841 reinforced images of New York as a dangerous and sinful place where women were increasingly vulnerable. Vagrancy, civic unrest, and prostitution were becoming ever more pressing urban problems.[5] At times, Child noted, the city seemed "a deep and tangled labyrinth," a place in which the bonds of human sympathy could be swept away in fiery waves of bloodthirsty feeling ignited by executions at the Tombs. Most unsettling of all, perhaps the city was becoming a site—as Edgar Allan Poe dramatized in "The Man of the Crowd" and "The Mystery of Marie Roget"—where individuals cut off from all social ties could slip into a rootless anonymity. In the face of such confusion, Child, like the fugitive slaves who played such an important role in her antislavery writing, searched for "a calm, bright pole-star . . . to guide their [and her] steps."[6]

Both Child and Fuller challenged their readers to weigh their investment in daily realities against utopian images of both human and social perfection. Asserting the existence of realities beyond what could be "proved to the senses," they opened up imaginary vistas of a refashioned world structured according to principles of social justice.[7] The effect of this reorientation, Child insisted, would be a transformation of "the medium through which the earth is seen," a process analogous to that which Thoreau would later characterize in *Walden* as "carv[ing] . . . the very atmosphere and medium through which we look."[8] Like Child and Thoreau, Fuller considered her task to be reconfiguring the ideological structures that shaped her readers' awareness and their sense of everyday reality. For example, it was an unexamined assumption that the accumulation of capital should benefit the rich, who displayed their wealth in the lavish mansions they built along the thoroughfares and parks of New York City. A sharply defined cultural geography of "sunshine and shadows" seemed to be solidifying in the minds of Fuller's contemporaries: the fashionable sidewalks of Broadway contrasting with the cellars of Five Points, the open spaces of Gramercy Park with the high walls of the Tombs. Writing on the "State of Society" in 1840s New York, Philip Hone observed "two extremes": on the one hand, "costly luxury in living, expensive establishments, and improvident waste"; on the other, "squalid misery and hopeless destitution."[9]

"Sunshine-and-shadow" writers depicted a city in which "the center no longer held."[10] Instead of locating consensus or patterns of interclass affiliation or even communication, they represented the wealthy and the poor as living on opposite sides of an inseparable divide. In the context of this growing sense of social division, Fuller's 1846 *New-York Tribune* essay "The Rich Man: An Ideal Sketch" is an important text. Challenging the widespread assumption that people were "mere calculating, money-making machines," Fuller began reshaping what she termed "public attention" by appealing to a vision of human beings' nobler nature.[11] Resorting to a vein of idealism, she projected for her readers an image of a city modeled on social justice, not the exploitation of the poor.

At the opening of "The Rich Man," Fuller detached her readers from the visual consumption of material reality by pairing the "sights" gleaned from her "walks through the city" with a "reverie" of a city founded on an ideal of social justice. This virtual landscape, Fuller commented, was stimulated by "the woes, difficulties and dangers of our present social system" — "mighty problems" that could be addressed only through a process of "radical reform."[12] Her response to the schisms dividing New York was to create a vision of a businessman who "sees the interests of all mankind engaged *with* his, and [who] remembers them while he furthers his own." Demonstrating a nobility of spirit, Fuller's imaginary businessman exhibits the extraordinary behavior of building a fine new home that he opens to anyone who shares his values, not just members of his own social circle. In contrast to the new urban elite insulating themselves in fine homes on Fifth Avenue and Gramercy Park, he allows neither "wealth" nor "fashion" to be "a cause of exclusion more than of admission," since "all depend[s] upon the person." Although he appreciates fine art and loves "the Beautiful," he also can perceive the "sharp and care-worn faces, the joyless lives that throng his busy street" — a "noble human sympathy" that motivates him to turn his house into a haven for artists, the poor, and the virtuous who are "suffering."

But the final sentence of Fuller's urban reverie underscores the vast distance between her idealized vision of a virtual city and the urban realities surrounding her: "'Please ye give me a penny,' screamed a ragged, half-starved little street sweep, and the fancied cradle of the American Utopia receded or rather proceeded fifty years at least into the Future."[13] Although most of this essay operates on the plane of an imagined future, this conclusion punctures Fuller's reverie on the ideal deployment of wealth in America with the jarring sounds of New York's streets—a vivid moment that intensifies the appeal to the heart's political sympathies. Unlike "sunshine-and-shadow" writers who complacently contrasted the luxurious lifestyle of the rich with the degradation of the poor, Fuller in this moment pulled representatives of *both* sides into the same frame. The "rich man" and the "half-starved street sweep" both have a life in her text and both make a claim on the reader's attention *and feelings*.

Fuller's appeal to her readers' feelings surprised some members of her audience, who expected to measure her writing against an austere model of Transcendentalist spirituality. This shift in emphasis was apparent in Fuller's first *New-York Tribune* article, a December 7, 1844, review of "Emerson's Essays." Maintaining Emerson's commitment to transformation, Fuller shifted its application from the self to society. The responsibility of the writer, she noted, was "to admonish the community . . . and arouse it to nobler energy." The writer of "genius" such as Emerson, she continued, should be "the natural priest, the shepherd of the *people*" not just, as Emerson had positioned himself, "a representative of the claims of *individual* culture." "Here is, undoubtedly," Fuller exclaimed, "the man of ideas, but we want the ideal man also; want *the heart* and genius of human life to interpret it." The problem, Fuller continued, was that life could be "chilled" if viewed only through "the critical intellect."[14]

A close reading of Fuller's New York essays reveals her growing conviction that the deployment of sentiment and sympathy played a key role in shaping public attention. Thus she observed in her January 25, 1845, review of James Russell Lowell's work that the "great Critic" "is not merely the surveyor, but the interpreter of what other minds possess; . . . he must have, no less, a refined imagination and *quick sympathies* to enter into each work in its own kind, and examine it by its own law."[15] In such passages, Fuller outlined a process of response that combined the intellect, emotions, and imagination. She linked both intellectual discernment *and* judicious feeling to form her ideal of critical response. For example, her portrait of Elizabeth Barrett Browning in a January 4, 1845, review captured the complex interconnection of thought *and* feeling that was beginning to inform her understanding of public attention. Unlike many women writers, Fuller observed, Barrett

Browning was "wholly free" of "morbid sentimentalism.... Personal feeling is in its place; enlightened by Reason, ennobled by Imagination."[16] Connecting feeling to reason and imagination, Fuller did *not* reject sentimental writing outright (as some scholars have claimed) but rather adapted it to her critical and political agendas.[17]

Given the dominant critical tendency to characterize Fuller as a Transcendentalist who gravitated toward socialism, it comes somewhat as a surprise to recognize that a powerful vein of sentiment tinges the political views of her New York essays.[18] As she wrote about the poor, the incarcerated, and the abandoned, Fuller adopted a sentimentalist moral tone that measured the response of the caring heart against the ideal of Christian love. What is unmistakable is the new vein of *Christianized* sentimentalism that interlaces Fuller's *New-York Tribune* articles. For example, she argued that social problems had to be addressed by an "open heart" that could avoid "callousness."[19] Society, she affirmed, should be directed by "the divine obligation of love and mutual aid between human beings."[20] The highest manifestation of this communal feeling, she asserted, was the "divine love of Jesus," a spirit of care that embodied "the miraculous power of Love ... guided by a pure faith."[21] Benevolent reformers, she observed, were motivated by a "God of Love."[22]

In place of multiple allusions to classical mythology, present in Fuller's writing as late as the fall of 1844, numerous biblical passages provide the grounding for her New York essays. Fuller cited all four of the gospels, as well as a number of Old Testament books—a shift in orientation that reflected the Christian ethos of sentimental writing (and, perhaps, the direct influence of William Henry Channing's urban ministry).[23] Fuller's essay on "Prison Discipline" exemplifies her use of Christian sentiment. "There are symptoms that mankind at large begin to have some sympathy with the divine love of Jesus," Fuller observed. "Harsh bigots may sneer at this spirit of mercy as 'sickly sentimentality,' but the spark has been struck, and, nothing daunted, the fire glows, grows, rises, and begins to cast a light around."[24]

Probably the most vivid example of the ways in which Fuller's New York writing began to defend the deployment of sentiment is found in "Asylum for Discharged Female Convicts," published June 19, 1845. This essay asks middle-class readers to attend to one of the most controversial sites of all—the home of women discharged from prison, many of them former prostitutes, who were attempting to find the means to resist a "return to their former suffering and polluted life." Overturning schematic social discourses that projected opposed images of "true women" and "fallen women," Fuller argued that all inhabitants of the city—the poor, the rich, men, and women—had a responsibility toward its weakest and most vulnerable inhabitants. Hoping "to awaken the heart" of each reader "to a deep and active interest in this matter," she actively resisted the ethos of middle-class respectability that led most of her contemporaries to turn away from individuals whom society was all too willing to exclude. Near the end of her essay, Fuller engaged her readers with society's outcasts by asking them to take their emotional response to literary texts as a model of sympathetic political vision. Exhorting them to displace their concern from the printed page to the suffering poor, she commented,

> Have you entertained your leisure hours with the Mysteries of Paris or the pathetic story of Violet Woodville? . . . Do you want to link these fictions, which have made you weep, with facts around you where your pity might be of use? Go to the Penitentiary at Blackwell's Island. . . . See them in the hospital where the worn features of the sick show the sad ruins of past loveliness, past gentleness. . . . See those little girls huddled in a corner, their neglected dress and hair contrasting with some ribbon of cherished finery held fast in a childish hand. Think what "sweet seventeen" was to you, and what it is to them, and see if you do not wish to aid in any enterprise that gives them a chance of better days.[25]

By the end of this passage, Fuller outlined a process of seeing that was not urban spectatorship but rather an attentiveness that measured human losses against the heart's moral register.

Fuller's deployment of sentiment in this passage illustrates the way in which she was forging a new mode of critical awareness in the city, what I term "sentimental Transcendentalism." Appealing to her readers' hearts as well as their minds, Fuller aimed to reshape their perceptions of the urban landscape by suggesting that they could read both contemporary novels and the pain legible on the faces of the institutionalized poor. Holding both literary and human texts together in a double exposure, she helped her audience rethink the boundaries of their own critical and cultural perceptions. Such a shift in readerly orientation is apparent in Fuller's March 1845 essay "Our City Charities," which focused on the reform institutions on Blackwell's Island.

Starting in the 1820s new institutions such as Bellevue Hospital and the Bloomingdale Asylum for the Insane emphasized the class differences between genteel visitors and the unfortunate inmates housed at public expense. Yet instead of reproducing an urban tourism that cast her readers as detached voyeurs visiting isolated enclaves of difference, Fuller demanded that public attention and sympathy be focused on individuals confined to institutions outside the boundaries of polite society. Curious visitors—such as Charles Dickens in 1842—had found New York's new benevolent institutions to be irresistible tourist attractions.[26] While Dickens's visit to Blackwell's Island had brought him face-to-face with what he characterized as the "moping idiot," "the gibbering manic," and "the terrible crowd," Fuller critiqued the spectatorial assumptions that distanced such viewers from the incarcerated persons they encountered.[27] Challenging the detached gaze of observers interested solely in gawking at amusing spectacles of poverty and vice, she reflected that the residents of Blackwell's Island were most often subjected to what she termed "careless scrutiny" and "the gaze of the stranger."[28] As passing curiosities embodying the "urban picturesque," the outcasts and failures of society were cut off from the caring reflection that might consider the human expense of their wasted lives.[29]

Isolated in institutions on the margin of the city, the poor, criminal, and insane had been removed from view and given a social invisibility that cut them off from public concern. Opposing such neglect, Fuller observed near the opening of "Our City Charities" that "the pauper establishments that belong to a great city take the place of the skeleton at the banquets of old. They admonish us of stern realities. . . . They should be looked at by all, if only for their own sakes, that they may not sink listlessly into selfish ease, in a world so full of disease. They should be looked at by all who wish to enlighten themselves as to the means of aiding their fellow creatures in any way, public or private." The key phrase in this passage is "They should be looked at by all." Rather than allowing her readers to maintain an impressionistic sense of urban outcasts exiled to locales beyond their own realms, Fuller situated the city's exiles within what she termed "public attention," a focused awareness that—she affirmed—had started to awaken.[30]

Representing herself as a journalist embedded *within* the city's institutions, she modeled for her readers processes of compassionate witnessing that would bring the poor and institutionalized into the perceptual field of middle-class urban consciousness. In so doing, she broke down barriers that relegated the disabled, insane, and criminalized to preserves cut off from the city's collective gaze. Such awareness, the continuation of this passage reveals, involved attending to "right principles" and the "heart of the community," invisible domains beyond the mere act of looking. Without such capacity to generalize from their perceptions, many people looked without really seeing. They were "short-sighted," Fuller showed us, as she constructed sustained acts of public attention that involved much more than the touristic desire for visual amusement, since they engaged a multifaceted response that linked social surfaces to hidden causes.[31]

Expanding her readers' awareness, Fuller shaped public attention by illuminating the blind spots that blocked sympathy and public care. It is striking that, in Fuller's theorizing, the antithesis of sympathetic public attention was "prejudice." In "St. Valentine's Day: Bloomingdale Asylum for the Insane," she argued that both "mania" and "the commonest forms of prejudice" revealed "a mind which does not see far enough to connect partial impressions." Both mental conditions, she explained, illustrated the way in which "attention" might be "distorted into some morbid direction."[32] In other words, the achievement of "clear light"—a clarity of public attention—necessitated focusing a balanced awareness that sidestepped the pitfalls of contention and blind prejudice, both of which led to overinvestment in "partial" concerns at the expense of a more judicious evaluation of social conditions. Fuller had begun to consider the link between what she termed "sincere and patient attention" and clarity of vision in *Woman in the Nineteenth Century*, the book she completed just before moving to New York. In that treatise, she paired the awakening of "attention" with the "aspiration of soul, of energy of mind, *seeking clearness* and freedom."[33] As she grappled with the pressing social problems of New York, Fuller learned that the clarity she sought was deeply linked to "aspiration" and "energy," two terms that point toward the central role that public affect plays in motivating social change. At the same time, however, her equation of "clearness" with "freedom" reflected a deep commitment to a critical awareness founded on intellectual discipline and careful thought.

Fuller, of course, defended the pairing of these two sides throughout *Woman in the Nineteenth Century*. She asserted that women must possess the stern independence of Minerva as well as the more familiar emotionality of the Muse. "Energy and Harmony," "Intellect and Love," she asserted elsewhere, represented the two faces of human character.[34] This dual orientation appears in the different *authorial* personae that Fuller adopted in her *Tribune* essays. On the one hand, she played the role of the gentle "mother" encouraging her readers to model their private lives on ideals of courtesy and political sympathy. On the other hand, especially when she was discussing public political affairs such as slavery or the relationship of the United States with Mexico, she played the role of the stern father figure who assumed a stance of prophetic admonition. The challenge in reading Fuller is to perceive both sides: to see that her vision of a more caring society was paired with the recognition that public events might call for stricter measures. It is tempting to conceptualize *both* personae as facets of Fuller's prophetic stance, since she frequently merged the call for Christian "love" with visionary vistas of social corruption and prophetic denunciations of social "pollution" in its various guises.

It is worth lingering over the term "pollution," which entered Fuller's writing as she expanded "The Great Lawsuit" into *Woman in the Nineteenth Century* at the end of 1844. Dating to Old Testament prophets such as Amos and Hosea, the term "pollution" carried an overdetermined charge that served Fuller's purposes well. It evoked the sexual exploitation of women (which Fuller diagnosed in a new, controversial section on prostitution), but it also registered the idolatry, the worship of false gods, that had been the target of biblical prophets. In the materialistic culture of 1840s America, traumatized by the Panic of 1837, money had become the ruling deity for many, a perversion of values that helped justify the continuation of slavery and the impending war with Mexico. For Fuller, this public corruption extended into the personal lives of her contemporaries, who occupied a world in which it seemed normal for a woman to "make an imperfect man her god, and thus sink to idolatry."[35]

Attending to the politics of daily life, Fuller espoused the values of social contact and care. While some genteel observers saw little connection between themselves and those who were beyond "charity and pity," Fuller took great pains to represent points of contact and exchange between opposed social classes.[36] In "The Rich Man: An Ideal Sketch," for example, where she asserted that "sharp and care-worn faces" and "joyless lives . . . throng his busy street," the verb "throng" is striking; it suggests that rich and poor, privileged and destitute, coexisted in the *same* urban environment.[37] They were not temporally or spatially separated from one another. Similarly, in "Prevalent Idea That Politeness Is Too Great a Luxury to Be Given to the Poor," Fuller dramatized the encounter of members of different social classes. "A few days ago," her sketch opens, "a lady, crossing in one of the ferry boats that ply from this city, saw a young boy, poorly dressed, sitting with an infant in his arms on one of the benches. She observed that the child looked sickly and coughed." Yet rather than exhibiting any kindliness toward these impoverished children, Fuller recorded, the lady began pestering them with rude questions. Chastising the lady for her rudeness toward the underprivileged, Fuller argued in her essay for an urban environment in which "a rich man is not . . . surprised to find himself in *contact* with a poor one," a society in which the wealthier classes pass through the city "with an open eye and an *open heart*, ready to cheer the downcast, and enlighten the dull by words of comfort and looks of love."[38] More controversially, the essay "Asylum for Discharged Female Convicts" documented contact between fallen women and "the ladies of the Prison Association," who were working "to save" society's female outcasts "from return to their former suffering and polluted life."[39] Espousing an urban ethic of "contact" and openness, Fuller directly opposed middle-class writers who saw themselves as members of a superior species who could lock both their doors and their hearts.

For many writers in the 1840s, the greatest challenge to sympathy was the swelling wave of immigration, especially from Ireland and Germany, that threatened to inundate the city with poverty, crime, and cultural difference. By this decade, more than 150,000 European immigrants arrived annually.[40] To the upper-class businessman Philip Hone, this rising tide of immigration was the root of many of the city's social problems. The "squalid misery and hopeless destitution" of New York's poor, he observed, "has been hastened ... by the constant stream of European paupers arriving upon the shores of this land of promise. . . . If we had none but our own poor to take care of, we should get along tolerably well."[41] Reinforcing such nativism, essays by John O'Sullivan in the *United States Magazine and Democratic Review* argued for the limitation of suffrage and civic opportunity along national and racial lines. In contrast to such views, Fuller saw clearly that the foreign-born residents of New York were not an *external* threat but had already become an essential part of the community and many household establishments. This was especially true of the Irish, who had already begun carving out a niche for themselves as grooms, cooks, and servants. While the presence of a foreign-born laboring class had become the source of inevitable misunderstanding and conflict, Fuller believed that the mixture of different nationalities and classes represented an opportunity for the nation to grow even stronger. "Our thoughts anticipate with eager foresight," she reflected in one essay, "the race that may grow up from this amalgamation of all races of the world which our situation induces. It was the pride and greatness of ancient nations to keep their blood unmixed, but it must be ours to be willing to mingle, to accept in a generous spirit what each clime and race has to offer us."[42] Reflecting upon the "mighty sea of life" that "swells within our nation," Fuller argued that her "community" must manifest "a soul of goodness" and "wise aspiration" that might "assimilate" and transform the good and bad, the wholesome and unwholesome. Fuller recognized that Europe was pouring both "corruptions" and "riches" on "our shores," but, in contrast to many of her contemporaries, she also saw the pool of new immigrants as a source of potential strength.[43]

In three 1845 essays on "The Irish Character," Fuller vigorously defended the proposition that the Irish would come to represent "a most valuable element in the new race."[44] In a number of ways, Fuller anchored her appeal for political sympathy in the daily interaction between "employer and employed." There was a failure of "mutual understanding," she asserted, because "people meet in the relations of master and servant who have lived in two different worlds." The "lack of acquaintance" (or contact) between "the upper and lower classes" had led to poorly founded charges of laziness, dishonesty, and ingratitude.[45] Attempting to correct this misunderstanding, Fuller developed both a personalized discourse of sympathy and a generalized analysis that related the development of character to cultural circumstances. Despite the fact that "the Irishman appeals to you eye to eye," Fuller observed a breakdown of reciprocity and courtesy. Her readers made no effort "to put thyself into the position of the poor man" or to identify with the position of a harried and overworked group of people.[46]

But in a striking modulation of her rhetoric, Fuller linked the plea for sympathy to a more generalized plane of analysis that connected character with culture—a move that crystallized itself elsewhere as a fully articulated stance of prophecy. The fault lay less in the individual, Fuller asserted, than in the social circumstances that had deformed a person's character. Exhibiting the "faults of an oppressed race," the Irish had developed "habit[s]" that had grown out of a servile position, so that "the expectation of being tyrannized over has rooted in their race for ages." "Under the weight of old feudalism," Fuller observed elsewhere, "their minds were padlocked by habits against the light."[47] In such passages, Fuller exhibited the primary characteristic of prophetic writing: the linkage of personal and social dysfunction to a larger corruption of values.

It was a very short step from critiquing the "feudalism" that deformed the Irish to denouncing the "pollution" that was corroding American culture. In her essays, Fuller affirmed the need for a "deeper religion at the heart of Society," of individuals "acting from intelligent sympathy—from love."[48] Asserting the political efficacy of what she characterized as "the divine love of Jesus," she envisioned the expansion of care and compassion throughout the body politic.[49] Yet the pathos of political sympathy, Fuller recognized, was that its "impulse" toward "social or political reform" was audible only to "those who have ears to hear."[50] Writing during a period of increasing political turbulence (manifested in the Mexican War, which broke out in 1846), a rising tide of cruelty and greed was drowning out the expression of universal love. As Fuller recognized in her short essay "Victory," "the flames of burning towns rise higher than those of the altar" while "the wolves of war rage abroad."[51] In a homeland scarred by slavery, she lamented that the "cause of right" was daily sacrificed "for the impure worship of idols," as her compatriots gave "their children to the fire in honor of Moloch."[52] Confronted with slavery, economic and sexual exploitation, and war fever, Fuller searched for louder tones.

In a number of significant essays, Fuller moved beyond the sphere of everyday life—the realm of sympathy—onto the rhetorical plateau of prophetic anger.[53] In "New Year's Day," "Fourth of July," "First of August, 1845" (commemorating the British abolition of slavery), and "1st January, 1846," she used the occasion of public anniversaries to monitor the condition of the nation's "heart" and the moral welfare of its citizens.[54] Taken together, these four essays map out Fuller's prophetic vision of the country's moral and political situation. In them, she defined the nation's divine destiny and its current declension into a condition of "shame." She offered the hope that widespread "pollution" might be cured if "ten just men" could still be found. To achieve that goal, she asserted, both the individual and the national character would need to be purified. Asserting that she declined the role of prophesy (which she purported to leave to others), Fuller actually lifted her readers onto the plane of prophetic vision, warning of divine retribution if the moral and political corruption of the country were not corrected.

In "New Year's Day" Fuller reminded her readers of the divine "destiny of our Country," marked by "the purposes of Heaven with regard to it," an assertion that lay at the heart of her prophetic discourse. Americans were "the Chosen People of the elder day," she continued; "Wo be to those who betray this trust. On their heads are to be heaped the curses of unnumbered ages!" Eight months later, in "First of August, 1845," Fuller continued her discussion of the nation's special relationship with God. A chosen few, she affirmed, "feel that the power of the Great Spirit and its peculiar workings in the spirit of the age are with them."[55] By neglecting this divine potential, Fuller lamented (in a stance analogous to that of the great prophets of the Old Testament), the country had been scarred with shame. In allowing the perpetuation of slavery, the nation was busy "contriving measures that may best rivet the fetters on those now chained, and forge them strongest for millions yet unborn." In such a world, "Selfishness and tyranny no longer wear the mask; they walk haughtily abroad. . . . National Honor is trodden under foot for a National bribe."[56] Slavery, Fuller asserted in "First of August, 1845," is "the most shameful deed . . . that ever disgraced a nation; because the most contrary to consciousness of right."[57] Witnessing the "tragic thread" that had darkened her country's destiny, Fuller bemoaned "the evil star looming up that threatened cloud and wreck to its future years."[58]

At the root of the nation's declension from its divine mission, Fuller believed, lay the corruption of individual character. Rather than living up to his potential, the "good man" had allowed "a spot of base indulgence, a fibre of brutality" to "canker a vital part" of his being.[59] In several striking passages, Fuller amplified this idea by referring to the chilling biblical episode of the "ten just men." Bargaining with the Lord not to destroy Sodom, Abraham asked if the city could be saved if he could locate "fifty righteous within the city," or perhaps "forty and five," "forty," "thirty," or "twenty;" could it be saved even if "ten shall be found there?"[60] Ultimately, not even one "just man" was found within the walls of Sodom, and the city was utterly destroyed because of its moral corruption. In *Letters from New-York*, Child had written, "I used to say, I knew not where were the ten righteous men to save the city; but I have found them now."[61] Returning to the original spirit of the biblical passage, Fuller observed in "New Year's Day," "If the nation tends to wrong, there are yet present the ten just men." Seven months later, in "Fourth of July," she proclaimed, "Things are still in the state when ten just men may save the city."[62] Impersonating the voice of Abraham, Fuller weighed her sense of civic and national corruption against this terrifying image of divine judgment. Her hope was that there still existed in the country a stream of purity that might counter the rising tide of moral corruption; "pure blood," she hoped, "flows yet within her veins."[63] "The safety of the country," she asserted, "must lie in a few . . . men who have achieved the genuine independence, independence of wrong, of violence, of falsehood."[64] Only if "the pure blood shown in the time of the Revolution still glows in our heart" might it be possible to resist the "foreign elements" of greed and corruption.[65]

In the face of the widespread pollution of American values, Fuller believed that the nation needed to undergo a radical process of transformation. The character, homes, and conscience of America needed to be purified, rekindling the glow that might illuminate the heart. Resorting to the alchemical imagery that had attracted her since her spiritual crisis of 1840–41, Fuller reflected that the corrosion of values had resulted because "there was no love to kindle the fire under the furnace." As a result, "the precious secret is not precipitated yet, for the pot will not boil to make gold . . . if love do not fan the fire."[66] Fuller's hope was that the "good man, once raised from his moral lethargy," might learn how to "deepen and purify his whole nature."[67] Only then might he become part of the "faithful band determined to expiate the crimes" that have corrupted the nation.[68] Evoking the "glowing eyes" of this dedicated company, Fuller returned to one of her key ideas. In her poem "Sub Rosa-Crux," at the end of *Woman in the Nineteenth Century*, and in her references to "ten just men," she asserted that the key to the country's moral destiny lay in the capacity of a select group of leaders to guide it back onto the path of social justice. Only then might the altar of national consciousness be rekindled with "sparks of new fire," instead of being "quench[ed]" by the "insatiate love of wealth and power."[69] Fuller's great fear was that those who supported slavery, as well as the self-serving materialism damaging the national character, might perpetuate indefinitely a "will alien from God."[70]

This sense of spiritual alienation was one of the defining characteristics of prophetic vision. It is thus highly significant that, in two of these essays, Fuller directly addressed the cultural function of prophesy. She did so through a classic rhetorical maneuver, widespread among nineteenth-century women writers, in which the author coyly suggested that the topic she was discussing was better suited to others (presumably men). Ostensibly distancing herself from the rhetorical power she was channeling, Fuller (as female prophet) thus simulated the gendered boundaries of literary decorum at the same time that she crossed them. At the end of "First of August, 1845," after asserting the necessity of purifying the nation, she added that "volumes may be preached from such a text." "We, however, preach not," Fuller added. "There are too many preachers already in the field, abler, more deeply devoted to the cause." Then, however, as she characterized the discourse of "those ardent 'sons of thunder,'" Fuller easily slipped into their prophetic style: "They cry aloud and spare not; they spare not others, but neither do they spare themselves, and such are ever the harbingers of *a new advent of the Holy Spirit*." Amplifying this strain of prophecy, Fuller concluded her essay with a stern warning. Asserting her "aspirations" for the country, she prayed that its "festivals" would no longer be "blacked by falsehood, tyranny, and a crime for which neither man below nor God above can much longer pardon thee." For such devotion to "Mammon," Fuller sternly warned, could lead only to "endless torment or final death."[71]

If such passages illustrate Fuller's willingness to adopt a prophetic mode of discourse, the conclusion of "1st January, 1846" is even more striking. In the middle of this essay, after denouncing the moral corruption of her contemporaries, Fuller bemoaned the way in which they had forgotten the wisdom of the "Fathers of the Revolution." "The vision of those prophetic souls," she cautioned, "must be realized, else the nation could not exist." Given this affirmation of the political value of prophecy, the conclusion of Fuller's essay takes on special interest. After evoking the apocalyptic and prophetic image of an "avalanche" rushing down a mountain to destroy a village, Fuller ostensibly negated the rhetorical mode she had just been using by asserting in the next paragraph that "the time of prophets is over, and the era they prophesied must be at hand." Yet despite this declaration, Fuller concluded her essay by returning to the mythical mode of high prophecy:

> Altogether, it looks as if a great time was coming, and that time one of Democracy. Our country will play a ruling part. Her Eagle will lead the van, but whether to soar upward to the sun or to stoop for helpless prey, who now dares promise? At present she has scarce achieved a Roman nobleness, a Roman liberty, and whether her Eagle is less like the Vulture and more like the Phoenix than was the fierce Roman bird, we dare not say. May the New Year give hopes of the latter, even if the bird need first to be purified by fire.[72]

Asking whether the nation would be reborn from its ashes or degenerate into a bird of prey, Fuller again reminded her readers that a fiery process of purification might be the gateway to regeneration. What she had no way of knowing was that the impending war with Mexico would be quickly followed thirteen years later by a devastating Civil War. What she could perceive, however, was that the maintenance of the nation's democratic promise required eloquent pleas for political sympathy and prophetic warnings about the consequences of moral decline.

The question that lingers, after this survey of Fuller's political writings in New York, is whether sympathy and prophecy are the twin faces of a single authorial orientation. While we distinguish the two as distinct rhetorical modes, they seem interconnected, as expressions of what William Cullen Bryant characterized as the gentle and stormy passions.[73] As this essay suggests (and as a poem such as Bryant's "A Winter Piece" confirms), it is very easy—indeed, almost compelling in Fuller's case—to gender these two styles as expressions of maternal and paternal sensibilities. Yet such gendering of language, as Fuller herself knew well, carries its own dangers. A more precise approach might consider the ways in which sentimentalized sympathy and prophecy were gendered in the nineteenth century. We now know, after the publication of the collection *Sentimental Men*, that sentimental rhetoric was widely used by both men and women.[74] The question that Fuller's *New-York Tribune* essays open up is whether prophecy could be practiced by women as well as by men. Fuller certainly seems to have thought so. In an October 1840 letter to William Henry Channing, she affirmed her desire to "preach the Holy Ghost."[75] In her mystical essay "Leila," she asserted her desire to express "the secret of moral and mental alchymy" so that "all Bibles" could pass "into one Apocalypse."[76] And in the pages of *Woman in the Nineteenth Century*, Fuller carefully traced a tradition of female religious leadership, including that of Teresa of Avila, Madame Guyon, Joanna Southcott, and Mother Ann Lee, among others. As Fuller knew from her classical reading, the figure of the female prophet was sometimes associated with Cassandra, doomed by Apollo to speak the truth and never be believed. It is intriguing to consider the extent to which Cassandra's fate influenced Fuller's own writing, especially the careful declarations that she was *not* writing prophecy. As Fuller understood all too well, women could safely be considered guardians of the heart of America. Whether or not they would be allowed to enter the sphere of public political discourse as prophets was a much more difficult question.

9

MARGARET FULLER AND URBAN LIFE

Robert N. Hudspeth

What is the great attraction in Cities? It is universally admitted that human beings invariably degenerate in them.
 —*Henry Thoreau*, Journal, *winter 1845–46*

The City also is a bed in God's garden.
 —*Margaret Fuller to her brother Richard*, Letters, *December 1841*

"Who can see these cities and say that there is any life in them?" asked Thoreau to himself in his *Journal* in 1843. The answer was ready at hand: Margaret Fuller, that's who. New York City was their common point of reference, for when Thoreau wrote his truculent query he was a tutor on Staten Island, but he occasionally made forays into Manhattan, excursions that were quite unsatisfactory. He went on in his *Journal* to complain, "I walked through New York yesterday—and met no real and living person."[1] Slightly more than a year later Margaret Fuller walked through the same Manhattan streets and found a complex, thriving city full of living persons. The authors' reactions to urban life made clear their opposing assumptions about the best means of obtaining self-culture: for Thoreau the self was to be found by distancing oneself from the distractions of other people; for Fuller the self was created in one's involvement with and reactions to others. Walden Pond was the adequate symbol of Thoreau's needs, but the city was Fuller's symbol, for a city woman she was.

Urban environments, it turns out, were life itself to Fuller, the necessary stimulation of both mind and emotions that drove a significant portion of her writing. While Margaret Fuller seldom wrote overtly about urban life, cities, replete with both possibilities and limitations, deeply stirred her imagination, and, save for a brief period early in her life, she always wrote from a city and to a city audience. This existence set her apart from Emerson and Thoreau, who were repulsed by urban life; their famous titles are, after all, *Nature* and *Walden*. Fuller's sensibilities placed her in contrast to other authors as well. The most memorable reform movements of the period involved attempts to flee urban living for the life-giving presence of "nature," attempts to reform the nature of "work" and to make possible the growth of a genuine human "self." Brook Farm and Fruitlands, both founded by friends of Margaret Fuller, were the most obvious examples. The ills of society—those of the body, the mind, and the soul—had to be renounced, and as everyone knew, such troubles were concentrated in urban environments. Thus George Ripley and Bronson Alcott both assumed that only by removing from city life could authenticity be found. It was all but axiomatic: "reform" was synonymous with "removal." Emerson, after all, had moved from Boston to Concord not only because village life was more thrifty but because it was more conducive to his work than city living. Boston offered him nothing but distractions.

Fuller's experience was just the opposite. Not only did she live her entire life (with the marked exception of her years in Groton) in and around cities, she embraced urban life; even more, she depended on it. Cities could teach her, and she in turn could teach them. In such diverse places as Boston, New York, and Rome, Fuller found opportunities to instruct her readers about topics unique to city experiences and central to self-growth: the fine arts, especially music, and social reform.[2] Cities blossomed with the fine arts—drama, sculpture, painting, and music—in Fuller's lifetime. Both the expensive structures of the arts (the studios, the musical ensembles, the galleries) and the patrons willing to pay for them were fixtures of city life. An author might live by a pond, at a remove from the publishing house through which works would find their audience, but a violinist needed a hall; a painter needed a gallery; an opera needed a company of performers. Nor did Fuller just stumble on the fine arts, for she made it clear again and again in her writing that the experiences of music and painting, of sculpture and dramatic performance, were necessary for human growth. Far from being merely pleasurable additions to daily life, they were essential to becoming fully human. In her 1842 *Dial* essay "Entertainments of the Past Winter," Fuller wrote that the arts teach individuals that "the desire for amusement" is "irrepressible," that the "love of the beautiful for its own sake" cannot be stifled, and that "the Power" that governs life "meant that all beings able to receive and feel should, with recreative energy, keep up the pulse of life and sing the joy it is to be,—to grow." As she went on to say, "Music is the great living, growing art. . . . We look out through this art into infinity."[3] Though she never put it quite so bluntly, change was life. Like Emerson, like Thoreau, she abhorred torpor. To be fully human was to embrace growth.

Fuller seldom discussed the city as such. In her writing, there was little overt description of either Boston or New York, little of London, little of Paris. Even in Rome, a city whose mystique seems always to elicit description, Fuller resisted the temptation to lapse into conventional travel writing. There were occasional moments when, as in the quotation at the head of this essay, she figuratively stepped back far enough to reflect on city life in an impartial manner, but those moments were rarer than one would have expected. What one found instead was that urban experiences consistently framed her writing, both public and private. Ever the observer, Fuller accepted her responsibility to scrutinize the performances before her, to judge both them and her responses to them, and to turn her experiences of art or of social reform into teachable moments that would lead to better human understanding, more cultivated tastes, better artistic performances, improved social structures, and finally, more effective political institutions.

For several decades scholars have focused on Fuller's growing interest in reform when she moved from New England to New York City in 1844, but this transition should be evaluated in the light of her ongoing experience of urban culture and viewed more clearly as part of a continuum that ended only with her sudden death.[4] I mean no teleology in Fuller's experiences in cities. Her supple ability to respond deeply and thoughtfully to the several cities that she experienced was remarkable. There was no inevitable arc of growth: Fuller simply made use of what she had previously seen and read and thought; she changed, of course, but there was no sudden eruption that severed her from her past. Many of her most important physical experiences were of urban life, and these in part shaped her evolution as a thinker. Of her major contemporaries only Fuller lived through the shelling of a city, only she talked directly to a prostitute. She was the only one to venture inside a prison (Thoreau's night in the Concord lockup notwithstanding), to attend Philharmonic concerts regularly, and to give birth.[5] Fuller began as a bookish young writer but matured into a sophisticated analyst of her contemporary world. Her recognition that one could actually change in deeply meaningful ways underlay her faith in human improvement. Through observation, thought, and empathy the writer could serve as a genuine teacher.

Margaret Fuller was not a Boston native, but she might as well have been one. She grew up in Cambridgeport, which was close enough to the city for her to ride in and out, visiting her expansive circle of friends, several of whom remained her intimates in later years. These relationships characterized her earliest experience of the city; as a young person she was part of a lively social scene that included such Boston girls as Almira Penniman, Elizabeth and Belinda Randall, and Amelia Greenwood. As she grew older these associations were expanded by the addition of a number of young men, and in her responses to them one can glimpse a nascent insight concerning what the city meant to her. Here was a place where minds could meet, as when the nineteen-year-old Fuller met Frederic Henry Hedge: "Ah!" she exclaimed, "What pleasure to meet with such a daring yet realizing mind as his!" Four years later, when Hedge deliberated taking a pulpit in Bangor, Maine, Fuller cautioned him, "With your habits of mind I think you will regret leaving the vicinity of Boston much and more."[6]

This seemingly offhand comment reminds us about Fuller's lifelong concern with mental stimulation. From an early age she was fearful of stasis. Like Emerson, she valued a process of always "becoming," always feeling herself to be growing. When she thought about Hedge's dilemma she quickly recognized the danger of isolation and its inevitable result — mental inactivity. As it turned out, she was prescient, for she was later forced to discover for herself what it meant to be cut off from such minds, when her father moved the family to Groton. There she found herself lacking the stimulation of good talk; as she bitterly wrote to Hedge, "this going into mental solitude is desperately trying."[7] Boston signified thoughtful and energizing conversation and intellectual give-and-take, all of which was far removed from a Middlesex farm. Fuller had her books, to which she turned with a vengeance, but she still longed for the pleasures of talks with people who stimulated her.

Her father's death changed everything: Fuller became the head of an impoverished household with no choice but to go back to a city to make a living. First she tried Boston, where she worked as a teacher for Bronson Alcott's Temple School, then she left for Providence to teach at Hiram Fuller's Greene Street School. Providence was not much to Fuller's liking; she found it restrictive and uninteresting. It did have music, however, and her responses to compositions provide an early insight into what music meant to Fuller and, beyond that, why cities mattered. In a lecture delivered to the Providence Athenaeum, she responded to a concert by Maria Caradori-Allan. Fuller prefaced her remarks by saying, "Music, is the best language known to man"; it was "the means of transmitting thought, best calculated to meet at once, the wants of both of sense, and soul." She claimed that music once built cities and that a society given over to money making needed its power even more. She used particularly active verbs to describe the power of music "to break the bonds of sensuality, or custom," to "dissipate the fog of a narrow, dull ability," to "call back souls." This was just the sort of stimulation Fuller most wanted. In music she found creativity in action, but more important, she determined music to be the means of unlocking personal creativity in its listeners. "Man needs the insight of taste, and imagination, as much as that of mere understanding, to fathom the shallowest marvel of his existence."[8]

Fuller's idea of "taste" is perhaps too large a topic to explore fully here, but it was of unquestioned importance to her. Taste was something acquired, not inherent, the product of experience. The more one heard performances, the more one looked at paintings, the more one read poetry and prose, the more dependable was the foundation of one's personal growth. Fuller thought that taste also enabled one to make distinctions, to judge the inferior from the superior. The aim of taste was not, however, to dismiss out of hand whatever one found wanting but rather to show what was needed to make it better. Fuller's notion of taste did not involve an imperial judgment but an exercise of sympathetic engagement to explore that "marvel" of "existence."

As meaningful as Fuller found Caradori's performance to be, it was one of only a limited number of opportunities that Providence offered. Boston was still the "Hub of the Universe" of fine arts in New England. Fuller was keenly aware, however, of the ill effects of the city's Puritan history and its commercial present. "There is no poetical ground-work ready for the artist in our country and time," she said in "A Record of Impressions," published in the first issue of the *Dial* in July 1840. "What is most dignified in the Puritanic modes of thought is not favorable to beauty." She immediately went on to indict "the habits of an industrial community" that "are not propitious to delicacy of sentiment."[9] Fuller even made fun of it all. In 1842 she began a comprehensive review of the arts in Boston in the winter of 1841–42 by asking, "What would the Puritan fathers say, if they could see our bill of fare here in Boston for the winter?" Four pages later she witheringly observed, "If New England thinks, it is about money, social reform, and theology."[10] Given this milieu, her writing aimed to be a countermeasure. As a critic Fuller wanted to make a case for "beauty" and "delicacy of sentiment" and to cause New Englanders to think about art. She knew that her readership was small, but she strove to make it larger, to create an audience not only for her writing but, more important, for art itself. Nor did she set herself up as a superior observer. In her "Record of Impressions" she admitted that she was "conscious of an eye and taste, not sufficiently exercised by study of the best works of art, to take the measure of one who has a claim to be surveyed from the same platform."[11] She implied that she and her audience would grow together, that she could model the habits of mind necessary to become a better audience for, in this case, Washington Allston's paintings.

Running through Fuller's criticism of the arts was a fundamental belief in the possibility of education and thus of growth. In fact, the very paintings, sculptures, and symphonies themselves could "gradually educ[ate] us to their own level."[12] Although Fuller detested the profession of teaching—her experiences with Alcott and Hiram Fuller had exhausted her and left her dissatisfied—she discovered that she could be a quite effective teacher outside of formal schools. She laid out her ambition in "Entertainments of the Past Winter": "the aesthetic side has not yet found an advocate of sufficiently commanding eloquence to give it due place in the councils of the people." In the essay she went on to comment on Fanny Elssler, the ballet dancer (then called an "opera dancer"), who had caused a minor scandal in Boston, because the more prudish considered it inappropriate to display the female body in public. Fuller lectured her audience about the difference between the artist and the work itself. In defending the performance, Fuller implicitly defined her own role, one that aimed to "rais[e] the standard of thought on the subject, and alte[r] the point of view" and thus "disarm it of its power to injure."[13] "Raise" and "alter" were words that lay at the core of Fuller's criticism, focused as they were on the audience members and their ability to grow and become adequate partners of the artist. She wanted to educate her readers about the possibility that art was a collaboration between creator and audience. Fuller tried to break down the assumption that the audience was a passive recipient of "genius" provided by the performer. She never wholly worked out her idea, but it was implicit in many of her reviews of music. As Tess Hoffman has pointed out, in Fuller's writings about music, "One voice answers the other—the musical voice turns into the poetic voice, a metamorphosis that suggests the inter-relationship between the fine arts as well as the intricate link and intense communication possible between the artist, the work of art, and the audience."[14]

The notion of collaboration extended into Fuller's experience and understanding of art, but most important, of music. Musical performances implied the presence of an audience, an assembly that varied in size from large (at symphonies) to small (in gatherings at private homes). But whether it was played in public or in private, music was a shared experience that drew together performers and an audience; to Fuller, in fact, it was a no less than a collaborative effort. Thoreau might play his flute to satisfaction for the fishes of Walden Pond, but Ole Bull required a Boston or New York audience for his violin. Fuller acknowledged that music was played everywhere, that "psalmody in country villages is a favorite and pleasing amusement of family and social circles" and that it "has certainly a tendency to cultivate the more pure and graceful feelings." But there was a limitation to simple enjoyment: "as to music, the exclusive care for time and tune thus cultivated is hostile to any free acceptance of the art in its more grand and creative movements."[15] What was needed was an audience at once more sophisticated and more tolerant, an audience that, like Fuller, was willing to enter into new aesthetic experiences.

Even before Fuller publicly became the critic and champion of the arts in Boston, she had explored another form of collaboration that the city had offered her when, in 1839, she began her five-year Conversations series. Fuller took advantage of the fact that a number of her friends and acquaintances lived in Boston and that these women longed for mental activity for which they had no ready leadership. If Boston had always been a world of "talk" for Fuller, discussion now became a professional activity, for her Conversations were structured events for women who paid for the opportunity to participate. Fuller set the agendas and took the lead, but her overall aim was to create a community of thinking women. As always, she wanted to achieve a better, more productive way of thinking about serious topics. She knew that women were seldom encouraged to consider ideas carefully or to trust their own perceptions, so she set out to make it possible for a group of middle-class women, all of whom were city dwellers, to grow, to develop their tastes, and to trust each other. For the most obvious reasons, these seminars could only occur in an urban setting, for they required a critical mass of women of a similar background and who had similar aims—even allowing for the diversity among them. A village, even one as sophisticated as Concord could be, could not muster a five-year experience of Conversations with Margaret Fuller. She and her participants lived in a culture that valued lectures (and, to her dismay, overvalued sermons) and that provided access to bookstores. This urban underpinning was crucial to her Conversations. She made it clear in her letters that she needed other minds and that she needed a wide range of opinions. Fuller understood in ways that Thoreau never did that friendship was, in Bell Gale Chevigny's apt phrase, a "collusion in prophetic activity—one helped the other to discern 'the law of one's being.'"[16]

On another level, Fuller's responses to cities reflected a deep fear of being too alone, a fear that probably originated in Groton. It is not at all surprising to discover that in 1844 as Fuller left the Hub for good, she wrote to her brother Richard, "I felt regret at leaving Boston, so many marks of friendship were shown me, at the last so many friendships true, though imperfect, were left behind."[17] She was never again to have the richness of friendship that she experienced in Boston, though New York and Rome offered other satisfactions that took her to new heights. She thought Boston was narrow, too provincial, and too smug, but it was the home of her youth, a city alive with personal connections.

Moreover, "home" is where one doesn't see clearly, and Fuller never truly "saw" Boston, a fact that became strikingly apparent when she moved to New York City. It has become commonplace in Fuller studies to note how much she became aware of urban poverty and oppression when she moved to New York, how much she was willing to devote herself to organized forms of social amelioration. But one wonders, had not Boston its poor? Its destitute? Its prostitutes? Of course it did, but Fuller, at least in the record that survives, never saw them, and truly, the reason is unknown. As she moved to New York, something happened to her consciousness, though there is no defining event, no watershed moment to suggest an explanation. Perhaps it was the experience of holding a Conversation with the imprisoned women at Sing Sing. In all likelihood Boston simply was too familiar. Fuller had grown up perceiving the city as she saw it from childhood. There was nothing "new" for her there. Such was not the case with New York City or, later, with Liverpool, London, Paris, and Rome.

A second guess is that she never had a companion with eyes focused on different realities. The American men who had the greatest effect on Fuller in Boston were probably George Davis and James Clarke (early in her life) and then Emerson (after 1836), none of whom was going to spend time among the derelicts in Scollay Square. In contrast, her growing friendships with William Henry Channing, who became Virgil to her Dante in New York City, and with Horace Greeley, also, as the editor of the crusading *New-York Daily Tribune*, her employer, influenced her to "see" more completely. One can gauge the change by contrasting her mockery of the Dorr Rebellion in Rhode Island, which she witnessed in the summer of 1842, with her responses to the women at Sing Sing two years later in the autumn of 1844.[18]

Rhode Islanders had been embroiled in a sometimes violent attempt to revise their archaic state charter that severely limited the franchise. From October 1841 to June 1842, Thomas Wilson Dorr led a people's rebellion to create a more democratic state constitution. The governor declared martial law, but on May 19, 1842, Dorr led an unsuccessful attack against a state arsenal in Providence. He was forced to flee Rhode Island, and his movement collapsed just as Fuller visited Providence. There she found "little cheer, in what I have seen," as she wrote to Channing, "a city full of grown-up people as wild, as mischief-seeking, as full of prejudice, careless slander, and exaggeration, as a herd of boys in the play-ground of the worst boarding-school." Even though she thought the demonstrators had a point, what she saw and heard repelled her: "These absurdities, of course, are linked with good qualities, with energy of feeling, and with a love of morality, though narrowed and vulgarized by the absence of the intelligence which should enlighten." In short, a political movement grounded in democratic principles, one that sought to end a severely restrictive state constitution, had devolved, for her, into near anarchy. In a striking conclusion to her response, she quoted Psalm 19: "'keep back thy servant from presumptuous sins; let them not have dominion over me.'"[19] It was as if she felt trapped by what she saw and heard, as if that political upheaval had the ability to soil her. She saw power in action and was frightened by it. In Providence she was writing as an outsider, a mere observer who had not the slightest sympathy with the actors she observed.

By the time she began to write for the *Tribune* Fuller exhibited the very sympathy she lacked in Providence. Before she actually arrived in New York, she met a group of prostitutes serving time in Sing Sing. In August 1844 Georgiana Bruce, a former resident of Brook Farm who was then working at the prison, lent to Fuller some journals written by the prisoners. Fuller's response demonstrated not only sympathy for the women but an understanding of the connection between them and the world surrounding them: "these women in their degradation express most powerfully the present wants of the sex at large. What blasphemes in them must fret and murmur in the perfumed boudoir, for a society beats with one great heart." When she met the women two months later, she described them in terms exactly opposite of those she had used to impale the Dorrites: "They were among the so called worst, but nothing could be more decorous than their conduct, and frank too. All passed much as in one of my Boston Classes."[20] In her own mind what she had accomplished in Boston was being repeated at Sing Sing. What she saw in Providence was political, public, abstract, and anonymous. What she found at Sing Sing was deeply personal, very concrete and human, and, as she said, "decorous." The nature of individuals who sought a reformed life, who were civil and self-respecting, was alluring to Fuller. She had found, as she said in a very early *Tribune* essay, that "if charity begin at home, it must not end there; and while purifying the innermost circle, let us not forget that it depends upon the great circle, and that again on it."[21] Her increasing understanding of the interdependence of what was most private and most public in her experiences characterized her different reactions to Boston and New York.

As she began her career in New York City, Fuller had modest aims for herself, despite the stimulation she found in her new field. Writing to a friend in mid-January 1845, she said, "I do not expect to do much, practically, for the suffering; but having such an organ of expression, any suggestions that are well-grounded may be of use."[22] The question of how "practical" a writer can actually be is an open and much contested problem. Fuller, like Emerson before her, will never wholly satisfy a reader deeply committed to social action. Chevigny made a forceful case when she said, "While New York enlarged the scope of Fuller's social concerns, it was not a place in which she either learned how to analyze social ills or modified her ideological orientation." But Chevigny's disdainful claim that for Fuller "domestic problems invited lame invocations of individualism" overshot the mark in understandable ways.[23] Far from being "lame," Fuller's invocations assumed a sturdy ability to resist the temptations of materialism and a willingness to march against the current of public opinion. Her ability to judge quickly from evidence at hand gave her the latitude to see and understand increasingly "foreign" examples of human misery. Fuller's idea of individualism was central to her thinking; that she conceived of a possible freedom was her first step toward that achievement.

This contribution is not intended to survey the whole of Fuller's several forays into reform, interests that she had revealed in both *Summer on the Lakes* and *Woman in the Nineteenth Century*, which expressed a keen understanding of oppression. Her New York essays included more sympathetic discussions of abolition than she had previously written; she scorned the Mexican War and generally opposed American expansionism. She quoted from European newspapers and commented favorably on radical reform movements. These topics in themselves did not represent the unique experience of New York, but the cosmopolitan, multicultural realities of the city freed her. Her work on the *Tribune* helped her to attain what Chevigny has called "a social cosmopolitanism to match her long-standing cosmopolitanism in literary criticism."[24] Her position on the *Tribune* gave her access to foreign journals; the freedom she had to write on whatever interested her allowed her to explore. There was, however, one body of her social commentary that sprang directly from New York: her observations about the several institutions devoted to the poor, the deranged, and the criminal. New York found her exploring these places for the first time.[25]

Fuller now had a real audience, one that even reached beyond New York City itself.[26] She was clear that her aims were larger than the merely personal, that her writing looked outward in specific ways. Fuller was quite aware of the changed condition she faced in New York, for she thought that in Boston and Cambridge she had "given almost all my young energies to personal relations" and that now she no longer felt "inclined to this, and wish to share and impel the general stream of thought."[27] By early 1845, then,

Fuller had moved from a familiar, smaller city to a "foreign," larger one; she had followed the lead of William Channing, an old friend who suddenly became important to her as he steered her toward new topics; she was employed by a man who valued social reform; she was free to choose her topics; and she had a large, receptive audience. And so she set to work.

At the heart of that enterprise was her ongoing faith in education. Her reviews of musical events continued to reflect her interest in creating a better audience, and her reactions to social reform efforts were attempts to raise the consciousness of her readers, to bring them to "see" what they would rather not see, to end the complacency that made it possible for those who had money to live in the midst of the poverty and wretchedness. As Jeffrey Steele put it, "she shattered the ideological complacency of her readers by modeling an intellectual mobility that freed them from unjust attitudes and values."[28] Corresponding with James Clarke, Fuller made her aim clear: in writing for the *Tribune* she was "well content for the present to aid in the great work of mutual education in this way."[29] She put it directly to her readers in "Our City Charities": "nothing can be done till the right principles are discovered" and "every establishment in aid of the poor should be planned with a view to their education."[30]

When it came to the public and private institutions charged with the care of the outcast part of society, the first fact to acknowledge is that Fuller actually went and looked. She took herself to insane asylums, to prisons, and to houses of refuge. She talked directly with prostitutes who had been convicted. Her actions showed a direct, empathetic interest in those on the margins of urban life, and she used her *Tribune* position as a bully pulpit to educate her readers. Her best-known essay, "Our City Charities," demonstrated how she could at once sympathize with the organized institutions of social reform and at the same time point out to her readers that further actions needed to be taken: the farm school paid too little attention to education; the alms house allowed nursing mothers to be ogled by visitors; the air of the Tombs was suffocating. While she took satisfaction that these institutions existed, she was clear that there needed to be improvements. "There is," she said, "no reason why New-York should not become a model for other States in these things. There is wealth enough, intelligence, and good desire enough, and *surely need enough*."[31]

Fuller focused on individuals' responsibility to extend charity to the helpless. As David Robinson has noted, "Fuller's discussion of progressive reform returns repeatedly to the fundamental principle of the integrity and worth of every human life."[32] Not only did Fuller make her own trips to the institutions, she routinely reviewed the public reports they issued, always taking care to quote voluminously from those parts that described how much individuals could be rescued from their predicaments. What she found in the best efforts, and what she urged from her readers, was a deep sympathy for those unlike her. But too often, instead of that sympathy she found a lust for vengeance: "Punishment is the necessary result of a bad choice," she wrote; it was not "meant by [God] as vengeance, but as an admonition to choose better."[33] Fuller steadfastly opposed the idea that vengeance was absolute; she argued for a sympathy for men and women who found little elsewhere, but she also knew how difficult it was to acquire that sympathy, because most Americans were driven by a fear of criminals. What was needed most was a triumph over that fear, one that she modeled in her essays: "Those who have understood and obeyed the laws," she wrote in a review of the Prison Association in February 1846, "are not afraid to look into the causes that have made their brothers outlaws. They are not afraid that sin will seem less hateful or less noxious, because it may be traced back to hereditary taint, bad education or corrupting influences of a half-civilized state." Here Fuller clearly argued for a causal understanding. Men committed crimes not because they were inherently evil but because of external forces. Change the forces, she argued, and change the man. Her best jailors were "not afraid to do all they can to help a fallen brother man to rise, but [by] putting his life under more healthful conditions both of body and mind."[34] Courage and sympathy were psychological states, not opinions, but they, too, might be open to education. In Philip Gura's words, "Personal ignorance perpetuated the misery seen on the city's streets."[35]

Margaret Fuller had a stubborn faith in benevolence, a faith that served her well as a writer for a major urban newspaper whose audience was large and varied. When she called for donations to support the newly established "Asylum" for discharged female convicts (many of whom had been prostitutes), she revealed the depth of her role in the reform effort. By writing her essay she hoped to end the inertia of those readers who had the money to help. "It has been our happiness," she wrote, "in not a few instances, by merely apprising such persons of what was to be done, to rouse that generous spirit which relieved themselves from ennui, dejection, and a gradual ossification of the whole system, into a thoughtful, sympathetic and beneficent existence."[36] Succinctly put, that was her self-defined role: to apprise and to rouse—that is, to educate and make sympathetic.

The general themes of education and sympathy lead to a discussion of Fuller's second powerful urban experience: her engagement with music. To her, however, "reform" and the fine arts were not separable, for in them the principle of self-reform was at work, especially when she attended musical performances. In a November 1845 review of the violinist Ole Bull, she directly claimed that music was a counterweight to the materialism she so disliked in American life: "We need unspeakably the beautiful arts to animate, expand, and elevate our life which rushes dangerously toward a coarse utilitarianism," she said. "We need them to exhibit the religion of universal love, the harmony in the designs of the Creative Spirit which the coldness of dogmatic theology hides from the heart of the votary." In other words, art, and especially music, had transforming power. It was the office of art "not to pamper the pride of wealth as a part of refined luxury, but to educate the heart and mind of all men by inspiring the purer and gentler emotions, by substituting a sense of spiritual beauty in place of the lust of the eye and the pride of life.[37] As she had argued in the *Dial* in Boston, she declared in the *Tribune:* the arts educate, they have power, they move us in ways that alter our very selves.

Music was perhaps the central satisfaction of Fuller's life in the United States. "Whatever is truly felt has some precious meaning," she wrote to Emerson in 1844, and surely it was in music that Fuller "truly felt" human possibility.[38] In one of her *Tribune* essays she was clear and succinct: "Music is not a mere entertainment, a means of sensuous or sentimental gratification, but the mode of expression of the human soul which penetrates deepest, circulates widest, and soars highest." "There is," she went on, "no branch of culture more important, and in our own country and age there is no influence so desirable, as that of musical expression in its higher forms," and it was in New York that such excellence could be found.[39] Early in her *Tribune* career, she heard the New York Philharmonic and reported that it was "music worthy the admiration of any mind, and performed with a degree of perfection worthy a great metropolis."[40] Her role as teacher of the arts in New York was similar to that in Boston, though in Gotham she focused most often on music: she touted coming performances; she praised excellence and damned mediocrity; she told her readers why she thought music was special; and she continually urged them to support the performers.

Her urban experience of music in both cities centered in part on her by now familiar need to engage other people. Fuller was a deeply social being, a fact that often caused her mental and bodily distress—too much stimulation from people often laid her low. Nevertheless, unlike her encounters with painting and sculpture, her experience of music involved being connected with the performers. People were in front of her making music; her aesthetic and emotional responses were, in part, buoyed by their presence. While she seems to have found her fellow audience members distracting, she engaged with the musicians.

None of the advantages that New York gave Fuller were apparent to her New England friends, many of whom very much regretted her decision to leave Boston. That choice was probably more complicated than we will ever be able to understand, but in part it was a business decision: Greeley could offer her a steady salary, and she would have a large audience for her ideas. Shortly after she settled in, she wrote to a Boston friend, saying simply, "I like living here. All flows freely." But she went on to characterize both Boston and New York in a witty way: "I find I don't dislike wickedness and wretchedness more than pettiness and coldness." Even a few weeks of New York clamor and dirt had shown Fuller that there were possibilities beyond the stiff and correct Boston world she had left. Moreover, she very much liked Greeley, whom she called "the man of the people and of the *Amer[ica]n* people," a man of "genuine excellence," who was "honorable" and "benevolent."[41] Moreover, Greeley's paper could be, in Steven Fink's words, "the tool, not the enemy, of her idealism and a potentially powerful instrument of reform—though the underlying profit motive that actually drove the market forces would always make this a delicate and strained alliance."[42]

It was the *Tribune* that helped Fuller become thoroughly urban, for in it she had an organ to speak as a member of the city to others of its citizens. She and her audience were to become one in her mind. In writing for the *Tribune* she could "address not our neighbor, who forces us to remember his limitations and prejudices, but the ideal presence of human nature as we feel it ought to be and trust it will be." At the same time, the *Tribune* was a national paper that spanned the distance between sections of the country as well as between urban readers and those in smaller towns. It allowed Fuller to "address America rather than Americans." Fuller knew that some of her friends thought newspaper writing was beneath her, but she perceived a more complex and satisfying reality. By the time she wrote her essay on American literature for her *Papers on Literature and Art*, she had arrived at the conclusion that "the life of intellect is becoming more and more determined to the weekly and daily papers," of which, naturally, the *Tribune* was the chief example. She claimed that "this mode of communication is susceptible of great excellence in the way of condensed essay, narrative, [and] criticism." Tellingly, she connected newspaper writing with two of her favorite and fundamental activities: education and conversation. To the population as a whole, the *Tribune* and papers like it could offer "instruction and thought" that could easily be assimilated into the mind. She acknowledged that newspaper writing needed to be scrupulous, because it could not elaborate meanings as could more sophisticated forms of prose. But, she said, "newspaper writing is next door to conversation, and should be conducted on the same principles."[43] This most urban form of writing offered Margaret Fuller a means of continued conversation, an organ to pursue her sympathy for those on the margins, a way to champion the fine arts. It was an ideal form of education. As Leslie Eckel has put it, "Fuller's 'conversational' approach to journalism actually feeds her transnational imagination, for it encourages the productive juxtaposition of ostensibly diverging viewpoints and generates a drive to seek common ground, whether linguistic or political."[44]

Fuller's access to Greeley's *Tribune* allowed her to write rapidly on topics that interested her. To understand the advantage Fuller enjoyed in writing for the *Tribune* one need only remember how long and frustrating was Thoreau's search for the publishers of his two books; he faced even more unhappy experiences with George Curtis and James Russell Lowell, the uncooperative editors of the journals that published his essays on Cape Cod and the Maine woods. The contrast between Greeley, who apparently gave Fuller a free hand in her choice of topics, and John Wiley, the publisher of *Papers on Literature and Art* who censored Fuller, is even more revealing.[45] At the *Tribune* she had to pass through no editorial gauntlet.

Fuller summarized this urban experience succinctly in her "Farewell" essay of July 1846: "Farewell to New-York City, where twenty months have presented me with a richer and more varied exercise for thought and life than twenty years could in any other part of these United States."[46] She had accomplished so much and so well that it was as if, in Barbara Packer's felicitous phrase, "there was some special magic in the city's soil."[47] Fuller's "farewell" was a bit of theater, a necessary and useful one of course, but still a gesture, for she continued to write for the *Tribune* as she moved on to experience very new urban environments, ones that were neither Boston nor New York. As suggested, Fuller very much lived *in* New York, though her stay was a short one.

Her encounters with British and French urban life were quite different, for abroad she was simply a tourist. Or perhaps not so simply: for though Fuller wrote what, on the surface, appeared to be conventional travel essays, she showed yet again how quickly she could respond to something new. For instance, she had seen poverty in New York, but she found that "Poverty in England has terrors of which I never dreamed at home." She observed filth in Edinburgh and "squalid and shameless beggars of Liverpool."[48] She was learning new lessons in human poverty, lessons that made it harder to sustain the notion of self-culture that had informed her previous writing. In Great Britain Fuller heard more about organized social reform, for intermingled with her anticipated accounts of the Roman ruins at Chester and a visit to Wordsworth were Fuller's exploration of the Corn Law controversy and accounts of her conversations with William Johnson Fox and James Martineau, formidable reformers of the time. The smaller cities of England and Scotland had an array of men and women who interested Fuller more than landscapes and monuments. As she wrote to Caroline Sturgis from Paris to summarize her experience in Great Britain, "As soon as I got to England, I found how right we were in supposing there was elsewhere a greater range of interesting character among the men, than with us."[49] Indeed, it was "men" who would come to dominate her travel letters that describe the English and French, and those were men in cities.

London surprised her. She was there during the off-season but found that she profited from the absence of the most affluent and prominent residents: "I am glad I did not at first see all that pomp and parade of wealth and luxury in contrast with the misery, squalid, agonizing, ruffianly, which stares one in the face in every street of London." A natural observer, Fuller had found a new urban center quite unlike Boston and New York, but one that she had no real chance to come to understand. Her London had "hieroglyphics which ages have been inscribing on the walls of this vast palace," marks that called out for interpretation, though she herself could only pass by. "It would be to me," she said, "an inexhaustible studio, and that if life were only long enough, I would live there for years . . . to watch the vast unobserved stream of life."[50] One might say that from her days in New York on, Fuller interpreted the "hieroglyphics" of urban life. Without a doubt the scene in London had captivated her. The Lake Country was nice, but it was London that lived. It had a history to interpret in the light of contemporary problems; it had the people who could stimulate her. For instance, she did encounter Thomas Carlyle, once an intellectual hero of hers, though it was a trying experience, for he allowed no one to talk but himself. More important, at Carlyle's she met Giuseppe Mazzini, who became to her the embodiment of heroic ideals when they were reunited in Rome in 1849. Fittingly, she later went to visit Mazzini at a school for poor immigrant Italian boys so that, for a moment, her ideal of education and her impending discovery of revolution were united in the person of the Italian exile.

After a month in London, Fuller arrived in Paris, which offered her very clear views of artistic excellence, mainly in the person of Elizabeth Félix, best known by her stage name, Rachel. The French capital provided Fuller with a theatrical experience beyond any she had previously known. Not only Rachel, but other actresses gave outstanding performances nightly, and in the smaller theaters Fuller could "see excellent acting and a sparkle of wit unknown to the world out of France."[51] Yet for all her satisfaction with the theater, as well as with the art galleries, Fuller again was taken by the persons she met, who were not only famous but deeply involved in social reform: Pauline Roland, Félicité Robert de Lamennais, Pierre-Jean de Béranger, and, most of all, George Sand, whose novels Fuller had been touting for years. Urban life again meant an array of people, minds of great power and range, individuals accomplished in the arts as well as in political thought.

Fuller was keenly aware of the political ferment just beginning to roil the French population: "While Louis Philippe lives, the gases, compressed by his strong grasp, may not burst up to light; but the need of some radical measures of reform is not less strongly felt in France than elsewhere, and the time will come before long when such will be imperatively demanded." Such a day did come, only months later, when the French king was overthrown in the revolution of 1848. Fuller was keenly attuned to the swirling political thought of the Paris she visited, and she took every opportunity to educate herself about what the French were doing for social reform. In her apostrophe to the city, Fuller turned yet again to a metaphor of education: "Paris! I was sad to leave thee, thou wonderful focus, where ignorance ceases to be a pain, because there we find such means daily to lessen it." The city was, she said, "the only school where I ever found abundance of teachers who could bear being examined by the pupil in their special branches." She had ever been the willing pupil, even in Boston and certainly in New York City, but it was in Paris "where the experience of others might accelerate our progress."[52] It is no wonder that she wrote to William Henry Channing, her guide and fellow New York reformer, that "Art is not important to me now. . . . I take interest in the state of the people, their manners, the state of the race in them. I see the future dawning."[53]

In the nine months between her departure from New York City and her arrival in Rome, Fuller had both extended her previous urban interests and found that if Europe had artistic excellence, it also had new, as yet not wholly understood, possibilities of radical reform. There was no abrupt change in Fuller, but each city had so far added to her growth. Boston had shown her both the possibilities of the fine arts and the opportunities for communal growth of her Conversations; New York had caused her to focus on reforming institutions. London and Paris had heightened her consciousness of poverty and of the possibilities of organized social reform. Urban life had paid off handsomely for Fuller, who in turn was educating her readers all the while.

Her experience of Rome was divided into two unequal parts: for two months, from March to May 1847, she was a conventional tourist. Then, after a four-and-a-half month tour of northern Italy, she returned to Rome, this time by herself, for her traveling companions, Marcus and Rebecca Spring, had gone their way into Germany. For the next eight months, Fuller was a committed resident of Rome, which now included her lover and husband-to-be, Giovanni Angelo Ossoli. After a five-month hiatus in Rieti to give birth to their son, Fuller returned to the city, only to be forced to leave on July 12, 1849, in the wake of the French defeat of the Roman Republic. If one counts her stay in Rieti as part of her Roman life (and in a way it was, for she considered herself an exile from the city), then Margaret Fuller spent twenty months in Rome, almost exactly the same amount of time that she resided in New York. But the nature of that residency was immeasurably different.

When she first arrived in Rome, Fuller did what all tourists do: she saw the sights, for she had "actually touched those shores to which I had looked forward all my life." She gazed at the paintings of Domenichino and Titian, and she visited the studios of American sculptors and painters working in Rome. She attended the Holy Week ceremonies in Saint Peter's, but she also wrote at length about Pope Pius IX, who at the time appeared to be a reforming pope; he was a man in whom the hopes of many were vested. Her letters to the *Tribune* kept up a steady discussion of political developments both on the Italian peninsula and in other European states. She offered her readers a mixture of artistic commentary and political reportage. It was, she said, news of the "old and new," the expected work of travel writing.[54] She was experiencing the urban areas of Italy exactly as she had those of England and France. She was an astute, sophisticated observer who found much in the city to interest her, and she was keenly alive to the increasingly powerful political pressures that she had first felt in France.

After this brief stay she continued her tourism. She went to Venice, twice to Milan and Florence, and to the smaller cities of northern Italy. Again she was traveling, observing, thinking, and reporting. She made it clear that in Milan she gained an entrée into liberal political circles and that she planned to keep up her correspondence with them to assess more accurately what was happening there. At another time that would have been it for Italy. Fuller would have gone on to Germany, which was, after all, her original passion. But instead, she went back to Rome, almost surely to rejoin Ossoli. The city had become something other than a tourist stop; what more that might be she did not yet know.

In the following months her relationship to urban Rome radically changed. Fuller quite understood the limitations of travel. After she settled down she admitted to her readers that she "went through the painful process of sight-seeing, so unnatural everywhere, so counter to the healthful methods and true life of the mind." Tourists never had the time "to think and study," which, she said, was "the natural way in which the mind is lured to cure its defects." Now she had time, and she surely thought and studied. She reported, "I now really live in Rome, and I begin to see and feel the real Rome." Fuller discovered the depths of ancient Rome but also the promise of a modern city. The seat of the Romans whom she so revered in her youth came to life for her: "the innumerable temples glitter, and the Via Sacra swarms with triumphal life once more." There still was a commonplace Rome, one with "taverns, lodging houses, cheating chambermaids . . . and fleas!!" and there was a papal Rome repellant to her American, Republican sensibility, but here was also a potential Rome "where bright hopes gleam now amid the ashes."[55]

In December 1847 Fuller was still able to believe in the possibility that Pius IX would be the leader the Italians needed. Never, she said, had a people before the Romans "showed a better heart than they do in this day of love, of purely moral influence. It makes me very happy," she continued, "to be for once in a place ruled by a father's love, and where the pervasive glow of one good, generous heart is felt in every pulse of every day." Rome was filled with cheerful spirits and holiday pleasure. Fuller walked from the Corso to Saint Peter's "to see the decorations of the streets, but it was impossible. In that dense but most vivacious, various and good-humored crowd, with all best will on their part to aid the foreigner, it was impossible to advance. So I saw only themselves; but that was a great pleasure. There is so much individuality of character here that it is a great entertainment to be in the crowd."[56] It was this Rome to which she committed herself: a city of life and promise, but one that became a city of betrayal and warfare. Pius might fail, but the ideal of Roman freedom endured.

Fuller was well equipped to live in Rome: she was widely read; she read and spoke Italian and French; she had become an apostle of reform; and she possessed a keen analytical mind. She had correspondents in Milan and Florence; she was already a friend of Mazzini's; and the *Tribune* gave her an outlet to organize and develop her ideas. Her essays and letters show that she continually enjoyed her walks through the city. She visited the churches often; she felt the past come alive. Once, in 1849, she wrote to her brother Richard about a stroll on which she passed Keats's house, the Casino of Raphael, "the Villa where Goethe lived when in Rome; afterwards the houses of Claude and Poussin." "Ah," she concluded, "what human companionship here, how everything speaks."[57] She had traded the living friends of Boston for the living presence of the Italian city. While she was now more physically isolated from her loved ones, she was more mentally stimulated by and engaged with the city itself.

More than ever, her *Tribune* articles became her vehicles for teaching her readers. In New York she could assume that she and they shared the city; in Rome she had to describe and analyze a world foreign to her readers. She wanted to illuminate the political realities of the city in the midst of radical changes; she wanted to create sympathy in American readers for the goals of the revolution. This city was rapidly becoming *hers* but it could not be *theirs*. The best Fuller could do was to enlist the aid of her readers to practice their American ideals of democratic freedom by supporting the Roman Republic. The realities of her Roman experience forced themselves into the center of not only her daily life but of her professional ideals. Gone were the appeals to art; gone were the reports of transcendent music. What remained was Fuller's intense sympathy with the oppressed.

Sometimes to make her point, Fuller cast Rome as a theater on whose stage great spectacles were being performed, an image natural to her, given her literary sensibilities. In January 1848 she wrote, "no day, scarcely no hour, has passed unmarked by some showy spectacle or some exciting piece of news." In May, when Pius finally renounced any intention of leading a reform movement, Fuller described the reaction: "A momentary stupefaction received this astounding performance, succeeded by a passion of indignation, in which the words *traitor* and *imbecile* were associated with the name that had been so dear to his people"[58] No dramas staged in Boston or New York could have matched these performances for Fuller.

While she was witnessing and recording all of this she was pregnant, so her identification with Rome was much more complex than any of her readers, whether of her public or her private letters, could imagine. She had identified with what she understood to be the aspirations of the common people in ways that outstripped her experience of New York. She was now ready for radical change. All of this was something of a surprise, for as she had been preparing to leave New York, she bitterly complained, "I do not look forward to seeing Europe now as so very important to me. My mind and character are too much formed. I shall not modify them much but only add to my stores of knowledge."[59] She could not have been more mistaken! At every level, from the most personal to the most intellectual, Fuller changed from 1846 to 1848, and that change was deeply rooted in her urban experience. She found herself in the most ironic position possible: she was both a committed Roman and yet a foreign American. If we accept Charles Capper's conclusion that her marriage to Ossoli occurred in April 1849, we could say that she married Rome before she married him.[60] It was no wonder that she wrote cryptically that the future "is more alive here at present than in America."[61] Rome to her had become "home" as no other city had ever been.

Then, she went into an enforced exile to bear the child. From May 28 to November 8, Fuller lived in the Abruzzi Mountains. Her letters to Ossoli showed that she was almost frantic for news not only of Rome but of other Italian cities, for this was the height of the 1848 European revolutionary period. When she returned to Rome she found a city that was "empty of foreigners" but that was on the verge of outright revolution.[62] To measure how differently Fuller now experienced urban politics, one might contrast her response to the Dorr Rebellion in Providence with her report of the murder of Pelligrino Rossi, the prime minister of the Papal States, as Bell Gale Chevigny has so effectively done.[63] Fuller was repelled by the vulgarity of mobs in Providence, but she came very close to approving of political murder in Rome. Moreover, it was again a moment of high theater for her. She did not actually witness the event, but she narrated it as if she were present: "[Rossi] turned abruptly and received as he did so the fatal blow. It was dealt by a resolute, perhaps experienced, hand; he fell and spoke no word more." Here, as often, Fuller emphasized the crowd, "the people" as she often called them. They acted almost as a chorus in a tragedy: "the sense of the people certainly was that it was an act of summary justice on an offender whom the laws could not reach."[64]

Fuller was not a dispassionate witness, for she was wholly given over to the revolution.[65] She was one of the dissidents, so she no longer wrote as a mere observer; she inhabited the city as she had none before. One of her strategies was to portray Rome as completely safe, even at the height of the revolutionary changes. "I go from one end to the other," she wrote, "where [are] the poorest and most barbarous of the population (barbarously ignorant, I mean) alone and on foot." This was a form of "urban innocence," as opposed to the conventional rural innocence that had so characterized previous American visions of Italy and especially of Rome. Fuller was able, when she wanted, to enter the traditional picturesque genre, as, for example, when she described Garibaldi's departure from a defeated Rome: "Never have I seen a sight so beautiful, so romantic and so sad," she said. She then described the scene in detail: "The sun was setting, the crescent moon rising, the flower of the Italian youth were marshaling in that solemn place. . . . They had all put on the beautiful dress of the Garibaldi legion, the tunic of bright red cloth, the Greek cap, or else round hat with Puritan plume."[66] This was all quite conventional in its perspective and its detail. But it was written by a woman who had lived through a war, who had tended to the wounded as the head of a field hospital, and who had borne a Roman son and was married to a Roman nobleman—a woman, finally, who was on the losing side of the war. In her picturesque portrait there was no hint of a detached observer who sentimentalized the young warriors. These were men who had fought and lost and who were leaving with the hopes of fighting another day.[67]

Fuller's final urban experience in Rome was of war. From the first battle on April 30, 1849, to the Roman capitulation on July 3, Fuller was both witness and participant. Daily she heard the bombs fall; she saw the shots explode. She was, of course, shocked: "War near at hand seems to me even more dreadful than I had fancied it." Unexpectedly the fighting brought out the worst in "the people," in ways she had not anticipated. While there was heroism, "still it breeds vice, too, drunkenness, mental dissipation, tears asunder the tenderest ties." The battles ravaged the beautiful city: "the trees of the Forum are fallen. Rome is shorn of the locks which lent grace to her venerable brow." The carnage was so great that Fuller suddenly "[felt] what I never expected to, as if I might by and by be willing to leave Rome." She stayed, however, until she was forced to leave. On April 30 Princess Cristina Trivulzio di Belgioso appointed her the director of the Fate Bene Fratelli Hospital; here she oversaw the care of the wounded. She lived in daily fear for her husband's life, for he was on the battle lines. She graphically reported the condition of the battlefield after the fighting ended: "A pair of skeleton legs protruded from a bank of one barricade; lower a dog had scratched away its light covering of earth from the body of a man, and discovered it lying face upward all dressed."[68] Urban life had become warfare for Fuller, complete with its horrors; the question of survival was foremost in her mind. The chance conditions of being in that place at that time obliterated her experiences of music and art; collaboration now was military, and reform was revolution.

The overmatched Romans finally capitulated to the French on July 3, and Fuller suddenly found herself in an occupied city. Now her theatrical vignettes were violent. After a priest dared cry "*Viva Pio Nono*" in public, he was overwhelmed as "the populace, roused to fury, rushed on him with their knives," only to be repelled by the French soldiers, bayonets at the ready.[69] This was no place for an American Roman woman and her Republican soldier husband. The Ossolis had to leave, for the city to which Fuller gave her heart, her "home" as no other had been, was closed to them.

The brief epilogue to the story of Margaret Fuller's responses to urban life is something of an anticlimax, for it was to Florence that she and Ossoli fled after leaving Rome. Though one of the great cities of Italy, Florence never appealed to Fuller: "Florence is a kind of Boston," she wrote in October after the Ossolis arrived. "It has not the poetic greatness of the other Italian cities." Great or not, it was a resting place, though miserably cold that winter. Fuller had friends among the Americans living in Florence, and she made new and strong friendships with Robert and Elizabeth Barrett Browning, whose poetry she had long admired. The Ossolis lived a quiet life. She read and wrote her history of the recent Italian revolutions; she played with her son; and she occasionally went to the theater. All in all she quite naturally retreated into a protective quietness. Although Tuscany was, of course, also occupied territory, the Austrian hand lay easier on Florence than did the French on Rome. Everywhere she looked she was reminded of the failure of her hopes. It seemed as if all her pleasures were hounded by memories of Rome. "You will love the Duomo, it is far more divine than St Peters, worthy of Genius, pure and unbroken," she wrote to an American friend. Yet she went on immediately to say, "I adore the Duomo, though no place can now be to me like St Peters, where has been the splendidest part of my life." In writing to Lewis Cass Jr., the American attaché in Rome who had been responsible for getting the Ossolis passports out of the city, Fuller pined for the spring flowers of the Campagna but concluded that "indeed Rome every day is worth ten million Florences."[70]

In the end, Rome had the ultimate triumph: it occupied Margaret Fuller's memory, her emotions, and her imagination. This urban place had seized her in her deepest being, and she was clear-eyed about what its future foretold. In her last *Tribune* essay, written on Epiphany Day 1850, Fuller spoke prophecy: "The seeds for a vast harvest of hatreds and contempts are sown over every inch of Roman ground, nor can that malignant growth be extirpated, till the wishes of Heaven shall waft a fire that will burn down all, root and branch, and prepare the earth for an entirely new culture. The next revolution, here and elsewhere, will be radical."[71] Fuller had traveled far in both body and spirit from the milder form of self-culture that she had first championed in Boston and from her disdainful dismissal of Dorr in Providence. Fuller's urban experiences were the means of her own education, her own self-development, but she turned them into prose that was published in a major American city newspaper for the education of all who would read.

Margaret Fuller was by far the most cosmopolitan of the American Transcendentalists. To be sure, Emerson was welcomed wherever he chose to go, and he circulated in even more august houses in London than Fuller had done. He was the guest of George Bancroft, the American ambassador; he met the best-known writers and thinkers. But Emerson cared little for art and apparently nothing for music. Writing from London to Fuller in Rome, he admitted that he had "studied with much curiosity" the English people but that "my interest already flags." He concluded, "My respect is the more generous that I have no sympathy with [them]."[72] In many ways that succinctly defines Emerson and Fuller's differences: he confessed a lack of sympathy for those he observed, those whom he lumped together as a race of people; she closely identified herself with the outcasts, with specific individuals who had to live on the margins of urban life.[73] I have already quoted the line Fuller used when describing the women at Sing Sing: "Society beats with one great heart," but it is worth noting that she used a slightly modified version of the same line ("Mankind is one / and beats with one great heart") three times in her European dispatches in the *Tribune*.[74] It is that identification that so defined Fuller's empathetic responses to cities. Emerson lived as quietly as he could in Concord; Fuller immersed herself in cities, made them, as she said to her brother Richard, "God's garden," which she assiduously cultivated.

She needed the stimulation of other people; she needed her own immersion in the arts. Her eye had to look, her ear to hear, and her tongue to speak—all of which could be accomplished only in an urban setting. She had no theory of urban life; actually, she thought about that life fairly little. Yet she valued her urban experiences and found in them a fulfillment that neither Waldo Emerson nor Henry Thoreau could ever have understood. Her entwined interests in the fine arts and in social amelioration steadily grew as she moved from one city to another. Finally, of course, the relationship between private and public changed under the pressures of her experiences in Rome. The city that was at first the embodiment of artistic accomplishment became the city of revolution; urban life became an experience of open warfare, and the lesson Fuller learned was that only a radical change was going to free the Italians. She could have learned this nowhere but in Rome and at that time. New York undoubtedly prepared the way, the deep poverty of London moved her consciousness along, but it took Pius IX's failures, the heroism of Giuseppe Mazzini, the bomb blasts she heard, and, above all, the blood of the wounded men she nursed to show Fuller what "reform" must finally be. There is evidence in her final *Tribune* dispatches that her faith in individualism shifted toward an idea of collective action. William Channing, himself a moderate socialist, had first led her away from an Emersonian individualism, but her experiences in Rome were more profound: "I believed before I came to Europe in what is called Socialism," she wrote from Florence, "as the inevitable sequence to the tendencies and wants of the era, but I did not think these vast changes in modes of government, education and daily life, would be effected as rapidly as I now think they will, because they must."[75]

At every step of her journey Fuller used her writing as her means of educating her fellow citizens about their common responsibilities, both public and private. In an 1846 letter to Sam and Anna Ward written in New York City, she reviewed her life and noted her early disappointment at not having gone to Europe in 1836: "I do feel that I have tried to make the best of life in every sense I could. Many sweet fruits has it brought me . . . and a liberal communion with the woful struggling crowd of fellow men."[76] That crowd was most visible to her in cities, and her communion was deepest when she shared their struggling. For good or for ill, cities meant an accumulation and concentration of money and people. Those facts poisoned the mind of many an imaginative writer, but not always; the same conditions enabled others to thrive, and Fuller was one of these. The character of cities made it hard for one to be left alone, to focus one's mind, to concentrate one's powers, as Thoreau and Emerson found, but as Fuller discovered, in equal measure cities could provide stimulations that opened up the imagination. Scholars have become so accustomed to accepting the Thoreauvian model of "Transcendentalism" that they underestimate the fact that, taken as a whole, the very large majority of writers and thinkers who are called "Transcendental" worked out of cities.[77] This should not be a surprise, for, after all, where one lives is in large part a result of how one makes a living. Fuller could not have supported her family had she stayed in Groton; both Ellery Channing and Bronson Alcott blighted their families by their devotion to rural simplicities. Emerson, though he lived in Concord, moved among cities for his entire career as a lecturer. None of his contemporaries presented so much to so many urban audiences. He was hardly oblivious to the possibilities of speaking to this group.

Fuller's work points us toward some conception of "urban Transcendentalism" that bears further scrutiny. This contribution has argued for her importance in three urban frames of reference: conversation; criticism of the arts, most specifically music; and social reform. It is reasonable to claim not only that Fuller excelled in all three but that she stood virtually at the head of the first two. Transcendentalism rode on a sea of talk; the prevalence of sermons, lectures, and "Conversations" points to the oral nature of the movement. There were differences among them, however: while sermons and lectures were in fact essays yet to be printed, Conversations were quite different. They led to no written artifact, and thus they are evanescent and hard to estimate. Fuller was fortunate in having her scribes, but if one turns, say, to Bronson Alcott's Conversations or to the later Boston meetings of John Weiss's Radical Club, one comes up short, for no one knows what was said or how the participants responded. The best one can do is to observe that people did pay for formal Conversations; they returned to club meetings; and the spoken word must have had its influences. Clearly, here the concentration of participants was central: no audience meant no Conversation.

Fuller's criticism of the fine arts had no rival save that of her friend John Dwight, and his work came somewhat later. As suggested earlier, books were available and easily transportable, but paintings and sculptures were not, even though there were published reproductions (always in black and white, one might remember). Symphonic music did not reach rural areas, nor did the flow of native and immigrant performers. One had to be in the city to see and hear. Part of Fuller's success lay in her understanding that readers wanted and needed commentaries on the fine arts. She trusted her impressions and thoughts, but she equally trusted her audience and knew that they valued a broader perspective than they would otherwise receive. In part, Fuller's criticism of the fine arts was an aspect of her larger cosmopolitan agenda, for her writing and that of the Transcendentalists in general was always on the attack against provincialism. Just as foreign books were important—German biblical criticism as well as Anglo-German philosophy underlay much of the assault on conventional Christianity, for instance—continental music was too. An unwillingness to be self-satisfied about their American culture and a drive always to discover new possibilities of human fulfillment were implicit in Fuller's work as well as that of her peers.

As social reformer, Fuller came late to an understanding of the squalor that cities bred. Their concentration of wealth inevitably resulted in a concentration of poverty, hunger, and disease. When she finally saw New York's poor, she did her best to make them present to her readership. Perhaps more important, when she was confronted with political repression in Italy, she never flinched. She combined analysis with testimony, judgment with sympathy, and finally a complete identification of her American selfhood with the human aspirations of the Romans whom she joined.

In each of Fuller's explorations, the city acted as a force to cause her reactions. She was not merely living in a city; she was responding to its opportunities. Unlike her friend William Henry Channing, she did not start a "Union" church whose mission was social amelioration; unlike another friend, Lydia Francis Child, she did not edit an abolitionist newspaper. She did, however, accomplish something more subtle and audacious: she brought her readers together into what one would now, perhaps too glibly, call a "virtual audience." She had, after all, acted the role of an audience both literally and symbolically.[78] She sat before Ole Bull in New York City, before Mazzini in Rome, and she watched the unfolding tragedy of the French occupation of the Italian city. She was, in both senses of the word, a "witness," for she not only saw, she testified—to the failures among individuals but also to their successes, to destruction but also to creation. Perhaps most of all Margaret Fuller was a witness to the succession of human visions that rose from the ever-shifting, ever-shaping experiences of living in and for that "woful struggling crowd of fellow men."

10

CIRCLES AROUND GEORGE SAND

Margaret Fuller and the Dynamics of Transnational Reception

Charlene Avallone

Scholarship on Margaret Fuller tends to stress her affinity for George Sand, finding Fuller's responses to the author unique and radical. Reader response studies, by contrast, maintain that acts of reading are shaped by readers' situation in interpretive communities and by interpretive approaches that vary historically and diversely comprehend codes of aesthetic, moral, and social significance in texts.[1] Yet Fuller's reading of Sand, like the meeting of the two women in Paris, appears more often cast as an exceptional face-to-face encounter of two Romantic geniuses, feminist sisters, or acolyte and hero. Howard Meyer long ago cautioned against representing Fuller as exceptional in her "approval and appreciation of the work of George Sand."[2] Scholars have also set aside the dramatic style of expressing affinity, evinced in Russell Durning's characterization of Fuller with her "enthusiasm for French literature" as a lone "voice crying in the wilderness" of New England, or Perry Miller's contention that Fuller "deliberately jeopardized her entire plea for woman suffrage by citing George Sand's life as a triumphant example of female emancipation." But the underlying assumption of Fuller's cultural transcendence continues, in feminist as well as Romantic critical paradigms.[3] A historicist approach to her reception of Sand reveals ways in which Fuller's response more complexly participated in reception circles on both sides of the Atlantic. This approach develops a model of reading thoroughly embedded in local and transatlantic dialogue, a model that might be extended to analyze Fuller's response to Goethe and other writers.

Fuller began recording her private responses to Sand's fiction and journalism in 1839 and circulated her notes among friends.[4] As a professional journalist at the *New-York Tribune* some half-dozen years later, she published literary criticism of Sand's writing. In the interim, in "The Great Lawsuit" (1843) and *Woman in the Nineteenth Century* (1845), Fuller's review of the international discussion of the woman question assessed Sand's title to a leadership role in the progressive movement. After meeting Sand in 1847, Fuller returned to writing only privately about her work. From the beginning, Fuller's considerations occurred within a transnational discussion already in progress.

As Fuller began reading Sand, the premier French critic Charles-Augustin Sainte-Beuve was poised to declare the writer the greatest literary sensation of the previous decade.[5] Sand was by much reckoning at the center of la jeune France, the progressive movement that emerged after the July Revolution of 1830 to become central in the intellectual life of Paris, the acknowledged heart of the Atlantic cultural world.[6] Sand's reputation had eddied out internationally from French reviews that inaugurated a complex critical dynamic of appreciation, attacks on her unconventional thought and "dangerous tendencies," and advocacy prompted by those attacks that, as her first English biographer observes, "enlarged her fame abroad."[7] On the appearance of Sand's first solo novels, *Indiana* and *Valentine*, in 1832, Sainte-Beuve had endorsed her achievement, his endorsement as weighty as "a nod from the Almighty."[8]

British journalists, too, gave favorable notices. Five early *Athenaeum* pieces, despite reservations about the morality of her life or texts, culminated in their crowning Sand in 1834 "the most gifted and most original female writer of her country and times, a sort of female Jean-Jacques Rousseau," then in 1837 simply "the greatest writer" in France.[9] John Wilson Croker's infamous 1836 attack in the Tory *Quarterly Review* met immediate opposition from the *Westminster* and from the *Revue des deux mondes*, two journals Fuller often read. In 1839 not only did Joseph Mazzini in the *Monthly Chronicle* again answer the *Quarterly*'s "anathema"; the more conformist Henry Chorley reacted with a "rehabilitation" of Sand in the *British and Foreign Review*.[10] That same year, William Makepeace Thackeray, writing for American readers as a correspondent from Paris where "Madame Sand is a god," anticipated that "many" of them had already read her latest work, *Spiridion*. Even as he hoped that the German-influenced "transcendentalism," epitomized by this "parable of the downfall" of Christianity would "take no hold in your country," Thackeray assumed that "most" readers shared his appreciation of Sand's "wonderful power of language," which made her "the best writer . . . now in France," the most "eloquent" woman ever.[11]

Not long before Thackeray wrote his review and Fuller made her notes, a circle of progressive reviewers in Britain had begun forming around Sand. After Sainte-Beuve questioned the competence of foreigners (such as Croker) to fathom the morality of contemporary French literature, several reviewers instructed their English audience that the writing of la jeune France called for expectations and methods of reading that were different from those applied to English works.[12] Sand's art, Mazzini observed, did not encode its "lesson of morality" in the style of either classical tragedies, which (he believed) plot the punishment of evil, or the novels of Maria Edgeworth, which plot the rewarding of virtue.[13] Unlike English writers who fabricate "almost impossible fictions" to didactic ends, George Reynolds explained, the modern "French author paints the truth in all its nudity."[14] Journals that Fuller mentioned frequently, such as the *Westminster* and the *Foreign Quarterly Review*, similarly counseled revised codes of reading. The *Westminster* urged more careful reading and translation, hoping to "lead those capable of drawing their own moral ... to look a little closer at French fiction" for an "antidote to the showy morality" of English novels. Close reading would establish that "it is against, and not for license, that Sand is contending." Her fiction, along with the philosophical and political writings of Young France, chronicled the search for "a new and more comprehensive form of religion"; the French romance had become a vehicle for the revelation of the soul and the ideal.[15] An English reader, according to John Stuart Mill, could best "understand" fiction such as Sand's *Leone Leoni* not as a conventional moral lesson or work of art, but rather as French readers would, as the expression of "an idea, ... some form of real life, or some conception respecting nature or society."[16]

This line of recuperative interpretation climaxed in the mid-1840s in the *Foreign Quarterly Review*, where George Henry Lewes denounced Croker, recommended Mazzini's "profound article," and affirmed that a critical reader inquiring into the "morality" of a Sandian text would discover nothing like "sermons in the style of Hannah More." Because Sand felt "bound to utter what she thought the truth, . . . in her own way," and a writer is "accountable, as [William Ellery] Channing well said, for the uprightness, not the rightness, of his doctrine," any immoral "tendency" of her texts should be understood as mistaken "convictions," not a flouting of "generally received" principles. The moral in a work of art, Lewes argued, citing Hegel, finally depends on the inference of a reader.[17]

By the time Fuller articulated her views privately, the progressive reception circle around George Sand extended across the Atlantic in Americans' published response to the French author. Samuel Ward, like transatlantic progressives, argued against applying conventional moral "codes of England and America" in reading modern continental fiction.[18] Characters in Henry

Wadsworth Longfellow's *Hyperion*, even as they professed not to admire la jeune France themselves, agreed that Sand and others should be read from the perspectives of their own national culture.[19] When Ward promoted his friend's novel as marking a shift in American literary values, he situated *Hyperion* in a modern tradition of ideal romance developed by Sand and Goethe and best appreciated by readers who sought poetry and thought, not sensation and adventure.[20] In Fuller's Boston Unitarian circle, Samuel Osgood in the *Christian Examiner* more cautiously negotiated the reputation of modern writers by appropriating the term "Satanic," not to define a "School" as Robert Southey famously used it, but rather to describe one of two "tendencies" in "many minds." A reader's work, Osgood implied, included discriminating between the "Satanic" tendency that led toward "rebellion and lawlessness" and a "nobler" one that "attained an independence . . . and a liberty, . . . founded upon law." Osgood preferred eclectic philosophers such as Victor Cousin and Théodore Jouffroy, yet his caution against "abandoning the movement party" in regressive "worship of the past" indicted readers who "throw aside . . . George Sand."[21]

Fuller's response to la jeune France entered the dynamic of Sand's reception in complicated ways, implicated in circles on both sides of the Atlantic. Her epistolary criticism of Sand, published posthumously in the *Memoirs*, credited her introduction to the movement writers to "absurd reports of English reviewers."[22] But English reviews also informed Fuller's opinion in positive ways. The *London and Westminster* article on journalist Armand Carrel that she admired in this early criticism, for example, conveyed ideas similar to those she expressed here: that French intellect had achieved greater maturity with the movement writers, exemplified by George Sand and "eclectic philosophy," and that France, taught by England, had some hope of progress toward equality under law.[23] Fuller's endeavor to keep abreast of current opinion could have led her to notices and translations of French writers not only in the *Westminster* and the *Foreign Quarterly*, but also in other periodicals, such as the *Quarterly Review* and local journals, including the *New England Magazine* and *North American Review*.[24] Thus Fuller likely knew some part of the transnational debate over Sand and her circle. Since some of the Sand texts that Fuller reported having read were then available only as serials in the *Revue des deux mondes*, she likely encountered there some of the French perspectives on that debate, as well as writings by other movement authors. At the same time, Fuller participated in a local circle that discussed la jeune France in conversation, correspondence, and print.

Along with Osgood, Orestes Brownson, George Ripley, John S. Dwight, and her close friends James Freeman Clarke and William Henry Channing,

Fuller figured in this liberal Unitarian cluster who extended the notice of French progressives and stimulated the sanction of Sand. Literary histories often submerge this group, with its particular interest in liberalizing American thought through engagement with modern continental literature, in the larger Transcendental Club. Furthermore, since Octavius Brooks Frothingham first synthesized the critical paradigm of Transcendentalism, histories have often depreciated both the status of this circle in the movement and its interest in French writing and socialism.[25] Although this coterie could not provide the financial support Fuller sought, to undertake "translations from the modern French novelists," it did encourage her to become more cosmopolitan and opened venues for Fuller's first professional critical publications: in the *Western Messenger*, edited variously by Clarke, Osgood, and Channing; in the *Boston Quarterly Review*, edited by Brownson; and in the translation series Specimens of Standard Foreign Literature, edited by Ripley.[26] The mediation of this circle is visible in Fuller's reading of Sand, from her first contacts recorded in what Ralph Waldo Emerson called "private folios" circulated among friends, to her professional reviews at the *Tribune*, which pronounced Sand "the best living prose writer."[27]

Brownson is significant as the early and most avid promoter of French progressivism before his conversion to Catholicism in 1842. He published a series of reviews and pamphlets, often including extensive translations, that disseminated the thought of the Saint-Simonians, Félicité Robert de Lamennais, Cousin, and Pierre Leroux in particular. If, as Brownson proclaimed, by 1834 "everybody [had] heard of the Saint-Simonians," it was due in part to his publicizing their "new Christianity," universal church, and understanding of their leader as "the type of an eternal progress toward perfection" that was "prophetic of the advance of humanity."[28] An 1838 review of *Affaires de Rome* and *Paroles d'un croyant* recognized Lamennais's thought as particularly "kindred" with progressive Unitarian thinking and social action in Boston. Brownson explained that Lamennais, in championing liberty against absolutism, interpreted the religious principle of spiritual equality under God to entail social and political equality. Spiritual equality takes "form" as "liberty," both in "the holiest and most imprescriptible laws of human nature" and in the organization of society and the state in "free association" within the bonds of moral law.[29] Against the despotism that used religion to maintain hierarchy and reserved knowledge and power for an elite, Lamennais endorsed Christianity as a revolutionary force and described society as progressive, ever advancing toward an ideal of perfectibility. Brownson approved Lamennais's interpretation of the Bible and Christianity as social code; "perfection," albeit impossible as a final achievement, was an important "duty" of society even more so than of individuals. In the United States, where political liberty was achieved, Brownson urged, the church had an obligation to preach democracy and social equality "to create a heaven here."[30]

Ripley's early promotion of the "progress of religious thought" in France, instanced by political liberal Benjamin Constant and popular writing, focused more on "religious sentiment" as a psychological verity independent of religious form.[31] Ripley and William Henry Channing published translations of Constant, Cousin, and Jouffroy in the Specimens of Standard Foreign Literature series in hopes of advancing eclecticism not only as a method of distilling elements of truth from all systems of philosophy but also as itself a philosophical system to counter materialism and skepticism. Their eclecticism viewed religious belief, moral law, and the perception of absolute truth as rooted in human psychology, in "some primary law" of the mind, as Channing put it, or, as Ripley did, in "the everlasting sentiments of the human heart."[32]

Ripley's statement of the aim of his translation series summed up another underlying interest in French progressive writers that he shared with Channing, Brownson, Fuller, and their circle. The editor and the translators sought to import modern continental classics in the interest of American cultural independence from England, a transnational project in support of enhanced nationalism. Americans, Ripley argued, "need[ed]" French idealism to reform politics, industry, and society, as well as religion and literature. Brownson's review of Ripley's first volume in the series stressed sociopolitical reform: French writers, the most "democratic," could aid in renovating "the faults of our own democracy."[33] Around the time that Fuller wrote her first observations on la jeune France, Channing took to the public platform with a speech endorsing the "free inquiry" that led Lamennais, Henri de St. Simon, and Charles Fourier to agree on the need for "radical reform," even as they proposed different means to attain it.[34] And, as evinced in Osgood's *Christian Examiner* essay, the views of perfectibility circulating within this circle, resonant with philosophical, psychological, religious, social, and political significance, that is to say, with French Transcendentalism, along with an emergent discourse of the "liberty of the law," were beginning to be linked with George Sand.

Fuller would have read some of this discussion and heard more from this circle in social parlors, in meetings of the Transcendental Club, and elsewhere. She agreed with the priority of renovated faith, invested in an ideal of perfectibility, and employed the discourse of a "law of liberty." After conversing with Ripley about the New Christianity, she concurred, "Xty [*sic*] needs to be reproduced" and appreciated that "every speculation which is founded on a sighing after perfectibility and a love for humanity lets in some light." Still she questioned the means: "Unitarianism is not exactly the thing—nay—nor St Simonianism—nor any other yet discovered ism."[35] Nor did Lamennais, despite his own lack of commitment to any Utopian "ism," afford "exactly the thing"; Fuller later publicly denied any personal "influence" from the man she privately acknowledged as the great "Apostle of Democracy" on the assumption that the "circumstances" of her national and religious background preempted anything of value he taught.[36] Yet Fuller committed to her circle's nationalist appropriation of continental writing. Her contribution to Ripley's translation series not only held up Schiller and Goethe as models that "we" might "learn from the Germans habits of more liberal" critical reading but also desired lessons in taste from "another school," the French, while as a professional critic she advised Americans on how to read George Sand for "valuable suggestions" for the nation.[37] Her initial interpretation of Sand, what Emerson labeled "criticism on her recent readings" directed "to an earlier friend," focused on other ideas of French Transcendentalism current in her circle.[38]

Fuller's initial remarks appear to have been part of an ongoing exchange with William Henry Channing, in which jeune France writers figured in the discussion of their own circle's reform and literary labors, with Fuller citing "your Jouffroy" to Channing and he encouraging her to emulate George Sand.[39] Channing, similar in "temperament" and "in perpetual quest," was the most important figure in Fuller's growing interest in reform, as Joan von Mehren demonstrates.[40] After Channing's "friendly intimacy" with Fuller intensified in the summer of 1839, around the time that she first read Sand, he assured her, "'You shall write nobler books than ever George Sand could conceive,'" and he advised Fuller to take as the subject for a novel "the growth of her own mind."[41] The religious growth of the mind was precisely the subject Fuller found to be of "unutterable interest" in reading *Spiridion*.[42]

Fuller reported reading the "religious sentiment" out of the first Sand texts she perused, particularly *Spiridion*. In Sand and other French writers she found parallels to her own circle's religious struggle with the "enigmas" of free will, necessity, and compensation and to the dilemmas that circle posited between emotions and intellect and between spiritual and active life. She also discovered similar "practical optimism" and even greater immediate "hope for the masses" among the French. Fuller found the larger "scope and bearing" of Sand's fiction difficult to discern, however, more than that of the readily explicable Wilhelm De Wette, who commanded the interest of Osgood and Clarke but whose *Theodor*, like *Spiridion* a narrative of religious crisis, Fuller put aside as insufficiently compelling in either thought or art. Fuller's own "unutterable interest" fixed rather on what she labeled the "Eclectic course" of the monk Alexis in *Spiridion*.[43] She interpreted his spiritual career in terms of Channing's and Ripley's explanations of the eclecticism of Jouffroy and Cousin. Alexis's quest (through reading the church fathers, heretical and Protestant writers, classical Western and Eastern philosophy, and the skeptical thought of his own eighteenth century) resulted not in any distillation of truth and morality, however, but rather in illness, a trope for the "despair" Fuller noted in the work, and in atheism. Yet Sand depicted the sense of moral law (*"un sentiment de justice"*) as enduring in Alexis's heart, and his faith was redeemed through mystical visions of the divine in nature and of the divine thought of perfectibility in all creation. Fuller appreciated that Alexis's rebirth came through the direct perception of sacred meaning in nature and of beauty in the arts, but her summary omitted an earlier insight crucial in his regeneration, that friendship was more valuable than genius, that humanity was made for love.[44]

As Fuller puzzled at Sand's meaning, reading *Spiridion* twice, the author of the fiction slid into "these persons in France," and Fuller thought that reading Lamennais or Eugène Lerminier would aid her not only in comprehending the "scope and bearing of this book" but in understanding "what they all want or intend." Made "more curious than ever" by this encounter with Sand, Fuller "beg[ged]" her addressee to send any copy of *Les paroles d'un croyant* he might encounter, a work that she appears to have believed would help to clarify parallels between "the faith of some of my friends here" and the French.[45] Her supposition that Lamennais's text could help to explain Sand and them "all" suggests that Fuller was making connections between her reading of Sand and her circle's discussion of other writers, even ones she appears not to have read much. Her mention of Lerminier with Lamennais here suggests that her cosmopolitan reading also may have introduced her to the debate in the *Revue des deux mondes* between Lerminier and Sand. There Sand answered the philosopher's criticism of Lamennais's *néo-christianisme* with a defense of the Abbé's religious principles, which she claimed as her own, including his democratic gospel, based on the words of Jesus alone, of perfectibility, human equality, spiritual immortality, and infinite progress toward a heaven on earth. Alternatively, Fuller could have read the sarcastic report of their debate in the *Foreign Quarterly Review*, which attacked all Modern Liberalism as blasphemy, especially Unitarianism, with its views of marriage more iconoclastic than those of the revolutionary Lamennais.[46] Whatever her sources, Fuller, having only enough context to arouse curiosity, shifted to a biographical explanation of the astonishing "life of thought" in Sand's work, adopting an interpretation that has prevailed into our own time: "She must know it through some man."[47]

Another fragment (labeled "George Sand, Again" in the *Memoirs* and dated 1839), also undertakes a biographical interpretation, this one informed by the moral discourse of Fuller's circle. The law inscribed in the moral sentiment, as Channing and Jouffroy understood it, is a law of liberty, for to act morally an agent must have freedom to choose the good. Yet at the same time, this liberty is "founded upon law," as they understood it and as Osgood described the ethical "tendency" of liberty in modern writers, including Sand. For the moral ideal operating in that sentiment, according to Jouffroy, "is obligatory and impersonal, that is, it has the authority of a law" making it "a law of obligation" that sways volition.[48] Fuller thus traced in *Les sept cordes de la lyre*, *André*, and *Jacques* "the same high morality of one who had tried the liberty of circumstance only to learn to appreciate the liberty of law, to know that license is the foe of freedom." From this reading, she concluded that Sand "had cast aside the slough of her past life." In *Lettres d'un voyageur*, however, Sand's autobiographical narrator's "bewailing" circumstances appeared to Fuller to abdicate moral responsibility.[49]

In yet another fragment, dated September 1839, Fuller claimed some success in interpreting a wider reading of the writers of la jeune France. As she read more and discerned relations between this school and Germany, she felt that she began "to divine the meaning of St. Simonianism, Cousinism, and the movement which the same causes have produced in belles-lettres." But she refrained from jotting what she called her "petty impressions of the movement writers," as "these things only glimmer at present upon me." Her impressions of Sand recorded in the previous fragments are the exception. Confidently, Fuller spelled out of Sand's writings—six titles in all—the significance of themes, characters, and moral; stylistic achievement equal to that of Rousseau; connections not only to other "movement" writers but also to Fuller's own experience and spiritual quest; and parallels to characters in her social circle. Fuller "loved" some of Sand's idealism.[50] Still, she preferred the fiction of a forerunner of the movement, Alfred de Vigny, a preference maintained in her professional criticism, which promoted his "manners, thoughts, and feelings" as those "of a cosmopolite gentleman" in contrast with the work of Sand and other iconoclasts.[51] In Fuller's first published responses, the *Dial* essay and its revision as *Woman in the Nineteenth Century*, Sand once more came off unfavorably in comparison to other writers, as Fuller, in the context of shifts in Sand's reputation, again took up issues of perfectibility and the liberty of law.

Soon Fuller recorded her private responses, her circle began to show a more extended public notice of Sand. Brownson, liberal enough to appreciate everything about Sand but her gender politics, commenced a paean to *Spiridion* and its author (in reaction to Croker's "denunciations") before turning his review into a rant against the women's movement. Sand's novel, with the same aim of tracing the progress from doubt to faith as his own *Charles Elwood*, merited study for its illustration of "religious speculation among the popular writers in France" and the "growing influence" of Saint-Simonians.[52] Sand's "powerful genius," "aesthetic and moral merits," "social democracy," and aspiration made her "in many respects the first and best of the authors of modern French Literature," as well as his own personal favorite. *Spiridion* deserved "a place in Mr. Ripley's series." But Brownson devoted the bulk of his pages to dismissing as "ultraism" the "nonsense" about women's "lot" and rights that he read in Sand's fiction and biography, as well as in the rising women's movement around him. Brownson's attack on "'Woman's Rights' people" through his review of Sand marks an emergent animosity that cut across the political, aesthetic, and moral spectra of the anglophone response to the writer.[53]

The previous year, Croker's parting shot at Sand in the *Foreign Quarterly Review* had warned against her advocacy of the "absolute emancipation of woman from all moral and social obligations" on the grounds of its spreading "contagion" to Britain; Christianity already guaranteed "equality . . . compatible with [woman's] destiny." Soon, the conservative Unitarian Francis Bowen, with whom Brownson seldom publicly agreed, also attacked Sand's revolutionary uniting of "fierce attachment to the doctrines of liberty and equality" with "the wildest form of . . . doctrine respecting the rights of woman." The liberal George Henry Lewes, in his 1844 essay that marked Sand's moral renovation in England, argued against notions that she "is riotous in favour of the emancipation of women"; yet even Lewes admitted some immoral "tendency" in "her fondness for making women independent of society."[54] Fuller's first public reading of Sand reflected this shift in the transatlantic and local reception of the author.

"The Great Lawsuit" addresses the destiny of human perfection through an enlarged ideal or "law" of woman's liberty and equality, which Fuller situated as part of a "universal, unceasing revelation" epitomized in Matthew's gospel: "Be ye perfect," the "text" from which all "deep-searching influence" was to be preached. The essay depreciates the extensive contribution to the women's movement of Sand's writing, describing her as "a woman whose existence better proved the need of some new interpretation of woman's rights, than anything she wrote." Rather than enrolling Sand among the "shining names of famous women" authors or endorsing her as a model of emancipation, Fuller classed her among the "outlaw[ed]," even while protesting the "bonds" of femininity that created such classification.[55]

Out of more than a dozen available works by Sand, Fuller approved only of *Mauprat*. Fuller read the novel as a morality tale of the power of woman's love to reform men, "depicting one raised . . . from the depths of savage sensualism to a moral and intellectual life."[56] Fuller's estimate was not far from that of the conservative Bowen, who also singled out the novel as Sand's "least exceptionable" work, "suffering hardly a taint from the writer's erratic . . . philosophy of woman's nature."[57] Fuller warned Sand to reform herself if she would revolutionize society; the lives of "those who would reform the world . . . must be unstained by passionate error; they must be severe lawgivers to themselves."[58] In revising the essay into the book-length *Woman in the Nineteenth Century*, Fuller added, "their liberty must be the liberty of law" and again affirmed the "right" of society "to outlaw" those who protest until "she has revised her law."[59] Fuller's revision further interpreted *Mauprat* as evidence that Sand was turning from criticism of "bad institutions" to envision "that the only efficient remedy must come from individual character," a reading that inflected Sand's thematics with the priorities of Fuller's Unitarian and Transcendentalist circles.[60] Fuller also added references to *Simon* and *Indiana*, but only as instances of a moral deficiency in their "author," not as earlier explorations of issues that Fuller also broached, such as the double standard of sexual morality and inequalities maintained by marriage law, nor as an earlier declaration of a woman's religious self-dependence.[61]

Of course, Sand was not outlawed by "society," as Fuller remarked when she later encountered Parisian opinion and met Sand. Rather, as Julie Ellison notes, Fuller, with her "moderate ethos," routinely balanced her considerations of rebellion with an "insistence on . . . the acceptance of existing moral judgments" and here exhibited what Ellison judges to be a "surprisingly explicit need for social integration and . . . acceptance of middle-class manners."[62] Not only did Fuller shift the code "liberty of law" away from her circle's emphasis on freedom of conscience to mean instead conformance to local social conventions, she also misrepresented Sand as one "who would trample on every graceful decorum and every human law for the sake of a sincere life." Other additions to the essay favor the reform "spirit" of Eugène Sue, who, unlike Sand in Fuller's view, perceived "what [women] need, and what causes are injuring them." Yet other additions find more promise of the perfectibility of humanity through woman in the mystical theory of Saint Simon and the progressive theory of Fourier, valuable not for his system of socialist association but explicitly for his vision of perfectibility, "what man can be." These additions, along with Fuller's generalization that "in reform, as in philosophy, the French are the interpreters to the civilized world," suggest that again she was thinking with her progressive circle about Sand and la jeune France, if in her own way.[63]

In the early 1840s, that circle expanded from its Cambridge center and acquired a significant new member. Ripley and Dwight moved to Brook Farm; Channing and Fuller took to visiting it; and Francis Shaw moved to the edge of the farm, where he translated three of Sand's novels: *Consuelo*, *La comtesse de Rudolstadt* (as *The Countess of Rudolstadt*), and *Le compagnon du tour de France* (as *The Journeyman Joiner*), the first two serialized in the *Harbinger* between 1845 and 1847.[64] The circle's new focus on socialism was reflected in Fuller's gradually enlarged appreciation of Sand and socialist writers. William Henry Channing, a self-described "confirmed Socialist" after a religious crisis in 1841, recalled discussing Associationism with Fuller during this time. Fuller, "always more enthusiastic than philosophical," he believed, valued the ideal of association, but "questioned" Fourierist "means." Although she desired "as earnestly as any Socialist 'Liberty and Law made one in living union'" and had "faith that [such] an era was coming," she did not commit herself either to any systematic social philosophy, such as Fourier's, or to collective action.[65] In 1844 Channing's editorials in the *Present*, detailing the progress of "heaven on earth," appropriated insights from Fuller's writing, as well as from the texts of Lamennais and Leroux, in describing "the Great Associative movements of the age."[66] Channing also took Fuller to Fourierist conventions, as Brook Farm was transformed into a phalanx. Yet even as Fuller read Fourier and heard him discussed; even as she rejoiced to see "liberty of law" replace freakish freedom at the farm; even as Shaw on her leave taking for New York confided in her "his 'excellent plans' for aiding socialist reform"; even as Channing brought her into close, material contact with severe economic inequalities on her remove to New York; and even as she circulated there among others interested in Associationism, notably Horace Greeley and Albert Brisbane, Fuller remained a "sympathetic" fellow traveler rather than a committed associationist.[67] Fuller's sympathy with association grew in her interactions with others in her circle, however, and her interest in the Romantic socialism of Sand and other French writers increased in tandem.

By 1845, when Fuller undertook professional reviews of Sand, the liberalizing effects of this circle, combined with changes in Sand's writing and international reception, showed in Fuller's increasing appreciation. Although *Le compagnon du tour de France* was published in 1840, it had not as quickly generated the wide reception typical of Sand's work, for the *Deux mondes*, the internationally distributed journal where much of Sand's work appeared in serial, refused to circulate such an iconoclastic combination of "socialism and evangelical egalitarianism."[68] Instead, Sainte-Beuve's celebration of Sand in that review's March 1840 issue as the most original new writer of the past decade, combined with the 1842 publication of her *Oeuvres complètes* and the positive British reception of her "calmer" *Consuelo* while still in serial, made Sand an unparalleled transnational literary celebrity by the time Fuller joined the *Tribune* staff.[69] Only during the midforties did critical attention shift to the socialism in Sand's writings. This shift in the focus of Sand's reputation coincided with Fuller's changing views at the *Tribune*. As Susan Belasco demonstrates, upon assuming the role of professional critic, Fuller at first restricted her commentary to aesthetic concerns, only gradually expanding to include social issues.[70] "French Novelists of the Day" accordingly presented a method of reading the best literature as the best defense against the imported fiction that Fuller reported Americans devoured, even as "good people" regretted its "corrupting . . . our youth."[71]

Fuller imagined the audience she addressed at the *Tribune* as "our nation," potential "translator and buyer" of French novels about which they knew little. She undertook to inform them about the novelists whom she believed to be preeminent in France, their critical reputation there, and the way to "assimilate" their work without "infection." The essay promoted a reading method that valued authors' literary talents while it could "understand" national "circumstances" that environed writers and (on the English model of Elizabeth Barrett [Browning]'s two sonnets on Sand that Fuller quoted) "look[ed] for virtue" in them. With this approach, Sand's premier "rank" in France, "influence abroad," and style signified more than her private life or her boldness in criticizing marriage. Explaining how social "circumstances" extenuated Sand's bohemianism, Fuller stressed the writerly achievement that for many critics made Sand the most artistically powerful of contemporary French novelists.[72]

Even as aesthetic interest motivated her essay, Fuller moved from the position of her protofeminist writings to account more for the power of social forces in her understanding of morality and therefore to appreciate Sand as a social critic. Sand saw the flaws in French "society" and protested them with "nobleness" of character, not "sinning against what she owned to be the rule of right." Still, Fuller regretted the not "quite clean" hands that she believed kept Sand merely a leader, not an apostle, in France and ended in praying over her, that Sand might be led to "harmony with the higher laws of life!" Fuller nonetheless observed a turn "towards philanthropic measures" in Sand's recent work and approved the "firmer," more serene "genius" exhibited in *Consuelo* and its sequel. Eugène Sue, by contrast, with "far inferior powers, on the whole, to Sand," would not be remembered as an artist, Fuller predicted, but rather as a "teacher of the ignorant" through his socialist theories. Fuller understood his socialism to have been evoked by the "corrupt society" of France and explained it in a sentimental trope from *Festus*, rather than in analytical terms, as "the means by which the heart of mankind may be made to beat with one great hope, one love." She positioned herself as an intellectual, above both the "deep interest" his socialism inspired in the United States and the conservative reaction to it: "it is well for the value of new thoughts to be tested by . . . resistance." Although Sand's imagining of "some form of life worthy to supersede the old" appeared in Fuller's description as less formed in "thought" than Sue's socialism, Sand's "philanthropic" fiction held for Fuller more of what she called "force" and "power."[73]

Between this February essay and Fuller's September review of *Consuelo* and *The Countess of Rudolstadt*, her views changed. Fuller now wrote closer to the perspective she described of "those who have looked upon Sand, for some years back, as one of the best exponents of the difficulties, the errors, and the aspirations, the weaknesses and the regenerative powers of the present epoch."[74] This was, as we have seen, not her own earlier perspective. Although Fuller remained interested in the theme of "perfection" in terms of individual talent, here she also evaluated Sand's thought on "Association as a means" of "reform," finding it "crude" yet approving its aim. Sand "proceed[ed] toward . . . a great Idea," that of "sincere democracy, universal religion." Fuller no longer positioned her interpretation at a remove above socialism, but nearer this author's version of it, where Sand's "still growing thoughts" made this fiction "a companion of rare value to one in the same phase of mind." Yet Fuller still struggled to grasp what *Consuelo* says about reform. Her focus on the character Albert as representing simply the "aristocratic democrat" suggests that the failure of "meaning" Fuller attributed to Sand's clumsy embodiment of "religion and philosophy" had as much to do with the insufficiency of her own method of unpacking the significance of this text's complex mélange of historical, gothic, and mystical fiction, including what "more" she recognized Albert signifies.[75] Fuller's criticism had advanced far from her first encounter with the French writer, when she judged *Spiridion* as simply too "bold" for undertaking to represent religious philosophy in fictional "character painting" at all.[76] Still, she had not arrived, as she implied, at the same phase of socialist thought as the author of *Consuelo*. Although Fuller understood that the theme of conflict "between the claims of Art and Life" in self-development was not the "main object" of Sand's fiction, her own interest centered more on that motif.[77] Others in Fuller's circle, more attached to socialist theory, managed more appreciative or comprehensive readings of Sand.

Shaw, defending both Associationists and Sand from the *Christian Examiner*, followed Sand in describing her early canon as deliberately questioning "false social institutions" rather than prescribing reforms. She "writes for the people and the people know the truth of her pictures," which "work to rouse" them "to a sense of the evils which lie at the basis of our social miseries," evils not touched by such "panaceas" of Unitarian Christianity and self-reform as the *Examiner* advocated.[78] Dwight, in the initial, June 1845 issue of the *Harbinger*, which devoted half of its pages to the first installment of Shaw's translation of *Consuelo*, focused on Sand's "master-piece."[79] While Dwight shared, perhaps even exceeded, Fuller's aesthetic appreciation of what "many" regarded as "the highest triumph of modern novel-writing," his interpretation also discerned more of the religious socialism represented through Sand's fable and characters. Although he relied on religious discourse without appealing to the rhetoric of socialism that Fuller engaged, Dwight understood the novel's meaning as pertaining to the collective human spirit, beyond individual self-development: "all thought of self is lost" in Consuelo's undertaking a "religious mission" of music, which expressed "the deepest, inmost life" of the "soul," that is the soul of humanity.[80] Fuller's ongoing resistance to "merging the individual in the mass" in spite of her "catholic sympathy" for socialism, as Channing put it, appeared in her more limited reading of Sand.[81]

That Fuller was working to reassess Sand through rereading, however, appears likely from her September review's echoes of Sand's own rhetoric in the 1842 preface to the collected *Lettres d'un voyageur*, a preface not yet written when Fuller recorded first reading from the *Lettres* some three years earlier.[82] Fuller's reference to the *Lettres* by name in her next and final *Tribune* review of the French writer, in June 1846, further suggests that she had in mind this earlier collection, which states Sand's love for Saint-Simonian faith and her respect for Fourier's theory, indeed for any scheme for the salvation of humanity, but also her resistance to the application of any system.[83] The September review observes the progress of the *Harbinger*'s serialization of Shaw's translation of *Consuelo*, suggesting that Fuller was reevaluating her opinion of Sand in dialogue with the Brook Farm circle, whose appreciation appeared in seven notices by Dwight, Shaw, Ripley, and others in the Associationist journal.

Fuller's final *Tribune* review of Sand, upon the completion of Shaw's translation of *Consuelo*, signals its embeddedness in both local and transatlantic reception circles. Fuller here backed her most unambivalent appreciation of Sand as "in some respects the best living prose writer" with reference to "one of the leading English Reviews," the *Foreign Quarterly*.[84] The definition she sketched of the critic's legitimate role as concerned only with Sand's "works and not her private life" paralleled the British rejection of biographical criticism marked by Lewes's 1844 article in the same periodical. The fact that Fuller reprinted the journal's translation of an extract from *Tévérino* to illustrate Sand's "great descriptive powers" and said little about the details of Shaw's translation of *Consuelo*, her ostensible subject, suggests that this review was more about promoting her friend's book—"to be found at . . . [the] Tribune Buildings"—than it was about evaluating Shaw's translation or interpreting Sand. Still, Fuller read out of Sand's fiction a gendered illustration of the theme of the liberty of internal law that so interested her circle, finding that *Consuelo* shows "how inward purity . . . secure[s] a genuine independence" to a woman. Reading an affirmation of artistic as well as moral independence in the novel, Fuller observed that Sand, in contrast with other novelists, encouraged women who have "a tendency to the intellectual life . . . in preference to the usual home duties."[85]

In this review Fuller expressed little interest in the novel's other "attempts to solve some problems of the time" that bore less directly on her own situation. Fuller did not follow up here on her previous reviews' focus on association, and there is no evidence to suggest that she ever interested herself in the treatment of "problems of the time" in Sand's *romans socialistes*.[86] Here Fuller opted to reprint the *Foreign Quarterly*'s translation from a "*fantaisie*" that the critic (Lewes, again) labeled an "abuse" of Sand's great "gifts" wasted "upon trivialities," rather than to engage his praise, despite his personal disapproval of socialism, of Sand's "well . . . conducted" "socialist discussions" in other recent fiction.[87] Inquiring of Shaw later from Rome about the success of his third translation, Fuller referred to "Le Compagnon &" as "a book in which only those who are in earnest and willing to think will take an interest;" even though her lack of commentary on this socialist novel suggests her own detachment, she did follow her circle's engagement of Sand and socialism.[88] In this last *Tribune* review of the author, Fuller seemed preoccupied as she prepared to leave for Europe later in the summer, where Sand and Pierre-Jean de Béranger were the only two French writers whom she expressed a desire to meet.[89]

Two other reception circles mediated Fuller's relation to Sand before their meeting, an international circle of critics and writers whom Fuller met in England and Paris and a women's reading circle that intersected the local circles described earlier. The notoriously fragmented archive of women's history tantalizes with glimpses of the latter group but frustrates efforts to reconstruct it.⁹⁰ Surviving evidence shows that women in Fuller's professional and social circles had access to texts and opportunities for discussing them together. Yet these fragments of evidence serve more to raise than answer questions about this circle's response to Sand and other French writers. How did Sophia Ripley respond to la jeune France beyond working with her husband on the translations he published? What did Elizabeth Peabody think of the half-dozen Sand volumes she arranged on the shelves of her Foreign Library before opening it in 1840? Or of Sand's other fiction and essays and reviews of her work that appeared in the French periodicals also in the library? Or of the other Sand titles later added to the collection as they appeared in print? What did the women who patronized this ladies' "literary lounge" for "literary intercourse" have to say to each other about Sand's works?⁹¹ What was the response of the "two young ladies" Fuller described as entering the library, while she "was sitting there," to request "Les Sept Chordes [*sic*] &c."?⁹² What part did Sand's publications and notices of her work in the *Revue des deux mondes* play in the conclusion drawn by "one of the bright girls who first saw it there" at the library that the journal constituted a "liberal education"?⁹³ Did the women who chatted over the Brook Farm experiment that was hatched at the library or in the Conversations that Fuller conducted there discuss the Sand texts? Did Elizabeth Hoar share her interpretation of the Dark Knight in *Consuelo* as the culmination of a transnational literary type with Fuller or other women, as she did with Emerson?⁹⁴ Did Fuller have anything to do with Caroline Dall's later inspiration to translate *Spiridion*, rather than some more obviously protofeminist text, for the *Una*?⁹⁵

The muted discussion among the women in Fuller's intellectual circle may be a consequence of the double standard that, as Lydia Maria Child privately protested both to Osgood's sisters, Lucy and Mary, and to Anna Loring stigmatized Sand for sexual nonconformance while winking at the conduct of male writers.⁹⁶ As with the author, so the double standard might serve to censure her female readers. Although women joined more in open approbation of Sand's writing after the publication of the irreprehensible *Consuelo* and of Barrett [Browning]'s 1844 sonnet expressing "Desire" for a miracle to bring a "stainless fame" for the writer, women continued to risk reproach through association with Sand.⁹⁷ While Child limited her discussion of Sand, even with female friends, to an intimate circle (Sarah Shaw, the Osgoods, and Loring), surviving evidence shows that Fuller also discussed Sand with women only in her inmost circle: Sarah Shaw, Caroline Sturgis, and Hoar.⁹⁸ Sand's nonconformance intrigued both of these groups. Fuller sent gossip from Paris to Hoar, who particularly "wished to hear of George

Sand," and to Sturgis about the writer's unconventional "private life" and the tolerance of "what are called errors" in Sand's social circles.[99] She warned Sturgis, however, "Do not speak of this in America."[100]

Sand's writing, as well, figured significantly in Fuller's close female circle, uniquely affording them entertainment, aesthetic pleasure, and a means of understanding and communicating their experience. As Shaw's *Consuelo* ran in the *Harbinger*, Fuller wrote Sarah to congratulate her and Frank on the birth of another daughter and the rightness of his translation "when he has so many daughters," suggesting that Sand's fiction held special import for female readers. Fuller assumed that while Frank would like "to have intercourse with the French socialists" in Paris, Sarah would rather visit Sand before the author's imaginative "fire . . . wane[d]."[101] Allusions to Sand in the correspondence between Fuller and Sturgis appear to have encoded experience in a symbolic discourse that presumed shared meanings between these two readers of the fiction. Fuller described a man in Italy simply as "seem[ing] the type of some of George Sand's characters" and sent from Venice a friendship token of shells, because "they *are* the same Consuelo used to gather," presuming that Sturgis would understand what she meant by that "reason" for sending them.[102] When Fuller first read Sand, she carried on intellectual correspondence about the writer with male friends, while she sent Sturgis Sand's fiction for the amusement that she later deprecated in the "French Novelists."[103] Yet Sturgis's later evaluation of that essay as a "good" one for readers in need of an "introduction" shows that she came to share something of the range of reading and the more critical reading method Fuller detailed there.[104] Sturgis, inquiring if Fuller had read the sequel to *Consuelo*, admired the *vraisemblance* of Sand's idealist art, as well as her types of womanhood. "What a stamp of reality there is upon all Sand's characters," Sturgis enthused. "I feel as if I had known Consuelo all my life—I wish I did know such women," unlike those of her experience.[105] In their inner circles, American women could share some of their enthusiasm and sympathy for Sand that was elsewhere tabooed, enthusiasm that Fuller damped in her professional criticism even behind its ostensible anonymity.

Across the Atlantic, Fuller entered an inner circle of professional Sand enthusiasts when she found herself in the company of England's two strongest advocates of Sand's work, Lewes and Mazzini. At one gathering hosted by the Carlyles, the discussion of jeune France marginalized women, not because of a double moral standard, but rather, Fuller reported, because Thomas Carlyle's "haranguing" silenced both her and his wife, Jane. At another gathering, which included Mazzini, Carlyle stifled discussion of "ideal subjects" and "progress" with a rant against such "rose-water imbecilities." Fuller found in Lewes only a "french flippant sort of man," not the anonymous *Foreign Quarterly* proponent of Sand whose translation of *Tévérino* she had quoted at length in the *Tribune*. She was nonetheless grateful that he contradicted Carlyle's railing against "modern French Literature."[106] In contrast, Mazzini, then writing for the reformist *People's Journal*, became an important professional contact for Fuller and her direct link to Sand.

Fuller left for Paris with his introduction to the *Revue indépendante* (founded by Sand with Leroux). This proved to be her entrée into French journalism, leading to the December *Revue*'s translating extracts from her work and putting her in touch with journalist and activist Pauline Roland, with whom Fuller began planning a project to write about Sand and other jeune France figures.[107] At the beginning of 1847 Mazzini invited Sand, then Fuller to write for the *People's Journal*, as he planned to make it an "organ" of the People's International League and convert English utilitarian democracy to a religious democracy. In addition, he provided letters that negotiated Fuller's meeting with Sand, apologizing lest his requests to receive his friends annoy Sand.[108] Not long before the February meeting, the *People's Journal*, to which Mazzini had become a principal contributor, began heavily promoting the work of both women. An article on Fuller's visit to his charity school identified her as the "authoress of *Woman in the Nineteenth Century*, the best work on the subject which has yet appeared." A bordered advertisement in the March 6 issue announced:

> *Our next Number will contain*
>
> A PORTRAIT OF GEORGE SAND
>
> WITH
>
> A PAPER BY JOSEPH MAZZINI.
>
> We are at the same time authorized to announce, that ORIGINAL CONTRIBUTIONS BY GEORGE SAND Will appear in future pages of the *People's Journal*.
>
> S. MARGARET FULLER
> Will contribute to the pages of the *People's Journal*.[109]

Mazzini's essay on Sand in the next issue cited the rehabilitation of her reputation in England as symbolic of progress in general, repeated his earlier ranking of Sand and Lamennais as the foremost French writers, and celebrated her as "an apostle of religious democracy."[110] Mazzini only touched on Sand's role in "the emancipation of woman, of the determinations of her duties and her rights." He reserved that topic, as well as an "appreciation [of] her numerous works, of her artistic genius, [and] subordinate ideas," for future articles, to coincide with the publication of a six-volume translation of Sand's *Works*, edited by Matilda M. Hays.[111] Although Mazzini's article sounds like a prospectus for Fuller's promised contributions, the journal carried only her short verse prayer that "woman" might inspire Italy to "higher honors."[112] Fuller later reported to Mary Howitt, to whom she had promised sketches on Lamennais and on Sand "in connection with these translations of Miss Hays," that she had confused *Howitt's Journal* with the *People's Journal* (from which the Howitts had broken in January) and had promised Mazzini the announced contribution for the *People's*. She now hoped to write for both, asking Howitt to wait until "next winter" and to consider adding sketches of Béranger and Leroux. Fuller had "learned and thought so much about [Sand's] position while in France" that she needed time and favorable "circumstances" to focus "full and strong" on a sketch of her.[113] At the end of 1847 Mazzini was still encouraging Fuller, "be *my* contributor." Yet given the editor's unwillingness to relinquish the *People's* to Mazzini's management, along with Mazzini's own anticipation of being called to the impending "struggle" in Italy, he cautioned Fuller "to wait a little longer before embarking in any series of articles."[114] Fuller became caught up in these conflicts in British reception circles, then in the adventure of Italy, never furnishing an essay on Sand to either journal. But why Fuller wrote only short private accounts of Sand from Paris and, subsequently, a single, brief indictment of Sand in the *Tribune* remains less clear.

Fuller's accounts of George Sand in Parisian circles disappoint expectations of significant Romantic or feminist encounter. In response to Hoar's request "to hear of George Sand," Fuller sent a letter intended for a circle of "*near* friends" that included gossip about Sand's divorce, lovers, family, and benevolence.[115] She observed with surprise the gap between American "feeling" and the French practice of receiving Sand in respectable society, where "like a man, . . . the weight of her thoughts," rather than her sexual conduct, determined her status. The other details Fuller described—specifics of Sand's pay, circulation, influence relative to her male counterparts, and her relations with Lammenais—bear on Sand's professional life. Their inclusion seems motivated more by the interests of the professional circles in which Fuller had been moving in England and France than by any particular curiosity of her "near" circle back home. Indeed, the information could all have come from Dr. Ferdinand François, editor of the *Revue indépendante*, with whom Fuller had been working on reprinting her essays and here called an "intimate" of Sand's.[116]

Nor does the account of the two personal encounters, which Fuller apparently recorded in a journal that ended up with Emerson, come much closer to Sand's "ardent . . . genius," which Fuller praised but did not detail. Fuller was relieved to encounter "a character" she found "so *really* good" in many ways, in "contrast to the vulgar caricature" of Sand. Of their talk, which touched on no "personal or private matters," Fuller recorded nothing beyond the exchange of politesse. After admiring a few details of Sand's appearance, Fuller's account focused on the same traits of character that her readings of Sand's works had already discovered in their author—the same characteristic style of expression in Sand's talking as in her writing, the same "nobleness" and "power" that the first *Tribune* notice stressed, the spirit of abandon wanting sufficient balance (here figured in mythic characters) that Fuller had seen in her early reading of Sand's early fiction, and the spiritual "purity" of Helena that Fuller had first observed years earlier in the author of *Les sept cordes de la lyre*. Fuller now added one detail. Helena and Consuelo acted on that inner law and so, as the third *Tribune* review remarked and Fuller reaffirmed here, secured a spiritual independence, a liberty of the moral law. Sand, by contrast, "ha[d] that purity in her soul" to such an extent that she could appreciate its value, but in her own life had rather "bravely acted out her nature," "naturally" changing lovers as no man "could command her throughout her range." So Fuller saw in her, "as one sees in her writings, the want of an independent, interior life." Yet Fuller no longer "fe[lt]" that this was "a fault."[117] Fuller's explanation of Sand's "nature" parallels the author's own description of the autobiographical title character of *Lucrezia Floriani* (1846) whose "nature" ("*ce naturel*") likewise needed no explanation, but only to be understood to be appreciated.[118] Sand's portrait of her heroine resembles Fuller's portrait of Sand as a generous, modest woman characterized by virtues at odds with her reputation. Sand, like Lucrezia, was motivated by her "heart" and good "intentions" to love "one man permanently," "break[ing] it off suddenly" as soon as love failed; thus, she was not "coarse" even as she undertook a series of affairs.[119]

The brief explicit notice that Fuller took of Sand's recent fiction, however, added little to what she had already said of Sand's art and gave no sense of how the writing of either woman might have figured as a subject of their discussion. In reiterating many of her earlier observations on Sand,

Fuller touched on topics that Mazzini had outlined for the projected *People's Journal* series. If, as it appears, however, Mazzini had arranged the meeting in part for Fuller to prepare for her promised contribution to the *People's Journal*, Fuller did not discover much new about her subject. The rest of her account is largely taken up with gossip about Sand's smoking and lovers, with Fuller's anxieties over Sand's celebrity and her own social and linguistic inadequacies, and with her identification of Sand's social place "in her circle" with Fuller's own "position," "the same as my own in the circle of my acquaintance as distinguished from my intimates," "the same position" of "intellectual woman and good friend."[120] A further description of this second meeting comes from Barrett Browning, who, characterizing Fuller as "one of the out and out *Reds* and scorners of grades of society," quoted her as nonetheless saying this "soirée was 'full of rubbish,'" in the way of its social composition, which George Sand likes."[121] Perhaps the most significant outcome of the meetings was, as Bell Gale Chevigny argues, that Fuller "enlarged her consciousness" of sexual "passion" in coming to accept that Sand "'acted out her nature'" in taking lovers, an interpretation of Sand's personal life that would inform Fuller's explanation of her own later liaison.[122]

Fuller's declaration in her journal after meeting Sand that she "loved, shall always love" her might better support claims that Sand was Fuller's "hero," were it not for the absence of any subsequent "friendship," solidarity, or public avowal of regard.[123] No correspondence appears to have passed between these two champion letter writers. On her part, Sand evidently left no mention of the American who had basked in her hospitality. Fuller maintained public silence on their meeting, although she provided *Tribune* readers with sketches of such male progressives whom she met as Lamennais.[124] The *Harbinger* reprinted Mazzini's essay on Sand from the *People's Journal* but carried no word on the writer from Fuller.[125] Fuller did not pass on to *Tribune* readers the praise of Sand that Mazzini wrote to her, that in organizing the Italian revolutionary movement he took "strength from personal intercourse with Mad. Sand."[126] And although Fuller's dispatches extolled the French Revolution, they did not circulate information about Sand's activism in it. Fuller's only subsequent mention of Sand in the *Tribune* charged her with failure as a feminist progressive.

The December 2, 1848, dispatch sketchily reported as hearsay that Sand refused to "act" with women whom Fuller identified only as those who "hold their clubs in Paris." Although Fuller herself did not take up the cause of those socialists, who, ten months earlier in their campaign for political rights for women had proposed Sand as a candidate for the National Assembly, she rebuked Sand for not doing so. Fuller did not dispute what "they say"

Sand said, that women "are too mean, too treacherous," but only argued that "not nature but misfortune" was the reason. Fuller confessed that her own exhaustion of "genius" and "energy" prevented her addressing "Woman's condition" but offered no such extenuation of Sand, only a reprimand: "She should not abandon" "women as they are."[127] This was Fuller's last public word on the woman she professed to "love."

The evidence of Fuller's response to George Sand over time and in transatlantic contexts, then, suggests the need to reevaluate claims of Fuller's avant-garde reception of the writer; indeed, it might prompt the reconsideration of Fuller's avant-garde status more broadly. As the phrasing that echoes throughout Fuller's writing on Sand makes clear, the French writer's chief appeal for Fuller lay in her Romantic "aspiration" and literary style. Fuller joined other readers on both sides of the Atlantic in paying homage to Sand's "genius" and aesthetic achievement, but she neither led the way nor went it alone, as her reviews openly acknowledge. Like others, she worked with more or less success to elaborate reading methods adequate to the codes of Sand's innovative writings. While her reading of some of Sand's work and of the criticism surrounding it contributed to Fuller's own developing progressivism, she also shared the era's reluctance to embrace Sand's more radical views. Fuller expressed more reservations than enthusiasm about Sand's gender critique. Her reading did not focus on the specifics of Sand's exploration of socialism, nor did it extend to much of the range of that exploration. A transnational reception study thus not only provides a complex sense of international cultural dynamics and historicity but also challenges idealizations of Fuller. In so doing, it challenges us to account more for the uneven process that brought Fuller to where we value her as an intellectual, feminist, and progressive, continually struggling to transcend the limits of her own liberalism.

Epilogue

"THE MEASURE OF MY FOOT-PRINT"

Margaret Fuller's Unfinished Revolution

Mary Kelley

In a letter that she wrote to William Henry Channing late in 1844, Margaret Fuller told her friend that she had completed *Woman in the Nineteenth Century*, the book that made her famous then and now. The final pages of the project behind her, Fuller acknowledged to Channing that she "felt a delightful glow as if I had put a good deal of my true life in it, as if, suppose I went away now, the measure of my foot-print would be left on the earth." Priced at fifty cents a copy, the original edition of fifteen hundred sold within two weeks of its publication in 1845. Another edition appeared in England before the end of that year. Whether they celebrated or condemned its contents, reviewers kept *Woman in the Nineteenth Century* in the public eye. The journalist and abolitionist Lydia Maria Child, who hailed the book's "noble aspirations," described its author as a woman of "powerful intellect, comprehensive thought, and thorough education." An anonymous reviewer disagreed vehemently, saying that the aspirations of *Woman in the Nineteenth Century* were actually heresies and that, having unsexed herself, Margaret Fuller was "no longer a woman."[1]

Why did her critics offer such diametrically opposed responses? Edgar Allan Poe suggested that Fuller's "way of independence, of unmitigated radicalism" made her an idol to some, a villain to others. Still, it was her claims for *Woman in the Nineteenth Century* that made Fuller controversial. During a century in which the world was divided on the basis of gender, in which marriage and motherhood were considered a female's sole occupation, Fuller insisted that women be able to develop their potential as individuals, each of whom had particular inclinations and talents. "We would have every arbitrary barrier thrown down. We would have every path laid open to woman as freely as to man," she declared. That would not be likely without a revolution in the values held by a majority of Fuller's contemporaries.[2]

In the twenty-first century, of course, Child and her fellow admirers have been vindicated. Or have they? What, we might ask, can Margaret Fuller say to us today? To what degree is her revolution unfinished? What lessons still resonate? Let us take a journey through Fuller's life and letters. To mark where progress stands today, we will slip into our baggage some newspaper and magazine articles and two recently published books, both of which register women's status in contemporary society. Published in the fall of 2009, Gail Collins's *When Everything Changed: The Amazing Journey of American Women* begins in 1960, when women were routinely paid less than men in the same positions, when newspapers divided classified ads into MEN: HELP WANTED and WOMEN: HELP WANTED, when women needed their husband's permission to apply for a credit card, when medical and law schools either banned female students or severely limited their numbers. It is of little wonder that in 1961 women constituted only 6 percent of the nation's doctors and 3 percent of its lawyers. Then, as Collins states, there was a national consensus that women could not be airplane pilots, television news anchors, firefighters, movie directors, combat soldiers, or heads of corporations. Then, there was the issue of reproductive choice. Abortion was illegal everywhere. What was women's status fifty years later? Americans witnessed Hillary Rodham Clinton's historic campaign for the presidency. She did not take the White House. She did become secretary of state. Two other women, Condoleezza Rice and Madeleine Albright, were her immediate predecessors. In sectors other than electoral politics, women held 51.4 percent of managerial and professional positions in 2010. They took 43 percent of the MBAs awarded in the United States.

Issued in the spring of 2010, Susan Douglas's *Enlightened Sexism* strikes a cautionary note. In a spirited and smashingly funny consideration of popular culture, Douglas shows how today's media are sending conflicting messages that feminism has met its objectives and is now nothing more than an albatross and that the genuine sources of power are highly sexualized beauty and unrelenting consumerism, not economic independence or professional achievement. "The seductive message that feminism's work is done," which Douglas takes for the subtitle of her volume, portrays women who still dare to call themselves feminists as "man-hating, child-loathing, hairy, shrill, humorless, [and, of course,] deliberately unattractive." These are the women who are the impediment to female happiness and fulfillment. Dismiss them—the battle for equality has been won, audiences are told. Sexist stereotypes may now be resurrected, only for amusement, of course. With these markers in place, let us begin our journey in Margaret Fuller's nineteenth century.[3]

CLAIMING AN EDUCATION

The social and cultural milieu of the antebellum decades and the individual circumstances of her life shaped Fuller's aspirations for herself and the women of her century. At the same time, in the choices she made, Fuller played a signal role in shaping those aspirations. Fuller's particular circumstances were exceptional, at least in terms of the formal learning she received and the informal learning she claimed for herself. At this juncture it is important to note the decisive role that education has played in determining what might be possible for a woman, whatever her aspirations and whatever her century. With the exception of Oberlin College, established in 1833, America's colleges and universities excluded women until the second half of the nineteenth century.[4] That was no obstacle as far as Fuller's father, himself a graduate of Harvard College, was concerned. Instructing his daughter as if she were a son preparing for his alma mater, Timothy Fuller began schooling Margaret in English and Latin grammar at the age of six. Three years later she was reading Virgil, Cicero, Horace, Livy, and Tacitus. Greek grammar was added to her daily studies, as were French and Italian. In an autobiographical sketch written when she was thirty, Fuller recalled that the Greek and Roman heroes had impressed upon her the importance of "earnest purpose," of "self-command," of "force of expression." She considered these luminaries her companions, their struggles her inspiration. In reading herself into these texts, Fuller laid claim to qualities of character that had been considered the possession of men. Equally notably, she made the classical heritage and Western culture her own. Yet Fuller did more. Counterpointing the daily study of languages with volumes in her father's library, she read Shakespeare, Cervantes, Molière, Fielding, Smollett, and Scott.[5]

In its particular character and intensity, Margaret Fuller's education was singular. But she was not alone among women in claiming the privilege of higher education. Thousands of others who shared her social and racial standing enrolled in postrevolutionary and antebellum female academies and seminaries, which welcomed women into the world of higher learning and schooled them in a course of study that matched the curriculum then being taught at the exclusively male colleges and universities. Students were expected to command mathematics, moral philosophy, logic, and the natural sciences. The curriculum at these female academies and seminaries was gendered in one telling respect. Students at many of these schools were invited to read books by and about learned women. As early as the 1790s Sarah Pierce, the head of Litchfield Academy in Litchfield, Connecticut, began to introduce her students to British luminaries such as Hannah More, Maria Edgeworth, and Hester Chapone. Mary Lyon, the founder of Mount Holyoke, honored Americans in pronouncing "Mrs. [Lydia] Sigourney the most finished and elegant writer of our country, and Miss [Catharine] Beecher the most strong and powerful." Fuller, who would teach at Greene Street School in Providence, Rhode Island, in the 1830s, celebrated French as well as British women. She told us "a great deal about the writings of distinguished females," one of her students recalled. Twenty years later, young women attending Miss Porter's School in Farmington, Connecticut, added Fuller to the ranks of their exemplars. Reporting in a letter to her sister that she was reading the *Memoirs of Margaret Fuller Ossoli*, one of the students paid tribute to Fuller, declaring, she "was a wonderful woman."[6]

What is the situation in the present? Today women and men sit together at the nation's institutions of higher education. Indeed, in 2010 women earned 57 percent of the nation's college and university degrees. Close to half of the law and medical degrees were awarded to women, an increase from 10 percent only four decades ago. Women made up 32 percent of the nation's lawyers and 28 percent of its physicians. Four out of eight presidents of the formerly all-male Ivy League were women. A woman presided at Timothy Fuller's alma mater. Women there led the schools of law, engineering, and education. Elena Kagan, the former dean of the law school, had been appointed to the United States Supreme Court. Today thousands of women's studies programs across the country are bringing to the fore the historical and contemporary experiences of women. At the University of Michigan, the Women's Studies Department has joint PhD programs in history, English, sociology, and psychology. All this said, consider a U.S. Department of Education study published in 2010 that shows the following: despite having earned higher college and university GPAs in every subject, young women will take home, on average across the professions, only 80 percent of their male colleagues' incomes. Women who have taken MBAs will make $4,600 less per year in their first position after graduation. A *New York Times* article published on April 12, 2010, is also telling. In reporting that academic salaries had risen only 1.2 percent in 2009, the smallest increase in fifty years, the author notes, "at every type of institution in almost every class of faculty, men were paid substantially more, on average, than women." Some careers remained decidedly gendered. In 2010 only 10 percent of the nation's civil engineers, 14 percent of its police officers, and 1 percent of its police chiefs were women. Fully 98 percent of kindergarten teachers and dental assistants were women.[7]

BECOMING A WOMAN OF LETTERS

Once the schooling with her father was completed, Fuller continued to pursue her studies by herself. There was the reading, always the reading, which filled her days. The breadth of that reading is striking: philosophy, Italian poetry, French novels, and Castilian ballads. Fuller and her friend James Freeman Clarke began reading Goethe together. Fuller's engagement with the German poet, playwright, and novelist was immediate and intense. Like other nineteenth-century women and men, Fuller approached reading and writing not as separate and autonomous acts but instead as continually intersecting and mutually constitutive habits. But now she was reading and writing with an eye to the literary marketplace. Fuller began a translation of *Torquato Tasso*, Goethe's verse drama about the deeply alienated Renaissance poet, and she began to write criticism, poetry, and fiction. In 1834 she published an essay in the *Boston Daily Advertiser*. The next year three articles appeared in Clarke's periodical, the *Western Messenger*. Margaret Fuller had taken command of her education and made it serve ends that she had determined. Her career as a woman of letters had begun.

Almost at the moment at which Fuller embarked on that career, it looked as if she might have to cast it aside. In October 1835 Timothy Fuller died from cholera, leaving his family with slender means of support. Fuller, the eldest child, lamented she had not been born a male. Had she been the eldest son, she would have been appointed head of the family and guardian of her younger brothers and sisters. Nonetheless, Fuller resolved to be that son, albeit as a surrogate. The challenges proved formidable: administering the estate, supervising the family's affairs, managing the education of her siblings, and earning an income. Fuller was also determined to keep pace with her intellectual aspirations, which included publishing literary essays and pursuing research for a biography of Goethe. Less than a year after her father's death, she had accomplished all of this except obtaining an income.

In the fall of 1836 Fuller implemented a series of strategies to support herself as a teacher. She settled in Boston and held two appointments, teaching German, French, and Italian literature to privately organized classes of young women and Latin, French, and Italian languages to children at Transcendentalist Bronson's Alcott's Temple School. The next fall she took a position at the Greene Street School in Providence, Rhode Island. She was paid the exceptional sum of one thousand dollars a year and taught women from eighteen to twenty years of age a challenging variety of courses, ranging from natural history to English poetry. "This is just what I wanted," she told Caroline Sturgis in January 1838. Fuller stamped her lessons with a pedagogy that rejected the memorization practiced at the male colleges and universities and instead called students to "get our lessons by mind—to give our minds and souls to the work," as Mary Ware Allen recalled. Collective acts of interpretation superseded daily recitation. "It is all talk," said Allen, who explained Fuller's reasoning: "She says we must *think* as well as *study*, and *talk* as well as *recite*." Fuller called her students to approach their learning through the cultivation of mental faculties: "activity of mind, accuracy in processes, constant looking for principles, and search after the good and beautiful," as she explained to Ralph Waldo Emerson.[8]

Instilling in those whom she taught the dual claim to intellectual authority and public voice, Fuller committed her students to lives of consequence. "She spoke upon what woman could do—said she should like to see a woman everything she might be, in intellect and character," one of her students remarked. After she had listened to Fuller describe a woman who had succeeded as a sculptor, another declared, "it makes me proud when I hear such things as this for it shows what our sex is capable of doing and encourages us to go on improving and doing all we can to show that we are not entirely incapable of intellectual cultivation as some think." Fuller also introduced her students to women of letters. In their eyes, Fuller herself was a model. Their teacher was an "incomparable woman," Louise Hunt exclaimed to Lucy Clark Allen. She was a "perfect wonder," Anna Gale told her brother Frederic, then a student at Harvard. It was the learning that Gale most admired: "I almost stand in awe of her, she is such a literary being."[9]

Although Fuller took satisfaction from the impact she had on her students, the demands of teaching made it increasingly difficult for her to remain, as Gale described her, "a literary being." She confessed to Ralph Waldo Emerson: "What grieves me too is to find or fear my theory a cheat—I cannot serve two masters." Fuller chose the master with whom she identified most deeply. She set aside teaching to focus on her career as a woman of letters. Income did remain an issue, and Fuller once again showed her inventiveness. She returned to teaching, albeit in a less formal setting. The site was the "Conversations," which were held at Elizabeth Peabody's bookshop on West Street in Boston. In the next five years, Fuller and other highly educated women addressed a series of subjects, including Greek mythology, the historical development of the fine arts, and contemporary definitions of masculinity and femininity. The subject of women's intellectual potential figured in all of these Conversations. Fuller suggested that, although women and men had the same mental attributes, they had been "combined in different proportions." Still, she insisted that there was no "essential difference — it was only more or less."[10]

Did the participants agree, Fuller asked? Did they subscribe to the opinion that the differences they had all observed were grounded in social prescriptions rather than biological differences? Fuller's rhetorical questions had revolutionary implications: "It would follow of course that we should hear no more of repressing or subduing faculties because these were not fit for women to cultivate." The radical individualism driving Fuller's insistence that a woman could design for herself the manner in which she cultivated her faculties liberated all women from the restrictions imposed by prevailing definitions of femininity and masculinity. Women could now look upon their intellectual potential as "a principle of our perfection and cultivate it accordingly — and not excuse ourselves from any duty on the ground that we had not the intellectual powers for it; that it was not for women to do, on *an intellectual ground*."

Whatever the topic of the Conversations, Fuller's colleagues were dazzled by their leader's ability to gather together threads from disparate sources and weave them together in a tapestry of larger meanings. "I never heard, read of, or imagined a conversation at all equal to this we have now heard," one participant exulted. As with her students at Greene Street School, Fuller herself made the most powerful imprint. Elizabeth Cady Stanton provides a telling illustration. The woman who would become the nineteenth century's most famous feminist theorist, Stanton attended a series of Conversations during a winter she spent in Boston and, returning to her home in western New York, inaugurated meetings "in imitation of Margaret Fuller's Conversationals," as she described them. Fuller's Conversations, in Stanton's opinion, constituted "a vindication of woman's right to think." They also validated Fuller as a model of *woman thinking*. In answering the questions she posed, "What were we born to do?" and then, "how shall we do it?" Fuller sought to activate that model among the other participants. Fuller's Conversations, then, were a rehearsal for the claim that she would make in *Woman in the Nineteenth Century* on behalf of "*women thinking.*"[11]

During these years, Fuller also made her mark with the *Dial*, a Transcendentalist periodical that she edited from 1840 until 1842. Convinced that her nation needed to reform itself intellectually and spiritually, Fuller told William Henry Channing that the *Dial*, "will not aim at leading public opinion, but at stimulating each man to think for himself, to think more deeply and more nobly by letting them see how some minds are kept alive by a wise self-trust." Fuller's translations, essays on critical theory, poems, and commentaries on Goethe appeared in the pages of the *Dial* during these years. As Megan Marshall shows, she even introduced readers to the relatively neglected art of music, contributing a total of seven articles, including the famous "Lives of Great Composers." Fuller's final essay, "The Great Lawsuit. Man versus Men. Woman versus Women," prepared the ground for *Woman in the Nineteenth Century*.

In the spring of 1844, Fuller completed another series of Conversations, her fifth in as many years. That summer she published *Summer on the Lakes*, a narrative of the journey she had made through Illinois, Wisconsin, and Michigan during the summer of 1843. Fuller seemed poised for change. Horace Greeley, the editor of the *New-York Daily Tribune*, spoke to two possibilities. Impressed with *Summer on the Lakes* and "The Great Lawsuit," the most controversial of Fuller's contributions to the *Dial*, Greeley invited her to become the literary editor at the *Tribune*. The evidence suggests that he also recommended that she expand the essay. Fuller did both, joining the ranks of the *Tribune's* journalists and making the "The Great Lawsuit" into *Woman in the Nineteenth Century*.[12]

In the same years that Fuller was becoming a prominent woman of letters, scores of other women were embarking on careers as writers. A significant number achieved as much if not more visibility than Emerson, Thoreau, Hawthorne, and Melville, all of whom would be canonized in the decades bridging the nineteenth and twentieth centuries. The beneficiaries of increasing literacy and expanding print circulation, women such as Catharine Maria Sedgwick, Lydia Maria Child, Louisa May Alcott, Maria Cummins, and Harriet Beecher Stowe commanded large readerships. Published in 1852, Stowe's *Uncle Tom's Cabin* became the nineteenth-century's most popular novel. And yet, and in making the canon and teaching it in classrooms across the country, literary critics and cultural historians erased these women and others, including Fuller. Galvanized by the aptly named Second Wave Feminism in the academy and beyond, scholars began recovering these writers and remaking the canon in the 1970s. Under the sponsorship of Rutgers University Press, the American Women Writers Series has returned to print sixteen writers, including Sedgwick, Child, Alcott, Cummins, and Stowe. The Schomburg Library of Nineteenth-Century Black Women Writers, published by Oxford University Press, has issued forty titles. Two pathbreaking biographies of Margaret Fuller appeared in 1976 and 1994. Bell Gale Chevigny's *The Woman and the Myth: Margaret Fuller's Life and Writings* was published by the Feminist Press, itself founded in 1970 to recover a lost women's literature; eighteen years later, Joan Von Mehren's *Minerva and the Muse: A Life of Margaret Fuller* appeared from the University of Massachusetts Press. The first volume of Charles Capper's magisterial biography had been published two years earlier by Oxford University Press; the second appeared in 2007.

There are also internationally and nationally recognized markers suggesting that female writers are beginning to receive the same consideration as their male counterparts. Awarded 102 times to 106 individuals between 1901 and 1990, the Nobel Prize in Literature went to women only 6 times. An equal number of women became Nobel Laureates in the next two decades. Awards for the Pulitzer Prize for Fiction have had a similar trajectory. Between 1949 and 1989, 9 women were awarded Pulitzers; 7 Pulitzers have gone to women in the two decades between 1990 and 2010. Yet there are still significant disparities, which have been documented by VIDA: Women in Literary Arts. All of Publisher Weekly's "Top Ten Books of 2009" were authored by men. The same year the National Book Award honored men exclusively in Fiction, Nonfiction, and Poetry. Slate's Best Reads of 2009 went to 15 men and 7 women, and only 23 women were cited in Amazon's Top 100 Editor's Picks for 2009.[13]

ACHIEVING AMERICA'S PROMISE:
MARGARET FULLER'S DECLARATION OF INDEPENDENCE

Manifesto, celebration, meditation, and declamation, *Woman in the Nineteenth Century* began on an optimistic note. Confident that individual and social perfection were possible, Fuller declared, "Now, no more, a glimmering consciousness. But assurance begins to be felt and spoken, that the highest ideal man can form of his own powers, is that which he is destined to attain." However, the male dominance that made the prevailing system of gender relations imbalanced stood as a basic obstacle. Despite asymmetries that highlighted the distance between the real and the ideal, Fuller believed that the achievement of the latter was inevitable. Comparing America with Europe, Fuller predicted, "this country is as surely destined to elucidate a great moral law, as Europe was to promote the mental culture of man." With the Declaration of Independence as her source, Fuller chose equality as the "moral law" that constituted America's destiny.[14]

America's first women's rights convention, which was held in Seneca Falls, New York, late in the summer of 1848; the conventions that followed almost yearly; and the movement on behalf of women's rights all looked to the nation's Declaration of Independence. In their pursuit of female equality, women's rights advocates focused on structural reforms that gave women control of the property they brought to marriage and the wages they earned thereafter. They sought equal rights in matters of divorce and the custody of children. They championed increased educational opportunity for women. Not least, they advocated female suffrage. Unsurprisingly, Fuller supported all of these structural reforms. Recall Fuller's radical claim with which this contribution began: "We would have every path laid open to woman as freely as to man." In that proclamation, as in other statements scattered through *Woman in the Nineteenth Century*, Fuller made the male public world women's domain. Fuller also understood the degree to which women's engagement with the public world depended on expanding educational opportunities. She contributed her mite with images of learned women. Presenting readers with a female tradition designed to stir their imaginations, she selected examples from history, folklore, literature, mythology, and contemporary society. Those from the last source were perhaps the most arresting. Fuller selected the French Romantic Germaine de Staël, who had been a luminous ideal for generations of American women. De Staël's influence had been pervasive; as Fuller tells us, her dazzling intellect had made "the obscurest school-house in New-England warmer and lighter to little rugged girls, who are gathered together on its wooden bench." Mary Somerville had warmed and lightened those schoolhouses in a similar manner. Highlighting the English scientist's accomplishments, Fuller asked readers, if she "has achieved so much, will any young girl be prevented from seeking a knowledge of the physical sciences, if she wishes it?" The question was rhetorical: Somerville had made manifest all that might be realized if women, no longer constrained by deference and dependence, freely pursued knowledge, whatever the subject.[15]

Today they do, after a powerful cultural awakening that delivered on its promise. In describing the impact of Second Wave Feminism, Gail Collins has declared, "It happened so fast that the revolution seemed to be over before either side could really find its way to the barricades." And that it did. *Time* magazine's editors devoted a 1972 special issue to investigating the status of women in the midst of the Second Wave, but it was still too early for this women's rights movement to have taken hold. *Time* found that women's average wages had actually fallen relative to men's. The editors noted that no woman had served in the Cabinet since the Eisenhower administration; no women were working as FBI agents, network news anchors, or Supreme Court justices. The Museum of Modern Art had done one thousand one-artist shows in the previous forty years: five of those shows had featured women. Only 7 percent of students playing high school sports were girls. College and university campuses were 60 percent male. "In terms of real power—economic and political—we are still just beginning," Gloria Steinem observed at the time. But, she added, "the consciousness, the awareness—that will never be the same." In terms of women's economic and political power, the changes since the early 1970s have been enormous. There has been a "revolution," as Collins says. But, after that "consciousness," that "awareness," mounted a powerful challenge to the inequalities that *Time* documented for its readers, have cultural attitudes changed all that much? Or has sexism simply been packaged differently? In a recent column in the *New York Times*, newspaper and magazine editor Joanne Lipman suggested, "We've focused primarily on numbers at the expense of attitudes." The latter are crucial, she added. "We've got to include popular perceptions in the equation as well. Progress in one area without the other is no progress at all." In this respect, Susan Douglas's *Enlightened Sexism* is on the mark. The media, she tells us, "have been giving us little more than fantasies of power." The most insidious of these fantasies is the assurance that "women's liberation is a fait accompli and that we are stronger, more successful, more sexually in control, more fearless and more held in awe than we actually are." But, one might ask, aren't the media simply addressing long-standing demands for more representations of female achievement? Perhaps. And yet what society is actually getting are portrayals of an imagined power that masks "how much remains to be done for girls and women, [portrayals] that make sexism seem fine, even fun, and insist that feminism is pointless."[16]

Margaret Fuller would have applauded Susan Douglas, and, in this regard, Fuller herself has much to tell us today. In a statement that embodies a cultural model of feminism that is the subject of Dorri Beam's essay, Fuller told her readers, "What woman needs is not as a woman to act or rule, but as a nature to grow, as an intellect to discern, as a soul to live freely and unimpeded, to unfold such powers as were given her when we left our common home." Fuller's woman did not need portrayals that deceive. She did not need fantasies. She needed more than the structural reforms claimed by women's rights advocates then and now. Americans, Fuller declared, needed to dismantle the system of gender relations that had secured female dependence. Grounded in a series of paired oppositions that juxtaposed private and public, household and marketplace, feminine and masculine, the nineteenth-century system of gender relations had made man the measure for all humanity. Inevitably, that yardstick had led to the conviction "that woman was made *for man*," as Fuller aptly described women's position relative to men. Some dismantling has been achieved; however, as Douglas shows, there is still plenty of work to be done.[17]

Any project that liberated women from strictures subordinating them to male authority challenged prevailing binaries of masculinity and femininity. Fuller did so, taking particular aim at the familiar juxtaposition of male strength and female frailty. Those who insisted on this mark of femininity, which signaled that women needed to be protected from rather than encouraged to participate in the world beyond the home, were illogical at best, hypocritical at worst. She charged sarcastically, they "who think that physical circumstances of woman would make a part in the affairs of national government unsuitable, are by no means those who think it impossible for the negresses to endure field work, even during pregnancy, or the semptresses to go through their killing labors." The mention of "negresses" and "semptresses," who were invisible to most of Fuller's readers, might well have brought a shock of recognition. Yes, and obviously, female African American field hands and working-class seamstresses were women. But in an antebellum America in which gender was used not only to mark sexual hierarchies but also to render invisible divisions of race and class, Fuller's white and relatively affluent readers might well have presumed that only those who shared their racial and social status were truly women. Fuller, who, as John Matteson has noted, considered womankind indivisible, did not hesitate to demolish that self-serving presumption.[18]

Fuller's other subjects included the social reformers Angelina Grimké and Abby Kelley, both of whom spoke on behalf of slaves. In highlighting the tribute she paid to Grimké and Kelley, Phyllis Cole notes that Fuller designated women the key to the achievement of antislavery's goals. How were they to accomplish this? Fuller told her readers that these Garrisonian abolitionists had spoken with such moral power that they had been able to subdue "the prejudices of their hearers and excite an interest proportionate to the aversion with which it had been the purpose to regard them." Grimké's and Kelley's impact on their culture derived from a nineteenth-century sensibility that they shared with their audiences. Speaking to the heart, they mobilized the public's "affections" as well as their "reason" on behalf of social reform. Fuller cited a letter she had received from a correspondent who had heard Kelley speak and had told her that Kelley had done "much good," "more than the men in her place could do, for woman feels more as being and reproducing, this brings the subject more into home relations." Men, this correspondent reported, spoke "through and mostly from intellect," a posture that led to "combative[ness]" in relations with their audiences. Readers of Fuller would have understood the larger meaning that resonated through this letter: allowing men sole control of antislavery discourse would result in failure. Women's expression of the "affections," or the heart, their emotionally powerful descriptions of slavery's sin—as much as if not more than the "reason," or the head, which proclaimed the institution's illegitimacy—were required to persuade citizens to return to the nation's founding principles.[19]

Margaret Fuller concluded *Woman in the Nineteenth Century* as she had begun it. Suggesting that the fulfillment of an individual's potential entailed the development of energy and harmony, of power and beauty, of intellect and love, Fuller employed these already familiar juxtapositions for an unusual purpose. In what Charles Capper described as Fuller's "proportional androgyny," differences remained, but they no longer marked the masculine as superior, the feminine as inferior. Instead, Fuller's juxtapositions signaled "unison in variety, congeniality in difference." Equally important, she emphasized that the "masculine" and the "feminine" were not fixed; instead, they were fluid and were "perpetually passing into one another." In offering an alternative system of gender relations, Fuller sought to have the "conditions of life and freedom recognized as the same for the daughters and sons of time." Today we look to her ideas in trying to craft a culture in which all individuals have the opportunity to achieve their potential.[20]

Little more than two weeks after she had completed *Woman in the Nineteenth Century*, Fuller's columns began appearing on the front page of the *New-York Daily Tribune*. Now living in New York City and occupying the post of the newspaper's literary editor, Fuller defined her position broadly, reviewing poetry, theology, fiction, philosophy, and history. Shortly after she joined Greeley at the newspaper, he asked her to report on New York City's prisons, almshouses, hospitals, and insane asylums. Published in March 1845, "Our City's Charities" contained that report and more. Fuller's reasoning can still be heard in debates about marginalized peoples and social welfare in contemporary America. Concerned that institutions for the destitute did not prepare their inmates for self-support, Fuller suggested that the residents be trained in various occupations. She extended this reasoning to those incarcerated in the city's penal institutions. Suggesting that punishment alone was not sufficient, Fuller called for rehabilitation as an objective. In this, she shifted the emphasis from the individual reformation of the self to the collective reform of society.[21]

Fuller was now a "city woman," as Robert Hudspeth remarks. Indeed, Hudspeth tells us, Fuller's reaction to the urban environment "set her apart from Emerson and Thoreau . . . [whose] famous titles are, after all, *Nature* and *Walden*." Already familiar with the asymmetry of power in gender relations, Fuller came to see more clearly the same imbalances in America's class and race relations. Telling her readers, "The ark of human hopes has been placed for the present in our charge," she made America's special destiny the basis for claims on behalf of the nation's disempowered. Sharply criticizing men and women who behaved with condescension toward those less fortunate than themselves, Fuller said the privileged should cultivate a more "expansive nature, a heart alive to affection, and some true notion, however imperfectly developed, of the nature of human brotherhood."[22] She called them to "compassionate witnessing," as Jeffrey Steele notes. This more generous behavior would not challenge the structural relationship between classes. Instead, Fuller's was an "ameliorative" vision, as Adam-Max Tuchinsky tells us. As he demonstrates, Fuller did not suggest that the political order be overthrown but that its obvious defects be addressed with cultural uplift, professional insight, and organized benevolence.

The racially based slavery that dominated the antebellum South was a different matter. Fuller wanted slavery ended. Not surprisingly, she turned to ideas as the place to begin the process. Exposing readers to the contradiction between the promise of equality and the nation's enslavement of African Americans, she focused on the sacred rather than the secular, on what Jeffrey Steele labels "Christianized sentimentalism." Fuller asked her readers to contemplate the words of the anonymous but readily identifiable character of Jesus Christ: "I came hither an uninvited guest, because I read sculptured above the door—'All men born Free and Equal,' and in this dwelling I hoped to find myself at home."[23] As Fuller's Christ made clear, slavery stood as a mockery not only of the Declaration of Independence, but also of the fundamental Christian tenet of the equality of the human soul. Written only four months after the annexation of Texas had extended slavery still further, Fuller's column made her condemnation of the institution equally clear.

Titled simply "Farewell," Fuller's last column as the *Tribune*'s literary editor appeared on August 1, 1846. Acknowledging to her readers that the twenty months spent in New York City had provided her "with a richer and more varied exercise for thought and life than twenty years could in any other part of these United States," she told them that Europe was her next destination.[24] Horace Greeley had agreed to supply the income, paying Fuller ten dollars for each of the dispatches that would appear in his *Tribune*. Twenty months later, Fuller was living amid the fires of revolution that blazed across Europe in 1848. A resident of Rome, she made an impassioned commitment to the cause of Italian unification and independence. With a passion that was equally strong, she pledged herself to Giovanni Ossoli, an Italian nobleman who shared her beliefs about the Italian Revolution. Their son, Angelo, was born two months before the establishment of the Roman Republic in November 1848. This victory on behalf of democratic principles was followed by a series of devastating defeats that culminated in the fall of the republic only seven months later.

Less than a year after their aspirations for unification and independence had been shattered, Fuller, Ossoli, and Angelo left Italy for America. Sailing on the *Elizabeth* on May 17, 1850, they reached Fire Island, New York, sixty-three days later. Only a few hundred yards from shore, the storm-tossed *Elizabeth* was wrecked on a sandbar. All three perished. Fuller's death stilled a voice that had challenged her contemporaries to create an America in which all individuals could fulfill their potential. When she told William Henry Channing that she felt as if she had left a footprint on the earth, Fuller was referring only to *Woman in the Nineteenth Century*. The same might be said about everything that came from her pen. Margaret Fuller's challenge remained *and remains* in the words she left behind.

NOTES

INTRODUCTION: FULLER AT TWO HUNDRED

Many thanks to Conrad Edick Wright and Katheryn P. Viens for their contributions to this introduction. Thanks are due as well to Joel Myerson and Charles Capper, who suggested that the Massachusetts Historical Society honor Fuller with a conference in 2010.

1. The title of Phyllis Cole's work in progress on Fuller is "The Afterlife of Margaret Fuller."
2. Kelley has placed Fuller in a history of late eighteenth- and early nineteenth-century female academies, elite women's increased access to reading and writing, and the growing expectation that this access would allow them to participate in the public sphere. See *Learning to Stand and Speak: Women, Education, and Public Life in America's Republic* (Chapel Hill: University of North Carolina Press, 2006). Cole has documented Fuller's persistent presence as an inspirational example and a cultural critic in women's rights expressions from Fuller's death in 1850 into the early twentieth century; Cole discusses celebrations of Fuller's birthday by women's groups and references to her works by feminist advocates from Paulina Wright Davis to Stanton. See "The Nineteenth-Century Women's Rights Movement and the Canonization of Margaret Fuller," *ESQ: A Journal of the American Renaissance* 44, nos. 1 and 2 (1998): 1–33. See also Judith Mattson Bean's article, which discusses the extensive influence Fuller had on women lecturers and writers who drew on the rhetoric of public speaking, in the same issue of *ESQ:* "'A Presence among Us': Fuller's Place in Nineteenth-Century Oral Culture" (79–123). For further discussion of the masculinizing of the canon of antebellum literature, see Kelley's epilogue to this volume. But Fuller continued to be the subject of some scholarship; see, for example, Madeleine B. Stern, *The Life of Margaret Fuller* (1942; repr., New York: Haskell House, 1968).
3. Cole notes in her contribution here that this integration of literary and political history in feminist studies of Fuller has been slow to emerge.
4. Joseph Jay Deiss, *The Roman Years of Margaret Fuller: A Biography* (New York: Crowell, 1969); Paula Blanchard, *Margaret Fuller: From Transcendentalism to Revolution* (New York: Delacorte/Lawrence, 1978); Margaret Vanderhaar Allen, *The Achievement of Margaret Fuller* (University Park: Pennsylvania State Univer-

sity Press, 1979); Bell Gale Chevigny, *The Woman and the Myth: Margaret Fuller's Life and Writings*, rev. and exp. ed. (1976; repr., Boston: Northeastern University Press, 1994).

5. Examples of connections between antebellum and late twentieth-century critical movements in different disciplines range from the parallels between the analyses of gender ideology by antebellum and Second Wave feminists—as in Elaine Showalter, ed., *The New Feminist Criticism: Essays on Women, Literature and Theory* (New York: Pantheon Books, 1985)—to the parallels between antebellum abolitionists' critiques of U.S. laws and the analysis of the intersections of law and race in contemporary critical legal studies, as in Kimberlé Crenshaw, Neil Gotanda, Gary Peller, and Kendall Thomas, eds., *Critical Race Theory: The Key Writings That Formed the Movement* (New York: New Press, 1995). On the rapid expansion of print culture in this period, see Robert A. Gross and Mary Kelley, *An Extensive Republic: Print, Culture, and Society in the New Nation, 1790–1840*, vol. 2 of *A History of the Book in America* (Chapel Hill: University of North Carolina Press/American Antiquarian Society, 2010); and Scott E. Caspar, Jeffrey D. Groves, Stephen W. Nissenbaum, and Michael Winship, eds., *The Industrial Book, 1840–1880*, vol. 3 of *A History of the Book in America* (Chapel Hill: University of North Carolina Press/American Antiquarian Society, 2007).

6. For Fuller's impact on the women's rights movement, see Cole, "Women's Rights Movement," and Bean, "*Presence* among Us." For approaches to Fuller's international perspectives, see Charles Capper and Cristina Giorcelli, eds., *Margaret Fuller: Transatlantic Crossings in a Revolutionary Age* (Madison: University of Wisconsin Press, 2007).

7. Robert Hudspeth edited *The Letters of Margaret Fuller*, 6 vols. (Ithaca, N.Y.: Cornell University Press, 1983–94). Susan Belasco Smith issued a reprint of Fuller's *Summer on the Lakes* (Urbana: University of Illinois Press, 1991). Judith Mattson Bean and Joel Myerson edited Fuller's New York journalism: *Margaret Fuller, Critic: Writings from the* New-York Tribune, *1844–1846* (New York: Columbia University Press), 2000. Larry J. Reynolds and Susan Belasco Smith edited her foreign correspondence: *"These Sad but Glorious Days": Dispatches from Europe, 1846–1850* (New Haven, Conn.: Yale University Press, 1991). *Woman in the Nineteenth Century* is available in part or in full in several anthologies; for the most thoroughly edited and annotated, see Jeffrey Steele, ed., *The Essential Margaret Fuller* (New Brunswick, N.J.: Rutgers University Press, 1992). Larry J. Reynolds contributed a Norton Critical Edition of *Woman in the Nineteenth Century* (New York: Norton, 1997).

8. Anthologies currently in print include Steele, *Essential Margaret Fuller;* Donna Dickenson, ed., *Margaret Fuller: Woman in the Nineteenth Century and Other Writings* (Oxford: Oxford University Press, 1994); and Mary Kelley, ed., *The Portable Margaret Fuller* (New York: Penguin, 1994). For other editions of her works meant for the classroom, see also Eve Kornfeld's *Margaret Fuller: A Brief Biography with Documents* (Boston: Bedford St. Martin's, 1997), published in

the Bedford Series in History and Culture. A measure of the way in which the recovery of Fuller's texts has gone hand in hand with the academy's revised understanding and undergraduate teaching of the antebellum period is the difference between her representation in the first *Norton Anthology of American Literature* in 1979, which contains excerpts from *Woman in the Nineteenth Century*, and in the 2007 edition of the Norton, which includes excerpts from "The Great Lawsuit" (the essay from which she developed *Woman in the Nineteenth Century*), *Summer on the Lakes*, and three examples of her columns for the *Tribune:* a review of Douglass's *Narrative*, a Fourth of July jeremiad on the state of the nation, and a column on Rome (New York: Norton, 2007).

9. This tally is taken from the list of dissertations on or partially on Fuller (1962–2010) in the *MLA International Bibliography*, Modern Language Association, accessed June 28, 2011, www.mla.org/bibliography.

10. Charles Capper, *Margaret Fuller: An American Romantic Life*, 2 vols. (New York: Oxford University Press, 1992–2007); Joan von Mehren, *Minerva and the Muse: A Life of Margaret Fuller* (Amherst: University of Massachusetts Press, 1994); Meg McGavran Murray, *Margaret Fuller, Wandering Pilgrim* (Athens: University of Georgia Press, 2008). See also Donna Dickenson, *Margaret Fuller: Writing a Woman's Life* (New York: St. Martin's, 1993).

11. Christina Zwarg, *Feminist Conversations: Fuller, Emerson, and the Play of Reading* (Ithaca, N.Y.: Cornell University Press, 1995); Jeffrey Steele, *Transfiguring America: Myth, Ideology, and Mourning in Margaret Fuller's Writing* (Columbia: University of Missouri Press, 2001). Essay collections, as well as individual essays and book chapters on Fuller and her writings, have grown substantially in number, as a glance at the MLA Bibliography will confirm. See also Joel Myerson's bibliographies of criticism of Fuller's texts in the 1970s and 1990s: *Margaret Fuller: An Annotated Secondary Bibliography* (New York: Franklin, 1977); and *Margaret Fuller: An Annotated Bibliography of Criticism, 1983–1995* (Westport, Conn.: Greenwood, 1998).

12. Bell Gale Chevigny and Larry J. Reynolds created the Margaret Fuller Society, which cosponsored the first all-Fuller conference with the New England American Studies Association at Babson College in 1995. The chief organizer of the conference was Fritz Fleischmann, who edited a volume of essays derived from the conference: *Margaret Fuller's Cultural Critique: Her Age and Legacy* (New York: Lang, 2000).

13. The review essay in *American Literary Scholarship*, written annually by David M. Robinson, has since the 1992 issue been titled "Emerson, Thoreau, Fuller, and Transcendentalism." See *American Literary Scholarship, Annual, 1992* (Durham, N.C.: Duke University Press, 1994).

14. John Matteson, *The Lives of Margaret Fuller: A Biography* (New York: Norton, 2012). Cole's study is cited in the first note; her coedited collection emerges out of a special issue titled *Exaltadas: A Female Genealogy of Transcendentalism, ESQ: A Journal of the American Renaissance* 57, nos. 1–2 (2011). In addition, I

am editing a special issue of the journal *Nineteenth-Century Prose* on Fuller. New work also includes a chapter on Fuller in Larry J. Reynolds's book *Righteous Violence: Revolution, Slavery, and the American Renaissance* (Athens: University of Georgia Press, 2011).

15. Many thanks to Reverend Dorothy Emerson for this information (e-mail correspondence, August 3, 2011). Reverend Emerson cochaired the Margaret Fuller Bicentennial Committee with Jessica Lipnack; their website on Fuller has received more than fourteen thousand hits.

16. See Joan D. Hedrick, *Harriet Beecher Stowe: A Life* (New York: Oxford University Press, 1994); Carolyn Karcher, *The First Woman in the Republic: A Cultural Biography of Lydia Maria Child* (Durham, N.C.: Duke University Press, 1994); and Megan Marshall, *The Peabody Sisters: Three Women Who Ignited American Romanticism* (Boston: Houghton Mifflin, 2005). For another collective biography, see Barbara A. White, *The Beecher Sisters* (New Haven, Conn.: Yale University Press, 2003). For examples of collections of essays, see Lucinda Damon-Bach and Victoria Clements, eds., *Catharine Maria Sedgwick: Critical Perspectives* (Boston: Northeastern University Press, 2003); Monika M. Elbert, Julie E. Hall, and Katharine Rodier, eds., *Reinventing the Peabody Sisters* (Iowa City: University of Iowa Press, 2006); and JerriAnne Boggis, Eve Allegra Raimon, and Barbara A. White, eds., *Harriet Wilson's New England: Race, Writing, and Region* (Hanover: University of New Hampshire Press, 2007).

17. The exception is Albert J. von Frank's contribution on Fuller and the antislavery movement, which the editors invited subsequently.

18. The conference was greatly benefited by Megan Marshall's exhibition of visual material, manuscripts, and artifacts associated with Fuller and her contemporaries, displayed at the Massachusetts Historical Society, Boston, in 2010.

19. Larry J. Reynolds, "Margaret Fuller," in *Prospects for the Study of American Literature*, vol. 2, ed. Richard Kopley and Barbara Cantalupo (New York: AMS, 2009), 50–71. This article represents an update of his earlier essay, "Prospects for the Study of Margaret Fuller," *Resources for the Study of American Literature* 26, no. 2 (2000): 139–58.

20. Reynolds, "Margaret Fuller," 62.

1. FULLER'S LAWSUIT AND FEMINIST HISTORY

1. Elizabeth Cady Stanton, Susan B. Anthony, Matilda Joslyn Gage, and Ida Usted Harper, eds., *History of Woman Suffrage*, 6 vols. (1881–1922; repr., New York: Arno, 1969), 1:801–2, 34, 39–40, 1. Their appendix on Fuller (1:801–2) was the only such biography added to this opening chapter of myriad names.

2. Charles Capper, *The Public Years*, vol. 2 of *Margaret Fuller: An American Romantic Life* (New York: Oxford University Press, 2007), 190; Robert N. Hudspeth, ed., *Letters of Margaret Fuller*, 6 vols. (Ithaca, N.Y.: Cornell University Press, 1983–94), 2:242; Caroline Healey Dall, *The College, the Market, and the Court;*

or, Woman's Relation to Education, Labor, and Law (1867; repr., New York: Arno, 1972), 83–130.

3. Early history anthologies suggest the relative unease with which Fuller has been entertained: Miriam Schneir, ed., *Feminism: The Essential Historical Writings* (New York: Random House, 1972), describes Fuller's manifesto as "a bewildering mix of mysticism and pragmatism" (63), while Alice S. Rossi, ed., *The Feminist Papers: From Adams to Beauvoir* (New York: Columbia University Press, 1973), includes Fuller in a section on "The Enlightenment Perspective" but comments only on her life rather than her text within that category. More recently, in her study of rhetoric at the women's rights conventions, Nancy Isenberg positions Fuller as a background figure through her journalism; however, without even mentioning *Woman in the Nineteenth Century*, she concludes that Fuller was "just one woman among the literati," choosing print over the "visible, decidedly more exposed domain of public speaking." *Sex and Citizenship in Antebellum America* (Chapel Hill: University of North Carolina Press, 1998), 57. Among the historians who scrutinize Fuller in depth are Capper in his biography and Mary Kelley, whose social history of women's civic emergence incorporates the influence of both Wollstonecraft and Fuller. *Learning to Stand and Speak: Women, Education, and Public Life in America's Republic* (Chapel Hill: University of North Carolina Press, 2006). Two exceptionally wide-ranging literary interpretations of Fuller's feminism are Susan Phinney Conrad, *Perish the Thought: Intellectual Women in Romantic America, 1830–1860* (New York: Oxford University Press, 1976), which proposes the influence of a "grammar of romanticism" on nineteenth-century woman's rights arguments, and Elaine Showalter, *Inventing Herself: Claiming a Feminist Intellectual Heritage* (New York: Scribner, 2001), though it ranges across generations of literary and philosophical writing without mentioning the political movement for women's rights.

4. Elizabeth Ann Bartlett, introduction to her edition of Sarah Grimké, *Letters on the Equality of the Sexes and Other Essays* (New Haven, Conn.: Yale University Press, 1988), 6–11. See also Bartlett, *Liberty, Equality, Sorority: The Origins and Interpretation of American Feminist Thought; Frances Wright, Sarah Grimké, and Margaret Fuller* (Brooklyn: Carlsen, 1994), 101, 158n69. Christina Zwarg, *Feminist Conversations: Fuller, Emerson, and the Play of Reading* (Ithaca, N.Y.: Cornell University Press, 1995), 24–28, 37–39, 52–55, 114–19, provides the best discussion of Fuller's Fourier-inspired socialism.

5. John Paul Gatta, *American Madonna: Images of the Divine Woman in Literary Culture* (New York: Oxford University Press, 1997), 42; Jeffrey Steele, *Transfiguring America: Myth, Ideology, and Mourning in Margaret Fuller's Writing* (Columbia: University of Missouri Press, 2001), 112.

6. Sarah Grimké published under the title *Letters on the Equality of the Sexes, and the Condition of Woman. Addressed to Mary S. Parker, President of the Boston Female Anti-Slavery Society* (Boston: Knapp, 1838); Angelina Grimké wrote *Appeal to the Christian Women of the Southern States* (New York: American Anti-Slavery

Society, 1836) and *An Appeal to the Women of the Nominally Free States* (New York: Dorr, 1837).

7. Margaret Fuller, "The Great Lawsuit. Man versus Men. Woman versus Women," in *Transcendentalism: A Reader*, ed. Joel Myerson (New York: Oxford University Press, 2000), 383–84, 422; Fuller, *Woman in the Nineteenth Century*, in *The Essential Margaret Fuller*, ed. Jeffrey Steele (New Brunswick, N.J.: Rutgers University Press, 1992), 245. Marie Olesen Urbanski began to describe this rhetorical strategy by calling Fuller's essay a "sermon," but with an antagonistic overtone that "suggests court action." "The Genesis, Form, Tone, and Rhetorical Devices of Woman in the Nineteenth Century," in *Critical Essays on Margaret Fuller*, ed. Joel Myerson (Boston: Hall, 1980), 268–69.

8. In *History of Woman Suffrage*, Stanton and her coauthors misrepresented the subtitle of Fuller's essay as "Man vs. Woman, Woman vs. Man" (1:801). The element of conflict they accentuated, however, was not wholly absent from Fuller's larger argument.

9. James Kent, *Commentaries on American Law* (1827; repr., New York: Da Capo, 1971), 2:129–30. On the response of literature to law in American culture, see Robert A. Ferguson, *Law and Letters in American Culture* (Cambridge: Harvard University Press, 1984); and Priscilla Wald, *Constituting Americans: Cultural Anxiety and Narrative Form* (Durham, N.C.: Duke University Press, 1995). Linda K. Kerber discusses the limited privileges of single as well as married women under the law of coverture. *Women of the Republic: Intellect and Ideology in Revolutionary America* (Chapel Hill: University of North Carolina Press, 1980), 120, 153.

10. Five years before William Seward and Ralph Waldo Emerson declared for a "higher law than the Constitution" that would invalidate the Fugitive Slave Law of 1850, Fuller elucidated both the authority of such a law and its dynamic openness to evolving interpretation. On the later crisis in legal and intellectual context, see Gregg D. Crane, *Race, Citizenship, and Law in American Literature* (Cambridge: Cambridge University Press, 2002), esp. the intro. and ch. 1.

11. Fuller, *Woman*, 253–54.

12. Ibid., 251–52.

13. See Robert D. Richardson Jr., *Myth and Literature in the American Renaissance* (Bloomington: Indiana University Press, 1978), 54–64, on Orpheus and Orphism in Transcendentalism; and Steele, *Transfiguring America*, 114–17, on the call of Eurydice.

14. Mary Wollstonecraft, *A Vindication of the Rights of Woman*, ed. Carol H. Poston, Norton Critical ed. (New York: Norton, 1975), 45; S. Grimké, *Letters*, 73; this and subsequent references are to the Bartlett edition.

15. Different lines from these letters are quoted in Charles Capper, *The Private Years*, vol. 1 of *Margaret Fuller: An American Romantic Life* (New York: Oxford University Press, 1992), 30; and Meg McGavran Murray, *Margaret Fuller: Wandering Pilgrim* (Athens: University of Georgia Press, 2008), 9.

NOTES

16. On this crossing of Transcendental and abolitionist company, see Phyllis Cole, "'Men and Women Conversing': The Emersons in 1837," in *Emersonian Circles: Essays in Honor of Joel Myerson*, ed. Wesley T. Mott and Robert E. Burkholder (Rochester: University of Rochester Press, 1997), 152–54.
17. Fuller, *Woman*, 284. Cf. Fuller, "Great Lawsuit," in Myerson, *Transcendentalism*, 407.
18. Quoted in Murray, *Margaret Fuller*, 9.
19. Fuller, *Woman*, 284, 286.
20. Ibid., 283–86.
21. Critical opinion is sharply divided on the portrayal of Wollstonecraft in Godwin's *Memoirs*. Among those valuing his candor and loyalty are Showalter in *Inventing Herself*, 31–38. Barbara Caine, in *English Feminism, 1780–1980* (Oxford: Oxford University Press, 1997), 40–41, instead calls the book a "positive gift" to antifeminists, as it emphasizes not only Wollstonecraft's sexual aberrations but also an entrapment in emotion that undercut her rational feminist argument.
22. Fuller, *Woman*, 284.
23. Pamela Clemit, ed., *St. Leon* (1799; repr., Oxford: Oxford University Press, 1994), xv–xvii, 75, 132–35.
24. Kelley, *Learning to Stand*, 235, 242. On Fuller's relation to Emerson, see Zwarg, *Feminist Conversations*, and Phyllis Cole, "Woman Questions: Emerson, Fuller, and New England Reform," in *Transient and Permanent: The Transcendentalist Movement and Its Contexts*, ed. Charles Capper and Conrad Edick Wright (Boston: Massachusetts Historical Society, 1999), 408–46.
25. Fuller, *Woman*, 347, cf. 308; Wollstonecraft, *Vindication*, 8, 26; Fuller, *Woman*, 260–61.
26. Fuller, *Woman*, 261–62; Wollstonecraft, *Vindication*, 20; Fuller, *Woman*, 346.
27. Wollstonecraft, *Vindication*, 12; Fuller, *Woman*, 309.
28. Gatta, *American Madonna*, 42. Bartlett shares this assumption of a divide between Enlightenment and Romantic thought.
29. Wollstonecraft, *Vindication*, 21.
30. Barbara Taylor, *Mary Wollstonecraft and the Feminist Imagination* (Cambridge: Cambridge University Press, 2003), 103–4. See Kenneth W. Cameron, *Transcendental Climate* (Hartford, Conn.: Transcendental Books, 1963), 1:154–55, 165–66, for Ralph Waldo Emerson's Harvard-bred knowledge of Price, and Phyllis Cole, *Mary Moody Emerson and the Origins of Transcendentalism: A Family History* (New York: Oxford University Press, 1998), 167–68, for the conversation between Mary and Waldo Emerson on Price's "immutable and eternal" principles of right and wrong.
31. Wollstonecraft, *Vindication*, 21, 25–26, 8; Fuller, *Woman*, 310–11.
32. Wollstonecraft, *Vindication*, 5; Fuller, *Woman*, 252–53.
33. Wollstonecraft, *Vindication*, 24–38, 175.
34. Fuller, *Woman*, 252–55.

35. Wollstonecraft, *Vindication*, 15; Taylor, *Mary Wollstonecraft*, 1–4, 151, 155; Wollstonecraft, *Vindication*, 57.
36. Fuller, *Woman*, 345; Wollstonecraft, *Vindication*, 147–48, 36.
37. Fuller, *Woman*, 262, 315, 243, trans. 452n1. This credo, from Schiller's 1789 poem "The Artists," affirms the correspondence of creative mind and universal law in the context of apparently imminent humanistic revolution, a hope prompted for Schiller by events in France. Schiller's German Romantic poetry has an important consonance with Wollstonecraft's 1792 manifesto. For Schiller's authorship (unnamed by Fuller) and a discussion of the poem's significance, see Marianna Wertz, "The Artists," Schiller Institute, 2002, accessed November 18, 2009, www.schillerinstitute.org/transl/schiller_artist_article.html.
38. Cf. his words in the "American Scholar" address: "It is a shame to [the scholar] if his tranquillity, amid dangerous times, arise from the presumption, that, like children and women, his is a protected class." Joel Porte, ed., *Ralph Waldo Emerson: Essays and Addresses* (New York: Library of America, 1983), 65.
39. Carol Strauss Sotiropoulos, "Revisiting Fuller, Goethe, and the German Romantics," paper presented at the annual meeting of the Modern Language Association of America, Philadelphia, December 28, 2009.
40. Fuller, *Woman*, 264.
41. Ibid., 296–97, 284, 285. Gary Williams, "George Sand and Margaret Fuller: 'Expansive Fellowship,'" paper presented at the conference "Transatlanticism in American Literature," Oxford University, Oxford, July 2006; Fuller, *Woman*, 285.
42. Meg McGavran Murray, introduction to unpublished ms. (1975). My thanks to her for permitting quotation from this document, an expansion from her dissertation comparing Wollstonecraft and Fuller: Margaret Ross McGavran, "Mary and Margaret: The Triumph of Woman" (PhD diss., Cornell University, 1973). Murray's recent biography, *Margaret Fuller*, while it does not sustain her earlier comparison to Wollstonecraft, comments again on their affinity as part of her larger study of Fuller's psychosexual development (193–94).
43. James Freeman Clarke, Ralph Waldo Emerson, and William Henry Channing, eds., *Memoirs of Margaret Fuller Ossoli*, 2 vols. (Boston: Phillips, Sampson, 1852), 2:281.
44. George Eliot, "Margaret Fuller and Mary Wollstonecraft," in Wollstonecraft, *Vindication*, 243–49; Gordon S. Haight, ed., *The George Eliot Letters*, 9 vols. (New Haven, Conn.: Yale University Press, 1954–78), 2:15. Eliot alluded to Fuller's words in Clarke, Emerson, and Channing, *Memoirs*, 1:237.
45. The original lectures were published in Caroline Healey Dall, *Historical Pictures Retouched: A Volume of Miscellanies* (Boston: Walker, Wise, 1860).
46. Dall, *College*, 89, 91, 116–17. For Dall's more personal record of thoughts about the desertion of her husband, Charles, and about Fuller, see *Selected Journals of Caroline Healey Dall*, ed. Helen R. Deese, vol. 1 (Boston: Massachusetts Historical Society, 2006). Upon first reading the *Memoirs* in 1852, Dall began her

multipage journal response by confessing, "In Margaret Fuller's Autobiography I see my own life renewed" (359–68).
47. Dall, *College*, 116; Eliot, "Margaret Fuller," 244.
48. Larry Ceplair, ed., *The Public Years of Sarah and Angelina Grimké* (New York: Columbia University Press, 1989), 139–141, and, for the text of the "Pastoral Letter," 211–12.
49. Fuller, *Woman*, 305–8.
50. Ibid., 259, 301–8, 341–42.
51. S. Grimké, *Letters*, 71–72, 74–75.
52. Ibid., 73.
53. Steele, *Transfiguring America*, 114, 119; Fuller, *Woman*, 257.
54. Elizabeth Cady Stanton, *Eighty Years and More: Reminiscences 1815–1897* (1898; repr., New York: Schocken Books, 1971), 31–32; Gerda Lerner, *The Grimké Sisters from South Carolina: Pioneers for Women's Rights and Abolition* (1967; repr., New York: Oxford University Press, 1998), 12, 15, 19.
55. Murray, *Margaret Fuller*, 17, 20–21.
56. Fuller, "Autobiographical Romance," in Steele, *Essential Margaret Fuller*, esp. 24, 26–27. This quote is from 28–29. Cf. Stanton, *Eighty Years*, 20, and Lerner, *Grimké Sisters*, 16.
57. Hudspeth, *Letters of Margaret Fuller*, 1:237.
58. Fuller, *Woman*, 256–58.
59. "The Legal Wrongs of Women," *United States Magazine and Democratic Review* 14, no. 71 (May 1844): 477–83; cf. Fuller, *Woman*, 454n33.
60. Fuller, *Woman*, 258.
61. Steele, *Transfiguring America*, 108, 117–20.
62. S. Grimké, *Letters*, 31–33, 89–95, 40–41.
63. Fuller, *Woman*, 248, 266–69, 249.
64. S. Grimké, *Letters*, 96, 103.
65. Fuller, *Woman*, 261, 254.
66. S. Grimké, *Letters*, 76; Wollstonecraft, *Vindication*, 201.
67. Fuller, *Woman*, 246, 345, 260.
68. Sarah Moore Grimké to Harriot Kezia Hunt, December 31, 1852, manuscript, Weld-Grimké Papers, William L. Clement Library, University of Michigan, Ann Arbor. Quotation of this manuscript is with permission. Cf. Gerda Lerner, ed., *The Feminist Thought of Sarah Grimké* (New York: Oxford University Press, 1998), 29–31, on the context for this letter.
69. Quoted in Stanton, Anthony, and Gage, *History of Woman Suffrage*, 1:355. The passage is from Clarke, Emerson, and Channing, *Memoirs*, 1:303.
70. Stanton, Anthony, and Gage, *History of Woman Suffrage*, 1:353.
71. S. Grimké, *Letters*, 135–36, 108.
72. Ibid., *Letters*, 164; emphasis added.
73. Paulina Wright Davis, *A History of the National Woman's Rights Movement, for Twenty Years* (New York: Journeymen Printer's Cooperative Association, 1871),

17, 14; cf. Phyllis Cole, "The Nineteenth-Century Women's Rights Movement and the Canonization of Margaret Fuller," *ESQ: A Journal of the American Renaissance* 44 (1998): 1–33. Information about 1850s Fuller publications is in Showalter, *Inventing Herself*, 58, and Capper, *Public Years*, 192.

74. Stanton, Anthony, and Gage, *History of Woman Suffrage*, 1:70–73; Dall, *Historical Pictures Retouched*, 249; "Address by ECS on Woman's Rights," *The Selected Papers of Elizabeth Cady Stanton and Susan B. Anthony*, ed. Ann D. Gordon, 5 vols. to date (New Brunswick, N.J.: Rutgers University Press, 1997–forthcoming), 1:107, 115–16 (cf. Fuller, *Woman*, 346, 349). On Stanton's 1848 echoing of Fuller and ongoing use of her work, see Phyllis Cole, "Stanton, Fuller, and the Grammar of Romanticism," *New England Quarterly* 73 (2000): 533–59.

75. Joan W. Scott, "The Imagination of Olympe de Gouges," in *Mary Wollstonecraft and 200 Years of Feminisms*, ed. Eileen Janes Yeo (London: Rivers Oram, 1997), 36.

2. FULLER AND THE PROBLEM OF FEMININE VIRTUE

1. Margaret Fuller to Caroline Sturgis, October 22, 1840, *The Letters of Margaret Fuller*, ed. Robert N. Hudspeth, 6 vols. (Ithaca, N.Y.: Cornell University Press, 1983–94), 2:168; emphasis in the original.

2. Ralph Waldo Emerson, "Journal D," in *Selected Journals: 1820–1842*, ed. Lawrence Rosenwald (New York: Library of America, 2010), 646; "Journal A," 322; "Journal Q," 206; "Journal A," 296.

3. Robert D. Habich, ed., "Margaret Fuller's Journal for October 1842," *Harvard Library Bulletin* 33 (Summer 1985): 287.

4. Habich, "Fuller's Journal," 286.

5. Fuller's thinking on this subject was not entirely removed from the philosophical position later announced by Tolstoy in his novella *The Kreutzer Sonata*, that sexual desire continually prevents humankind from ascending to its divine potential and that the millennium will be achieved only when men and women stop having babies and start focusing on achieving moral perfection in the current generation. Although Fuller never traced out her thought to such a radical conclusion, her notion of sexual desire as lowering the status of heterosexual relationships has similar undertones.

6. Margaret Fuller, "Credo," in *Margaret Fuller and Goethe: The Development of a Remarkable Personality, Her Religion and Philosophy, and Her Relation to Emerson, J. F. Clarke, and Transcendentalism*, ed. Frederick Augustus Braun (New York: Holt, 1910), 248.

7. Ibid., 250.

8. Margaret Fuller, *Woman in the Nineteenth Century* (New York: Greeley and McElrath, 1845), 10. I have used the original texts of *Woman in the Nineteenth Century* and *Summer on the Lakes* with the supposition that these versions are the

most authoritative and, thanks to computer technology, the least expensive and most readily accessible. The 1845 *Woman in the Nineteenth Century* can be found in Google books.
9. Habich, "Fuller's Journal," 290.
10. Jeffrey Steele, *Transfiguring America: Myth, Ideology, and Mourning in Margaret Fuller's Writing* (Columbia: University of Missouri Press, 2001), 140, 150; Fuller to William H. Channing, March 29, 1841, in Hudspeth, *Letters of Margaret Fuller*, 2:205; Cheryl J. Fish, *Black and White Women's Travel Narratives: Antebellum Explorations* (Gainesville: University Press of Florida, 2004), 109.
11. Margaret Fuller, *Summer on the Lakes in 1843* (Boston: Little and Brown, 1844), 26. This original text of *Summer on the Lakes* can be found in Google books.
12. Fuller, *Summer on the Lakes*, 81, 85, 90, 91.
13. Ibid., 99, 97, 99.
14. Ibid., 94, 95.
15. Ibid., 15; Fish, *Women's Travel Narratives*, 102.
16. Fuller, *Summer on the Lakes*, 145, 128.
17. Fuller to Ralph Waldo Emerson, July 11, 1848, in Hudspeth, *Letters of Margaret Fuller*, 5:86.
18. Fuller, *Summer on the Lakes*, 138, 139; Fish, *Women's Travel Narratives*, 128.
19. Fuller, *Summer on the Lakes*, 159–60.
20. Fuller to Ralph Waldo Emerson, July 11, 1848, Hudspeth, *Letters of Margaret Fuller*, 5:86.
21. Fuller, *Summer on the Lakes*, 160.
22. Margaret Fuller, "The Great Lawsuit. Man versus Men. Woman versus Women," *Dial* 4 (July 1843): 43, 44.
23. Professor Dorri Beam's contribution in this volume speaks sagely of Fuller's perception of "the great radical dualism" between male and female.
24. Georgiana Bruce Kirby, *Years of Experience: An Autobiographical Narrative* (New York: Putnam's Sons, 1887), 190.
25. Fuller to Georgiana Bruce, October 20, 1844, in Hudspeth, *Letters of Margaret Fuller*, 3:236.
26. Ibid.
27. Kirby, *Years of Experience*, 218–19.
28. Fuller to Elizabeth Hoar, October 28[?], 1844, in Hudspeth, *Letters of Margaret Fuller*, 3:237.
29. Fuller to Georgiana Bruce, August 15, 1844, in Hudspeth, *Letters of Margaret Fuller*, 3:223.
30. Fuller to the Women Inmates at Sing Sing, early November [?] 1844, in Hudspeth, *Letters of Margaret Fuller*, 3:238.
31. Kirby, *Years of Experience*, 221.
32. Fuller to Georgiana Bruce, July 27[?], 1845, in Hudspeth, *Letters of Margaret Fuller*, 4:143–44.
33. Fuller, *Woman*, 106.

34. Fuller, "Great Lawsuit," 10.
35. Fuller, *Woman*, 118, 119.
36. Ibid., 120.
37. Ibid., 132.
38. Fuller to Georgiana Bruce, in Hudspeth, *Letters of Margaret Fuller*, 3:236.
39. Fuller, *Woman*, 132.
40. Ibid., 133.
41. Ibid., 159, 162.
42. Fuller, *Summer on the Lakes*, 129.
43. Margaret Fuller, "Great Lawsuit," 30; Fuller, *Woman*, 65.

3. FULLER, FEMINISM, PANTHEISM

1. Perry Miller, "Jonathan Edwards to Emerson," *New England Quarterly* 13 (December 1940): 589–617 (see 616, 617, 611).
2. Ibid., 600, 591.
3. Miller's primary motivation was to show that Transcendentalist mysticisms were "restatements of a native disposition," that is, "less an oriental ecstasy and more a natural reaction of some descendants of Puritans and Quakers to Unitarian and commercial times" ("Jonathan Edwards to Emerson," 596, 595). While his argument about the "dual heritage" of Calvinism is convincing and his historicizing of mystical enthusiasms important, the exceptionalist logic he uses to protect Transcendentalism from foreign ("oriental") influences is unnecessarily shortsighted and of course truncates the feminist import of Fuller's work.
4. Perry Miller, *Margaret Fuller: American Romantic* (Ithaca, N.Y.: Cornell University Press, 1963), xvii. For a discussion of the critical reception of Fuller, see my *Style, Gender, and Fantasy in Nineteenth-Century American Women's Writing* (Cambridge: Cambridge University Press, 2010), which discusses at length gender and "highly wrought" writing.
5. Miller, "Jonathan Edwards to Emerson," 591.
6. Judith Butler's *Gender Trouble: Feminism and the Subversion of Identity* (New York: Routledge, 1990) most notably restored continental thinkers to change the shape of American feminist critique. Saba Mahmood's *The Politics of Piety: The Islamic Revival and the Feminist Subject* (Princeton, N.J.: Princeton University Press, 2005) is one recent critique of the limitations of "secular" Western feminism. The nineteenth-century writing I examine here requires a similar rethinking of the gendered commitments entailed in the ecstasy and passion it foregrounds. This writing demands a treatment of gender and sexuality as in part disembodied phenomena that reverberates with Butler's work and an open recognition of the subjective forms available in nonsecular epistemologies.
7. Margaret Fuller, review of *Etherology; or, The Philosophy of Mesmerism and Phrenology*, by J. Stanley Grimes, *New-York Daily Tribune*, February 17, 1845,

1, reprinted in *Margaret Fuller, Critic: Writings from the New-York Tribune, 1844–1846*, ed. Judith Mattson Bean and Joel Myerson, with CD-ROM (New York: Columbia University Press, 2000).
8. Fuller reviewed Leger's *Animal Magnetism; or, Psychodunamy* for the *Tribune* in 1846. Fuller, review of *Animal Magnetism; or, Psychodunamy*, by Theodore Leger, *New-York Daily Tribune*, May 30, 1846, supplement, 1, in Bean and Myerson, *Margaret Fuller, Critic*. See Georgiana Bruce Kirby's description of Fuller's treatment by Leger in Kirby, *Years of Experience* (New York: Putnam, 1887), 213–14. Joan von Mehren's biography of Fuller reports that Fuller's friends Sam and Anna Ward were so shocked by the transformation in Fuller that Anna put herself into Leger's care. By the doctor's account, Fuller's shoulders had evened out and she had gained four inches in height. Joan von Mehren speculates on the curative powers of Fuller's romance with James Nathan, whom she would regularly meet outside Leger's office after her appointments; see Joan von Mehren, *Minerva and the Muse: A Life of Margaret Fuller* (Amherst: University of Massachusetts Press, 1994), 206. For Fuller's interest in Mesmerism around the time of the earlier review of Grimes, see Susan Belasco's account of Fuller's 1844 epistolary exchanges with Emerson, in which she teased him about avoiding evenings with a clairvoyant at the home of James Freeman and Sarah Clarke. "'The Animating Influences of Discord': Margaret Fuller in 1844," *Legacy* 20 (2003): 76–93.
9. Julian Hawthorne discusses the drugs administered to his mother in *Nathaniel Hawthorne and His Wife, a Biography* (Boston: Osgood, 1884), 1:64. Taylor Stoehr discusses Sophia's interest in Mesmerism and her morphine addiction in *Hawthorne's Mad Scientists: Pseudoscience and Social Science in Nineteenth-Century Life and Letters* (Hamden, Conn.: Shoestring Books/Archon, 1978), 45.
10. Ralph Waldo Emerson, "Self-Reliance," in *Emerson's Prose and Poetry*, ed. Joel Porte and Saundra Morris (New York: Norton, 2001), 123.
11. Harriet Martineau, *Letters on Mesmerism*, 2nd ed. (London: Moxon, 1845), 40, 25.
12. Chauncy Hare Townshend, *Facts in Mesmerism, with Reasons for a Dispassionate Inquiry into It* (New York: Harper, 1841), vii, viii.
13. Ibid., 7, 131, 160, 261, 160, 223.
14. Joseph Haddock, *Psychology; or, The Science of the Soul, Considered Physiologically and Philosophically* (New York: Fowler and Wells, 1850), 60, 62.
15. Townshend, *Facts in Mesmerism*, 327.
16. Haddock, *Psychology*, 63, 65.
17. Fuller, *Woman in the Nineteenth Century* (1845), in *The Essential Margaret Fuller*, ed. Jeffrey Steele (New Brunswick, N.J.: Rutgers University Press, 1995), 302.
18. Leigh Kirkland, "A Human Life: Being the Autobiography of Elizabeth Oakes Smith; A Critical Edition and Introduction" (Ph.D. diss., Georgia State University, 1994), 245.
19. Barbara Welter, *Dimity Convictions: The American Woman in the Nineteenth Century* (Athens: Ohio University Press, 1976), 96. For an account of Fuller's in-

terest in mysticism as a site for alternative constructions of female identity throughout her life and writing, see Jeffrey Steele, *Transfiguring America: Myth, Ideology, and Mourning in Margaret Fuller's Writing* (Columbia: University of Missouri Press, 2001). Charles Capper's biography, *Margaret Fuller: An American Romantic Life*, 2 vols. (New York: Oxford University Press, 1992–2007), offers fine-grained analyses of the cosmopolitan intellectual and cultural influences behind Fuller's mystical commitments. Fuller's interest in a variety of nontraditional and occult beliefs is surveyed in Deshae Lott, "Preaching Mysticism: Margaret Fuller and the Veiled Lady," *Studia Mystica* 20 (1999): 57–112. Christina Zwarg's *Feminist Conversations: Fuller, Emerson, and the Play of Reading* (Ithaca, N.Y.: Cornell University Press, 1995) treats Fuller's interest in Mesmerism in relation to the Seeress of Prevorst in Fuller's *Summer on the Lakes* (116–19).

20. Elizabeth Oakes Smith, *Woman and Her Needs* (New York: Fowler and Wells, 1851), 20.
21. Ibid., 28, 22.
22. Ibid., 24, 28, 43.
23. Fuller, *Woman*, 302, 309.
24. This was particularly the case in debates about Fuller's positioning in the "separate" literary spheres. Ann Douglas inaugurated a pervasive view that describes Fuller as a heroine of masculinity combating the rancid "feminization" of American culture. *The Feminization of American Culture*, 1977 (New York: Macmillan, 1988). Critics have more recently argued for the continuities between Fuller and "feminine" cultures of sentimentality or domesticity. Yet Fuller's distinction and distance from any construction of the feminine is still often asserted: Sandra Gustafson focuses on Fuller's use of "sentimental ideals to justify antisentimental forms" — in fact to justify a genderless rhetorical form. "Choosing a Medium: Margaret Fuller and the Forms of Sentiment," *American Quarterly* 47 (1995): 34–65 (esp. 50). Jeffrey Steele's work on Fuller's development of a personal mythology of feminine figures and zones, as well as his attention to her mystical modes, has been one notable exception to critical discomfort with Fuller's interest in a notion of feminine difference (Steele, *Transfiguring America*), as is Julie Ellison's *Delicate Subjects: Romanticism, Gender, and the Ethics of Understanding* (Ithaca, N.Y.: Cornell University Press, 1990), though here Fuller's embrace of femininity is sometimes made to seem compensatory, an effect of her alienation from Romantic cultures dominated by men as she struggled to make "genius" compatible with her gender. This contribution attempts to take Fuller's theory of gender and interest in Transcendental modes in *Woman in the Nineteenth Century* at face value, historically reconstructing how these operate, rather than positing them as symptomatic of ideological or psychological conflict.
25. Cynthia J. Davis, "What 'Speaks in Us': Margaret Fuller, Woman's Rights, and

Human Nature," in *Margaret Fuller's Cultural Critique: Her Age and Legacy*, ed. Fritz Fleischmann (New York: Lang, 2000), 45; emphasis in the original.
26. Fuller, *Woman*, 310.
27. Oakes Smith, too, insisted on gender fluidity in the flesh while continuing to pursue her theory of gendered essence. She also paid homage to "the infinitude of shades in either sex by which they blend into each other, and those great occasions in life which may transform a woman into a Medea" and (in a valiant attempt to better Fuller's example of Hercules spinning) transform "the American savage into a nursing mother to his bereaved child" (*Woman and Her Needs*, 41). Indeed, in this example of the lactating father, even the dimorphism of biological sex was challenged.
28. Fuller, *Woman*, 310.
29. Ibid., 309.
30. Pheng Cheah and Elizabeth Grosz, "The Future of Sexual Difference: An Interview with Judith Butler and Drucilla Cornell," *Diacritics: A Review of Contemporary Criticism* 28 (1998): 19–42 (esp. 22).
31. John Edmonds, *Intercourse with Spirits of the Living* (New York, 1858), 7; Lydia Maria Child, *The Progress of Religious Ideas, through Successive Ages*, 3 vols. (New York: Frances, 1855), 1:26, 2:176. Haddock's *Psychology* said much the same: "Metaphysicians have studied mind irrespective of form or matter; and some philosophers would resolve all things into material operation, irrespective of mind. I believe that fact and demonstrative evidence will prove both classes of philosophers to be wrong. From Divine Revelation we know that there is both spirit or mind, and matter; both a spiritual body and a natural body" (10). Sarah Helen Whitman—friend of Oakes Smith, spiritual kindred of Poe, professed Spiritualist, and poet—also expressed interest: "The idea of an existing spiritual body enshrined within, and veiled by the material, has long attracted my attention." Quoted in Eliab Wilkinson Capron, *Modern Spiritualism: Its Facts and Fanaticisms, Its Consistencies and Contradictions* (1855; repr., New York: Arno, 1976), 238.
32. Elizabeth Oakes Smith, *Shadow Land; or, The Seer* (New York: Fowler and Wells, 1852), 14.
33. Caroline Chesebro,' "The Clairvoyant," in *Dream-Land by Daylight: A Panorama of Romance* (Clinton Hall, N.Y.: Redfield, 1851), 77.
34. Child, *Progress of Religious Ideas*, 1:364–65; emphasis in the original.
35. Elizabeth Oakes Smith, *Bertha and Lily; or, The Parsonage of Beech Glen: A Romance* (New York: Derby, 1854), 283.
36. Quoted in J. C. Derby, *Fifty Years among Authors, Books, and Publishers* (Hartford, Conn.: Winter and Hatch, 1886), 549; emphasis in the original.
37. Haddock, *Psychology*, 67; emphasis in the original.
38. Martineau, *Letters on Mesmerism*, 16.
39. Cora Hatch, *The Day after Death: A Discourse by Epes Sargent, Delivered through*

the Medial Instrumentality of Mrs. Cora L. V. Richmond (Boston: Colby and Rich, 1881), 8.
40. Oakes Smith, *Shadow Land*, 34–35.
41. Mary Clemmer, *Victoire: A Novel* (New York: Carleton, 1864), 45.
42. Ibid., 44.
43. Ibid., 96–97.
44. Ibid., 223.
45. See Robyn Wiegman, "Feminism's Apocalyptic Futures," *New Literary History* 31 (2000): 805–25, for a discussion of the uses of a "meantime" in contemporary feminist impasses.
46. Judith Butler, *Undoing Gender* (New York: Routledge, 2004), 29.
47. Clemmer, *Victoire*, 99.
48. Fuller, *Woman*, 309.
49. Robert C. Fuller, *Mesmerism and the American Cure of Souls* (Philadelphia: University of Pennsylvania Press, 1982), 59.
50. Butler, *Undoing Gender*, 28, 33.
51. Ibid., 16.

4. MARGARET FULLER, SELF-CULTURE, AND ASSOCIATIONISM

1. Bruce A. Ronda, *Elizabeth Palmer Peabody: A Reformer on Her Own Terms* (Cambridge: Harvard University Press, 1999), 261, 370n60. This is an often repeated story, and as Ronda notes, there are at least two versions of it among the historical sources.
2. Laura E. Richards, *Stepping Westward* (New York: Appleton, 1931), 65–66. In Richards's account, John Sullivan Dwight recounts this story about Alcott.
3. Henry David Thoreau, *Walden*, ed. J. Lyndon Shanley (Princeton, N.J.: Princeton University Press, 1971), 171.
4. William Ellery Channing, "Self-Culture," in *William Ellery Channing: Selected Writings*, ed. David M. Robinson (Mahwah, N.J.: Paulist, 1985), 226, 227.
5. James Freeman Clarke, Ralph Waldo Emerson, and William Henry Channing, eds., *Memoirs of Margaret Fuller Ossoli*, 2 vols. (Boston: Phillips, Sampson, 1852), 1:132; emphasis in the original; 1:117.
6. Ralph Waldo Emerson, *The Collected Works of Ralph Waldo Emerson: Nature, Addresses, and Lectures*, vol. 1, ed. Robert E. Spiller and Alfred R. Ferguson, 9 vols. to date (Cambridge: Belknap Press of Harvard University Press, 1971–), 45.
7. Robert N. Hudspeth, ed., *The Letters of Margaret Fuller*, 6 vols. (Ithaca, N.Y.: Cornell University Press, 1983–94), 5:58.
8. Charles Capper, *The Private Years*, vol. 1 of *Margaret Fuller: An American Romantic Life* (New York: Oxford University Press, 1992), 41; Margaret Fuller, "Autobiographical Romance," in *The Essential Margaret Fuller*, ed. Jeffrey Steele (New Brunswick, N.J.: Rutgers University Press, 1992), 24–43.
9. Elizabeth Ware Rotch Farrar was born in Europe to American parents. Raised a

Quaker, she later converted to Unitarianism. She married Harvard mathematician and astronomer John Farrar in 1828 and was a well-liked and influential member of Cambridge society, a hostess for conversations and lectures who brought together many men and women with literary and artistic interests. She was a mentor to Fuller and introduced her to several people who would have a large place in Fuller's life, including Samuel Gray Ward, Elizabeth Barker, Harriet Martineau, and Emerson. For discussions of her life and achievements, see Elizabeth Bancroft Schlesinger, "Two Early Harvard Wives: Eliza Farrar and Eliza Follen," *New England Quarterly* 38 (June 1965): 147–67; Schlesinger, "Eliza Ware Rotch Farrar," in *Notable American Women, 1607–1950: A Biographical Dictionary*, ed. Edward T. James, Janet Wilson James, and Paul S. Boyer, 3 vols. (Cambridge: Belknap Press of Harvard University Press, 1971), 1:601–2; and Farrar's memoir, *Recollections of Seventy Years* (Boston: Ticknor and Fields, 1865).

10. Thomas Wentworth Higginson, *Margaret Fuller Ossoli* (Boston: Houghton Mifflin, 1899), 35.
11. Joan von Mehren, *Minerva and the Muse: A Life of Margaret Fuller* (Amherst: University of Massachusetts Press, 1994), 35.
12. Eliza Farrar, *The Young Lady's Friend: A Manual of Practical Advice and Instruction to Young Females on Their Entering upon the Duties of Life, after Quitting School* (1836; London: Parker, 1837), 5, 8, 6.
13. Ibid., 2, 1, 3, 24–25.
14. Ibid., 244.
15. Margaret Fuller, trans., *Conversations with Goethe in the Last Years of His Life, Translated from the German of Eckermann* (Boston: Hilliard, Gray, 1839), vii–xxvi. Key information on the series is provided in Mathew David Fisher's "Specimens of Foreign Standard Literature," in *Encyclopedia of Transcendentalism*, ed. Wesley T. Mott (Westport, Conn.: Greenwood, 1996), 200–201. For discussions of Ripley's series, see Perry Miller, *The Transcendentalists: An Anthology* (Cambridge: Harvard University Press, 1950), 291–94; Henry A. Pochmann, *German Culture in America* (Madison: University of Wisconsin Press, 1961), 556n338, 617n585, and various comments on individual volumes; Barbara Packer, *The Transcendentalists* (Athens: University of Georgia Press, 2007); and Philip F. Gura, *American Transcendentalism: A History* (New York: Hill and Wang, 2007), 136–37.
16. Fuller, *Conversations with Goethe*, x, xvii.
17. Ibid., xiii.
18. For a reading of *Woman in the Nineteenth Century* as a feminist articulation of the Transcendentalist theory of self-culture, see David M. Robinson, "Margaret Fuller and the Transcendental Ethos: *Woman in the Nineteenth Century*," *PMLA* 97 (1982): 83–98.
19. For important readings of the "Autobiographical Romance," see Jeffrey Steele, *Transfiguring America: Myth, Ideology, and Mourning in Margaret Fuller's Writing*

(Columbia: University of Missouri Press, 2001), 25–46, and Katherine Adams, *Owning Up: Privacy, Property, and Belonging in U.S. Women's Life Writing* (Oxford: Oxford University Press, 2009), 40–50.

20. Sidonie Smith, "Resisting the Gaze of Embodiment: Women's Autobiography in the Nineteenth Century," *American Women's Autobiography: Fea(s)ts of Memory*, ed. Margo Culley (Madison: University of Wisconsin Press, 1992), 85, 84.
21. Margaret Fuller, "Autobiographical Romance," in Jeffrey Steele, ed., *The Essential Margaret Fuller* (New Brunswick, N.J.: Rutgers University Press, 1992), 24, 26.
22. Ibid., 24.
23. Ibid., 25, 26.
24. Ibid., 27.
25. For readings of the "transparent eye-ball" passage, see Jonathan Bishop, *Emerson on the Soul* (Cambridge: Harvard University Press, 1964), 9–15; David M. Robinson, *Apostle of Culture: Emerson as Preacher and Lecturer* (Philadelphia: University of Pennsylvania Press, 1982), 87–90; Merton M. Sealts Jr., *Emerson on the Scholar* (Columbia: University of Missouri Press, 1992), 67–73; Lee Rust Brown, *The Emerson Museum: Practical Romanticism and the Pursuit of the Whole* (Cambridge: Harvard University Press, 1997), 43–58; and Laura Dassow Walls, *Emerson's Life in Science: The Culture of Truth* (Ithaca, N.Y.: Cornell University Press, 2003), 98–101. The publication of a manuscript cartoon of a barefoot eyeball in top hat and tails by Emerson's friend and disciple Christopher Pearse Cranch, a poet and landscape painter, boosted the fame of Emerson's metaphor. See F. DeWolfe Miller, *Christopher Pearse Cranch and His Caricatures of New England Transcendentalism* (Cambridge: Harvard University Press, 1951). See in particular illustration 3, following page 36.
26. Fuller, "Autobiographical Romance," 27.
27. Ibid., 27.
28. Ibid., 27, 26.
29. David M. Robinson, ed., *William Ellery Channing: Selected Writings* (Mahwah, N.J.: Paulist, 1985), 228.
30. Fuller, "Autobiographical Romance," 28, 30.
31. Ibid., 31. For an illuminating discussion of Fuller's use of Greek mythology, see Andrew P. White, "'Expanding in the Sun': Margaret Fuller's 'Autobiographical Romance' and the Hellenic Topography of Early American Feminism," in *Anglo-American Perceptions of Hellenism*, ed. Tatiani Rapatzikou (Newcastle upon Tyne: Cambridge Scholars, 2007), 116–28.
32. Fuller, "Autobiographical Romance," 34, 28.
33. Ibid., 31, 32.
34. For a discussion of flowers and women's culture, see Beverly Seaton, *The Language of Flowers: A History* (Charlottesville: University Press of Virginia, 1995).
35. Fuller, "Autobiographical Romance," 32.
36. On the question of Transcendental friendship, see Carl F. Strauch, "Hatred's

Swift Repulsions: Emerson, Margaret Fuller, and Others," *Studies in Romanticism* 7 (1968): 65–103; Jeffrey Steele, "Transcendental Friendship: Emerson, Fuller, and Thoreau," in *Cambridge Companion to Ralph Waldo Emerson*, ed. Joel Porte and Saundra Morris (Cambridge: Cambridge University Press, 1999), 121–39; Caleb Crain, *American Sympathy: Men, Friendship, and Literature in the New Nation* (New Haven, Conn.: Yale University Press, 2001), 177–237; David M. Robinson, *Natural Life: Thoreau's Worldly Transcendentalism* (Ithaca, N.Y.: Cornell University Press, 2004), 64–72; William Rossi, "Performing Loss, Elegy, and Transcendental Friendship," *New England Quarterly* 81 (2008): 252–77; John T. Lysaker, *Emerson and Self-Culture* (Bloomington: Indiana University Press, 2008); and various essays in John T. Lysaker and William Rossi, eds., *Emerson and Thoreau: Figures of Friendship* (Bloomington: Indiana University Press, 2010).

37. For a philosophical analysis of friendship and self-culture, see Lysaker, *Emerson and Self-Culture*.
38. Fuller, "Autobiographical Romance," 158.
39. For the definitive history of Brook Farm, see Sterling F. Delano, *Brook Farm: The Dark Side of Utopia* (Cambridge: Belknap Press of Harvard University Press, 2004).
40. Steele, *Transfiguring America*, 65–104.
41. Margaret Fuller, "The Great Lawsuit. Man versus Men. Woman versus Women," *Dial* 4 (July 1843): 1–47. For a perceptive discussion of Fuller's development of the essay into *Woman*, see Larry J. Reynolds, "From *Dial* Essay to New York Book: The Making of *Woman in the Nineteenth Century*," in *Periodical Literature in Nineteenth-Century America*, ed. Kenneth M. Price and Susan Belasco Smith (Charlottesville: University of Virginia Press, 1995), 17–34.
42. For an informative portrait of Fuller at this turning point, see Susan Belasco, "'The Animating Influences of Discord': Margaret Fuller in 1844," *Legacy* 20 (2003): 82–91.
43. Margaret Fuller, *Summer on the Lakes, in 1843*, with an introduction by Susan Belasco Smith (Urbana: University of Illinois Press, 1991), 109.
44. Ibid., 70, 75.
45. Ibid., 75–76.
46. Ibid., 76–77.
47. Ibid., 77.
48. Hudspeth, *Letters of Margaret Fuller*, 2:216.
49. Emerson, *Collected Works*, 212.
50. Hudspeth, *Letters of Margaret Fuller*, 2:126.
51. Charles Fourier, *Selections from the Works of Fourier*, trans. Julia Franklin (1910; repr., New York: Gordon, 1972). Selections reprinted in *The Blithedale Romance*, by Nathaniel Hawthorne, ed. William E. Cain, Bedford Cultural Edition (Boston: Bedford Books, 1996), 338, 339.
52. For a history of Fourier's impact in America, see Carl Guarneri, *The Utopian*

Alternative: Fourierism in Nineteenth-Century America (Ithaca, N.Y.: Cornell University Press, 1991), and Gura, *American Transcendentalism*, 160–71. For an important recent interpretation of the ideologies underlying the Brook Farm experiment, see Richard Francis, *Transcendental Utopias: Individual and Community at Brook Farm, Fruitlands, and Walden* (Ithaca, N.Y.: Cornell University Press, 1997). See also Guarneri's "Brook Farm, Fourierism, and the Nationalist Dilemma in American Utopianism," in *Transient and Permanent: The Transcendentalist Movement and Its Contexts*, ed. Charles Capper and Conrad Edick Wright (Boston: Massachusetts Historical Society, 1999), 447–70. For insightful discussions of Fuller's engagement with Fourierism and Associationism, see Christina Zwarg, *Feminist Conversations: Fuller, Emerson, and the Play of Reading* (Ithaca, N.Y.: Cornell University Press, 1995), 50–58, 113–19, 187–205.

53. On Channing's relation to Brook Farm, see Lindsay Swift, *Brook Farm: Its Members, Scholars, and Visitors* (New York: MacMillan, 1900), 217–22.

54. Ralph Waldo Emerson, *The Journals and Miscellaneous Notebooks of Ralph Waldo Emerson*, vol. 9, ed. Ralph H. Orth et al., 16 vols. (Cambridge: Belknap Press of Harvard University Press, 1960–82), 54. Christina Zwarg has shown persuasively how "Fourierism," loosely defined, allowed Fuller and Emerson to engage in "a type of philosophical engagement with feminism *before the letter*." Zwarg, *Feminist Conversations*, 4.

55. Margaret Fuller, *Woman in the Nineteenth Century* (1845), reprinted in Steele, *Essential Margaret Fuller*, 282 and 289. For further discussion of Fuller's views on marriage, see Bell Gale Chevigny, *The Woman and the Myth: Margaret Fuller's Life and Writings*, rev. ed. (1976; Boston: Northeastern University Press, 2004), 24–29; and Zwarg, *Feminist Conversations*, 139–41.

56. William Henry Channing, "Heaven on Earth," *Present*, March 1, 1841; and "Heaven on Earth: Number II," *Present*, April 1, 1841. References to this two-part article use pagination following the printed version of the American Periodical Series online archive of the journal. These quotes are from March 1, 1841, 4, 10; and April 1, 1841, 6.

57. Ibid., April 1, 1841, 14.

58. Ibid., April 1, 1841, 13, 11.

59. On Channing's political development, see David M. Robinson, "The Political Odyssey of William Henry Channing," *American Quarterly* 34 (1982): 165–84.

60. Hudspeth, *Letters of Margaret Fuller*, 2:205.

61. Fuller, *Woman in the Nineteenth Century* (1845), reprinted in Steele, *Essential Margaret Fuller*, 249, 252, 306, 260.

62. Hudspeth, *Letters of Margaret Fuller*, 3:257.

63. Chevigny, *Woman and the Myth*, 291.

64. See Jeffrey Steele, "Purifying America: Purity and Disability in Margaret Fuller's New York Reform Writing," *ESQ: A Journal of the American Renaissance* 52 (2006): 301–17; and David M. Robinson, "Margaret Fuller, New York, and the

Politics of Transcendentalism," *ESQ: A Journal of the American Renaissance* 52 (2006): 271–99.

65. On Fuller's growing self-understanding as a social critic, see Adam-Max Tuchinsky, "'Her Cause Against Herself': Margaret Fuller, Emersonian Democracy, and the Nineteenth-Century Public Intellectual," *American Nineteenth Century History* 5 (Spring 2004): 66–99.

66. Larry J. Reynolds, *European Revolutions and the American Literary Renaissance* (New Haven, Conn.: Yale University Press, 1988); Margaret Fuller, *"These Sad but Glorious Days": Dispatches from Europe, 1846–1850*, ed. Larry J. Reynolds and Susan Belasco Smith (New Haven, Conn.: Yale University Press, 1991); Capper, *Public Years*, 320–497; Joan von Mehren, "Margaret Fuller, the Marchese Giovanni Ossoli, and the Marriage Question: Considering the Research of Dr. Roberto Colzi," *Resources for American Literary Study* 30 (2006): 104–43.

67. Hudspeth, *Letters of Margaret Fuller*, 5:58.

68. Pamela Pilbeam, *French Socialists before Marx* (Montreal: McGill-Queen's University Press, 2000); Jonathan Beecher, *Victor Considerant and the Rise and Fall of French Romantic Socialism* (Berkeley: University of California Press, 2001).

69. Roman Koropeckyj, *Adam Mickiewicz: The Life of a Romantic* (Ithaca, N.Y.: Cornell University Press, 2008); Ursula Phillips, "Apocalyptic Feminism: Adam Mickiewicz and Margaret Fuller," *Slavonic and East European Review* 87 (2009): 1–38.

70. Fuller, *Sad but Glorious Days*, 321.

5. AMERICAN SOCIALISM AND MARGARET FULLER'S 1848

1. Julian Hawthorne, *Nathaniel Hawthorne and His Wife*, vol. 1 (Boston: Houghton, Mifflin, 1884), 257; quoted in Joel Myerson, *New England Transcendentalists and the* Dial: *A History of the Magazine and Its Contributors* (Rutherford, N.J.: Fairleigh Dickinson University Press, 1980), 249n.

2. *New-York Daily Tribune*, January 1, 1848.

3. Bell Gale Chevigny, *The Woman and the Myth: Margaret Fuller's Life and Writings* (Old Westbury, N.Y.: Feminist Press, 1994), 365–401.

4. Larry J. Reynolds, *European Revolutions and the American Literary Renaissance* (New Haven, Conn.: Yale University Press, 1988), 58.

5. Margaret V. Allen, "The Political and Social Criticism of Margaret Fuller," *South Atlantic Quarterly* 72 (Autumn 1973): 560–73; Chevigny, *Woman and the Myth*, 282–303; Paula Blanchard, *Margaret Fuller: From Transcendentalism to Revolution* (New York: Delcorte, 1978), 225–44; Madeline B. Stern, *The Life of Margaret Fuller* (New York: Dutton, 1942), 336–75; Margaret Fuller, *"These Sad but Glorious Days": Dispatches from Europe, 1846–1850*, ed. Larry J. Reynolds and Susan Belasco Smith (New Haven, Conn.: Yale University Press, 1991).

6. Many historians have rejected this framework in a variety of ways. Some eco-

nomic historians suggest that there was very little, ideologically or institutionally, that was revolutionary about it. Some reject the periodization, noting in some cases the existence of markets and consumer cultures in the eighteenth century; others point out that markets did not penetrate some regions of the country until after the Civil War. The most persuasive and influential of these critics is Daniel Walker Howe, whose synthesis *What Hath God Wrought: The Transformation of America, 1815–1848* (New York: Oxford University Press, 2007) nonetheless describes a series of fellow *transformations* in communications, politics, urbanization, manners, religion, education, the organization of labor, gender, and the family, and even within the confines of the self that suggests the revolutionary character of the period, whatever its root cause.

7. See Anne C. Rose, *Transcendentalism as a Social Movement, 1830–1850* (New Haven, Conn.: Yale University Press, 1981); Richard Francis, *Transcendental Utopias: Individual and Community at Brook Farm, Fruitlands, and Walden* (Ithaca, N.Y.: Cornell University Press, 1997); Barbara L. Packer, *The Transcendentalists* (Athens: University of Georgia Press, 2007); Philip F. Gura, *American Transcendentalism: A History* (New York: Hill and Wang, 2007).

8. See Perry Miller, ed., *The Transcendentalists: An Anthology* (Cambridge: Harvard University Press, 1950), 464; Carl Guarneri, *The Utopian Alternative: Fourierism in Nineteenth-Century America* (Ithaca, N.Y.: Cornell University Press, 1991), 46. Rose, *Transcendentalism*, 130; Francis, *Transcendental Utopias*, ix–xi, 42–43; Emerson to Ripley, December 15, 1840, *Letters of Ralph Waldo Emerson*, ed. Ralph L. Rusk, vol. 2 (New York: Columbia University Press, 1939), 369.

9. Quoted in Charles Capper, *The Private Years*, vol. 1 of *Margaret Fuller: An American Romantic Life* (New York: Oxford University Press, 1992), x.

10. David Leverenz, *Manhood and the American Renaissance* (Ithaca, N.Y.: Cornell University Press, 1989), 43.

11. Ralph Waldo Emerson, *The Collected Works of Ralph Waldo Emerson: Nature, Addresses, and Lectures*, vol. 1, ed. Robert E. Spiller and Alfred R. Ferguson, 9 vols. to date (Cambridge: Belknap Press of Harvard University Press, 1971–), 53, 62, 150.

12. Ralph Waldo Emerson, *The Journals and Miscellaneous Notebooks of Ralph Waldo Emerson*, vol. 7, ed. A. W. Plumstead et al., 16 vols. (Cambridge: Belknap Press of Harvard University Press, 1960–82), 343.

13. Emerson, *Collected Works*, 62, 67, 63, 150, 158–59.

14. Fuller to Emerson, May 9, 1844, in Robert N. Hudspeth, ed., *Letters of Margaret Fuller*, 6 vols. (Ithaca, N.Y.: Cornell University Press, 1983–94), 3:196; Fuller to [?], 1845, in Hudspeth, *Letters of Margaret Fuller*, 4:39.

15. Ralph Waldo Emerson, "The Divinity School Address," in *Selections from Ralph Waldo Emerson*, ed. Stephen Whicher (Boston: Houghton, Mifflin, 1972), 112.

16. Ripley to Emerson, November 9, 1840, quoted in Octavius Brooks Frothingham, *George Ripley* (Boston: Houghton, Mifflin, 1882), 307–8.

17. This sensibility pervades most scholarship on Transcendentalism, but see in particular Gura, *American Transcendentalism*; Miller, *Transcendentalists*.
18. Emerson, *Selections*, 167.
19. Sterling F. Delano, *Brook Farm: The Dark Side of Utopia* (Cambridge: Harvard University Press, 2004), 157–58, 172–73.
20. Charles Capper, *The Public Years*, vol. 2 of *Margaret Fuller: An American Romantic Life* (New York: Oxford University Press, 2007), 64; Ralph Waldo Emerson, William Henry Channing, James Freeman Clarke, *Memoirs of Margaret Fuller Ossoli*, vol. 2 (Boston: Roberts, 1874), 58–59.
21. Capper, *Public Years*, 63–65, 103–6.
22. Emerson, Channing, and Clarke, *Memoirs*, 69, 71–72, 80.
23. Emerson to William Emerson, December 21, 1840, *Ralph Waldo Emerson*, 371.
24. Emerson to William Emerson, March 30, 1841, and June 1, 1841, *Ralph Waldo Emerson*, 389, 402.
25. Dorothy Ross, "Liberalism and American Exceptionalism," *Intellectual History Newsletter* 24 (2002): 74. See also Gerald Izenberg, *Impossible Individuality: Romanticism and the Origins of Modern Selfhood, 1787–1802* (Princeton, N.J.: Princeton University Press, 1992).
26. Capper, *Public Years*, 283; *New-York Daily Tribune*, November 7, 1861; June 25, 1863.
27. Ralph Waldo Emerson, "Historic Notes of Life and Letters in New England," in *The Works of Ralph Waldo Emerson: Lectures and Biographical Sketches*, vol. 10 (Boston: Fireside, 1883), 357–58.
28. For the connection between the labor question and the slavery question, see Adam Tuchinsky, *Horace Greeley's New-York Tribune: Civil War-Era Socialism and the Crisis of Free Labor* (Ithaca, N.Y.: Cornell University Press, 2009), 126–64.
29. Fuller, *Sad but Glorious Days*, 211.
30. For Fourier, see Guarneri, *Utopian Alternative*; Jonathan Beecher, *Charles Fourier: The Visionary and His World* (Berkeley: University of California Press, 1990).
31. Fuller to Samuel and Anna Ward, March 3, 1846, in Hudspeth, *Letters of Margaret Fuller*, 4:192.
32. Synthetic historical treatments of the 1848 revolutions include Eric J. Hobsbawm, *The Age of Revolution: Europe, 1789–1848* (London: Abacus, 1977); Jonathan Sperber, *The European Revolutions, 1848–1851* (New York: Cambridge University Press, 1994); Charles Breunig, *The Age of Revolution and Reaction, 1789–1850* (New York: Norton, 1977); and Roger Price, *The French Second Republic: A Social History* (Ithaca, N.Y.: Cornell University Press, 1972).
33. Sperber, *European Revolutions*, 74–75; Priscilla Robertson, *Revolutions of 1848: A Social History* (Princeton, N.J.: Princeton University Press, 1952), 322.
34. Fuller, *Sad but Glorious Days*, 41, 72, 88.

35. Capper, *Public Years*, 310–14.
36. Fuller, *Sad but Glorious Days*, 119, 120.
37. Fuller to Mary Rotch, May 29, 1848, in Hudspeth, *Letters of Margaret Fuller*, 5:71.
38. Fuller to William Henry Channing, March 10, 1849, and May 7, 1848, in Hudspeth, *Letters of Margaret Fuller*, 5:206, 271.
39. Fuller, *Sad but Glorious Days*, 211.
40. Ibid., 225.
41. Reynolds and Smith, introduction to Fuller, *Sad but Glorious Days*, 17.
42. Capper, *Public Years*, 280.
43. Fuller, *Sad but Glorious Days*, 281; Robertson, *Revolutions*, 313. See also Capper, *Public Years*, 376–77.
44. Fuller to Emerson, July 11, 1848, in Hudspeth, *Letters of Margaret Fuller*, 5:86.
45. Fuller to Richard Fuller, August 16, 1848; Fuller to G. Ossoli, October 18, 1848, both in Hudspeth, *Letters of Margaret Fuller*, 5:104, 134.
46. Guarneri, *Utopian Alternative*, 65.
47. See the *Harbinger* 6 (March 25; April 1, 8, 15, 1848); *Harbinger* 7 (May 13, 27; July 22, 29, 1848).
48. Fuller, *Sad but Glorious Days*, 154.
49. Ibid., 156. See Robert N. Hudspeth, "Margaret Fuller and the Ideal of Heroism" in *Margaret Fuller: Transatlantic Crossings in a Revolutionary Age*, ed. Charles Capper and Cristina Giorcelli (Madison: University of Wisconsin Press, 2007), 45–65.
50. *New-York Weekly Tribune*, March 25, 1848; *National Intelligencer*, March 21, 27, 1848. For a general survey of Americans' response, see Timothy Mason Roberts, *Distant Revolutions: 1848 and the Challenge to American Exceptionalism* (Charlottesville: University of Virginia Press, 2009); Roberts, "'Revolutions Have Become the Bloody Toy of the Multitude': European Revolutions, the South, and the Crisis of 1850," *Journal of the Early Republic* 25 (Summer 2005): 259–83; Roberts and Daniel Walker Howe, "The United States and the Revolutions of 1848," *The Revolution in Europe 1848–1849: From Reform to Reaction* (New York: Oxford University Press, 2000); Paola Gemme, *Domesticating Foreign Struggles: The Italian Risorgimento and Antebellum American Identity* (Athens: University of Georgia Press, 2005); Eugene N. Curtis, "American Opinion of the French Nineteenth-Century Revolutions," *American Historical Review* 29 (January 1924): 249–70; Merle Curti, "Impact of the Revolutions of 1848 on American Thought," *Proceedings of the American Philosophical Society* 93 (June 1949): 209–15; and Reynolds, *European Revolutions*.
51. *New-York Daily Tribune*, April 4, 1848.
52. For additional American responses to 1848, see Tuchinsky, *Greeley's* New-York Tribune, 82–107; and Roberts, *Distant Revolutions*, 21–62.
53. Curtis, "American Opinion," 255.

54. Margaret Fuller, "The War of the Races in Hungary," *North American Review* 70 (January 1850): 80.
55. Josiah C. Nott and George R. Gliddon, *Types of Mankind* (Philadelphia: Lippincott, 1854), 404. See also Gemme, *Domesticating Foreign Struggles*, 113. The *Tribune* would become the main organ of Radical Republicanism, and the debates about the capacity of various European peoples and "races" would anticipate American racial discourse during the Civil War and Reconstruction. Fuller made the connection directly: "They talk about the corrupt and degenerate state of Italy as they do about that of our slaves at home. They come ready trained to that mode of reasoning which affirms that, because men are degraded by bad institutions, they are not fit for better." Fuller, *Sad but Glorious Days*, 159.
56. *New-York Weekly Tribune*, May 6, 13; June 3, 1848.
57. *Harbinger* 6, no. 21 (March 25, 1848): 164. See the *Harbinger*, March 25; April 1, 8, 15; May 13, 27; and July 22, 29, 1848.
58. *New-York Weekly Tribune*, November 4, 18, 1848.
59. *New-York Daily Tribune*, April 24, 1848.
60. *New-York Weekly Tribune*, April 29, 1848, November 18, 1848.
61. Fuller's letter is dated March 29, but was not published in the *New-York Weekly Tribune* until May 6, 1848. The *Advertiser* is quoted in the *Harbinger*, April 15, 1848, 187. See also *Courier and Enquirer*, April 8, 1848. On the conservative turn of American opinion, see *Courier and Enquirer*, March, 28, 22; April 1, 14, 1848; *Republican* (Savannah), April 4, 1848; Curtis, "American Opinion," 258–59; Curti, "Impact of the Revolutions," 211; and *New-York Weekly Tribune*, May 13, 1848.
62. Engels to Marx, August 19, 1846, in *Collected Works*, 49 vols. (New York, 1975–), 38:55. See also Engels to Joseph Weydemeyer, February 27, 1852, in *Collected Works*, 39:52. Carl Wittke, *Refugees of Revolution: The German Forty-Eighters in America* (Philadelphia: University of Pennsylvania Press, 1952), 263, 265, 270–71. *Daily Tribune*, January 6, 25, 27; August 5, 1845. See also Tuchinsky, *Greeley's* New-York Tribune, 88–95; and Adam-Max Tuchinsky, "'The Bourgeoisie Will Fall and Fall Forever': The *New-York Tribune*, the 1848 French Revolution, and American Social Democratic Discourse," *Journal of American History* 92 (September 2005): 470–97.
63. Heinrich Börnstein, *Fünfundsiebzig Jahre in der Alten und Neuen Welt: Memoiren eines Unbedeutenden*, vol. 1, edited with an English introduction by Patricia A. Herminghouse (New York: Lang, 1986), 383. See also Herminghouse, *Memoirs of a Nobody: The Missouri Years of An Austrian Radical, 1840–1866*, trans. and ed. Steven Rowan (Saint Louis: Missouri Historical Society, 1997).
64. Fuller, *Sad but Glorious Days*, 294.
65. *New-York Daily Tribune*, May 9, 1848.
66. *Evening Express* (New York), May 23, 1848; *New-York Weekly Tribune*, May 6, 13; June 3, 1848.

67. *New-York Daily Tribune*, May 20, 1848.
68. *New-York Weekly Tribune*, April 22, 1848; *New-York Daily Tribune*, August 5, 1845.
69. Louis Blanc, *History of Ten Years, 1830–1840*, vol. 1 (London: Chapman and Hall, 1844–45), 50, 13, 14, 31, 46, 47. William Hamilton Sewell, *Work and Revolution in France: The Language of Labor from the Old Regime to 1848* (Cambridge: Cambridge University Press), 232–36.
70. Hudspeth, *Letters of Margaret Fuller*, 6:51. Bell Gale Chevigny speculates that her reading "suggests she was preparing to write something more broadly historical and possibly theoretical than her impressions of the Italian struggle" and in so doing may have "analyzed the difference between nationalist and social revolution." *Woman and the Myth*, 395. Charles Capper concurs that this sort of history was possible, rooted in Blanc's "democratic socialism," but also sees "classic Whig liberalism" and Romantic "set pieces, dramatic narratives, and piquant anecdotes" as equally strong possibilities. See *Public Years*, 485–89.
71. *Harbinger* 6 (April 15, 1848): 187.
72. *New-York Weekly Tribune*, October 28, 1848.
73. Donald Grant Mitchell, *The Battle Summer* (New York: Scribner, 1849), 253.
74. Albert and Redelia Brisbane, *Albert Brisbane: A Mental Biography* (Boston: Arena, 1893), 269.
75. Sewell, *Work and Revolution*, 222.
76. Chevigny, *Woman and the Myth*, 367.
77. Fuller, *Sad but Glorious Days*, 98.
78. Sperber, *European Revolutions*, 222–23, 230–36; Clara M. Lovett, *The Democratic Movement in Italy, 1830–1876* (Cambridge: Harvard University Press, 1982), 49–50, 127–30, 133–43; Fuller, *Sad but Glorious Days*, 98.
79. Capper, *Public Years*, 322.
80. S. Margaret Fuller, *Woman in the Nineteenth Century* (New York: Greeley and McElrath, 1845), 103.
81. Fuller, *Sad but Glorious Days*, 165.
82. Fuller, "Publishers and Authors," *New-York Daily Tribune*, February 3, 1846.
83. Fuller, *Sad but Glorious Days*, 129, 153.
84. Fuller, "The Irish Character," *New-York Daily Tribune*, July 24, 1845; review of *Narrative of the Life of Frederick Douglas*, *New-York Daily Tribune*, June 10, 1845. See also "Italy," *New-York Daily Tribune*, November 13, 1845.
85. Fuller, "Consecration of Grace Church," *New-York Daily Tribune*, March 11, 1846.
86. Orestes Brownson, "Church Unity and Social Amelioration," *Brownson's Quarterly Review*, July 1844. See David Joseph Voelker, "Orestes Brownson and the Search for Authority in Democratic America" (Ph.D. diss., University of North Carolina, Chapel Hill, 2003). Fuller later mocked Transcendental converts when clerical forces began to undermine the Roman Republic. See Capper, *Public Years*, 378.
87. Emerson, "American Scholar," in Emerson, *Collected Works*, 53; Alexis de

Tocqueville, *Democracy in America* (New York: Appleton, 1904), 2:586; Karl Marx and Frederick Engels, *The Communist Manifesto* (Chicago: Charles H. Kerr, 1906), 17.
88. Fuller, *Sad but Glorious Days*, 136, 155.
89. Ibid., 229, 278.
90. Ibid., 186, 188, 187, 205, 278, 279.
91. Ibid., 232, 237, 238, 277–78, 320, 321.
92. Elizabeth Barrett Browning, *The Letters of Elizabeth Barrett Browning*, vol. 1 (London: Smith, Elder, 1897), 460.
93. Larry Reynolds makes this argument recently in Larry J. Reynolds, *Righteous Violence: Revolution, Slavery, and the American Renaissance* (Athens: University of Georgia Press, 2011), esp. 38–56. See also Larry J. Reynolds, "Righteous Violence: The Roman Republic and Margaret Fuller's Revolutionary Example," in *Margaret Fuller: Transatlantic Crossings in a Revolutionary Age* (Madison: University of Wisconsin Press, 2007), 172–94.
94. Henry David Thoreau, *Walden and Civil Disobedience* (New York: Penguin Classics, 1983), 396.

6. MARGARET FULLER AND ANTISLAVERY

Ralph Waldo Emerson, *The Journals and Miscellaneous Notebooks of Ralph Waldo Emerson*, vol. 4, ed. Alfred R. Ferguson et al., 16 vols. (Cambridge: Belknap Press of Harvard University Press, 1960–82), 306; Harrison Hayford, Hershel Parker, and G. Thomas Tanselle. eds., *Moby-Dick*, in *The Writings of Herman Melville* (Chicago: Northwestern University Press/Newberry Library, 1988), 6:6.

1. "She did not indeed devote herself to this great cause with the singleness of purpose and intense zeal of Maria Weston Chapman and Lydia Maria Child. The influences about her early life were not of this character, and the movement had not then taken the active form which it did after her departure from America." Ednah Dow Cheney, *Reminiscences* (Boston: Lee and Shepard, 1902), 211. The "active form" refers to the revolutionary turn given to antislavery when the Fugitive Slave Law seemed to implicate the North in the legal workings of the southern system.
2. "But of all these plague-spots there is none for which we feel such burning pain of shame and indignation, as for the conduct of this nation toward the Indians." Review of *Memoirs, Official and Personal*, by Thomas L. McKenney, in *Margaret Fuller, Critic: Writings from the* New-York Tribune, *1844–1846*, ed. Judith Mattson Bean and Joel Myerson (New York: Columbia University Press, 2000), 465. On Margaret Fuller and Native Americans, see Susan Gilmore, "'Receiving' the 'Indians,'" in *Margaret Fuller's Cultural Critique: Her Age and Legacy*, ed. Fritz Fleischmann (New York: Lang, 2000), 191–227; and Jeffrey Steele, *Transfiguring America: Myth, Ideology, and Mourning in Margaret Fuller's*

Writing (Columbia: University of Missouri Press, 2001), 157–66. On Timothy Fuller, see Marion Mills Miller, ed., *Slavery from 1790 to 1857*, vol. 4 of *Great Debates in American History*, 14 vols. (New York: Current Literature, 1913), 51–54; "The existence of slavery in any State is so far a departure from republican principles" (51). This speech shows that Fuller supported the Colonization Society and that he denied the right of the federal government to interfere with slavery in states where it existed when the Constitution was adopted. For Fuller's speech on the Seminole War, see *Annals of Congress*, 15th Cong., 2nd sess., 985–1006: "Let us then examine, without fear, any existing practice which militates against the rights of humanity, and, whenever it should be found substantially unnecessary, let us boldly explode it, and not doubt that our example will be approved and adopted by other nations" (1002). See also Leona Rostenberg, "Diary of Timothy Fuller in Congress," *New England Quarterly* 12 (September 1939): 521–29.

3. Catharine E. Beecher, *Essay on Slavery and Abolitionism, with Reference to the Duty of American Females* (Philadelphia: Perkins, 1837), 100.

4. Over the past quarter century researchers have developed a peculiarly vibrant area of historical scholarship meant to show that antislavery, earlier depicted as a male reform, was in fact crucially shaped by women. So cumulatively successful has this revisionist effort been that a kind of reverse causation emerges, and we begin to see that antislavery had an important bearing on the lives and destinies of nineteenth-century American women. See, for example, Alma Lutz, *Crusade for Freedom: Women in the Antislavery Movement* (Boston: Beacon, 1968); Blanche Glassman Hersh, *The Slavery of Sex: Feminist-Abolitionists in America* (Urbana: University of Illinois Press, 1978); Jean Fagan Yellin, *Women and Sisters: The Antislavery Feminists in American Culture* (New Haven, Conn.: Yale University Press, 1990); Lori D. Ginzberg, *Women and the Work of Benevolence: Morality, Politics and Class in the Nineteenth-Century United States* (New Haven, Conn.: Yale University Press, 1990); Wendy Hamand Venet, *Neither Ballots nor Bullets: Women Abolitionists and the Civil War* (Charlottesville: University Press of Virginia, 1991); Debra Gold Hansen, *Strained Sisterhood: Gender and Class in the Boston Female Anti-Slavery Society* (Amherst: University of Massachusetts Press, 1993); Jean Fagan Yellin and John C. Van Horne, eds., *The Abolitionist Sisterhood: Women's Political Culture in Antebellum America* (Ithaca, N.Y.: Cornell University Press, 1994); Julie Roy Jeffrey, *The Great Silent Army of Abolitionism: Ordinary Women in the Antislavery Movement* (Chapel Hill: University of North Carolina Press, 1998); Gerda Lerner, *The Feminist Thought of Sarah Grimké* (New York: Oxford University Press, 1998); Anna M. Speicher, *The Religious World of Antislavery Women: Spirituality in the Lives of Five Abolitionist Lecturers* (Syracuse, N.Y.: Syracuse University Press, 2000); Deborah Bingham Van Broekhoven, *The Devotion of These Women: Rhode Island in the Antislavery Network* (Amherst: University of Massachusetts Press, 2002); Susan Zaeske, *Signatures of Citizenship: Petitioning, Antislavery, and Women's Political Identity*

(Chapel Hill: University of North Carolina Press, 2003); Beth A. Salerno, *Sister Societies: Women's Antislavery Organizations in Antebellum America* (DeKalb: Northern Illinois University Press, 2005); and Sandra Harbert Petrulionis, *To Set This World Right: The Antislavery Movement in Thoreau's Concord* (Ithaca, N.Y.: Cornell University Press, 2006).

5. Regarding her father's instigation, see Fuller's letter of March 6, 1835, to Frederic Henry Hedge, in Robert N. Hudspeth, ed., *The Letters of Margaret Fuller*, 6 vols. (Ithaca, N.Y.: Cornell University Press, 1983–1994), 1:226.

6. [George Bancroft], "Slavery in Rome," *North American Review* 39 (October 1834): 432, 433.

7. James Freeman Clarke, Ralph Waldo Emerson, and William Henry Channing, eds., *Memoirs of Margaret Fuller Ossoli*, 2 vols. (Boston: Phillips, Sampson, 1852), 1:17–28.

8. Charles Capper, *The Private Years*, vol. 1 of *Margaret Fuller: An American Romantic Life* (New York: Oxford University Press, 1992), 47.

9. Clarke, Emerson, and Channing, *Memoirs*, 1:14. See Robert N. Hudspeth, "Margaret Fuller and the Ideal of Heroism," in *Margaret Fuller: Transatlantic Crossings in a Revolutionary Age*, ed. Charles Capper and Cristina Giorcelli (Madison: University of Wisconsin Press, 2007), 45–65.

10. Hudspeth, *Letters of Margaret Fuller*, 1:151. Carolyn L. Karcher, *The First Woman in the Republic: A Cultural Biography of Lydia Maria Child* (Durham, N.C.: Duke University Press, 1994), 40, and Karcher, "Margaret Fuller and Lydia Maria Child," in Fleischmann, *Margaret Fuller's Cultural Critique*, 75–89.

11. Hudspeth, *Letters of Margaret Fuller*, 1:297; 3:183.

12. Harriet Martineau noted that Child was "a lady of whom society was exceedingly proud before she published her 'Appeal,' and to whom society has been extremely contemptuous since." *The Martyr Age of the United States* (Boston: Weeks, Jordan, 1839), 15. On the social cost to Child of her abolitionism, see, in addition to Karcher, *First Woman*, Kirk Jeffrey, "Marriage, Career, and Feminine Ideology in Nineteenth-Century America: Reconstructing the Marital Experience of Lydia Maria Child, 1828–1874," *Feminist Studies* 1 (1975): 113–30. In a private letter of 1845 apropos of Fuller's just-published *Woman in the Nineteenth Century*, Child wrote, "She ought to be at work with us. If there is anything in her (as there does seem to be by Jove!), she will be with us" (quoted in Lutz, *Crusade for Freedom*, 199).

13. Martineau would later say, "We were there intimate friends." See her *Autobiography*, ed. Linda H. Peterson (Toronto: Broadview, 2007), 378. In December Fuller wrote that "Miss Martineau encourages me to my Life of Goethe" (Hudspeth, *Letters of Margaret Fuller*, 6:272).

14. Fuller's friends included many who were active in the antislavery movement. It is not clear just when her friendship with the abolitionist lawyer Ellis Gray Loring began, but it was well established within a year of his successful argument in the celebrated case of *Commonwealth v. Aves*, an action brought in 1836

by the Boston Female Anti-Slavery Society. Judge Lemuel Shaw's decision in *Aves* set at liberty the six-year-old slave child Med, brought to Massachusetts by her Louisiana owner on a visit. Loring was a close colleague of William Lloyd Garrison's and was one of the small group that four years earlier had founded the New England Anti-Slavery Society. In the wake of Martineau's address to the BFASS, Loring explained to Garrison that her endorsement of the Society's *principles* (and not, at the time, of their measures) reflected her concurrence with William Ellery Channing that individual action was preferable to associated action. Along with Fuller's friend Caroline Sturgis, Loring led private readings of Emerson's lectures in 1838, but his most notable connection with the Transcendentalists came in 1844 when he assisted Emerson with the legal arguments in the revised version of the "Address on Emancipation in the West Indies." Len Gougeon, *Virtue's Hero: Emerson, Antislavery, and Reform* (Athens: University of Georgia Press, 1990), 29, 88–90. See also Gougeon, "1838: Ellis Gray Loring and a Journal for the Times," *Studies in the American Renaissance 1990*, ed. Joel Myerson (Charlottesville: University Press of Virginia, 1990), 33–47. On *Commonwealth v. Aves*, see Paul Finkelman, *An Imperfect Union: Slavery, Federalism, and Comity* (Union, N.J.: Lawbook Exchange, 2000), 103–14.

15. Capper, *Private Years*, 66–67; cf. Hudspeth, *Letters of Margaret Fuller*, 1:237.
16. Fuller's first reference to Channing's *Slavery* (the first of two) avoided making a judgment. It occurred in a letter to her brother Eugene, then teaching at a school in Virginia run by a family acquaintance, Samuel Appleton Storrow, the uncle of Thomas Wentworth Higginson. A Massachusetts native, Storrow had married into the prominent Carter family and so may have had complicated views on the subject of slavery. Fuller simply asked Eugene, "What says Col. Storrow to the Faneuil hall resolutions [opposing the abolitionists], to the Boston Mob [that went after Garrison], and Dr Channing's new book on slavery" (Hudspeth, *Letters of Margaret Fuller*, 1:240). Although Martineau was soon much bolder in her pronouncements, her deference to Channing in the immediate aftermath is not surprising, he being then America's foremost Unitarian, just as Harriet's brother James was Britain's.
17. Fuller, *Woman in the Nineteenth Century*, in *The Essential Margaret Fuller*, ed. Jeffrey Steele (New Brunswick, N.J.: Rutgers University Press, 1992), 307–8.
18. Hudspeth, *Letters of Margaret Fuller*, 1:218; Capper, *Private Years*, 146.
19. Hudspeth, *Letters of Margaret Fuller*, 1:221.
20. Clarke, Emerson, and Channing, *Memoirs*, 1:129–30.
21. Hudspeth, *Letters of Margaret Fuller*, 1:309–10. Fuller's letter to Martineau was sent in November 1837, the month of Emerson's first antislavery lecture, an address in which Len Gougeon finds "more emphasis upon the need to allow and encourage a free discussion of the question than upon the problem of slavery itself" (*Virtue's Hero*, 38).
22. Hudspeth, *Letters of Margaret Fuller*, 1:309–10.

23. Kathryn Kish Sklar, *Women's Rights Emerges within the Antislavery Movement, 1830–1870* (Boston: Bedford/St. Martin's, 2000), is largely concerned with the career of the Grimké sisters. Sklar is editor also (with James Brewer Stewart) of *Women's Rights and Transatlantic Antislavery in the Era of Emancipation* (New Haven, Conn.: Yale University Press, 2007), a collection of essays by several hands that derives American feminism from the efforts of antislavery reformers, effectively excluding Fuller from the narrative.
24. Child to Angelina Grimké, September 2, 1839, quoted in Sklar, *Women's Rights Emerges*, 162.
25. Gilbert H. Barnes and Dwight L. Dumond, eds., *Letters of Theodore Dwight Weld, Angelina Grimké Weld, and Sarah Grimké, 1822–1844*, 2 vols. (1934; repr., Gloucester, Mass.: Smith, 1965), 1:429.
26. The split in the abolitionist ranks was immediately precipitated by the appointment of Abby Kelley to the business committee of the American Anti-Slavery Society at its 1840 meeting in New York. A large contingent of the men insisted that the appointment was out of order because offices were reserved in the bylaws to "persons"—a category always previously understood to mean, exclusively, men. When Kelley tried to address the assembly in defense of her rights, she began by saying, "I rise because I am not a slave." Secession and the new organization followed. See Dorothy Sterling, *Ahead of Her Time: Abby Kelley and the Politics of Antislavery* (New York: Norton, 1991), 104–6.
27. Quoted in Larry Ceplair, ed., *The Public Years of Sarah and Angelina Grimké: Selected Writings, 1835–1839* (New York: Columbia University Press, 1989), 211–12.
28. Gerda Lerner, *The Grimké Sisters of South Carolina: Rebels against Slavery* (Boston: Houghton Mifflin, 1967), 199–200.
29. Sarah Grimké, *Letters on the Equality of the Sexes and Other Essays*, ed. Elizabeth Ann Bartlett (New Haven, Conn.: Yale University Press, 1988), 31, 37.
30. One of the first things Fuller did after her father's death was to cancel the family's subscription to the *Christian Examiner* (Hudspeth, *Letters of Margaret Fuller*, 1:238).
31. Jeffrey Steele observes that, following her removal to New York in 1845, Fuller adopted a more consistently Christian diction and dropped from her public writings (i.e., her *Tribune* articles) the old terminology of classical myth. Steele regards this as an excursion into the American demotic, necessitated by her journalist's role, but it was congenial also to the new social realism that her urban environment brought out and conducive in new ways to reform commitments (*Transfiguring America*, ch. 9). This shift in vocabulary prompts a further speculation that the classical structures, already personalized in Fuller's youth, as we have seen, were easily co-opted into an essentially non-Christian Transcendental ideology after 1836, becoming in effect the lingua franca of the Emerson wing of the New England movement. Cyrus Bartol, for example, complained of Emerson that "He talks of 'the gods' as an old Roman would

do." Joel Myerson, ed., *Emerson and Thoreau: The Contemporary Reviews* (Cambridge: Cambridge University Press, 1992), 154). Everything Steele has to say on this point tends to support the hypothesis that Fuller's increasing openness to social reform after the *Dial* years was materially aided by her close tracking of Christian-socialist language, bespeaking perhaps an influence from William Henry Channing. Along with abolitionists such as Garrison and Douglass, however, Fuller saw that less progressive forms of Christianity—as in the "Pastoral Letter"—offered no help to reform. This point became a tradition with American reformers, such that, for example, Elizabeth Cady Stanton, a figure much influenced by Fuller, years later boycotted a suffrage meeting that was to have opened with Isabella Beecher Hooker's hymn, "Guide Us, O Thou Great Jehovah." Stanton pointed out that Jehovah "had never taken any active part in the suffrage movement." Elisabeth Schüssler Fiorenza, *In Memory of Her: A Feminist Theological Reconstruction of Christian Origins* (New York: Crossroad, 1986), 7.

32. Fuller, *Woman*, 307. Steele's edition accurately reproduces the first-edition text at this point, and yet the language is certainly garbled; the emended form quoted here is taken from the 1855 edition, because it makes better sense. See Arthur B. Fuller, ed., *Woman in the Nineteenth Century and Kindred Papers* (Boston: Jewett, 1855), 111.

33. "We believe there has been no female lawyer, and probably will be none" (Bean and Myerson, *Margaret Fuller, Critic*, 236).

34. Fuller, *Woman*, 250.

35. See Henry Mayer, *All on Fire: William Lloyd Garrison and the Abolition of Slavery* (New York: St. Martin's, 1998), 199, and Walter M. Merrill and Louis Ruchames, eds., *The Letters of William Lloyd Garrison*, 6 vols. (Cambridge: Belknap Press of Harvard University Press, 1971–81), 1:544.

36. Charles Capper, *The Public Years*, vol. 2 of *Margaret Fuller: An American Romantic Life* (New York: Oxford University Press, 2007), 39.

37. Elaine Pagels, *The Gnostic Gospels* (New York: Random House/Vintage, 1981), 84–122; quotation on page 122. On the parallelism of gnostic and Transcendental thought, see Albert J. von Frank, "Emerson and Gnosticism," in *Emerson: Bicentennial Essays*, ed. Ronald A. Bosco and Joel Myerson (Boston: Massachusetts Historical Society, 2006), 289–314.

38. Emerson, "Introductory Lecture" (1841), in Emerson, *The Collected Works of Ralph Waldo Emerson: Nature, Addresses, and Lectures*, vol. 1, ed. Robert E. Spiller and Alfred R. Ferguson, 9 vols. to date (Cambridge: Belknap Press of Harvard University Press, 1971–), 179.

39. Fuller, *Woman*, 253–54.

40. Emerson, *Collected Works*, 20–21.

41. Fuller, *Woman*, 254–55.

42. Emerson, *The Collected Works of Ralph Waldo Emerson: Nature, Addresses, and*

Lectures, vol. 2, ed. Joseph Slater, Alfred R. Ferguson, and Jean Ferguson Carr, 9 vols. to date (Cambridge: Belknap Press of Harvard University Press, 1971–), 30.
43. Fuller, *Woman*, 286.
44. Ibid., 256, 257–58, 337, 258, 259, 277.
45. Ibid., 309.
46. Ibid., 335, 340–41.
47. Ibid., 341.
48. Ibid., 343, 347, 349.
49. Fuller, "New and Old World Democracy," in *"These Sad but Glorious Days": Dispatches from Europe, 1846–1850*, ed. Larry J. Reynolds and Susan Belasco Smith (New Haven, Conn.: Yale University Press, 1991), 164–65.
50. Ibid., 166.
51. Hudspeth, *Letters of Margaret Fuller*, 2:197–98. See also Phyllis Cole, "Woman Questions: Emerson, Fuller, and New England Reform," in *Transient and Permanent: The Transcendentalist Movement and Its Contexts*, ed. Charles Capper and Conrad Edick Wright (Boston: Massachusetts Historical Society, 1999), esp. 425–26.
52. Hudspeth, *Letters of Margaret Fuller*, 3:213. Fuller heard Emerson deliver the address on August 1; her complex and very different response to the live performance included being moved to tears. See Martha L. Berg and Alice de V. Perry, "'The Impulses of Human Nature': Margaret Fuller's Journal from June through October 1844," *Proceedings of the Massachusetts Historical Society*, 3rd ser. 102 (1990): 107, 109.
53. I am here suggesting a version of Larry J. Reynolds's argument in "Righteous Violence: The Roman Republic and Margaret Fuller's Revolutionary Example," in *Margaret Fuller: Transatlantic Crossings in a Revolutionary Age*, ed. Charles Capper and Cristina Giorcelli (Madison: University of Wisconsin Press, 2007), 172–92. A revised version of this contribution is included in Reynolds's *Righteous Violence: Revolution, Slavery, and the American Renaissance* (Athens: University of Georgia Press, 2011).
54. Martineau, *Autobiography*, 378.

7. MARGARET FULLER ON MUSIC'S "EVERLASTING YES"

Margaret Fuller, "Lives of the Great Composers," *Art, Literature, and the Drama* (New York: Tribune Association, 1869), 283.
1. John Sullivan Dwight, "The Concerts of the Past Winter," *Dial* 1 (July 1840): 124–34.
2. Robert N. Hudspeth, ed., *The Letters of Margaret Fuller*, 6 vols. (Ithaca, N.Y.: Cornell University Press, 1983–94), 5:54.
3. Margaret Fuller, "Mr. Fontana's Concert," *New-York Daily Tribune*, January 3, 1846, 1, reprinted in *New-York Weekly Tribune*, January 10, 1846, 6.

4. Hudspeth, *Letters of Margaret Fuller*, 4:262n. It seems a striking coincidence that both Fuller and Chopin were born in 1810 and that Chopin also died young, less than a year before Fuller, in October, 1849.
5. Ora Frishberg Saloman, "Margaret Fuller on Musical Life in Boston and New York, 1841–1846," *American Music* 6 (1988): 428–41; Saloman, "Margaret Fuller on Beethoven in America, 1839–1846," *Journal of Musicology* 10, no. 1 (Winter 1992): 89–105. Ruth Solie provides valuable context for an excerpt from Fuller's *Dial* essay "Lives of the Great Composers" in *The Nineteenth Century*, vol. 6 of *Source Readings in Music History*, ed. Ruth A. Solie (New York: Norton, 1998), 30–34.
6. Michael Broyles, *"Music of the Highest Class": Elitism and Populism in Antebellum Boston* (New Haven, Conn.: Yale University Press, 1992), 27, 8.
7. Hudspeth, *Letters of Margaret Fuller*, 1:81, 83, 86.
8. Ibid., 1:86.
9. Ralph Waldo Emerson, William Henry Channing, and James Freeman Clarke, eds., *Memoirs of Margaret Fuller Ossoli* (Charleston, S.C.: BiblioBazaar, 2006), 1:28.
10. Hudspeth, *Letters of Margaret Fuller*, 1:107, 116.
11. Ibid., 1:133, 151.
12. Ibid., 1:201, 2:58.
13. Quoted in Ruth Solie, "'Girling' at the Parlor Piano," *Music in Other Words* (Berkeley: University of California Press, 2004), 90. I am indebted to Solie for her research and writing on this topic.
14. Ibid., 89.
15. Arthur Loesser, *Men, Women, and Pianos: A Social History* (New York: Dover Publications, 1990), 291.
16. Quoted in Solie, "Parlor Piano," 88–89.
17. Loesser, *Men, Women, and Pianos*, 291.
18. Margaret Fuller, *Summer on the Lakes, in 1843* (Urbana: University of Illinois Press, 1991), 40.
19. Quoted in Solie, "Parlor Piano," 89.
20. Hudspeth, *Letters of Margaret Fuller*, 1:107.
21. Ibid., 6:359.
22. Tess Hoffman, "Miss Fuller among the Literary Lions: Two Essays Read at 'the Coliseum' in 1838," *Studies in the American Renaissance* (Charlottesville: University Press of Virginia, 1988), 42.
23. Ibid., "Miss Fuller," 42, 52n.
24. Hudspeth, *Letters of Margaret Fuller*, 2:69.
25. Irving Lowens, "Writings about Music in the Periodicals of American Transcendentalism (1835–50)," *Journal of the American Musicological Society* 10 (1957): 74, 85; Saloman, "Margaret Fuller on Beethoven," 92.
26. Broyles, *"Highest Class,"* 199, 306.
27. Saloman, "Margaret Fuller on Beethoven," 96.

28. Hudspeth, *Letters of Margaret Fuller*, 2:206.
29. Fuller, "Great Composers," 222, 224, 267.
30. Hudspeth, *Letters of Margaret Fuller*, 6:357.
31. Margaret Fuller, "Entertainments of the Past Winter," *Dial* 3 (July 1842): 62.
32. Fuller, "Great Composers," 224.
33. Fuller, *Summer on the Lakes*, 40.
34. Fuller, "Great Composers," 225.
35. Hudspeth, *Letters of Margaret Fuller*, 6:191, 189.
36. Margaret Fuller, "Music in New-York," *New-York Daily Tribune*, January 18, 1845, 2, reprinted in *New-York Weekly Tribune*, January 25, 1845, 1.
37. Saloman, "Margaret Fuller on Beethoven," 91.
38. Charles Capper, *The Public Years*, vol. 2 of *Margaret Fuller: An American Romantic Life* (New York: Oxford University Press, 2007), 58.
39. Quoted in Saloman, "Margaret Fuller on Beethoven," 97.
40. Fuller, "Music in New-York."
41. Dwight, "Past Winter," 126.
42. Fuller, "Entertainments," 53.
43. Fuller, "Great Composers," 225.
44. Hoffman, "Miss Fuller," 41.
45. Review of *Music Explained to the World; or, How to Understand Music and Enjoy Its Performance*, by Francis James Fetis, *Dial* 3 (April 1843): 533.
46. Jeffrey Steele, ed., *The Essential Margaret Fuller* (New Brunswick, N.J.: Rutgers University Press, 1992), 12.
47. Hudspeth, *Letters of Margaret Fuller*, 2:191, 258.
48. Steele, *Essential Margaret Fuller*, 45, 51.
49. Fuller, "Mr. Fontana's Concert."
50. Margaret Fuller, "Music," *New-York Daily Tribune*, January 31, 1846, 1, reprinted in *New-York Weekly Tribune*, February 7, 1846, 6.
51. Steele, *Essential Margaret Fuller*, 406.
52. Hudspeth, *Letters of Margaret Fuller*, 4:263.
53. Ibid., 2:89, 3:111, 2:113.
54. Emerson, Channing, and Clarke, *Memoirs*, 1:181.
55. Margaret Fuller, *Woman in the Nineteenth Century* (New York: Norton, 1971), 79, 121, 170, 179.
56. Fuller, *Summer on the Lakes*, 40, 106.
57. Fuller, "Entertainments," 52.
58. Fuller, *Summer on the Lakes*, 127, 149.
59. Ibid., 149.

8. SYMPATHY AND PROPHECY

1. Introduction to Lydia Maria Child, *Letters from New-York*, ed. Bruce Mills (Athens: University of Georgia Press, 1998), xxvii.

2. Ibid., 43, 109.
3. Charles Dickens, "New York," in *American Notes for General Circulation*, ed. Patricia Ingham (1842; repr., London: Penguin Books, 2000), 90, 99.
4. "New York (Manhattan) Wards: Population and Density, 1800–1910," Demographia, 2001, accessed May 16, 2006, www.demographia.com.
5. For a discussion of social conditions in antebellum New York, see Edwin G. Burrows and Mike Wallace, *Gotham: A History of New York City to 1898* (New York: Oxford University Press, 1999), chs. 35–37.
6. Child, *Letters from New-York*, 60, 137, 102.
7. Ibid., 83.
8. Henry David Thoreau, *Walden and Civil Disobedience*, ed. Owen Thomas (New York: Norton, 1966), 61.
9. Allan Nevins, ed., *The Diary of Philip Hone, 1828–1851* (New York: Dodd, Mead, 1936), 785.
10. Burrows and Wallace, *Gotham*, 697.
11. The phrase "public attention" is found in Fuller's essay "Our City Charities," in *Margaret Fuller's New York Journalism*, ed. Catherine C. Mitchell (Knoxville: University of Tennessee Press, 1995), 91.
12. Fuller, "The Rich Man: An Ideal Sketch," in *Margaret Fuller, Critic: Writings from the New-York Tribune, 1844–46*, ed. Judith Mattson Bean and Joel Myerson (New York: Columbia University Press, 2000), 359.
13. Ibid., 360–66.
14. Fuller, "Emerson's Essays," *New-York Daily Tribune*, December 7, 1844, in Bean and Myerson, *Margaret Fuller, Critic*, 2, 5, 6; emphasis added.
15. Fuller, review of *Conversations on Some of the Old Poets*, by James Russell Lowell, *New-York Daily Tribune*, January 21, 1845, in Bean and Myerson, *Margaret Fuller, Critic*, 36; emphasis added.
16. Fuller, "Miss Barrett's Poems," *New-York Daily Tribune*, January 4, 1845, in Bean and Myerson, *Margaret Fuller, Critic*, 20.
17. In *Delicate Subjects: Romanticism, Gender, and the Ethics of Understanding* (Ithaca, N.Y.: Cornell University Press, 1990), Julie Ellison argues that Fuller's writing exhibits a repeated "parody of the sentimental (234).
18. Bean and Myerson, *Margaret Fuller, Critic*, xxi; Larry J. Reynolds, *European Revolutions and the American Literary Renaissance* (New Haven, Conn.: Yale University Press, 1988), 60.
19. Fuller, "Prevalent Idea That Politeness Is Too Great a Luxury to Be Given to the Poor," *New-York Daily Tribune*, May 31, 1845, in Bean and Myerson, *Margaret Fuller, Critic*, 130; "The Poor Man: An Ideal Sketch," *New-York Daily Tribune*, March 25, 1846, in Bean and Myerson, *Margaret Fuller, Critic*, 377.
20. Fuller, "Caroline," *New-York Daily Tribune*, April 9, 1846, in Mitchell, *New York Journalism*, 122.
21. Fuller, "Prison Discipline," *New-York Daily Tribune*, February 25, 1846, in Mitchell, *New York Journalism*, 105; "St. Valentine's Day–Bloomingdale Asy-

lum for the Insane," *New-York Daily Tribune*, February 22, 1845, in Mitchell, *New York Journalism*, 81.
22. Fuller, "Prison Discipline," 106.
23. For a discussion of Fuller's use of Christian references and the influence of William Henry Channing, see chapter 9 of Jeffrey Steele, *Transfiguring America: Myth, Ideology, and Mourning in Margaret Fuller's Writing* (Columbia: University of Missouri Press, 2001).
24. Fuller, "Prison Discipline," 105.
25. Fuller, "Asylum for Discharged Female Convicts," *New-York Daily Tribune*, June 19, 1845, in Bean and Myerson, *Margaret Fuller, Critic*, 134, 136; emphasis added.
26. For a discussion of the rise of urban tourism, see Catherine Cocks, *Doing the Town: The Rise of Urban Tourism in the United States, 1850–1915* (Berkeley: University of California Press, 2001).
27. Dickens, *American Notes*, 104.
28. Fuller, "Our City Charities," in Bean and Myerson, *Margaret Fuller, Critic*, 99.
29. See Carrie Tirado Bramen, "The Urban Picturesque and the Spectacle of Americanization," *American Quarterly* 52 (September 2000): 444–77.
30. Fuller, "Our City Charities," 98, 102.
31. Ibid., 148.
32. Fuller, "St. Valentine's Day," 80.
33. Fuller, *Woman in the Nineteenth Century*, in *The Essential Margaret Fuller*, ed. Jeffrey Steele (New Brunswick, N.J.: Rutgers University Press, 1992), 246, 324, 287; emphasis added.
34. Ibid., 343.
35. Ibid., 346.
36. In "Open-Air Musings in the City," Nathaniel Parker Willis would characterize streetwalkers as "the unfortunate outlaws of charity and pity"; see *Rural Letters and Other Records of Thought at Leisure* (Auburn, N.Y.: Alden and Beardsley, 1856), 232.
37. Fuller, "Rich Man," 360.
38. Fuller, "Prevalent Idea That Politeness Is Too Great a Luxury to Be Given to the Poor," *New-York Daily Tribune*, May 31, 1845, in Bean and Myerson, *Margaret Fuller, Critic*, 128, 129–30, emphasis added.
39. Fuller, "Asylum," 134.
40. Burrows and Wallace, *Gotham*, 543, 736.
41. Nevins, *Diary of Philip Hone*, 785.
42. Fuller, "Italy" [Alfieri], *New-York Daily Tribune*, November 13, 1845, in Bean and Myerson, *Margaret Fuller, Critic*, 253.
43. Fuller, "French Novelists of the Day," *New-York Daily Tribune*, February 1, 1845, in Bean and Myerson, *Margaret Fuller, Critic*, 54–55.
44. Fuller, "The Irish Character," pt. 1, *New-York Daily Tribune*, June 28, 1845, in Mitchell, *New York Journalism*, 166.

45. Fuller, "The Irish Character," pt. 2, *New-York Daily Tribune*, July 15, 1845, Mitchell, *New York Journalism*, 170.
46. Fuller, "Irish Character," 1:167; 2:169, 171.
47. Fuller, "Irish Character," 1:166; 2:169, 168.
48. Fuller, "Our City Charities," 89.
49. Fuller, "Prison Discipline," 105.
50. Fuller, "Thanksgiving," *New-York Daily Tribune*, December 12, 1844, in Mitchell, *New York Journalism*, 179.
51. Fuller, "Victory," *New-York Daily Tribune*, May 21, 1846, in Bean and Myerson, *Margaret Fuller, Critic*, 425.
52. Fuller, "Cassius M. Clay," *New-York Daily Tribune*, January 14, 1846, in Bean and Myerson, *Margaret Fuller, Critic*, 339.
53. Later in her career, this prophetic stance morphed into the "fierce . . . martial pose" that Fuller adopted in her Roman dispatches; see Reynolds, *European Revolutions*, 74–75.
54. Fuller, "New Year's Day," *New-York Daily Tribune*, December 28, 1844, 14–19; "Fourth of July," *New-York Daily Tribune*, July 4, 1845, 149–51; "First of August, 1845," *New-York Daily Tribune*, August 1, 1845, 183–88; "1st January, 1846," *New-York Daily Tribune*, January 1, 1846, 323–32, all in Bean and Myerson, *Margaret Fuller, Critic*.
55. Fuller, "New Year's Day," 16, 17; Fuller, "First of August, 1845," 185.
56. Fuller, "New Year's Day," 15.
57. Fuller, "First of August, 1845," 185.
58. Fuller, "1st January, 1846," 325.
59. Ibid., 325.
60. Genesis 18:23–32.
61. Child, *Letters from New-York*, 13.
62. Fuller, "New Year's Day," 17; Fuller, "Fourth of July," 150.
63. Fuller, "New Year's Day," 17.
64. Fuller, "Fourth of July," 150.
65. Fuller, "1st January, 1846," 328.
66. For an extended analysis of Fuller's 1840–41 spiritual crisis and the alchemical symbolism that grew out of it, see Steele, *Transfiguring America*, chs. 2–4.
67. Fuller, "1st January, 1846," 326.
68. Fuller, "First of August, 1845," 184.
69. Fuller, "New Year's Day," 15; "Fourth of July," 150.
70. Fuller, "New Year's Day," 18.
71. Fuller, "First of August, 1845," 187, 188.
72. Fuller, "1st January, 1846," 328, 331, 332.
73. William Cullen Bryant's "A Winter Piece" alternates between soothing, maternal landscapes and a stern, patriarchal energy that he associates with winter storms; see Jane Donahue Eberwein, *Early American Poetry* (Madison: University of Wisconsin Press, 1978), 273–77.

74. Mary Chapman and Glenn Hendler, eds., *Sentimental Men: Masculinity and the Politics of Affect in American Culture* (Berkeley: University of California Press, 1999).
75. Robert N. Hudspeth, ed., *The Letters of Margaret Fuller*, 6 vols. (Ithaca, N.Y.: Cornell University Press, 1983–94), 2:173.
76. Fuller, "Leila," in Steele, *Essential Margaret Fuller*, 57.

9. MARGARET FULLER AND URBAN LIFE

Henry David Thoreau, *Journal: The Writings of Henry D. Thoreau*, vol. 2, *1842–1848*, ed. Robert Sattelmeyer (Princeton, N.J.: Princeton University Press, 1984), 147; Margaret Fuller to her brother Richard, December 1841, in *The Letters of Margaret Fuller*, ed. Robert N. Hudspeth, 6 vols. (Ithaca, N.Y.: Cornell University Press, 1983–94), 2:263.

1. Henry David Thoreau, *Journal: The Writings of Henry D. Thoreau*, vol. 1, *1837–1844*, ed. Elizabeth Hall Witherell, William L. Howarth, Robert Sattelmeyer, and Thomas Blanding (Princeton, N.J.: Princeton University Press, 1981), 465.
2. Reform activity occurred outside of cities, to be sure, but in urban areas the scale of poverty and abuse was larger; the common conception, which had its truth, was that urban crowding increased crime and squalor. Yet the resources for an organized response were also more readily at hand. Those same cities made it possible to plan some relief for the destitute, even if the efforts were halting or ineffective.
3. Margaret Fuller, "Entertainments of the Past Winter," *Dial* 3 (July 1842): 46, 53.
4. See the most recent biographies: Joan von Mehren, *Minerva and the Muse: A Life of Margaret Fuller* (Amherst: University of Massachusetts Press, 1994); Charles Capper, *Margaret Fuller: An American Romantic Life*, 2 vols. (New York: Oxford University Press, 1992–2007); and Meg McGavran Murray, *Margaret Fuller: Wandering Pilgrim* (Athens: University of Georgia Press, 2008), but see also the works of Bell Gale Chevigny, Julie Ellison, Larry Reynolds, David Robinson, Jeffrey Steele, and Christina Zwarg cited in the following notes.
5. As an aside, one might claim that it was Whitman, not Emerson, Thoreau, or Alcott, who had the most parallel experience of urban life.
6. Robert N. Hudspeth, ed., *The Letters of Margaret Fuller*, 6 vols. (Ithaca, N.Y.: Cornell University Press, 1983–94), 6:163, 1:214.
7. Ibid., 1:223.
8. Tess Hoffmann, "Miss Fuller among the Literary Lions: Two Essays Read at 'The Coliseum' in 1838," *Studies in the American Renaissance 1988*, ed. Joel Myerson (Charlottesville: University Press of Virginia, 1988), 42.
9. Margaret Fuller, "A Record of Impressions," *Dial* 1 (July 1840): 75.
10. Fuller, "Entertainments," 46, 49.
11. Fuller, "Record of Impressions," 73.

12. Ibid.
13. Fuller, "Entertainments," 46, 64.
14. Hoffman, "Miss Fuller," 41.
15. Fuller, "Entertainments," 53.
16. Bell Gale Chevigny, "Mutual Interpretation: Margaret Fuller's Journeys in Italy," in *Margaret Fuller: Transatlantic Crossings in a Revolutionary Age*, ed. Charles Capper and Cristina Giorcelli (Madison: University of Wisconsin Press, 2007), 101.
17. Hudspeth, *Letters of Margaret Fuller*, 3:234.
18. For Fuller's reaction to the Dorr Rebellion, see Bell Gale Chevigny, "To the Edges of Ideology: Margaret Fuller's Centrifugal Evolution," *American Quarterly* 38 (Summer 1986): 177–80.
19. Hudspeth, *Letters of Margaret Fuller*, 3:74.
20. Ibid., 3:223, 237.
21. Judith Mattson Bean and Joel Myerson, eds., *Margaret Fuller, Critic: Writings from the New-York Tribune, 1844–1846* (New York: Columbia University Press, 2000), 9–10.
22. Hudspeth, *Letters of Margaret Fuller*, 4:46.
23. Chevigny, "Edges of Ideology," 186.
24. Ibid.
25. Treatments of Fuller's intellectual growth are, of course, abundant. On the specific questions of Fuller's social concerns, see Larry J. Reynolds, *European Revolutions and the American Literary Renaissance* (New Haven, Conn.: Yale University Press, 1988); Julie Ellison, *Delicate Subjects: Romanticism, Gender, and the Ethics of Understanding* (Ithaca, N.Y.: Cornell University Press, 1990); and Christina Zwarg, *Feminist Conversations: Fuller, Emerson, and the Play of Reading* (Ithaca, N.Y.: Cornell University Press, 1995), as well as Chevigny, "Edges of Ideology." The authors work from differing assumptions and thus arrive at disparate conclusions.
26. Although Fuller erroneously claimed the *Tribune* readership to be "half a hundred thousand" (Hudspeth, *Letters of Margaret Fuller*, 4:56), it was closer to twenty-eight thousand, according to Catherine C. Mitchell, *Margaret Fuller's New York Journalism* (Knoxville: University of Tennessee Press, 1995), 9. Though the *Tribune* would become the largest American newspaper, those days were to come in the 1850s. Mitchell estimates that during Fuller's time in New York the *Tribune* was the third largest newspaper, trailing the *Herald* and probably the *Sun*, a one-cent paper.
27. Hudspeth, *Letters of Margaret Fuller*, 4:54.
28. Jeffrey Steele, *Transfiguring America: Myth, Ideology, and Mourning in Margaret Fuller's Writing* (Columbia: University of Missouri Press, 2001), 231. Steele emphasizes Fuller's Christian commitments to reform: "Representing herself as a vehicle for public consciousness and reform, she constructed a persona whose

authority rested in part upon use of a religious discourse that intersected with recognizable theological values."

29. Hudspeth, *Letters of Margaret Fuller*, 6:359. In *Feminist Conversations*, 207–12, Christina Zwarg uses Fuller's potent phrase from *Papers on Literature and Art*, "the great mutual system of interpretation" to derive a convincing argument about Fuller's developing understanding of reading as a means of social reform. She made, Zwarg says, "a direct correlation between the activity of reading and the process of social change, for reading can offer a way to disrupt certain ideological assumptions" (211).
30. Bean and Myerson, *Margaret Fuller, Critic*, 98.
31. Ibid., 103.
32. David M. Robinson, "Margaret Fuller, New York, and the Politics of Transcendentalism," *ESQ* 52 (2006): 289. Robinson goes on to say, "Self-culture remains, then, an essential value for Fuller. But in prison and asylum reform, as in women's rights, she has come to see that its sustained and widespread achievement is undoubtedly a social and political question, and must in some respects be pursued through means of civic education, political advocacy, public policy, and social reorganization" (292). My argument throughout is that "civic education" was always in the forefront of Fuller's thinking.
33. Margaret Fuller, "Darkness Visible," C-253. I cite by bibliographic number the CD-ROM edition of the complete *Tribune* New York essays that accompanies Bean and Myerson, *Margaret Fuller, Critic*.
34. Fuller, "Prison Discipline," C-249.
35. Philip F. Gura, *American Transcendentalism: A History* (New York: Hill and Wang, 2007), 232. Gura goes on to say that Fuller's new commitment to social reform "testifies to New York's indelible impact on her. . . . Awakened to the inequalities that gave the lie to America's purportedly egalitarian society, she subordinated her transcendent ego to her social conscience."
36. Bean and Myerson, *Margaret Fuller, Critic*, 135.
37. Fuller, "Ole Bull," C-207.
38. Hudspeth, *Letters of Margaret Fuller*, 3:209.
39. Fuller, "Music," C-240.
40. Fuller, "Music in New-York," C-88.
41. Hudspeth, *Letters of Margaret Fuller*, 5:51, 4:46.
42. Steven Fink and Susan S. Williams, eds., *Reciprocal Influences: Literary Production, Distribution, and Consumption in America* (Columbus: Ohio State University Press, 1999), 69.
43. S. Margaret Fuller, "American Literature: Its Position in the Present Time, and Prospects for the Future," in *Papers on Literature and Art* (New York: Wiley and Putnam, 1846), 2:140, 139, 140.
44. Leslie E. Eckel, "Margaret Fuller's Conversational Journalism: New York, London, Rome," *Arizona Quarterly* 63 (2007): 32.

45. Wiley objected to her essay on Philip Bailey's *Festus*, which caused Fuller to say that "there are probably sentences in every piece, perhaps on every page, which, when the books are once published, will lead to censure" (Hudspeth, *Letters of Margaret Fuller*, 4:212). She later regretted the publisher's unwillingness to publish more of her writing on continental literature and others of "a radical stamp" (Hudspeth, *Letters of Margaret Fuller*, 4:234, 235).
46. Fuller, "Farewell," C-316.
47. Barbara L. Packer, *The Transcendentalists* (Athens: University of Georgia Press, 2007), 205. Packer goes on to note that "the effect on Fuller's prose style was striking" (206).
48. Larry J. Reynolds and Susan Belasco Smith, eds., *"These Sad but Glorious Days": Dispatches from Europe, 1846–1850* (New Haven, Conn.: Yale University Press, 1991), 88, 47.
49. Hudspeth, *Letters of Margaret Fuller*, 4:240.
50. Reynolds and Smith, *Sad but Glorious Days*, 88.
51. Ibid., 106.
52. Ibid., 119, 126, 127.
53. Hudspeth, *Letters of Margaret Fuller*, 4:271.
54. Reynolds and Smith, *Sad but Glorious Days*, 129, 139.
55. Ibid., 167–68, 169.
56. Ibid., 169, 175.
57. Hudspeth, *Letters of Margaret Fuller*, 5:181.
58. Reynolds and Smith, *Sad but Glorious Days*, 199, 228.
59. Hudspeth, *Letters of Margaret Fuller*, 4:193.
60. Charles Capper, *The Public Years*, vol. 2 of *Margaret Fuller: An American Romantic Life* (New York: Oxford University Press, 2007), 367.
61. Reynolds and Smith, *Sad but Glorious Days*, 230.
62. Ibid., 239.
63. Chevigny, "Edges of Ideology," 176–78.
64. Reynolds and Smith, *Sad but Glorious Days*, 240.
65. See Francesco Guida, "Realism, Idealism, and Passion in Margaret Fuller's Response to Italy," in Capper and Giorselli, *Margaret Fuller*, 156–71. Guida comments on Fuller's point of view and claims that "her observations were sometimes idealized and sometimes wholly foreign to the actual Italian situation." He says that her "vision of the European political scene and, more deeply, of the Italian scene, did not go much beyond the observations of the Italian democratic press at the time" (156, 167).
66. Reynolds and Smith, *Sad but Glorious Days*, 284, 304.
67. For a thorough discussion of Fuller and artistic representation see Brigitte Bailey, "Representing Italy: Fuller, History Painting, and the Popular Press," in *Margaret Fuller's Cultural Critique: Her Age and Legacy*, ed. Fritz Fleischmann (New York: Lang, 2000), 229–45. "In her depiction of Garibaldi," Bailey says, "Fuller uses an image of temporary defeat as an originating moment for a future

national identity, or, rather, she seeks to make his exit from Rome visible to her readers as such a 'birth-event'" (242).
68. Reynolds and Smith, *Sad but Glorious Days*, 280, 310.
69. Ibid., 306.
70. Hudspeth, *Letters of Margaret Fuller*, 5:273–74, 305, 6:69.
71. Reynolds and Smith, *Sad but Glorious Days*, 321.
72. Ralph Waldo Emerson, *The Letters of Ralph Waldo Emerson*, ed. Ralph L. Rusk, 6 vols. (New York: Columbia University Press, 1939): 4:62.
73. See Reynolds, *European Revolutions*, 58–60 for a discussion of the different reactions of Fuller and Emerson.
74. Reynolds and Smith, *Sad but Glorious Days*, 98, 271, 311.
75. Ibid., 320.
76. Hudspeth, *Letters of Margaret Fuller*, 4:192.
77. The list is long, but it would include Theodore Parker after he moved to Boston, Thomas Wentworth Higginson, William Henry Channing, John Weiss, Harrison Gray Otis Blake and his friends in Worcester, and Orestes Brownson before his conversion to Catholicism.
78. Emerson was right to say—and Fuller would have understood his full meaning—when he first heard of her death: "I have lost in her my audience." Ralph Waldo Emerson, *The Journals and Miscellaneous Notebooks of Ralph Waldo Emerson*, vol. 11, ed. A. W. Plumstead et al., 16 vols. (Cambridge: Belknap Press of Harvard University Press, 1975), 258.

10. MARGARET FULLER AND THE DYNAMICS OF TRANSNATIONAL RECEPTION

1. For recent discussions of reading communities and codes, see, for example, Janice Radway, "What's the Matter with Reception Study? Some Thoughts on the Disciplinary Origins, Conceptual Constraints, and Persistent Viability of a Paradigm," *New Directions in American Reception Study*, ed. Philip Goldstein and James L. Machor (Oxford: Oxford University Press, 2008), 327–51; and Brian Richardson, "The Other Reader's Response: On Multiple, Divided, and Oppositional Audiences," *Criticism* 39 (1997): 31–53. Christina Zwarg's inquiry into reading situates Fuller in postmodern theory as a "proto-deconstructor" rather than in history; see *Feminist Conversations: Fuller, Emerson, and the Play of Reading* (Ithaca, N.Y.: Cornell University Press, 1995), 28. Zwarg addresses Fuller's "response toward . . . Sand" without analyzing any text by Sand.
2. Howard N. Meyer, "The Sisterhood of George Sand and Margaret Fuller," *Friends of George Sand Newsletter* 6 (1983): 45n8. For ways in which an appreciation of Sand did influence Fuller's writing, see Charlene Avallone, "Margaret Fuller and 'the Best Living Prose Writer,' George Sand," *Nineteenth-Century Prose*, special Fuller bicentennial issue, ed. Brigitte Bailey (forthcoming).
3. Russell E. Durning, *Margaret Fuller: Citizen of the World; An Intermediary between European and American Literatures*, Beihefte zum Jahrbuch für Ameri-

NOTES

kastudien, Heft 26 (Heidelberg: Winter, 1969), 55; Perry Miller, headnote, *Margaret Fuller: American Romantic: A Selection from Her Writings and Correspondence*, ed. Perry Miller (Garden City, N.Y.: Doubleday/Anchor, 1963), 260. For an exception, see Julie Ellison, *Delicate Subjects: Romanticism, Gender, and the Ethics of Understanding* (Ithaca, N.Y.: Cornell University Press, 1990).

4. Gary Williams makes the most concerted effort to untangle the chronology of Fuller's comments on Sand from documents mangled by the editors of the *Memoirs*; see "George Sand and Margaret Fuller: 'Expansive Fellowship'" (Paper presented at the conference "Transatlanticism in American Literature," Rothermere American Institute, University of Oxford, United Kingdom, July 2006, accessed May 19, 2008, www.class.uidaho.edu); and see James Freeman Clarke, Ralph Waldo Emerson, and William Henry Channing, eds., *Memoirs of Margaret Fuller Ossoli*, 2 vols. (Boston: Phillips, Sampson, 1852), 1:244–50.

5. Charles-Augustin Sainte-Beuve, review of *Indiana*, October 5, 1832, reprinted as "George Sand," *Portraits contemporains* (1845), tome 1, nouvelle édition (Paris: Calmann-Lévy, 1868), 470–81; review of *Valentine*, December 31, 1832, reprinted as "George Sand," 482–94; "Dix ans après en littérature," *Revue des deux mondes* 21, no. 4e (March 1840), http://fr.wikisource.org/wiki/Dix ans après en littérature.

6. Fuller uses the term "jeune France" (Young France) in its expansive reference, much as Frances Trollope explained it, to include the larger progressive movement and connote "something great, terrible, volcanic, and sublime." Frances Milton Trollope, *Paris and the Parisians in 1835*, 2nd ed. (London: Bentley, 1836), 1:14.

7. Bertha Thomas, *George Sand* (Boston: Roberts Brothers, 1883), 66; see also 75. This dynamic has been obscured, as the reception study of Sand is largely organized by a model of nationality. For an example of how quickly American periodicals picked up this discussion, see "From 'the Athenaeum, No. 309,'" *Select Journal of Foreign Periodical Literature* 3 (April 1834): 3.

8. Frances Winwar, *The Life of the Heart: George Sand and Her Times* (New York: Harper, 1945), 117.

9. Review of *Jacques*, *Athenaeum* (December 1834), quoted in Patricia Thomson, *George Sand and the Victorians: Her Influence and Reputation in Nineteenth-Century England* (New York: Columbia University Press, 1977), 12; Jules Janin, "Literature of the Nineteenth Century: France," *Athenaeum* 502 (June 10, 1837): 426.

10. Thomson, *Sand and the Victorians*, 18; on the *Westminster*, see 16–17; Charles-Augustin Sainte-Beuve, "Jugements sur notre littérature contemporaine a l'étranger," *Revue des deux mondes* 6 (1836), http://fr.wikisource.org/wiki/Jugements_sur_notre_littérature_contemporaine_à_l'étranger; Joseph Mazzini, "George Sand," *Monthly Chronicle* 4 (1839): 23–40. See also F. B., "Philosophy of Fiction," *London and Westminster Review*, American ed., 40 (April 1838): 38–51; Henry F. Chorley, "The Works of George Sand," *British and Foreign Review* 8 (1839): 360–90.

11. William Makepeace Thackeray, "Letters from London, Paris, Pekin, Petersburg, &c.," *Corsair*, September 14, 1839, 429–30; September 21, 1839, 447. *Spiridion* appeared in five installments in the *Revue des deux mondes* between October 1838 and February 1839.
12. Sainte-Beuve, "Jugements sur notre littérature," n.p.
13. Mazzini, "George Sand," *Monthly Chronicle*, 29.
14. George W. M. Reynolds, *The Modern Literature of France* (London: Henderson, 1839), intro., 1:xvii.
15. F. B., "Philosophy of Fiction," 49, and see 51, 45, 40, 38.
16. John Stuart Mill, review of *Oeuvres de Alfred de Vigny*, *London and Westminster Review*, April 1838, 15.
17. [George Henry Lewes], review of *Oeuvres complètes de M. de Balzac* and *Oeuvres complètes de George Sand*, *Foreign Quarterly Review*, American ed., 33 (July 1844): 297, 291, 266.
18. "Modern French Romance," *New-York Review* 4 (April 1839), quoted in John Stafford, "Samuel Ward's Defense of Balzac's 'Objective' Fiction," *American Literature* 24 (1952): 174.
19. Henry Wadsworth Longfellow, *Hyperion* (1839), in *Hyperion and Kavanagh*, vol. 8 of *The Works of Henry Wadsworth Longfellow*, ed. Samuel Longfellow, Standard Library ed. (New York: AMS, 1966).
20. Samuel Ward, Review of *Hyperion, a Romance, by the Author of Outre-Mer*, *New-York Review* 5 (October 1839): 455.
21. Samuel Osgood, "The Satanic School in Literature," *Christian Examiner* 27 (November 1839): 146, 153.
22. Clarke, Emerson, and Channing, *Memoirs*, 1:251.
23. [John Stuart Mill], "Armand Carrel," *London and Westminster Review*, October 1837, reprinted in *Dissertations and Discussions* (London: Parker, 1859), 234.
24. See, for example, Fuller to James Freeman Clarke, and Fuller to Caroline Sturgis, Robert N. Hudspeth, ed., *Letters of Margaret Fuller*, 6 vols. (Ithaca, N.Y.: Cornell University Press, 1983–94), 1:220, 221, 2:48–49; also see Joan von Mehren, *Minerva and the Muse: A Life of Margaret Fuller* (Amherst: University of Massachusetts Press, 1994), 62, 105; Charles Capper, *The Private Years*, vol. 1 of *Margaret Fuller: An American Romantic Life* (New York: Oxford University Press, 1992), 115.
25. Octavius Brooks Frothingham, *Transcendentalism in New England: A History* (New York: Putnam's, 1876).
26. Fuller to Clarke, April 28, 1835, in Hudspeth, *Letters of Margaret Fuller*, 6:260.
27. Clarke, Emerson, and Channing, *Memoirs*, 1:244; Margaret Fuller, review of *Consuelo*, by George Sand, *New-York Daily Tribune*, June 24, 1846, reprinted in *Margaret Fuller, Critic: Writings from the New-York Tribune, 1844–1846*, ed. Judith Mattson Bean and Joel Myerson (New York: Columbia University Press, 2000), 457.
28. Orestes Brownson, "Memoir of Saint-Simon," *Unitarian* 1 (June 1834), re-

printed in *The Free Thought and Unitarian Years, 1830–35*, vol. 2 of *The Early Works of Orestes A. Brownson*, ed. Patrick W. Carey (Milwaukee, Wisc.: Marquette University Press, 2000), 320, 333.

29. Orestes Brownson, "The Democracy of Christianity," *Boston Quarterly Review* 1 (October 1838): 444–73, reprinted in Carey, *The Transcendentalist Years, 1838–39*, vol. 4 of *Early Works* (2003), 74, 78–79.

30. Brownson, "The Democracy of Christianity," in Carey, *Transcendentalist Years*, 78, 96.

31. George Ripley, review of *Vues sur le Protestantisme en France*, *Christian Examiner* n.s. 15 (July 1831): 273; *Philosophical Miscellanies: Translated from the French of Cousin, Jouffroy, and B. Constant. . . . by George Ripley* (Boston: Hilliard, Gray, 1838), 2:282.

32. William H. Channing, "Translator's Preface," *Introduction to Ethics . . . , Translated from the French of Jouffroy*, trans. William H. Channing (1838; repr., Boston: Dennet, 1873), 1:xvii; Ripley, "Introductory Notice," *Philosophical Miscellanies*, 42.

33. Orestes Brownson, review of *Philosophical Miscellanies, translated from the French of Cousin, Jouffroy, and Benjamin Constant . . . by George Ripley*, *Boston Quarterly Review* 1 (October 1838): 438, 439.

34. Octavius Brooks Frothingham, *Memoir of William Henry Channing* (Cambridge: Riverside; Boston: Houghton Mifflin, 1886), 202.

35. Fuller journal, fall 1836, quoted in Capper, *Private Years*, 183.

36. Clarke, Emerson, and Channing, *Memoirs*, 2:202; Fuller, Dispatch 10, undated, *"These Sad but Glorious Days": Dispatches from Europe, 1846–50*, ed. Larry J. Reynolds and Susan Belasco Smith (New Haven, Conn.: Yale University Press, 1991), 111.

37. Margaret Fuller, "Translator's Preface," *Conversations with Goethe, in the Last Years of His Life: Translated from the German of Eckermann by S. M. Fuller* (Boston: Hilliard, Gray, 1839), xvii; Fuller, "French Novelists of the Day: Balzac, George Sand, Eugene Sue," *New-York Daily Tribune*, February 1, 1845, reprinted in Bean and Myerson, *Margaret Fuller, Critic*, 58.

38. Clarke, Emerson, and Channing, *Memoirs*, 1:244.

39. Fuller to William H. Channing, April 19, 1840, in Hudspeth, *Letters of Margaret Fuller*, 2:131. Fuller's desire upon reading Sand, to "try whether I have the hand to paint" and "write like a woman," first published in Higginson's biography, may have been part of that correspondence or a journal entry; Thomas Wentworth Higginson, *Margaret Fuller Ossoli*, American Men of Letters series, ed. Charles Dudley Warner (Boston: Houghton, Mifflin, 1884), 188.

40. Von Mehren, *Minerva and the Muse*, 149.

41. Frothingham, *William Henry Channing*, 180, 181.

42. Clarke, Emerson, and Channing, *Memoirs*, 1:246.

43. Ibid., 1:245–46.

44. George Sand, "*Spiridion*: Quatrième partie," *Revue des deux mondes* 17 (January 1839): 40, see esp. 42; on perfectibility, see 38.
45. Clarke, Emerson, and Channing, *Memoirs*, 1:246.
46. See Eugène Lerminier, "Radicalisme évangélique," revue de *Le livre du peuple*, in *Revue des deux mondes* 13, January 15, 1838; George Sand, "Lettre à M. Lerminier," *Revue des deux mondes* 13, February 15, 1838; and Lerminier, "Réponse à George Sand," *Revue des deux mondes* 13, February 15, 1838; all at http://fr.wikisource.org/wiki/Revue_des_Deux_Mondes /1829–1848#Tome_13_:_janvier_.C3.A0_mars_1838; "The Abbé de La Mennais," review of *Affaires de Rome: Paroles d'un croyant*, and *Le livre du peuple*, *Foreign Quarterly Review*, American ed., April 1838, 65–72. *Lettres d'un voyageur*, which Fuller read in serialization, celebrated Lamennais's inspiration for a heaven on earth and apotheosized him as one leader of the republican march that Sand joined as a writer; see "Lettres d'un voyageur III" and "Lettres d'un voyageur IV," *Revue des deux mondes* 3, September 15, 1834, 714–35; 2, June 15, 1835, 692–731.
47. Clarke, Emerson, and Channing, *Memoirs*, 1:247. Criticism now disputes the attribution of Sand's thought to Lamennais and Leroux; see Kristina Wingard Vareille, *Socialité, sexualité et les impasses de l'histoire: L'évolution de la thématique sandienne d'*Indiana *(1832) à* Mauprat *(1837)* (Stockholm: Uppsala, 1987); and Pierre Macherey, "George Sand's *Spiridion*: A Pantheist Novel," *The Object of Literature*, trans. David Macey (Cambridge: Cambridge University Press, 1995), 38–56.
48. Channing, *Introduction to Ethics*, 2:250, 249.
49. Clarke, Emerson, and Channing, *Memoirs*, 1:248, 249.
50. Ibid., 1:251–52, 248.
51. Fuller, "French Novelists," 55.
52. Orestes Brownson, "Modern French Literature. Art. V Spiridion," *Boston Quarterly Review* 5 (April 1842): 230, 250.
53. Ibid., 239, 232, 239, 251, 241, 243, 241.
54. John Wilson Croker, "Rousseau's *Nouvelle Heloise* and the Modern Littérature Extravagante," *Foreign Quarterly Review* 27 (April 1841): 131, 133; Francis Bowen, review of *Oeuvres de George Sand*, *North American Review* 53 (July 1841): 109, 110; [Lewes], review of *Oeuvres complètes*, 274, 271.
55. Fuller, "The Great Lawsuit. Man versus Men. Woman versus Women," *Dial* 4 (July 1843): 4, 29, 34, 29.
56. Ibid., 30.
57. Bowen, review of *Oeuvres de George Sand*, 113, 114.
58. Fuller, "Great Lawsuit," 30.
59. Fuller, *Woman in the Nineteenth Century* (1845), reprinted in *Margaret Fuller: Essays on American Life and Letters*, ed. Joel Myerson (New Haven, Conn.: College and University Press, 1978), 133. Zwarg defends Fuller's phrasing as merely "a rhetorical strategy," buffering references to the more "radical" Fourier (*Femi-*

nist Conversations, 172). Such phrasing in Fuller's appraisals of Sand from 1839, when neither audience nor Fourier was at issue, to 1847 suggests that Fuller's moral evaluation exceeded strategy. It is not only that Fuller "cannot condone" what Zwarg calls "Sand's sexual promiscuity"; she also slighted Sand as a writer and contributor to the women's movement. Zwarg's argument that Fuller developed a radical theory of reading at the *Tribune* does not consider the reviews of Sand.

60. Fuller, *Woman*, 132. See also George Sand, *Mauprat*, ed. Jean-Pierre Lacassagne (Paris: Gallimard, 1981).
61. Fuller, *Woman*, 131; see also George Sand, *Simon* (Paris: Dodo, 2008); Sand, *Indiana*, ed. Béatrice Didier (Paris: Gallimard, 1984).
62. Ellison, *Delicate Subjects*, 265, 10.
63. Fuller, *Woman*, 186, 168.
64. Lorien Foote, *Seeking the One Great Remedy: Francis George Shaw and Nineteenth-Century Reform* (Athens: Ohio University Press, 2003), 37 and 48–50.
65. Clarke, Emerson, and Channing, *Memoirs*, 2:81, 52, 81–82. Fuller's final description of herself as a "Socialist" used the same term, "enthusiastic"; she was "only blundering observing," not active in reform (Fuller to Marcus and Rebecca Buffum Spring, December 12, 1849, in Hudspeth, *Letters of Margaret Fuller*, 5:295). She confessed to Channing that she did not "like" any European Fourierites she met, so "terribly wearisome" they were in their attention to "system," and that her "interest" in socialism was as "shallow" as she judged all socialist "plans" to be (Fuller to Channing, May 23, 1847, March 10, 1849, in Hudspeth, *Letters of Margaret Fuller*, 4:271, 5:206). With Adam-Max Tuchinsky, I thus find Fuller's views of association less developed than scholars have recently maintained; see, in this volume, his "'More anon': American Socialism and Margaret Fuller's 1848." For other assessments of Fuller's interest in socialism, see Bell Gale Chevigny, "To the Edges of Ideology: Margaret Fuller's Centrifugal Evolution," *American Quarterly* 38 (1986): 173–201; Larry J. Reynolds, *European Revolutions and the American Literary Renaissance* (New Haven, Conn.: Yale University Press, 1988), 60–62; Reynolds and Smith, introduction to *Sad but Glorious Days*, 16–18; Zwarg, *Feminist Conversations*, esp. 54–55, 114–119, and 189–220; and David M. Robinson, "Margaret Fuller, Self-Culture, and Associationism," in this volume.
66. "Heaven upon Earth: No. 2," *The Present* 1 (April 1844): 425.
67. Clarke, Emerson, and Channing, *Memoirs*, 2:134; Charles Capper, *The Public Years*, vol. 2 of *Margaret Fuller: An American Romantic Life* (New York: Oxford University Press, 2007), 168; Clarke, Emerson, and Channing, *Memoirs*, 2:81.
68. Curtis Cate, *George Sand: A Biography* (New York: Avon, 1975), 490.
69. Review of *Consuelo*, by George Sand, *Foreign Quarterly Review* 30 (January 1843): 428.
70. See Susan Belasco, "'The Animating Influences of Discord': Margaret Fuller in 1844," *Legacy* 20 (2003): 76–93.

71. Fuller, "French Novelists," 54.
72. Ibid., 55, 54, 55, 58, 59, 57, 58.
73. Ibid., 58, 61, 60, 61, 63, 61, 62, 58, 60.
74. Fuller, "Jenny Lind . . . the Consuelo of George Sand," *New-York Daily Tribune*, September 19, 1845, reprinted in Bean and Myerson, *Margaret Fuller, Critic*, 227.
75. Ibid., 230, 229, 230.
76. Clarke, Emerson, and Channing, *Memoirs*, 1:245.
77. Fuller, "Jenny Lind . . . *Consuelo*," in Bean and Myerson, *Margaret Fuller, Critic*, 230.
78. Francis G. Shaw, "The Writings of George Sand. Art. IV of the *Christian Examiner* for March," *Harbinger* 4 (March 13, 1847): 223–24.
79. John S. Dwight, review of *Consuelo*, by George Sand, *Harbinger* 1 (June 14, 1845): 11. Georges J. Joyaux concluded that the journal gave equal coverage to Sand and Sue, overlooking that it published two of Sand's novels and nothing by Sue. "George Sand, Eugène Sue and *The Harbinger*," *French Review* 27 (December 1935): 122–31.
80. Dwight, review of *Consuelo*, 12.
81. Clarke, Emerson, and Channing, *Memoirs*, 2:81.
82. See Avallone, "Best Living Prose Writer."
83. Sand, "Lettres d'un voyageur VII," *Revue des deux mondes* 8, November 15, 1836, 429–30.
84. Fuller, review of *Consuelo*, 457; see [George Henry Lewes], "George Sand's Recent Novels," *Foreign Quarterly Review* 37 (April 1846), 32–34.
85. Fuller, review of *Consuelo*, 457, 462, 463, 457, 461.
86. Ibid., 461.
87. [Lewes], "George Sand's Recent Novels," 31, 29.
88. Fuller to Frank Shaw, October 25, 1847, in Hudspeth, *Letters of Margaret Fuller*, 4:307.
89. Clarke, Emerson, and Channing, *Memoirs*, 2:202.
90. Fuller noted that she wrote fifty letters in one three-month period in the year that she began reading Sand; of these, only sixteen appear in the collected letters. The archive is slimmer yet in the case of less celebrated women. See Fuller to Caroline Sturgis, March 4, 1839, in Hudspeth, *Letters of Margaret Fuller*, 2:58–59.
91. Elizabeth P. Peabody, *Reminiscences of Reverend William Ellery Channing* (Boston: Roberts, 1880), 409; For holdings in the library, see "Catalogue of the Foreign Library, No. 13 West Street," 1840, reprinted in Madeleine B. Stern, "Elizabeth Peabody's Foreign Library (1840)," *Books and Book People in Nineteenth-Century America* (New York: Bowker, 1978), 124–35.
92. Fuller to Ralph Waldo Emerson, November 7, 1840, in Hudspeth, *Letters of Margaret Fuller*, 2:182.
93. Quoted in *James Freeman Clarke: Autobiography, Diary and Correspondence*, ed. Edward Everett Hale, 3rd ed. (Boston: Houghton, Mifflin, 1891), 306.

94. See Ralph Waldo Emerson, *The Journals and Miscellaneous Notebooks of Ralph Waldo Emerson*, vol. 9, ed. Ralph H. Orth et al., 16 vols. (Cambridge: Belknap Press of Harvard University Press, 1960–82), 79.

95. On Dall, see Helen R. Deese, ed., *Daughter of Boston: The Extraordinary Diary of a Nineteenth-century Woman, Caroline Healey Dall* (Boston: Beacon, 2005), 224, 237.

96. Lydia Maria Child to Lucy Osgood, June 28, 1846; to Anna Loring, February 12, 1857, in *Selected Letters, 1817–1880*, ed. Milton Meltzer and Patricia G. Holland (Amherst: University of Massachusetts Press, 1982), 227, 305; Lydia Maria Child to Lucy and Mary Osgood, January 30, 1859, quoted in Carolyn Karcher, *The First Woman in the Republic: A Cultural Biography of Lydia Maria Child* (Durham, N.C.: Duke University Press, 1994), 412.

97. Quoted in Fuller, *Woman*, 131; cf. Fuller, "French Novelists," 59.

98. See Meltzer and Holland, *Selected Letters*, 305, 12, 315.

99. Fuller to Elizabeth Hoar, January 18, 1847, in Hudspeth, *Letters of Margaret Fuller*, 4:256.

100. Fuller to Caroline Sturgis, November 28, 1846, in Hudspeth, *Letters of Margaret Fuller*, 4:252.

101. Fuller to Sarah Shaw, July 1, 1845, March 18, 1849, in Hudspeth, *Letters of Margaret Fuller*, 5:127, 5:215.

102. Fuller to Caroline Sturgis, August 22, 1847, January 11, 1847, in Hudspeth, *Letters of Margaret Fuller*, 4:291, 5:42; emphasis in the original. The original note accompanying the gift was lost. Consuelo and her lover gather the shells to make ornaments that she sells to support her mother.

103. See Fuller to Caroline Sturgis, ca. March 1840, in Hudspeth, *Letters of Margaret Fuller*, 2: 124.

104. Caroline Sturgis to Fuller, March 4, 1845, in Francis B. Dedmond, "The Letters of Caroline Sturgis to Margaret Fuller," *Studies in the American Renaissance*, ed. Joel Myerson (Charlottesville: University Press of Virginia, 1988), 239.

105. Caroline Sturgis to Fuller, March 5, 1845, in Dedmond, "Letters of Caroline Sturgis," 242.

106. Fuller to Ralph Waldo Emerson, November 15, 1846, in Hudspeth, *Letters of Margaret Fuller*, 4:248, 246.

107. See von Mehren, *Minerva and Muse*, 242–43.

108. Joseph Mazzini to Sand, January 16, 1847, in George Sand, *Correspondance* 7 (juillet 1845–juin 1847), textes réunis, classés, et annotés par George Lubin (Paris: Garnier Frères, 1970), 604; and see Mazzini to Fuller, January 17, 1847, quoted in Capper, *Public Years*, 324. On Mazzini's arranging the meeting, see von Mehren, *Minerva and the Muse*, 242, 245–46.

109. *People's Journal* 3 (March 6, 1847): 5, 18. Editor John Saunders also listed Fuller among those who would "regularly" contribute "papers" to the journal. *William Howitt and the People's Journal: An Appeal to the Press and the Public* (London: People's Journal Office, 1847), 16. This work can be found in Google books.

110. Joseph Mazzini, "George Sand," *People's Journal* 3 (1847): 134. The version of Mazzini's essay in the *Harbinger* adds a notice of the Hays translation "in publication," regretting that its order "destroy[ed] all idea of . . . the moral and philosophical relationship of her works." "George Sand," *Harbinger* 4 (May 29, 1847): 392; *The Works of George Sand*, trans. Matilda M. Hays, Edmund R. Larkin, and Eliza A. Ashurst, ed. Matilda M. Hays, 6 vols. (London: Churton, 1847).

111. Mazzini, "George Sand," *People's Journal*, 134.

112. Fuller, "To a Daughter of Italy," *People's Journal* 4 (1847): 327.

113. Fuller to Mary Howitt, April 18, 1847, in Hudspeth, *Letters of Margaret Fuller*, 4:267. *Howitt's* also promoted Sand, the Hays series, and Hays's independent translation of *The Companion of the Tour of France*. The journal also accused the Parlor Library of pirating the Shaw translation of *Consuelo* to compete with Hays and published a confirmation from Shaw; see *Howitt's*, 1847, 14, 219, 317; also, 119, 317.

114. Joseph Mazzini to Fuller, December 1847, in Leona Rostenberg, "Documents: Mazzini to Margaret Fuller, 1847–1849," *American Historical Review* 47 (October 1941): 76, 77; emphasis in the original.

115. Fuller to Elizabeth Hoar, January 18, 1847, Fuller to Richard Fuller, February 8, 1848, in Hudspeth, *Letters of Margaret Fuller*, 4:256, 5:51; emphasis in the original.

116. Fuller to Elizabeth Hoar, January 18, 1847, in Hudspeth, *Letters of Margaret Fuller*, 4:256.

117. Clarke, Emerson, and Channing, *Memoirs*, 2:195–97; emphasis in the original.

118. Ibid., 197. Fuller's description of Sand summarizes the main points in Sand's description of Lucrezia as possessing "*un caractère aussi clair. . . . Vous apprécierez, comme vous l'entendrez, ce naturel.*" *Lucrezia Floriani* (Bruxelles: Meline, Cans, 1846), 41.

119. Clarke, Emerson, and Channing, *Memoirs*: 2:197–98. Again, Fuller summarizes Sand: Lucrezia describes her conduct, "*Je n'ai jamais aimé deux hommes à la fois, je n'ai jamais appartenu de fait et d'intention qu'à un seul pendant un temps donné, suivant la durée de ma passion. Quand je ne l'aimais plus. . . . Je rompais avec lui d'une manière absolue.*" Sand, *Lucrezia Floriani*, 42–43.

120. Clarke, Emerson, and Channing, *Memoirs*, 2:196.

121. Elizabeth Barrett Browning to Mary Russell Mitford, December 1, 1849, in *The Letters of Elizabeth Barrett Browning*, ed. Frederick G. Kenyon (New York: Macmillan, 1898), 1:428; emphasis in the original.

122. Bell Gale Chevigny, "Mutual Interpretation: Margaret Fuller's Journeys in Italy," *Margaret Fuller: Transatlantic Crossings in a Revolutionary Age*, ed. Charles Capper and Cristina Giorcelli, *Studies in American Thought and Culture*, ed. Paul S. Boyer (University of Wisconsin Press, 2007), 105; and see Chevigny, "Edges of Ideology," 188.

123. Clarke, Emerson, and Channing, *Memoirs*, 2:196; Bonnie S. Anderson, *Joyous Greetings: The First International Women's Movement, 1830–1860* (Oxford:

Oxford University Press, 2000), 147; Margaret H. McFadden, *Golden Cables of Sympathy: The Transatlantic Sources of Nineteenth-Century Feminism* (Lexington: University Press of Kentucky, 1999), 79.

124. See Fuller, Dispatch 10, undated, *Sad but Glorious Days*, 110–11.
125. Joseph Mazzini, "George Sand," *Harbinger* 4 (May 29, 1847): 392–94.
126. Rostenberg, "Documents," 75.
127. Fuller, Dispatch 26, December 2, 1848, *Sad but Glorious Days*, 245–46. On Sand and the socialist clubwomen, see Elizabeth Harlan, *George Sand* (New Haven, Conn.: Yale University Press, 2004), 243–57. The clubwomen apologized for the unauthorized use of Sand's name, suggesting that her response was more complicated than either Harlan or Fuller depicts. For a nuanced account of Sand's position on women and collectivity, see Naomi Schor, *George Sand and Idealism* (New York: Columbia University Press, 1993), 68–82. Phyllis Cole, in the present volume, addresses the ambivalence of Fuller's engagement with the women's movement.

EPILOGUE: MARGARET FULLER'S UNFINISHED REVOLUTION

1. Conrad Edick Wright, Nancy Frankenberry, Linda Kerber, Sidonie Smith, and Katheryn P. Viens offered suggestions that were key to my revisions. Philip Pochoda helped me think through the larger implications of this contribution. The intrepid Marie Stango provided ideas and sources in equal measure. I thank them and I am grateful as well to Conrad Edick Wright and Brigitte Bailey, who organized "Margaret Fuller and Her Circles" and assembled the scholars who participated in the conference.

    Margaret Fuller to William Ellery Channing, November 17, 1844, reprinted in *The Portable Margaret Fuller*, ed. Mary Kelley (New York: Viking Portable Library, 1994), 512; [Lydia Maria Child], "Woman in the Nineteenth Century," *Broadway Journal* 1, no. 7 (February 15, 1845): 1; A. G. M., "The Condition of Woman," *Southern Quarterly Review* 10, no. 19 (July 1846): 170. Portions of this contribution have been adapted from my introduction to *The Portable Margaret Fuller*.

2. Edgar Allan Poe, "The Literati of New York City," *Godey's Lady's Book* 33 (August 1846): 72; Fuller, *Woman in the Nineteenth Century* (1845), reprinted in Kelley, *Portable Margaret Fuller*, 243.

3. Gail Collins, *When Everything Changed: The Amazing Journey of American Women from 1960 to the Present* (Boston: Little, Brown, 2009), 3–8; Susan J. Douglas, *Enlightened Sexism: The Seductive Message That Feminism's Work Is Done* (New York: Holt, 2010), 11. On the criticism of the feminist movement and the assault on its activists, past and present, see Susan Faludi, "American Electra: Feminism's Ritual Matricide," *Harper's Magazine*, October 2010, 29–42; on Hillary Rodham Clinton's campaign for the presidency, the significance of gender, and the renewal of feminism among a younger generation of women involved in

the media, see Rebecca Traister, *Big Girls Don't Cry: The Election That Changed Everything for American Women* (New York: Free Press, 2010).

4. Other institutions that are now known as "colleges" and were established for women, such as Mount Holyoke College, founded in 1837, continued to call themselves "seminaries" until later in the century.

5. Fuller, *Woman*, 6.

6. Emily Noyes Vanderpoel, comp., *Chronicles of a Pioneer School from 1792–1833, Being the History of Miss Sarah Pierce and Her Litchfield School*, ed. Elizabeth C. Barney Buel (Cambridge, Mass., 1903), 219; letter transcripts of Lucinda Gifford, Mount Holyoke College Archives and Special Collections, South Hadley, Massachusetts, 10; Mary Ware Allen, *Greene Street Journal*, no. 1, p. 77, quoted in Judith Strong Albert, "Margaret Fuller and Mary Ware Allen: 'In Youth an Insatiate Student'—A Certain Kind of Friendship," *Thoreau Journal Quarterly* 22 (July 1980): 13; [Unknown student] to "My dearest Sister," November 26, 1859, in *Miss Porter's School: A History in Documents, 1847–1948*, ed. Louise L. Stevenson, 2 vols. (New York, Garland, 1987), 1:169.

7. Jessica Bennett, Jesse Ellison, and Sarah Bell, "Are We There Yet?," *Newsweek*, March 10, 2010, accessed April 3, 2012, www.newsweek.com; Tamar Lewin, "Study Finds a 1–2 Percent Increase in Faculty Pay, the Smallest in Fifty Years," *New York Times*, April 12, 2010, A12; Nancy Gibbs, "What Women Want Now," *Time*, October 14, 2009, accessed April 9, 2012, www.time.com.

8. Margaret Fuller to Caroline Sturgis, January 3, 1838, in *The Letters of Margaret Fuller*, ed. Robert N. Hudspeth, 6 vols. (Ithaca, N.Y.: Cornell University Press, 1983–94), 1:322; Mary Ware Allen, *Greene Street Journal*, no. 1, p. 4, quoted in Albert, "Margaret Fuller," 17; Fuller to Ralph Waldo Emerson, July 3, 1837, in Hudspeth, *Letters of Margaret Fuller*, 1:288.

9. Mary Ware Allen, January 18, 1838, quoted in Harriet Hall Johnson, "Margaret Fuller as Known by Her Scholars," in *Critical Essays on Margaret Fuller*, ed. Joel Myerson (Boston: Hall, 1980), 136; Mary Ware Allen, *Greene Street Journal*, no. 1, p. 77, quoted in Albert, "Margaret Fuller," 13; Journal of Evelina Metcalf, quoted in Laraine R. Ferguson, "Margaret Fuller in the Classroom: The Providence Period," in *Studies in the American Renaissance*, ed. Joel Myerson (Charlottesville: University Press of Virginia, 1987), 137; Louise Hunt to Lucy Clark Allen, n.d., Allen Johnson Family Papers, American Antiquarian Society, Worcester, Massachusetts; Anna Gale to Frederic Gale, December 30, 1837, Gale Family Papers, American Antiquarian Society.

10. Margaret Fuller to Ralph Waldo Emerson, March 1, 1838, reprinted in Kelley, *Portable Margaret Fuller*, 492; Nancy Craig Simmons, "Margaret Fuller's Conversations, the 1839–1840 Series," in Myerson, *American Renaissance*, 214–15.

11. Simmons, "Margaret Fuller's Conversations, 214–15; Ralph Waldo Emerson, William Henry Channing, and James Freeman Clarke, eds., *Memoirs of Margaret Fuller Ossoli*, 2 vols. (Boston: 1869), 338; Elizabeth Cady Stanton, *Eighty Years and More (1815–1897): Reminiscences of Elizabeth Cady Stanton* (New York:

Fisher Unwin, 1898), 152; "Address by ECS on Woman's Rights," in *The Selected Papers of Elizabeth Cady Stanton and Susan B. Anthony*, ed. Ann D. Gordon, 2 vols. (New Brunswick, N.J.: Rutgers University Press, 1997), 115–16.

12. Fuller to William Henry Channing, March 22, 1840, reprinted in Kelley, *Portable Margaret Fuller*, 503–4.
13. "The Count," *Amy King's Alias*, accessed April 9, 2012, www.amyking.wordpress.com. See also www.nobelprize.org and www.pulitzer.org.
14. Fuller did remark on the much starker asymmetry based on race, noting the abuse of African Americans in what she described as the "monstrous display of slave-dealing and slave-keeping." Fuller, *Woman*, 232, 236.
15. Ibid., 280.
16. Collins, *When Everything Changed*, 8; Douglas, *Enlightened Sexism*, 5, 6; Nancy Gibbs, "What Women Want Now: A *Time* Special Report," *Time*, October 14, 2009, 25–33; Joanne Lipman, "The Mismeasure of Woman," *New York Times*, October 24, 2009, accessed April 3, 2012, www.nytimes.com.
17. Fuller, *Woman*, 244.
18. Ibid., 242.
19. Ibid., 290–91.
20. Ibid., 1, 255. On "proportional androgyny," see Charles Capper, *The Public Years*, vol. 2 of *Margaret Fuller: An American Romantic Life* (New York: Oxford University Press, 2007), 118–19, 179.
21. Margaret Fuller, "Our City Charities: Visit to Bellevue Alms House, to the Farm School, the Asylum for the Insane, and Penitentiary on Blackwell's Island," reprinted in Kelley, *Portable Margaret Fuller*, 370–76.
22. Joel Myerson, *Transcendentalism: A Reader* (New York: Oxford University Press, 2000), 475; Jeffrey Steele, ed., *The Essential Margaret Fuller* (New Brunswick, N.J.: Rutgers University Press, 1992), 393.
23. Steele, *Essential Margaret Fuller*, 401.
24. Margaret Fuller, "Farewell," *New-York Daily Tribune*, August 1, 1846.

CONTRIBUTORS

CHARLENE AVALLONE is an independent scholar based in Kailua, Hawai'i, and is a former faculty member of the University of Notre Dame, where she taught gender studies, and the University of Hawai'i at Manoa. She serves on the editorial board of *Leviathan: A Journal of Melville Studies*. She is the author of numerous essays on nineteenth-century literary figures, including Margaret Fuller, Herman Melville, George Sand, and Catharine Maria Sedgwick.

BRIGITTE BAILEY is Associate Professor of English at the University of New Hampshire and a past president of the Margaret Fuller Society. She has published numerous essays on Catharine Maria Sedgwick, Nathaniel Hawthorne, Margaret Fuller, Harriet Beecher Stowe, and other nineteenth-century literary figures. Her research focuses on travel and urban writing.

DORRI BEAM is Associate Professor of English at Syracuse University. She is the author of *Style, Gender, and Fantasy in Nineteenth-Century American Women's Writing* (Cambridge University Press, 2010) and has recently contributed essays to *ESQ: A Journal of the American Renaissance* and to *American Literature's Aesthetic Dimensions*, edited by Christopher Looby and Cindy Weinstein.

PHYLLIS COLE is Professor of English, Women's Studies, and American Studies at Penn State, Brandywine. She is a past president of the Ralph Waldo Emerson Society and current first vice president of the Margaret Fuller Society. She is the author of *Mary Moody Emerson and the Origins of Transcendentalism: A Family History* (Oxford University Press, 1998; paperback reprint 2002), as well as numerous essays and book chapters. She is coeditor with Jana Argersinger of *Exaltadas: A Female Genealogy of Transcendentalism*, a special issue of *ESQ: A Journal of the American Renaissance* (2011).

ROBERT N. HUDSPETH is Research Professor of English at Claremont Graduate University. He is the editor of the six-volume *Letters of Margaret Fuller*, as well as *"My Heart Is a Large Kingdom": Selected Letters of Margaret Fuller* (Cornell University Press, 2001). He is currently editing *The Correspondence of Henry D. Thoreau*, three volumes of *The Writings of Henry D. Thoreau*, for Princeton University Press.

CONTRIBUTORS

MARY KELLEY is the Ruth Bordin Collegiate Professor of History at the University of Michigan. She is the author or editor of numerous publications, including *Private Woman, Public Stage: Literary Domesticity in Nineteenth-Century America* (Oxford University Press, 1984) and *The Portable Margaret Fuller* (Viking/Penguin, 1994). She coedited *An Extensive Republic: Print, Culture, and Society in the New Nation*, volume 2 of *History of the Book in America* (University of North Carolina Press, 2010). She has served as the president of both the American Studies Association and the Society for Historians of the Early American Republic and is currently a member of the executive board of the Organization of American Historians.

MEGAN MARSHALL is Assistant Professor of Writing, Literature, and Publishing at Emerson College. Her biography *The Peabody Sisters: Three Women Who Ignited American Romanticism* (Houghton Mifflin Harcourt, 2005) won the Francis Parkman Prize of the Society of American Historians and was a finalist for the Pulitzer Prize in biography and memoir. She is also the author of *Margaret Fuller: A New American Life* (Houghton Mifflin Harcourt, 2013).

JOHN MATTESON is Distinguished Professor of English at John Jay College of Criminal Justice, CUNY, where he teaches literature and legal writing. He received the 2008 Pulitzer Prize in biography for his book *Eden's Outcasts: The Story of Louisa May Alcott and Her Father* (Norton, 2007). His most recent book is *The Lives of Margaret Fuller: A Biography* (Norton, 2012).

DAVID M. ROBINSON is Oregon Professor of English and Distinguished Professor of American Literature and Culture at Oregon State University. He is the author or editor of four books on Ralph Waldo Emerson, in addition to his recent book on Henry David Thoreau, *Natural Life: Thoreau's Worldly Transcendentalism* (Cornell University Press, 2004).

JEFFREY STEELE is Professor of English at the University of Wisconsin, Madison. He is the author of numerous essays and three books, including *Transfiguring America: Myth, Ideology, and Mourning in Margaret Fuller's Writing* (University of Missouri Press, 2001) and *The Essential Margaret Fuller* (Rutgers University Press, 1992), which was named a *Choice* "Outstanding Academic Book." Steele is a past president of the Margaret Fuller Society.

ADAM-MAX TUCHINSKY is Associate Professor of History at the University of Southern Maine. He is the author of *Horace Greeley's New-York Tribune: Civil War–Era Socialism and the Crisis of Free Labor* (Cornell University Press, 2009).

KATHERYN P. VIENS is Research Coordinator at the Massachusetts Historical Society. As Assistant Editor of Publications, she coedited *Entrepreneurs: The Boston Business*

Community, 1700–1850 (Massachusetts Historical Society, 1997). She is a former editorial assistant of the *New England Quarterly* and has nearly two decades of independent historical editing experience, including publications of the Colonial Society of Massachusetts.

ALBERT J. VON FRANK is emeritus Professor of English and American Studies at Washington State University. He is the author of *The Sacred Game: Provincialism and Frontier Consciousness in American Literature, 1630–1860* (Cambridge Studies in American Literature and Culture, 1985) and *The Trials of Anthony Burns: Freedom and Slavery in Emerson's Boston* (Harvard University Press, 1998). More recently he has edited (with Tom Wortham) volume 9 of the *Collected Works of Ralph Waldo Emerson: Poems: A Variorum Edition* (Harvard University Press, 2011).

CONRAD EDICK WRIGHT is Director of Research and Ford Editor of Publications at the Massachusetts Historical Society. He is the author of two books and the editor or coeditor of eight essay collections, including *American Unitarianism, 1805–1865* (Massachusetts Historical Society and Northeastern University Press, 1989) and *Transient and Permanent: The Transcendentalist Movement and Its Contexts* (Massachusetts Historical Society, 1999).

INDEX

abolitionism. *See* antislavery movement
Alcott, Bronson, 35, 77, 103, 106, 127, 135, 180, 182, 184, 203, 233
Alcott, Louisa May, 236
Allen, Lucy Clark, 234
Allen, Margaret, 101
Allen, Mary Ware, 234
Allston, Washington, 184
American Revolution, Fuller's appeal to ideals of, 14, 19, 23, 173–78, 237
American Scholar (Emerson, 1837), 104, 105, 252n38
American Women Writers Series, 236
André (Sand, 1833), 214
anticlericalism of Fuller, 123–27
antislavery movement, 5–6, 128–47; Bancroft's "Slavery in Rome" (1834), Fuller's reply to, 130–32; Channing, William Ellery, and, 134–35, 140, 141, 274n14, 274n16; Child and, 130, 132–33, 135, 136, 137, 140, 204, 273n12; Christian martyrdom narrative of, 140–42; Compromise of 1850, 128; French abolition of slavery in its colonies (1848), American reaction to, 118; Fugitive Slave Law of 1850, 110, 128, 250n10, 271n1; Fuller's earliest attitudes about, 128–29; Fuller's initial lack of involvement with, 128–37; Grimké sisters and, 25, 130, 136, 137–39, 141, 146; Italian Risorgimento (1848), Fuller's radicalization by, 145–46; Martineau and, 133–36, 141, 145–47, 273n12–14; Mexican-American War (1846) and, 110, 128, 171, 173, 177, 188; modern legacy of Fuller and, 240–41, 242; radicalization of Transcendentalists by, 110; rhetoric of, Fuller's distaste for, 134–36, 140–43, 145, 146; social justice writings of Fuller and, 174; Tallmadge amendment (1819), 129; violence directed at, 133–34, 135, 140–41; *Woman in the Nineteenth Century* and, 6, 143–45; women's rights and, 129–30, 132, 136–39, 143–45, 240–41, 272n4
Appeal in Favor of That Class of Americans Called Africans (Child, 1833), 130, 132, 133, 135
Argersinger, Jana, 3
"The Artists" (Schiller, 1789), 252n37
Associationism: rise and fall of, 110–11; self-culture and, Fuller's commitment to, 5, 79, 89, 90, 93–97, 98, 107–8; socialism and, 107–8, 110–11, 116, 217
"Asylum for Discharged Female Convicts" (Fuller, 1845), 167–68, 171–72, 190
Athenaeum, 207
"Autobiographical Romance" (Fuller, 1840), 5, 79, 82, 83–89, 131
Autobiography (Martineau, 1877), 147
Avallone, Charlene, 6, 7, 9, 206, 299

Bailey, Brigitte, 1, 299
Bailey, Philip, *Festus* (1839), 219, 286n45
Bakunin, Michael, 120
Bancroft, George, 130–32, 134, 201
Barbes, Armand, 112
Barker, Anna, later Ward, 35, 37, 80, 203, 257n8

303

Bartlett, Elizabeth Ann, 12
Bartol, Cyrus, 275–76n31
Beam, Dorri R., 4–5, 9, 10, 52, 239, 299
Bean, Judith Matson, 245n2
Beecher, Catherine, 129, 232
Beecher, Jonathan, 98
Beecher, Lyman, 134
Beethoven, Ludwig van, Fifth Symphony, 154
Belasco, Susan (Susan Belasco Smith), 115, 218
Belgioso, Cristina Trivulzio di, 115, 116, 200
Béranger, Pierre-Jean de, 195, 221, 225
Bertha and Lily (Oakes Smith, 1852), 65
Blackstone, Sir William, 24, 27
Blackwell's Island, 161, 168, 169
Blake, Harrison Gray Otis, 287n77
Blanc, Louis, 112, 121, 270n70
Blanqui, Louis Auguste, 112, 121
Bloom, Harold, 104
body, separation of gender from, 56, 61–64
Boeckh, Philipp August, 131
Börnstein, Henry, 119–21
Boston Academy of Music, 153, 154, 155
Boston Daily Advertiser, 130, 233
Boston Female Anti-Slavery Society (BFASS), 134, 136, 145, 274n14
Boston, Fuller in, 181–82, 183–86
Bowen, Francis, 118, 215, 216
Brisbane, Albert, 110, 111, 118, 122, 217
Brontë, Charlotte, 29
Brook Farm, 5, 90, 94–96, 103, 105–8, 180, 217
Brown, John, 127, 141
Browning, Elizabeth Barrett, 20, 29, 127, 166–67, 201, 218, 222, 227
Browning, Robert, 201
Brownson, Orestes, 124, 209, 210–11, 214–15, 287n77
Broyles, Michael, 149
Bruce, Georgiana, 43–47, 49, 51, 187
Bryant, William Cullen, 177, 282n73
Buchanan, James, 118

Bull, Ole, 184, 191, 204
Burke, Edmund, 18
Burns, Anthony, 127
Butler, Judith, 74, 75, 256n6

Cabet, Etienne, 121
Cady, Daniel, 25
Caine, Barbara, 251n21
Capper, Charles, 2, 11, 79, 98, 106, 116, 123, 132, 134, 141, 198, 237, 241, 270n70
Captain P.'s wife (from *Summer on the Lakes*), 39–40
Caradori-Allan, Maria, Fuller's essay to Coliseum Club on, 152–54, 156, 182–83
Carlyle, Jane, 223
Carlyle, Thomas, and Carlylism, 125, 133, 135, 151, 194, 223–24
Carrel, Armand, 209
Cass, Lewis, Jr., 201
Catholicism, Fuller on, 123–27, 196–97, 198, 202
Channing, William Ellery: antislavery movement and, 134–35, 140–41, 211, 274n14, 274n16; Grimké sisters and, 23; rural simplicities, devotion to, 203; Sand, George, transatlantic reception of, 208; on self-culture, 78, 79, 82, 87; Transcendental model of feminism and, 52, 56
Channing, William Henry: Associationism and self-culture, 5, 90, 93–97, 98; Brook Farm, Fuller's reaction to, 106, 107; Christian-socialist language of, 276n31; feminine virtue, problem of, 38; music criticism of Fuller and, 154, 157, 159; in New York, 186, 189, 204, 287n77; Sand, George, transatlantic reception of, 209, 210, 212–14, 217, 220; social justice writings of Fuller and, 96, 167, 177, 186, 195; socialism and, 96, 115, 202, 217
Chapman, Maria Weston, 136, 146
Chapone, Hester, 232

Charles Albert (king of Piedmont-Sardinia), 114, 123, 126
Charles Elwood (Brownson, 1840), 215
chastity, female. *See* feminine virtue and female sexuality
Cheney, Ednah Dow, 271n1
Chesebro,' Caroline, 55, 65
Chevigny, Bell Gale, 1, 97, 100, 122, 185, 188, 199, 227, 236, 247n12, 270n70
Child, David Lee, 133
Child, Lydia Maria (née Francis): antislavery movement and, 130, 132–33, 135, 136, 137, 140, 204, 273n12; on Sand, 222; scholarship on, 3; social justice and, 161–64, 175; Transcendentalist model of feminism and, 64, 65; on *Woman in the Nineteenth Century*, 229, 230; as woman of letters, 236. *See also specific works*
Chopin, Frederick, 148
Christian diction in Fuller's writing, 162, 167, 170–71, 175, 176, 242, 275–76n31, 284–85n28
Christian Examiner, 209, 211, 219–20
Christian martyrdom narrative of antislavery movement, 140–42
"The Clairvoyant" (Chesebro,' 1851), 65
Clarke, James Freeman: antislavery movement and, 146; feminine virtue, problem of, 40; Fuller's reading program with, 233; Mesmerism and, 257n8; music criticism of Fuller and, 152, 154, 155; Sand, George, transatlantic reception of, 209, 210, 212; self-culture and, 79, 90, 93; socialism and, 103; urban culture and, 186, 189
Clarke, Sarah, 257n8
classical mythology, Fuller's employment of: antislavery movement and, 131–32, 144–45, 275–76n31; Christian diction, move to, 162, 167, 170–71, 175, 176, 242, 275–76n31, 284–85n28; feminism and women's rights, in writings about, 12, 25, 238, 258n24; Sand, George, transatlantic reception of,

226; in social justice writings, 162, 167, 176–77, 178; teacher, Fuller as, 234
Clemmer, Mary, 5, 55, 56, 68–73, 74, 75
Cole, Phyllis, 1, 3, 4, 5, 9, 11, 240, 245n2, 299
Coliseum Club, Fuller's music criticism essay delivered to, 152, 153, 154, 156, 182–83
The College, the Market, and the Court (Dall, 1867), 21
Collins, Gail, 230, 238, 239
Le compagnon du tour de France (Sand, 1840), 217
La comtesse de Rudolstadt (Sand, 1843), 217, 219
Congregational Church Pastoral Letter (1837) condemning public speech by women, 22–23, 27, 137–38
Conrad, Susan Phinney, 249n3
Considerant, Victor, 98, 114, 121
Constant, Benjamin, 211
Consuelo (Sand, 1842), 217–23, 226
Conversations, of Bronson Alcott, 203–4
Conversations, of Fuller (Boston, 1839–1844), 7, 29, 93, 133, 146, 159, 185, 222, 234–35, 236
Cousin, Victor, and Cousinism, 209, 211, 213, 214
coverture, common law of, 13, 24, 26
Cranch, Christopher Pearse, 262n25
Crandall, Prudence, 140
Creation (Haydn), 157
creative expression and self-culture, 82–88
"Credo" (Fuller, 1842), 36
Croker, John Wilson, 207, 208, 214, 215
Cummins, Maria, 236
Curtis, George, 193
Czerny, Carl, 150

Dall, Caroline Healey, 12, 21–22, 30, 222, 252–53n46
Dana, Charles, 111
Davis, Cynthia J., 61

Davis, George, 186
Davis, Paulina Wright, 30
De Wette, Wilhelm, 212
Dial: association and community, evidence of Fuller's interest in, 89–90; as countercultural publication, 103; editor, Fuller as, 2, 133, 159, 183–85, 235–36; music criticism of Fuller in, 6, 148, 149, 152, 153–55, 157, 160; mystical pieces written by Fuller for, 89, 157–58, 177. *See also specific articles*
Dickens, Charles, 164, 169
"Divinity School Address" (Emerson, 1838), 105, 141
Domenichino, 196
Dorr Rebellion, Rhode Island, 186–87, 199, 201
Dorr, Thomas Wilson, 186–87
Douglas, Ann, 258n24
Douglas, Susan, 230
Douglass, Frederick, 3, 124, 276n31
Durning, Russell, 206
Dwight, John Sullivan, 148, 149, 155–56, 204, 209, 217, 220
Dwight's Journal of Music, 149

Eckel, Leslie, 193
Eckermann's Conversations with Goethe, Fuller's translation of (1839), 82–83, 89
Economy of Athens (Boeckh, 1831), 131
Edgeworth, Maria, 208, 232
education: of Fuller, 25, 85–88, 231, 233; Fuller as teacher, 152, 182–84, 232, 233–34; Greene Street School, Providence, 152–53, 182–83, 232–33, 234; Litchfield Academy, Litchfield, Connecticut, 232; Miss Porter's School, Farmington, Connecticut, 232; Miss Prescott's School, Groton, 150; Mount Holyoke College, 232, 297n4; musical education of nineteenth-century girls, 149–52; Oberlin College, 134, 231; popular education, Fuller's journalism as form of, 105, 184, 203; Temple School, Boston, 135–36, 182, 233; of women, modern legacy of Fuller regarding, 231–33
electricity, as metaphor, 17, 42, 59–62, 64, 69, 92
Eliot, George, 21, 22, 30
Elizabeth, shipwreck of (1850), 146, 148, 243
Ellison, Julie, 216
Elssler, Fanny, 184
embodied soul, concept of, 64–68, 71–73
Emerson, Dorothy, 3
Emerson, Lidian, 15
Emerson, Ralph Waldo: antislavery movement and, 128, 140, 141, 146, 250n10; Brook Farm, response to, 105–6, 107–8; clairvoyant evenings, avoidance of, 257n8; classical mythology, Transcendentalist use of, 275–76n31; on death of Fuller, 287n78; dialogic engagement of Fuller with writings of, 3, 19; "Divinity School Address" (1838), 105, 141; education, Fuller's letters to Emerson on, 234; on feminine virtue, 34–35; meeting of Fuller with, 15, 80; modernity, heroic individualism as counter to effects of, 125; music criticism of Fuller and, 153, 155, 191; "new world," vision of, 99; Oversoul, concept of, 53, 57, 63–64; pantheistic and mystical elements of Transcendentalism of, 52–53; political awareness of, 96; Sand, George, transatlantic reception of, 210, 212, 222, 226; on self-culture and self-reliance, 78; social justice issues, Fuller's awareness of, 186; socialism of Fuller and, 5, 101, 103–6, 108–9, 127; urban culture and, 180, 181, 201–2, 203; *Woman in the Nineteenth Century,* not mentioned in, 16–17, 19–20. *See also specific works*
"Emerson's Essays" (Fuller, 1844), 166
Engels, Friedrich, 120

England. *See* Great Britain
Enlightened Sexism (Douglas, 2010), 230, 239
"Entertainments of the Past Winter" (Fuller, 1842), 155–56, 160, 180, 184
Etherology; or, The Philosophy of Mesmerism and Phrenology (Grimes, 1845), 56–57
Europe, Fuller in, 97–99, 111, 114–15, 148, 158, 193–202. *See also* France; Great Britain; Italian Risorgimento; revolutions of 1848; socialism
European Revolutions and the American Literary Renaissance (Reynolds, 1988), 98
Eurydice, 12, 14, 23
Everett, Edward, 134
Exaltadas, 24, 30, 144

Facts in Mesmerism (Townshend, 1841), 57–58
"Farewell" (Fuller, 1846), 193, 242
Farnham, Eliza, 43–44, 45, 46
Farrar, Eliza, 80–81, 133, 260–61n9
Farrar, John, 133, 261n9
Félix, Elizabeth (Rachel), 194–95
feminine virtue and female sexuality, 4, 32–51; afterlife, love in, 36; Emerson's views on, 34–35; Fourierism and, 95; free love, 68–71, 74; frustrations of Fuller's own love life, 35; Fuller's sexual relationship, birth of child, and marriage in Italy, 20–21, 35, 50–51, 100, 116, 158, 196, 198–201, 242–43; Groton, Fuller at bedside of girl dying from botched abortion in, 32–33, 37, 39, 44, 51; homosexual love, Fuller on, 35–36; as philosophical problem, 32–35; Sand, George, transatlantic reception of, 222, 225–27; Sing Sing, Fuller's interactions with prostitutes incarcerated in, 4, 34, 43–47, 49, 51, 187, 202; social definition of women hostile to their spiritual growth, 34–35, 42–43; spiritual progression, Fuller's natural philosophy regarding, 36–37; in *Summer on the Lakes*, 37–42, 50; Transcendentalist model of feminism, erotic and sexual registers of, 54, 65–66, 68–73; Wollstonecraft, personal life and reputation of, 15–16, 21–22; in *Woman in the Nineteenth Century*, 37, 43, 46, 47–50
feminism and women's rights, 4, 11–31; antislavery movement and, 129–30, 132, 136–39, 143–45, 240–41, 272n4; Enlightenment rights language and rhetoric of religious perfectionism combined in, 4, 12; Grimké sisters and Fuller (*See* Grimké sisters); modern legacy of Margaret Fuller regarding, 7–8, 237–43; music criticism, Fuller's feminism informed by, 159–60; precursors, feminist recognition of, 11–12, 21–22; radicalism of Fuller and, 123–24; rediscovery of Fuller by Second Wave Feminism, 1, 236–37, 246n5; rhetoric of expectancy as Fuller's gift to, 28–29; Romantic approach of Fuller to, 12, 14, 17, 19, 20, 22, 24, 26, 27, 29, 249n3; Sand, George, transatlantic reception of, 215, 227–28; self-culture and self-reliance, ideology of, 5, 17–18, 19, 27–31; Seneca Falls convention (1848), 11, 30, 237–38; transatlantic exchanges regarding, 4, 15, 30; Wollstonecraft and Fuller (*See* Wollstonecraft, Mary); *Woman in the Nineteenth Century*, influence of, 11–15, 21–22, 30–31. *See also* Transcendentalist model of feminism
Festus (Bailey, 1839), 219, 286n45
Fetis, James, 157
Fifth Symphony (Beethoven), Fuller on, 154
Fink, Steven, 192
"1st January, 1846" (Fuller, 1846), 174
"First of August, 1845" (Fuller, 1845), 174, 176
Fish, Cheryl J., 38, 40

Fleischmann, Fritz, 247n12
Florence, Fuller in, 196, 200–201
Foreign Quarterly Review, 208, 209, 213, 215, 220, 221, 223
Foster, George, 122
Fourier, Charles, and Fourierism: Fuller's knowledge of, 12; Sand, George, transatlantic reception of, 211, 217; self-culture and, 5, 90, 94–95; socialism and, 110–11, 114–15, 116, 119, 217
"Fourth of July" (Fuller, 1845), 174
Fox, William Johnson, 194
France: abolition of slavery in its colonies (1848), American reaction to, 118; Fuller in, 111, 114–15, 194–95; revolution of 1830 in, 207; revolution of 1848 in, 111–12, 116, 117–22, 195; Sand, George, French reception of, 207–9; Sand, George, Fuller's meeting in France with, 114, 195, 206, 225–28. *See also* French Revolution
François, Ferdinand, 226
free love, 68–71, 74
French Revolution (1789): Fuller's appeal to ideals of, 14, 19, 23, 227; Sand and, 227; Wollstonecraft and, 18–19, 21, 22
"Friendship" (Emerson, 1841), 89
friendship, Transcendentalist discourses on, 89, 185
Frothingham, Octavius Brooks, 210
Fruitlands, 90, 103, 106, 180
Fugitive Slave Law of 1850, 110, 128, 250n10, 271n1
Fuller, Eugene (brother), 274n16
Fuller, Hiram, 182, 184
Fuller, Julia (sister), death of, 84, 86
Fuller, Lloyd (brother), 106
Fuller, Margaret: bicentennial celebrations, 3, 8; death of, 21, 30, 100, 146, 148, 243, 287n78; in Europe, 97–99, 111, 114–15, 148, 158, 193–202 (*see also* France; Great Britain; Italian Risorgimento; revolutions of 1848; socialism); father, relationship with, 25–26, 80, 82–88; heroism for, 6, 133, 139–41, 142–43; in historical and literary context, 1–2, 4; language acts as medium of exchange for, 4, 9–10; Leger, medical treatment by, 56, 257n8; mother, relationship with, 80, 84, 86, 88, 106; as music critic, 6, 148–60 (*see also* music criticism); mysticism, attraction to, 52–56, 73–76, 98–99, 157–58; nightmares of, 85–86; personal and professional connections, importance of studying, 8–10, 79–80, 89; reform movements, involvement in, 5–6 (*see also* antislavery movement; self-culture and self-reliance; social justice; socialism); relationship, birth of child, and marriage in Italy, 20–21, 35, 50–51, 100, 116, 158, 196, 198–201, 242–43; republication of works of, 2, 8; Sand and, 7, 206–28 (*see also* Sand, George, transatlantic reception of); scholarship on, 1–3, 8–10, 97–98, 236–37; on urban culture, 7, 179–205 (*see also* urban culture); on women and gender ideology, 4–5 (*see also* feminine virtue and female sexuality; feminism and women's rights; Transcendentalist model of feminism). *See also specfic works*
Fuller, Richard (brother), 179, 185, 197, 202
Fuller, Timothy (father): antislavery movement and, 5, 129, 130–32, 271–72n2; in "Autobiographical Romance," 82–88; death of, 25–26, 32, 83, 86, 132, 133, 134, 150, 182, 233; education of Margaret Fuller by, 25, 85–88, 231; musical training of Margaret Fuller and, 149; relationship with Margaret Fuller, 25–26, 80, 82–88; on Wollstonecraft, 15, 17

Gale, Anna and Frederic, 234
Garibaldi, Giuseppe, 199

INDEX

Garner, Margaret, 143
Garrison, William Lloyd, 130, 131, 133–41, 240, 274n14, 276n31
Gatta, John Paul, 12, 17
gender. *See* women and gender ideology
Germany, revolution of 1848 in, 118
Gioberti, Vicenzo, 125
gnosticism and Transcendentalism, 104, 141
Godkin, Edwin Lawrence, 108
Godwin, William, 16, 20, 21, 251n21
Goethe, Johann Wolfgang von: dialogic engagement of Fuller with writings of, 3, 19, 20, 206, 212, 233; Fuller's translations of, 82–83, 233; Longfellow compared, 209; Martineau's interest in, 133, 273n13; Rome, house in, 197; self-culture, Fuller's concept of, 5, 79, 82–83
Gougeon, Len, 274n21
Great Britain: conservative reportage from, 118, 120; Corn Law controversy in, 108, 193; Emerson in, 201–2; Fuller in, 111, 114, 193–94; Sand, George, reception of, 207–9
"The Great Lawsuit" (Fuller, 1843): as confrontation with power, 13; feminine virtue, problem of, 38, 42–43, 47, 50; legal language, use of, 4; on Sand, 207, 214, 215–16; self-culture in, 89–90, 95; *Woman in the Nineteenth Century* as expansion of, 4, 38, 47, 90, 137, 162, 171, 216, 236
Greeley, Horace, 47, 114, 118–19, 186, 192, 193, 217, 236, 241, 242
Greene Street School, Providence, 152–53, 182–83, 232–33, 234
Greenwood, Amelia, 182
Gregory XVI (pope), 113
Grimes, Stanley, 56–57
Grimké, John Faucheraud, 25
Grimké sisters (Sarah and Angelina), 4, 22–30; antislavery movement and, 25, 130, 136, 137–39, 141, 146; Congregational Church Pastoral Letter (1837) condemning public speech by women and, 22–23, 27, 137–38; Fuller's discussion of, 15, 23–24, 139, 240; Fuller's influence on, 29–30; influence on Fuller's writings, 23, 24–30; legal analysis, Sarah's interest in, 24–27, 29; *Letters on the Equality of the Sexes* (Sarah Grimké, 1838), 12, 23, 24, 27, 28, 29, 138, 139; as precursors of feminist movement, 11–15, 30; Quaker grounding and religious sensibilities of, 22, 27–28; retirement from public life, 29, 30; Wollstonecraft compared, 27
Guarneri, Carl, 116
Guida, Francesco, 286n65
Gura, Philip, 190, 285n35
Gustafson, Sandra, 258n24
Guyon, Madame, 71, 177

Haddock, Joseph, 58–59, 259n31
Hallam, Martha, 46–47, 48
Harbinger (journal), 116, 118, 122, 149, 217, 220, 223, 227
Hatch, Cora, 55, 67, 75
Hawthorne, Nathaniel, 86
Hawthorne, Sophia, 56, 100, 257n9
Hayes, Woody, 104, 109
Hays, Matilda M., 225
"Heaven on Earth" (William Henry Channing, 1841), 96, 217
Hedge, Frederic Henry, 159, 182
Hegel, Georg Wilhelm Friedrich, 208
Heine, Heinrich, 120
Helps, Sir Arthur, 151
Hermotimus, 64
heroism, Fuller's understanding of, 6, 133, 139–41, 142–43
Higginson, Thomas Wentworth, 80, 127, 274n16, 287n77
Hoar, Elizabeth, 222, 225
Hobomok (Child, 1824), 133
Hoffman, Tess, 156, 184
homosexual love, Fuller on, 35–36

Hone, Philip, 165, 172
Hooker, Isabella Beecher, 276n31
Howe, Daniel Walker, 266n6
Howitt, Mary, 225
Hudspeth, Robert N., 6, 7, 9, 179, 299
Hungary, 1848 revolution in, 117, 118
Hunt, Harriot, 29
Hunt, Louise, 234
Hyperion (Longfellow, 1839), 209

Imlay, Gilbert, 15, 16, 21
immigration and immigrants, 91, 161, 164, 172–73
Indiana (Sand, 1832), 207, 216
individualism. *See* self-culture and self-reliance
"The Irish Character" (Fuller, 1845), 172–73
Irish immigrants, 172–73
Irish independence movement, 144
Isenberg, Nancy, 249n3
Italian Risorgimento (1848): antislavery movement, Fuller's radicalization and, 145–46; Catholicism, Fuller on, 123–27, 196, 197, 198, 202; commitment of Fuller to socialism and, 21, 79, 98; dedication of Fuller to, 21, 98; French revolution of 1848 compared, 122; liberal socialism of Fuller and, 120–23, 127, 203; Mazzini and, 7, 115, 123, 125, 194, 197, 202, 204; modern legacy of Fuller and, 242–43; nationalism of Fuller and, 123–24, 125; *New-York Tribune*, Fuller's coverage for, 5, 122–23, 145, 197–98, 201, 202, 242; radicalism of Fuller and, 123–27; relationship, birth of child, and marriage of Fuller in Italy, 20–21, 35, 50–51, 100, 116, 158, 196, 198–201, 242–43; rise and fall of, 112–14; socially revolutionary elements in, 122–23; urban culture and Fuller's experience of Italy, 195–201, 202; war, Fuller's experience of, 199–200, 202

Jackson, Andrew, 129
Jacques (Sand, 1833), 214
James, Henry, 67
Jameson, Anna, 23, 29
Jesuits, 126, 127
la jeune France, 7, 207–9, 211, 214, 216, 222, 223, 288n6
Jewett, Helen, 164
Jouffroy, Théodore, 209, 211, 212, 213, 214
Joyaux, Georges J., 293n79

Karcher, Carolyn, 133
Kelley, Abby, 23, 24, 26, 136, 139, 240, 275n26
Kelley, Mary, 1, 7–8, 9, 10, 16, 229, 245n2, 300
Kent, James, 13
Kilshaw, Ellen, 79, 89, 149, 150–51, 152
Knapp, Isaac, 141
Koropeckyj, Roman, 98
Kossuth, Lajos, 117

Lamartine, Alphonse Marie-Louis de, 121
Lamennais, Félicité Robert de, 114, 195, 210–13, 217, 225, 227, 291n46
Lane, Charles, 103, 106
Lee, Mother Anne, 24, 177
Leger Theodore, 56, 257n8
"Leila" (Fuller, 1841), 89, 157–58, 177
Leone Leoni (Sand, 1833), 208
Lerminier, Eugène, 213
Lerner, Gerda, 25
Leroux, Pierre, 114, 210, 217, 224, 225
Letters from New York (Child, 1843), 175
letters of Margaret Fuller, modern publication of, 2
Letters on Mesmerism (Martineau, 1845), 57, 66
Letters on the Equality of the Sexes (Sarah Grimké, 1838), 12, 23, 24, 27, 28, 29, 138, 139
Letters to a Young Lady, on the Art of Playing the Pianoforte (Czerny, 1840), 150

Lettres d'un voyageur (Sand, 1834–1836), 214, 220, 291n46
Leverenz, David, 104
Lewes, George Henry, 208, 215, 221, 223
liberal socialism of Fuller, 101–2
Liberty Party, 137
Linnaeus, Carl, and daughter, 63
Lipman, Joanne, 239
Liverpool, Fuller in, 114, 193
Lives of the Great Composers (Fuller, 1841), 148, 152, 154–55, 156, 158, 236
Longfellow, Henry Wadsworth, 209
Loring, Anna, 222
Loring, Ellis Gray, 134, 273–74n14
Louis-Philippe (king of France), 112, 118, 121, 195
Lovejoy, Elijah, 140
Lowell, James Russell, 166, 193
Lucrezia Floriani (Sand, 1846), 226
Lyon, Mary, 232

"The Magnolia of Lake Pontchartrain" (Fuller, 1841), 89, 157
"The Man of the Crowd" (Poe, 1840), 164
"Man the Reformer" (Emerson, 1841), 104
Marcus Brutus, Fuller's defense of, 131–32, 140
Margaret Fuller Bicentennial Committee, 3
Margaret Fuller Society, 3, 247n12
Mariana (from *Summer on the Lakes*), 38, 39–41
Marshall, Megan, 3, 6, 7, 148, 236, 248n18, 300
Martineau, Harriet: antislavery movement and, 133–36, 141, 145–47, 273n12, 274n14; *Autobiography* (1877), 147; *Letters on Mesmerism* (1845), 57, 66; *Society in America* (1837), 135, 146; Transcendentalist model of feminism and, 5, 55, 57, 66, 67, 74, 75; in *Woman in the Nineteenth Century*, 23

Martineau, James, 194
martyrdom narrative of antislavery movement, 140–42
Marx, Karl, and Marxism, 102, 108, 119–20, 125
Mary (Emerson's aunt), 32
Matteson, John, 3, 4, 9, 32, 240, 300
Mauprat (Sand, 1837), 216
Mazzini, Giuseppe (Joseph): Italian Risorgimento and, 7, 115, 123, 125, 194, 197, 202, 204; Sand, George, reviews of, 207, 208, 223–25, 227
Melville, Herman, 128
Memoirs of Margaret Fuller Ossoli (Clarke, Emerson, and Channing, 1852), 21, 22, 29, 30, 79, 146, 209, 214, 232
Memoirs of the Author of the Vindication of the Rights of Woman (Godwin, 1798), 16, 251n21
Mesmerism, 55, 56–60, 64, 66, 69, 71, 73, 74
Mexican-American War (1846), 110, 128, 171, 173, 177, 188
Meyer, Howard, 206
Mickiewicz, Adam, 98–99
Midwest, Fuller in. See *Summer on the Lakes*
Mill, John Stuart, 208
Miller, Perry, 52–54, 55, 75, 103, 206, 256n3
Minerva and the Muse: A Life of Margaret Fuller (von Mehren, 1994), 236
Miranda, as Fuller's alter ego, 17, 19, 27, 30
Mitchell, Donald, 122
More, Hannah, 208, 232
Moscheles, Ignaz, 151
Mott, Lucretia, 136
Mount Holyoke College, 232, 297n4
Mount Pleasant (Sing Sing), Fuller's interactions with prostitutes incarcerated in, 4, 34, 43–47, 49, 51, 187, 202
Murray, Meg McGavran, 2, 252n42

music criticism, 6, 148–60; in the *Dial*, 6, 148, 149, 152, 153–55, 157, 160, 236; "Entertainments of the Past Winter" (Fuller, 1842), 155–56, 160, 180, 184; in Europe, 158; feminism of Fuller informed by, 159–60; Fuller's early predilection for, 151–52; Fuller's musical aesthetic, 155–57; Fuller's use of musical metaphor in other writings, 158–59; girls, musical education of, 149–52; Greene Street School, Providence, written at, 152–53; *Lives of the Great Composers* (Fuller, 1841), 148, 152, 154–55, 156, 158, 236; mystical pieces by Fuller and, 157–58; in the *New-York Tribune*, 6, 148, 153, 155, 158; "Some Remarks on Madame Caradori" (Fuller, 1838; Coliseum Club essay), 152, 153, 154, 156, 182–83; urban culture and, 180–85, 190–91, 204

Music Explained to the World; or, How to Understand Music and Enjoy Its Performance (Fetis, 1843), 157

"*Music of the Highest Class*": *Elitism and Populism in Antebellum Boston* (Broyles, 1992), 149

"The Mystery of Marie Roget" (Poe, 1842), 164

mysticism, Fuller's attraction to, 52–56, 73–76, 98–99, 157–58

Nathan, James, 257n8
nationalism of Fuller, 123–24, 125
Native Americans, Fuller's sympathy for, 91, 129, 142
Nature (Emerson, 1836), 86, 142, 145, 180
"New Year's Day" (Fuller, 1845), 174, 175
New York, Fuller in, 161–65, 186, 187–93. *See also* social justice; urban culture
New York by Gaslight (Foster, 1850), 122
New York Philharmonic, 155, 191
New-York Tribune: book reviews of Fuller in, 56–57; Börnstein (Paris correspondent), on French revolution of 1848, 119–21; French revolution of 1848 and, 119; Italian Risorgimento, Fuller's coverage of, 5, 122–23, 145, 197–98, 201, 202, 242; modern publication of Fuller's correspondence with (1844–1850), 2; music criticism of Fuller in, 6, 148, 153, 155, 158; as pivotal phase in Fuller's intellectual career, 90–91, 97, 187–93, 236; popular education, Fuller's articles as form of, 105, 184, 203; Radical Republicanism, as main organ of, 269n55; readership of, 284n26; Sand, Fuller's literary criticism of, 207, 210, 217–21, 223, 225, 226, 227–28; social justice writings of Fuller in (*see* social justice). *See also specific articles*

Norton, Caroline, 26
Novalis, 99

Oakes Smith, Elizabeth: *Bertha and Lily* (1852), 65; embodied soul, concept of, 65–66, 67; on gendered essence, 59–61, 63, 259n27; on Mesmerism, 56, 59–60; mystical and pantheistic elements of Transcendentalism, feminist use of, 5, 55, 74, 75; *Shadow Land; or The Seer* (1852), 59–60, 65, 67; *Woman and Her Needs* (1851), 60

Oberlin College, 134, 231
O'Connell, Daniel, 144
Oeuvres complètes (Sand, 1842), 218
The Organization of Labor (Blanc, 1840), 112
Orpheus and Orphism, 14, 20, 22, 79
Osgood, Lucy and Mary, 222
Osgood, Samuel, 209, 210, 211, 212, 214, 222
Ossining (Mount Pleasant, Sing Sing), Fuller's interactions with prostitutes incarcerated at, 4, 34, 43–47, 49, 51, 187, 202
Ossoli, Giovanni Angelo, 21, 35, 158, 196, 198–201, 242–43

"Our City Charities" (Fuller, 1845), 168–69, 189
Oversoul, concept of, 53, 57, 63–64

Packer, Barbara, 193
Pagels, Elaine, 141
pantheistic approach to feminism, 52–56, 73–76
Papers on Literature and Art (Fuller, 1846), 192, 193, 285n29, 286n45
Paris, Fuller in, 111, 114–15, 194–95
Parker, Theodore, 96, 287n77
Les paroles d'un croyant (Lamennais, 1838), 210, 213
Peabody, Elizabeth Palmer, 32, 77, 103, 222
Peabody sisters, 3
Penniman, Almire, 182
People's International League, 224
People's Journal, 224, 227
perfectionism and perfectibility, 4, 6, 14, 36, 50, 96, 137, 145, 154, 155, 162, 210–16, 219, 235, 237
Phelps, Elizabeth Stuart, 52
Phillips, Ursula, 98–99
Philothea (Child, 1836), 133
Pierce, Sarah, 232
Pilbeam, Pamela, 98
Pius IX (pope), 113, 125, 196, 197, 198, 200, 202
Plutarch, 131, 132
Poe, Edgar Allan, 86, 164, 229
"pollution," Fuller's use of, 171, 173, 174
popular education, Fuller's journalism as form of, 105, 184, 203
Prescott, Miss, 150
Present (journal), 95, 217
Price, Richard, 17–18, 22
Prison Association, 172, 190
The Progress of Religious Ideas, through Successive Ages (Child, 1855), 64
prophetic vision of American values in Fuller's social justice writings, 173–78
prostitutes incarcerated in Mount Pleasant (Sing Sing), 4, 34, 43–47, 49, 51, 187, 202

Providence, Fuller in, 152–53, 182–83, 186–87
Psychology; or, The Science of the Soul, Considered Physiologically and Philosophically (Haddock, 1850), 58–59, 259n31

Randall, Elizabeth and Belinda, 182
reform movements, Fuller's involvement in, 5–6. *See also* antislavery movement; self-culture; social justice; socialism
Revolution, French, of 1789. *See* French Revolution
revolution of 1830, France, 207
Revolutionary War, Fuller's appeal to ideals of, 14, 19, 23, 173–78, 237
revolutions of 1848, 110–12, 116–22, 195. *See also* Italian Risorgimento
Revue des deux mondes, 207, 209, 213, 217, 222
Revue indépendante, 224, 226
Reynolds, George, 208
Reynolds, Larry J., 8, 10, 98, 101, 115, 247n12
Rice, Condoleezza, 230
"The Rich Man: An Ideal Sketch" (Fuller, 1846), 165–66, 171
Ripley, George, 7, 95, 96, 105, 180, 210, 211, 212, 215, 217, 220
Ripley, Sophia, 159, 222
Robinson, David M., 3, 5, 6, 9, 77, 189, 285n32, 300
Rogers, Mary, 164
Roland, Pauline, 195, 224
Roman Revolution. *See* Italian Risorgimento
Romanticism: dark side, Fuller's experience of, 85–86; of Emerson, 104, 108; feminism, Fuller's Romantic understanding of, 12, 14, 17, 19, 20, 22, 24, 26, 27, 29, 144, 249n3; nationalism of Fuller and, 123–24, 125; pro-Catholic sentiments and, 124; of Sand, 206, 217, 225, 228; socialism, Romantic, 114–15, 217

Rome, Fuller in, 195–202. *See also* Italian Risorgimento
Ross, Dorothy, 108
Rossi, Pelligrino, 199
Rotch, Mary, 115
Rousseau, Jean-Jacques, 18, 20, 207, 214
Ruge, Arnold, 119–20

Sainte-Beuve, Charles-Augustin, 207, 208, 217
Saint Simon, Henri de, and Saint-Simonians, 210, 211, 212, 214, 215, 216, 220
Saloman, Ora Frishberg, 148, 155
Sand, George, transatlantic reception of, 7, 206–28; dialogic engagement of Fuller with Sand's work, 3, 20; European Sand enthusiasts, Fuller's interaction with, 223–27; feminine virtue and female sexuality, 222, 225–27; feminism and women's rights, 215, 227–28; France, Fuller's meeting with Sand in, 114, 195, 206, 225–28; French, British, and American reviewers informing Fuller's opinions, 207–9; "The Great Lawsuit" and *Woman in the Nineteenth Century* on, 207, 214, 215–16; historiographical approaches to Fuller's appreciation of Sand, 206–7; la jeune France, critical reception of, 7, 207–9, 211, 214, 216, 222, 223, 288n6; *New-York Tribune*, Fuller's literary criticism of Sand in, 207, 210, 217–21, 223, 225, 226, 227–28; private writings of Fuller on Sand, 206–7, 209, 212–14, 225–26; Romanticism of Sand, 206, 217, 225, 228; socialism and, 217–21; Unitarian cluster interested in Sand, 209–12, 214–15, 217, 220; women's reading circle, Fuller's participation in, 221–23. *See also specific works*
Sargent, Epes, 67
Satira, 44, 46, 48
Schelling, Wilhelm Joseph, 36

Schiller, Friedrich, 19, 20, 212, 252n37
Schindler, Anton, 154
schools. *See* education
Scott, Joan W., 31
Sedgwick, Catharine Maria, 3, 236
Seeress of Prevorst (Frederica Hauffe, from *Summer on the Lakes*), 24, 38, 41–42
self-culture and self-reliance, 5, 77–99; Associationism and, 5, 79, 89, 90, 93–97, 98, 107–8; creative expression and, 82–88; as guiding principle for Fuller, 78–81; as ideology of Transcendentalism and New England, 78; origins of feminist models of, 5, 17–18, 19, 27–31; political significance of Transcendentalism and, 77; property rights, Emerson on, 106; relational and communal aspects of, 5, 79, 89–93; social justice and, 91, 188; socialism and, 79, 97–99; Transcendentalist model of feminism and, 4, 54–56; Unitarian concept of, 5, 17–18
"Self-Reliance" (Emerson, 1841), 78
Seneca Falls convention (1848), 11, 30, 237–38
Les sept cordes de la lyre (Sand, 1840), 20, 214, 222, 226
Seward, William, 250n10
sexuality of women. *See* feminine virtue and female sexuality
Shadow Land; or The Seer (Oakes Smith, 1852), 59–60, 65, 67
Shakespeare, William, 87–88, 131, 231
Shaw, Francis, 217, 219–20, 221, 223
Shaw, Lemuel, 274n14
Shaw, Sarah, 222, 223
Showalter, Elaine, 249n3
Sigourney, Lydia, 232
Simon (Sand, 1835), 216
Sing Sing, prostitutes incarcerated in, 4, 34, 43–47, 49, 51, 187, 202
Sklar, Kathryn Kish, 136–37, 275n23
slavery, opposition to. *See* antislavery movement

"Slavery in Rome" (Bancroft, 1834), 130–32
Smith, Sidonie, 83
Smith, Susan Belasco, 115, 218
social justice, 6–7, 161–78; Boston, Fuller's failure to respond to poverty and oppression in, 186; Channing, William Henry, and, 96, 167, 177, 186, 195; Child and, 161–64, 175; Dorr Rebellion, Rhode Island, Fuller's reaction to, 186–87; Groton, Fuller at bedside of girl dying from botched abortion in, 32–33, 37, 39, 44, 51; immigration and immigrants, 91, 161, 164, 172–73; modern legacy of Fuller regarding, 241–42; modern legacy of Fuller's writings on, 8; "pollution," Fuller's use of, 171, 173, 174; prophetic vision of American values and, 173–78; self-culture and self-reliance, Fuller's ethic of, 91, 188; sensitization of Fuller to issues of, 111; sentiment and sympathy, deployment of, 161–62, 166–74, 177–78, 190, 242; Sing Sing, prostitutes incarcerated in, 4, 34, 43–47, 49, 51, 187, 202; "sunshine and shadow" writing, 165, 166; Transcendentalism and, 161, 162, 166, 168; urban environment of New York and, 161–65, 186, 187–93, 204; *Woman in the Nineteenth Century* and, 170–71, 175, 177. *See also* Margaret Fuller, works of, *for specific essays*
"The Social Movement in Europe" (Fuller, 1845), 120
Social Pressure (Helps, 1875), 151
socialism, 5, 100–127; Associationism and, 107–8, 110–11, 116, 217; Börnstein's reporting on, 119–21; Brook Farm, Emerson's and Fuller's reactions to, 105–8; Channing, William Henry, and, 96, 115, 202, 217; Emerson and, 5, 101, 103–6, 108–9; Fourier, Charles, and Fourierism, 110–11, 114–15, 116; France, Fuller in, 111, 114–15; Great Britain, Fuller in, 111, 114; left-right, radical-conservative political divide, absence of, 102, 108–9, 125; liberal socialism of Fuller, 101–2, 114–17, 120–23, 127, 217, 292n65; "market revolution" in America and, 103, 116, 265–66n6; radicalism of Fuller versus, 101–2, 123–27; revolutions of 1848 (*see* Italian Risorgimento; revolutions of 1848); Romantic socialism, 114–15, 217; Sand, George, transatlantic reception of, 217–21; self-culture, role in Fuller's conception of, 79, 97–99; Thoreau and, 89, 99, 103, 106, 107–8, 127; Transcendentalism's radicalization and turn to social issues, 100–103, 110–11, 127
Society in America (Martineau, 1837), 135, 145
"Some Remarks on Madame Caradori" (Fuller, 1838; Coliseum Club essay), 152, 153, 154, 156, 182–83
Somerville, Mary, 238
Sotiropoulos, Carol Strauss, 20
Southcott, Joanna, 24, 177
Southey, Robert, 209
Spiridion (Sand, 1839), 20, 207, 212–13, 214–15, 219, 222
Spring, Marcus and Rebecca, 79, 115–16, 195
Staël, Germaine de, 20, 238
Stanton, Elizabeth Cady, 1, 11, 12, 25, 30–31, 235, 276n31
Steele, Jeffrey, 3, 6, 7, 10, 12, 27, 38, 75, 89, 161, 189, 242, 258n24, 275–76n31, 284–85n28, 300
Steinem, Gloria, 238–39
Stewart, Maria, 136
St. Leon (Godwin, 1799), 16
Stone, Lucy, 136
Storrow, Samuel Appleton, 274n16
Stowe, Harriet Beecher, 3, 52, 236
Sturgis, Caroline, 7, 32, 33, 150, 194, 222, 223, 233, 274n14

"St. Valentine's Day: Bloomingdale Asylum for the Insane" (Fuller, 1845), 170
Sue, Eugène, 216, 218, 293n79
Summer on the Lakes, in 1843 (Fuller, 1844), 2, 37–42, 50, 53, 90–93, 95, 151, 159–60, 188, 236

Talleyrand, Charles Maurice, 18
Tallmadge amendment (1819), 129
taste, Fuller's notion of, 183
Taylor, Barbara, 17, 19
teaching. *See* education
Temple School, Boston, 135–36, 182, 233
Teresa of Avila, 177
Tévérino (Sand, 1845), 221
Texas, annexation of (1845), 24, 128, 144, 242
Thackeray, William Makepeace, 207
Theodor (De Wette, 1822), 212
Thompson, George, 134, 136
Thoreau, Henry David: antislavery movement and, 145; publication woes of, 193; self-culture and, 78, 89, 99; social justice writings of Fuller and, 164; socialism and, 103, 106, 107–8, 127; urban culture and, 179, 180, 181, 184, 185, 202, 203; *Walden* (1854), 78, 109, 145, 164, 180; *A Week on the Concord and Merrimack Rivers* (1849), 89
Tocqueville, Alexis de, 121, 125
Tombs, New York City, 163, 165
Torquato Tasso (Goethe, 1790), Fuller's translation of, 233
Towianism, 98
Towianski, Andrzej, 98
Townshend, Chauncy, 57–58, 59, 60
transatlantic exchanges: in feminism, 4, 15, 30; Fuller scholarship involving, 1; as preoccupation of Fuller, 4. *See also* Sand, George, transatlantic reception of
Transcendental Club, 15, 210, 211
Transcendentalism: classical mythology, use of, 275–76n31; dark side, Fuller's experience of, 85–86; friendship, discourses on, 89, 185; gnosticism and, 104, 141; music criticism of Fuller and, 155; pantheistic and mystical elements of, 52–56; political awareness of, 77, 95–96, 99; radicalization and focus on social issues, 100–103, 110–11, 127; self-culture as ideology of, 78; social justice writings of Fuller and, 161, 162, 166, 168; "transparent eye-ball" as key visual image of, 86, 163, 262n25; urban culture and, 203–4; vocational crisis and, 93
"The Transcendentalist" (Emerson, 1841), 93
Transcendentalist model of feminism, 4–5, 52–76; body, separation of gender from, 56, 60, 61–63, 64; Clemmer's *Victoire* and, 68–73, 74; embodied soul, concept of, 64–68, 71–73; erotic and sexual registers of, 54, 65–66, 68–73; gendered essence, 59–64, 73–74, 258n24; Mesmerism as science of spirit and, 55, 56–60, 64, 66, 69, 71, 73, 74; Oakes Smith and (*see* Oakes Smith, Elizabeth); Oversoul, concept of, 53, 57, 63–64; pantheistic and mystical elements, Fuller's use of, 52–56, 73–76; self-culture and self-reliance, 4, 54–56
"transparent eye-ball" as key visual image of Transcendentalism, 86, 163, 262n25
Trollope, Frances Milton, 288n6
Tuchinsky, Adam-Max, 5, 6, 9, 100, 242, 300

Uncle Tom's Cabin (Stowe, 1852), 236
Unitarianism, 5, 17–18, 22, 52, 56, 78, 209–12, 214–15, 217, 220
urban culture, 7, 179–205; Boston, Fuller in, 181–82, 183–86; Fuller's affinity for, 179–81, 201–5; Great Britain, Fuller in, 193–94; mental stimulation, Fuller's concern with, 182; music and

the arts, 180–85, 190–91, 194–95, 196, 204; New York, Fuller in, 161–65, 186, 187–93; Paris, Fuller in, 111, 114–15, 194–95; Providence, Fuller in, 152–53, 182–83, 186–87; Rome and other Italian cities, Fuller in, 195–201, 202; social justice writings of Fuller and Child and, 161–65, 187–93, 204; taste, Fuller's notion of, 183; Transcendentalism and, 203–4

Urbanski, Marie Olesen, 250n7

utopianism: Brook Farm, 5, 90, 94–95, 96, 103, 105–8, 180, 217; of Channing, William Henry, and Associationism, 95, 96; in feminism, 12, 14, 19, 28, 31, 95, 144–45; Fruitlands, 90, 103, 106, 180; Lamennais's lack of commitment to, 212; Mesmerism and, 57; of Mickiewicz, 98–99; social justice writings of Fuller and, 164, 166; socialism and, 98–99, 116; Western frontier and, 90, 91, 93

Valentine (Sand, 1832), 207
Victoire (Clemmer, 1864), 68–73, 74
"Victory" (Fuller, 1846), 173
Viens, Katheryn P., 300–301
Vigny, Alfred de, 214
Vigoureaux, Clarisse, 114
Vindication of the Rights of Man (Wollstonecraft, 1790), 18
Vindication of the Rights of Woman (Wollstonecraft, 1792), 11–13, 15, 17, 18, 20, 21, 31, 252n37
virtue, feminine. *See* feminine virtue and female sexuality
von Frank, Albert J., 5–6, 9, 10, 128, 301
von Mehren, Joan, 236

Walden (Thoreau, 1854), 78, 109, 145, 164, 180
Ward, Anna, née Barker, 35, 37, 80, 203, 257n8
Ward, Samuel Gray, 80, 203, 208–9, 257n8

Webster, Daniel, 134
A Week on the Concord and Merrimack Rivers (Thoreau, 1849), 89
Weiss, John, 203, 287n77
Weld, Theodore Dwight, 29, 134, 138
Welter, Barbara, 60
"West Indian Emancipation Address" (Emerson, 1844), 146, 274n14
Western Messenger, 210, 233
Westminster, 207, 208, 209
When Everything Changed: The Amazing Journey of American Women (Collins, 2000), 230
Whitman, Sarah Helen, 259n31
Whitman, Walt, 283n5
Whittier, John Greenleaf, 137
Wiley, John, 193
Willis, Nathaniel Parker, 67, 281n36
Wilson, Harriet, 3
"A Winter Piece" (Bryant, 1854), 177, 282n73
Wollstonecraft, Mary, 4, 15–22; death of, 21, 30; French Revolution and, 18–19, 21, 22; Fuller, Timothy, and, 15, 17; Fuller's opinion of, 15–16; Godwin and, 16, 20, 21, 251n21; Grimké sisters compared, 27; influence on Fuller's writings, 16–20, 28; *Memoirs of the Author of the Vindication of the Rights of Woman* (Godwin, 1798), 16, 251n21; personal life and reputation of, 15–16, 21–22; as precursor of feminist movement, 11–15, 21–22, 30, 31; on Rousseau, 18, 20; Schiller's poetry and, 252n37; symmetries of Fuller's life with, 20–21; *Vindication of the Rights of Man* (1790), 18; *Vindication of the Rights of Woman* (1792), 11–13, 15, 17, 18, 20, 21, 31, 252n37
Woman and Her Needs (Oakes Smith, 1851), 60
The Woman and the Myth: Margaret Fuller's Life and Writings (Chevigny, 1976), 236

Woman in the Nineteenth Century (Fuller, 1845): antislavery movement and, 6, 143–45; Biblical patterns of prophecy and millennial possibility in, 27–28; concluding poem, 31; Conversations as rehearsal for claims of, 235; *Dial* article "The Great Lawsuit," expansion of, 4, 38, 47, 90, 137, 162, 171, 216, 236; edition of 1855, 30; electricity as symbol in, 92; epigraphs, 19; feminine virtue and female sexuality in, 37, 43, 46, 47–50; feminism and gender ideology in, 4, 5, 10, 237, 238, 241, 243; First Wave Feminist movement, relationship to, 11–15, 21–22, 30–31; Fuller on completion of, 229, 243; on gender and feminine essence, 61, 62, 63, 73, 241, 258n24; Grimké sisters and, 15, 23–30, 139; initial publication and reception of, 229–30; as "lawsuit," 13–14, 24–27; "let them be sea captains" remark, 19, 22, 28, 50; on marriage, 95; Mesmerism in, 57; modern legacy of Fuller and, 8, 229, 237, 238, 241, 243; modern publication of, 2; personal life of Fuller and moral sentiments of, 20–21; reform modalities described in, 140; on Sand, 207, 214; self-culture and self-expression in, 82–83; social justice writings of Fuller and, 170–71, 175, 177, 188; utopian thinking in, 96; Wollstonecraft and, 15–16

Woman's Bible (Stanton, 1895/1898), 31

women and gender ideology, 4–5; antislavery movement and, 6; body, separation of gender from, 56, 60, 61–63, 64; fluidity of gender, Fuller's beliefs regarding, 43, 62, 73, 241; legacy of Fuller regarding, 7–8. *See also* feminine virtue and female sexuality; feminism and women's rights; Transcendentalist model of feminism

Women's Rights Emerges within the Antislavery Movement, 1830–1870 (Sklar, 2000), 136–37, 275n23

Woodville, Violet, 168

Wordsworth, William, 193

Workers' Commission in France, 112

Wright, Conrad Edick, 301

Wright, Frances, 12

The Young Lady's Friend (Farrar, 1836), 80–81

"Yuca Filamentosa" (Fuller, 1842), 89, 157–58

Zwarg, Christina, 3, 264n54, 285n29, 291–92n59